# OXFORD CLASSICAL MONOGRAPHS

*Published under the supervision of a Committee of the
Faculty of Classics in the University of Oxford*

The aim of the Oxford Classical Monograph series (which replaces the Oxford Classical and Philosophical Monographs) is to publish books based on the best theses on Greek and Latin literature, ancient history, and ancient philosophy examined by the Faculty Board of Classics.

# Motivation and Narrative in Herodotus

EMILY BARAGWANATH

OXFORD
UNIVERSITY PRESS

# OXFORD

## UNIVERSITY PRESS

Great Clarendon Street, Oxford OX2 6DP

Oxford University Press is a department of the University of Oxford.
It furthers the University's objective of excellence in research, scholarship,
and education by publishing worldwide in

Oxford  New York

Auckland  Cape Town  Dar es Salaam  Hong Kong  Karachi
Kuala Lumpur  Madrid  Melbourne  Mexico City  Nairobi
New Delhi  Shanghai  Taipei  Toronto

With offices in

Argentina  Austria  Brazil  Chile  Czech Republic  France  Greece
Guatemala  Hungary  Italy  Japan  Poland  Portugal  Singapore
South Korea  Switzerland  Thailand  Turkey  Ukraine  Vietnam

Oxford is a registered trade mark of Oxford University Press
in the UK and in certain other countries

Published in the United States
by Oxford University Press Inc., New York

© Emily Baragwanath 2008

The moral rights of the author have been asserted
Database right Oxford University Press (maker)

First published 2008
First published in paperback 2012

British Library Cataloguing in Publication Data
Data available

Library of Congress Cataloging in Publication Data
Data available

Typeset by SPI Publisher Services, Pondicherry, India

ISBN 978–0–19–923129–4 (Hbk)
ISBN 978–0–19–964550–3 (Pbk)

*For my parents, Barbara and David Baragwanath*

*There can never be a single story. There are only ways of seeing.*
Arundhati Roy, 'Come September'

# Acknowledgments

This is the revised version of an Oxford D.Phil. thesis completed in 2005, written with the support of a scholarship funded by the Rhodes Trust, in the hospitable environment of Magdalen College. A Junior Research Fellowship at Christ Church, funded by the Christopher Tower Fund, allowed me to finish the project in the most welcoming and collegial of settings. I am extremely grateful to the Dean and Students of Christ Church for electing me to the position. The department of Classics at the University of North Carolina at Chapel Hill has provided much support and assistance with the final preparations for publication.

Many individuals have helped with this book. My sincere thanks go first of all to Chris Pelling: a most extraordinary supervisor, to whom I owe a vast debt. I thank him especially for the warmth and humanity of his scholarship, which has been an inspiration to me from beginning to end. Hugely generous with his time, he enabled me to refine my thinking at every stage of the thesis. I thank warmly my examiners, John Marincola and Angus Bowie, for their generous engagement with the thesis and many detailed and perceptive comments, which helped me enormously in improving it. My adviser Rosalind Thomas has overseen the process of transition from thesis to book with her inspiring, meticulous gaze. Ian McAuslan has been a tremendous help in copy-editing it, and the team at OUP in overseeing the whole process with great efficiency. For reading or discussing my work on Herodotus I am extremely grateful also to Stephanie West (who assisted me especially with what is now chapter nine), Tim Rood, Peter Parsons, Oliver Taplin, Pietro Vannicelli, Elton Barker, and the audiences at several conferences and seminars. Special thanks are due to Mathieu de Bakker for many stimulating Herodotus discussions and for his careful reading of a draft. Vivienne Gray first introduced me to Herodotus with her sparkling teaching, and she suggested to me this area of research. For inspiring teaching at an earlier stage I thank Sue Haywood, †Ken Trembath, Tom Stevenson, and Paul McKechnie.

None of these people is to be held in any way accountable for the shortcomings that remain in the book.

The warmest of thanks are due also to my friends and family for their support, especially to my parents, to whom this book is dedicated, and to my twin Paul. And a final large thank you to Sean, for a thousand things, including his help with this project from beginning to end, but particularly for his encouragement and companionship.

# Contents

# Abbreviations

Abbreviations follow those of LSJ and (for journal titles) *L'Année Philologique*. For ease of reference I abbreviate texts, translations, commentaries, and lexica as below (to the name of the scholar and a reference to the lines in question). These are not replicated in the References.

Asheri           D. Asheri (introduction and commentary), *Le storie: Libro III, la Persia*, tr. A. Fraschetti, text edited by S. M. Medaglia (Milan, 1990); *Le storie: Libro VIII, la vittoria di Temistocle*, additional comm. P. Vannicelli, tr. A. Fraschetti, text edited by A. Corcella (Milan, 2003); *Le storie: Libro IX, la battaglia di Platea*, additional comm. P. Vannicelli, tr. A. Fraschetti, text edited by A. Corcella (Milan, 2006).

Blakesley       J. W. Blakesley, *Herodotus*, 2 vols. (London, 1854).

Blanco           W. Blanco (tr.), W. Blanco and J. T. Roberts (eds.), *Herodotus: The Histories* (New York and London, 1992).

Bowen            A. J. Bowen, *Plutarch: The Malice of Herodotus* (Warminster, 1992).

Bredovius       F. J. C. Bredovius, *Quaestionum Criticarum de Dialecto Herodotea Libri Quatuor* (Leipzig, 1846).

Corcella         A. Corcella (introduction and commentary), *Le storie: Libro IV, la Scizia e la Libia*, tr. A. Fraschetti, text edited by S. M. Medaglia (Milan, 1993).

Dewald *Comm.*   See Waterfield (below).

Flower/Marincola   M. A. Flower and J. Marincola (eds.), *Herodotus: Histories Book IX* (Cambridge, 2002).

Godley           A. D. Godley (tr.), *Herodotus*, 4 vols. (Cambridge, Mass. and London, 1920–5).

How/Wells       W. W. How and J. Wells, *A Commentary on Herodotus* (Oxford, 1912).

Hude             C. Hude, *Herodoti Historiae*[3] (Oxford, 1927).

| | |
|---|---|
| de Jong *Comm.* | I. J. F. de Jong, *A Narratological Commentary on the Odyssey* (Cambridge, 2001). |
| Legrand | P.-E. Legrand, *Hérodote: Histoires*, 9 vols. (Paris, 1932–54). |
| LSJ | H. G. Liddell and R. Scott, *A Greek-English Lexicon*[9], rev. by H. Stuart Jones (Oxford, 1940). |
| Macan | R. W. Macan (ed.), *Herodotus: The Fourth, Fifth, and Sixth books* (London, 1895); *Herodotus: The Seventh, Eighth, and Ninth books* (London, 1908). |
| Maidment | K. J. Maidment, *Minor Attic Orators*, vol. 1 (Cambridge, Mass. and London, 1941). |
| Masaracchia | A. Masaracchia (ed.), *Le storie: Libro VIII, la battaglia di Salamina* (Milan, 1977); *Le storie: Libro IX, la sconfitta dei Persiani* (Milan, 1978). |
| Medaglia | See Asheri (above) and Corcella (above). |
| Nenci | G. Nenci (ed.), *Le storie: Libro V, la rivolta della Ionia* (Milan, 1994); *Le storie: Libro VI, la battiglia di Maratona* (Milan, 1998). |
| Ogilvie | R. M. Ogilvie, *A Commentary on Livy, Books 1–5* (Oxford, 1965). |
| van Ophuijsen/ Stork | J. M. van Ophuijsen and P. Stork, *Linguistics into Interpretation: Speeches of War in Herodotus VII 5 & 8–18* (Leiden, Boston, and Cologne, 1999). |
| *PMG* | D. L. Page (ed.), *Poetae melici Graeci* (Oxford, 1962). |
| Powell | J. E. Powell, *A Lexicon to Herodotus* (Cambridge, 1938). |
| Rosén | H. Rosén, *Herodoti Historiae*, 2 vols. (Leipzig, 1987–97). |
| de Sélincourt/ Marincola | A. de Sélincourt (tr.), rev. with notes by J. Marincola, *Herodotus: The Histories*, rev. ed. (London, 1996). |
| Stein | H. Stein (ed.), *Herodotos* (Berlin, 1881–96). |
| Waterfield | R. Waterfield (tr.), introduction and notes by C. Dewald, *Herodotus: The Histories* (Oxford, 1998). |

## *Note on texts and translations*

All translations of Herodotus and Plutarch are my own (unless otherwise noted), aided in particular by Powell and Waterfield. Translations of Homer are those of A. T. Murray (Loeb) as revised by W. F. Wyatt (*Iliad*) and G. E. Dimock (*Odyssey*), at times adapted. I use C. Hude's OCT text for Herodotus, B. Häsler's Teubner for Plutarch, and M. West's Teubner for Homer, unless otherwise specified. All references to Plutarch concern *de Malignitate Herodoti* (= *DMH* or *Malice*), and refer to the *Moralia*, unless I specify otherwise. I follow conventional English usage in spelling the more familiar of Greek proper names (e.g. Demaratus), but for the rest I follow more closely the Greek (e.g. Pittakos).

# 1

## The *Histories*, Plutarch, and reader response

### 1.1 INTRODUCTION

Construing a text entails dealing in differing degrees of certainty. At one end of the spectrum, we may employ an author's more or less explicit guidance: that expressed in direct comment, for example, or in programmatic passages. At the other end, we interpret what remains implicit, inferring meaning from a matrix of narrative pattern, lexical usage, historical background, and so on; and in doing so we at times impute to the text what cannot with certainty be taken as representing the author's intended meaning. In Herodotus' case we know far more about a segment, at least, of his original audience than we do of the man himself,[1] and so we are better equipped, at such moments of interpretative difficulty, to suggest a range of probable responses that the *Histories* is likely to have engendered in that audience than we are to speculate upon the author's intended meaning. We are especially entitled to do so in the *Histories*' case, since Herodotus has *invited* interpretations that potentially differ from his own.

First, Herodotus chose to orient his *Histories* not only to the past and to the present,[2] but also towards future time and future audiences, even implicitly inviting them to bring to bear their own

---

[1] Apart, of course, from what surfaces from his text; but the question of the extent to which Herodotus' persona in the narrative maps on to the historical individual is unanswerable.

[2] Fornara (1971), 75–91; Corcella (1984), 186–235; Raaflaub (1987); Stadter (1992); Moles (1996); Munson (2001).

experiences in its interpretation.[3] Their further knowledge as to 'how things turned out' he doubtless expected would cast different light on various aspects of his narrative—in accordance with Solon's advice (1.32.9) 'to consider the end (σκοπέειν... τὴν τελευτήν) of every matter, and see how it will turn out' (which is also a principle played out within the Histories). This decision is significant in inviting us to recognize that the meaning of his text is not to be bounded *diachronically* by the limits of his authorial intentions. And the same appears to be true also on a *synchronous* level, for Herodotus foregrounds the fact that history is contested territory: that differing interpretations and explanations of historical events and personalities arise from the perspectives of different individuals or groups.[4] His frequent inclusion in his text of a range of versions, including those with which he explicitly disagrees, furnishes others with the material they need, potentially to challenge his personal verdict. As Paul Veyne observes, 'chaque lecteur est non moins qualifié qu' Hérodote pour faire le dernier pas vers la vérité vraie'.[5] Thus Herodotus has constructed his text as inviting a multiplicity of perspectives on the part of readers from his present time to far into the future. This implies that, of the triangle 'author-text(/performance)-reader',[6] the point of the 'reader' deserves particular recognition in Herodotus' case. The way in which Herodotus empowers readers to contribute to imputing meaning to his Histories invites an approach that recognizes a wide range of potential responses: an approach that does not shy from operating

---

[3] Cf. 1.5.4: Herodotus' account will cover both small and large cities equally, τὰ γὰρ τὸ πάλαι μεγάλα ἦν, τὰ πολλὰ αὐτῶν σμικρὰ γέγονε, τὰ δὲ ἐπ' ἐμεῦ ἦν μεγάλα, πρότερον ἦν σμικρά ('since the majority of cities that in earlier times were important have become small, and those that **were** important in my time were formerly small'). See Rösler (1991); Dewald (1997), 62–82; Naiden (1999) for the openness of the ending as inviting future interpretations. Bakker (2002a), 3–32 argues that in speaking of *apodexis hēde* Herodotus orients his work towards the future as much as Thucydides does in calling his a *ktēma es aiei* ('possession for all time') (31); the Histories casts future readers into Herodotus' own role, inviting them 'to listen critically, to question, and to judge' (32).

[4] Kurke (1999) explores the Histories as a site of egalitarian v. elitist struggle to champion conflicting (historical) interpretations. Ch. 9 below considers the difference made by Greek v. Persian perspectives.

[5] Veyne (1987), 10 ('each reader is no less qualified than Herodotus to take the final step towards real truth').

[6] Abrams (1953).

on a level of conjecture, moving past what is explicit and authorially signalled to what is less so and casts upon the reader greater responsibility for contribution. An issue throughout our discussion will be the extent to which the interpretative strands we uncover are to be regarded as conscious authorial strategy.

This is a study of the representation of human motivation in the *Histories*. It examines how the narrator articulates people's thoughts, which is a major aspect of Herodotus' research into cause and explanation and thus central to his historical inquiry. Explanation on the human level is crucial to Herodotus' aim of making his *Histories* intelligible to readers: to his desire to communicate an understanding of the phase of history he recounts, but also a sensitivity to the methodological challenges faced by the historian in reconstructing it. Herodotus displays an overwhelming interest in the reasons behind actions.[7] He constantly sketches in the background of motives, frequently supplying multiple and various possibilities, and generally shows a concern to draw readers' attention to questions of motivation and to problematize such questions. Though it is concerned essentially with motivation, this study at the same time—through the point of entry provided by its particular focus—illuminates Herodotus' narrative techniques generally. It is concerned both with how Herodotus motivates his *Histories* and, more broadly, with how he motivates his readers in their process of reading it. Thus it provides a technique for reading Herodotus.

Herodotus recognized that those targeted by his oral research at times held differing, or irreconcilable, opinions about the way past events unfolded—or even about whether they had happened at all. The thoughts and motives that inspired a particular course of action were doubly concealed: in the past, and within the minds of those involved. And yet this background of human motivation was crucial to Herodotus in conferring intelligibility upon the course of history he recounts, since individuals played a vital role at frequent junctures in shaping its outcome. The historian's main recourse in accessing knowledge about the minds and motives of past individuals will have been personal conjecture: his own, along with that of his informants.

---

[7] 'Herodotus' denotes the Herodotean narrator, unless I make explicit reference to the historical individual.

At times he perhaps had access to oral traditions supplying reasons—or retrospective justifications—for action, remembered by the groups to which the actors belonged, and so naturally partial in perspective.[8] The limits and subjective nature of such recourses are evident.

Our study examines this tension between Herodotus' desire to ascribe motivation for purposes of intelligibility, and his desire to expose readers to the qualified and provisional character of such ascriptions. This situation (which will be introduced in the context of Homeric precedent in chapter two) echoes a broader dialectic: that between Herodotus' conviction that truth about the past is accessible and worth preserving, and his recognition—doubtless sharpened by the sophists' speculations—that much of importance remains partially concealed. This is very much the case when it comes to questions surrounding human and—even more so—divine motivations. In such challenging instances Herodotus develops strategies of engaging his readers in grappling with and piecing together the evidence themselves. He lays out before them the difficulties and contradictions, while at the same time offering hints in his narrative that a particular interpretation is the most plausible and closest to the truth. His ascriptions of motivation work effectively to this end, especially in the case of unresolved alternative (or multiple) possibilities, but also in that of single conjectures where they present a contrast with what the reader already knows, has heard in explicit authorial comment, or has assumed from the surrounding narrative. Or Herodotus invites readers to observe a complex skein of possible motivations, and their possible resolutions, keeping before their eyes the fact that polarized views of motivation rarely map directly on to complex realities. Or again, he prompts consideration not only of a multiplicity of possible motivations but also of the relevance of different perspectives—of different groups, and across time. Our study describes and illuminates strategies of this kind. What surfaces most strikingly is the active response from his readers that Herodotus

---

[8] Thus the situation in Herodotus' case presents a contrast with that of Thucydides, writing in large part about the motives of contemporaries he was in a position to question personally (Dover (1973), 31; Westlake (1989)) even if his ultimate analysis must in large part be based on his own conjectures; see below, ch. 4 n. 1 with text.

invites and rewards, and the *Histories'* polyvocal and dialogic character:[9] how it complicates rather than simplifies. Herodotus the inquirer into human motivation is never reductionist. As we shall see, the different possibilities he sets forth, as well as uncertainty itself, feed into the *Histories'* wider historical (and narrative) themes—most broadly, that of the elusiveness of wisdom.

We also examine Herodotus the narrative artist, exploring the broader functions and effects of his depiction of motivation. For regardless of their truth status, ascriptions of motivation can contextualize events, by illuminating the broader psychology that underlay past human action, and even painting a picture of a people's character across time (as we find in the case of the Athenians and Pelasgians, discussed in chapter five). Specific conjectures may feed into the text's wider patterns of human behaviour, and so come to express general truths. Most generally they may hint at 'the way the world works'. Thus they are a further means by which Herodotus 'hover(s) between the particular and the general'.[10] Ascriptions of motivation serve narrative functions, as transitional devices or tools to promote narrative coherence. They may underline significant themes, deepen readers' understanding of individual psychology, expand the background and context, allude to contemporary discussions and experience, and model interpretative method. In some ways Herodotus' techniques present a parallel to those of Homer—an important narrative predecessor, discussed in chapter two—and of the tragedians. Indeed, in its use of such techniques in presenting the *truth* about *recent* history, the *Histories* can contribute to modern debates on the boundaries between history and fiction.[11] In many respects this first work of the genre that would become 'history' diverges from the characteristics traditionally regarded as typical of historical narrative. It is all the more alluring, to twenty-first century eyes, for this reason. Our findings contribute to the case (against Detlev Fehling and others[12]) for Herodotus the poet—in the techniques he employs—as being wholly compatible with Herodotus the truth seeker.

---

[9] Cf. below, n. 57 with text.   [10] Lateiner (1989), 225.
[11] Cf. below, n. 93 with text.   [12] See below, n. 31 with text.

In describing Herodotus' narrative technique I borrow from certain modern theories where they prove especially useful in analysing Herodotean narrative. Reader response criticism articulates a process of moving through the text that in modified form is appropriate to Herodotus, and allows us tools and terminology that are helpful in describing the processes of Herodotean narrative. Wolfgang Iser's model of communication is valuable in the flexible negotiation it envisages between the poles of text and reader. His distinction between narrator and implied author provides a means of dealing with inconsistencies in a text, such as where Herodotus' comments appear to contradict what readers have assumed from the events he has described.[13] Narratology proves extremely useful in its sensitivity to changing perspectives, expressed with the concept 'focalization' (the question of 'who sees': whose gaze focalizes the narrative), and in its sensitivity to time, particularly to chronological displacements ('analepses', flashbacks and 'prolepses', flashforwards).[14]

The following chapters explore the range of narrative techniques that Herodotus employs to draw his readers into reflecting upon actorial motives in the *Histories*.[15] In keeping with the 'open', multifaceted quality I consider characteristic of the *Histories*, my discussion seeks to offer *additional* potential levels of interpretation through its focus on the presentation in the *Histories* of human motives and psychology—which is one of Herodotus' several ex-

[13] The case for the usefulness of reader response criticism in analysing the *Histories* is set out below, §1.3. For 'implied author', see n. 97 below with text.

[14] Narratology and the *Histories*: see esp. de Jong (1999); (2001a); (2002); (2004a); Munson (2001). Focalization: ch. 7 n. 17 below with text.

[15] Throughout, I use 'readers' to refer both to listeners to the text as it is performed orally or read out (as in the case of the original mid to late fifth-century BC audience), and to those reading it for themselves (e.g. Plutarch, moderns). If my argument appears at times to make large demands of listeners, it must be borne in mind that the original audience was far more practised in this role than a modern one is. Naturally there will have been a spectrum of responses to the *Histories*, ranging from the attentive to the more casual, with more subtle levels of meaning apparent to the first group. The term 'reader' also allows the possibility that the audience have the text reread to them or reread sections themselves. Though sections of the *Histories* will have been performed by Herodotus work-in-progress style, the focus in my discussion is the finished written text. Herodotus conceived of it as a completed work in the hands of a future audience (cf. n. 3 above with text), and as fixed for the future through its being written down—as at 7.214.3 he fixes in writing the guilt of the traitor of Thermopylae: 'I write this man (as) guilty' (τοῦτον αἴτιον γράφω). He refers to it as a *sungraphē*, 'written record' (1.93.1).

planatory strategies.[16] At times this focus may, of course, suggest qualifications to existing interpretations. And again, explanation on the human level *does* at times stand in tension with broader, for example cosmic, principles. In the case of Xerxes, for example, the alternative possible views of his personal motives may fall into the opposition of cautious and rational versus hubristic and irrational (as I suggest in chapter nine)—whereas on the broader cosmic level, Persian imperialism seems invariably to entail *hybris*. Amasis' motivation in breaking off his friendship with Polykrates remains paradoxical on the human level even while it makes perfect sense in the broader scheme.[17] Again, Herodotus' deduction that Helen was never in Troy (or the Trojans would have returned her) and stress on Paris' sole responsibility, together with the later account of Theseus' abduction with impunity of Helen (9.73), seems in tension with the moral interpretation he offers at 2.120: that the gods contrived Troy's annihilation to make clear to men that severe injustices meet with severe punishments from the gods. Divine causation represents a crucial aspect of explanation in the *Histories*, which operates in parallel to human explanation,[18] though its precise workings remain elusive.[19] Only occasionally does Herodotus in his authorial voice suggest its probable involvement; more often he supplies the reports of others. I deal with this important area indirectly, on occasions where Herodotus presents it interacting either with or against human motivations, or where humans are seen to be motivated by their impression of it. Equally hard to pin down is Herodotus' conception of the more general category of fate: its relation to human decisions and its role in determining historical outcomes.[20]

---

[16] See below, n. 39 with text.

[17] See below, ch. 4 n. 27 with text, and for a further example ch. 4 n. 48.

[18] See e.g. Gould (1989), 70.

[19] Cf. Scullion (2006), 196: '[b]eyond the narrow realm of sacrilege there is nothing automatic or straightforward about the operation of "divinity".' Modern opinion on the role of the divine in the *Histories*, as Scullion ibid. 204 observes, ranges from Herodotus the 'rationalist who keeps his residue of belief distinct from his analysis of historical causation', to the 'pious sceptic', to the 'pious believer', with e.g. Lateiner (1989) in the first camp; Scullion (2006) and Burkert (1990) in the second; and Gould (1994), Mikalson (2002), and Harrison (2000) in the third.

[20] Modern scholars hold divergent views, e.g. Fornara (1990) and Harrison (2000), 223–42 proposing a strongly fatalistic Herodotus; contra, e.g. Lateiner (1989), 189–210. For Mikalson (2003) the force behind "what must be" 'is simply

In this introduction I address the nature of the response the *Histories* elicits, arguing that Herodotus' reader is motivated to take a particular, active stance towards his text. The Homeric background (presented in chapter two) then provides a perspective in which to view Herodotus' methods, strengthening the case and pointing further to the crucial importance of questions of motives. In chapter three I examine Herodotus' portrayal of inquirers whose interest in the psychological parallels his own. This metatextual perspective implies that the inquiry into human motivation is a crucial complement to the record of *erga* (deeds)—as Herodotus indeed makes clear in his proem, with its mention of a focus on the *aitiē* (cause) of the conflict between Greeks and Persians.[21] It also furthers our characterization of Herodotus, who at first sight appears a polarized personality, concerned to confer *kleos* (fame, glory), but at the same time intent also on uncovering underlying and often disreputable motives. We then move on to consider (in chapter four) how Herodotus exposes the difficulties involved in determining motives. I contend that his ascriptions of motives can be sites of destabilization that point to dissonance between intention and outcome—in stark contrast with the pattern of congruence in Thucydides' history between intention and resulting action, or the similar restricting of the range of motives open to the audience's reflection that is characteristic of forensic oratory. Herodotus' ascriptions may hint at variant readings or may foreground ironies.

Herodotus' polarizing technique of presentation is discussed in chapter five, while chapter six focuses on his treatment of ideal motives and the role of rhetoric in the Ionian Revolt narrative. It becomes ever clearer that people's motives may *not* emerge straightforwardly from what they say: the rhetorical context complicates and problematizes.

---

"what will happen" and "what does in fact happen"' (150), and is not associated with the gods or a god. Gould (1989), 67–78 suggests that supernatural causation does not override human, but is invoked to answer different sorts of questions. In Immerwahr's attractive formulation (1956), Herodotus' focus is human explanation, but present in the background of the working of history are 'metaphysical causes and their equivalents...: necessity, retribution, change of fortune, balance', which perhaps, for Herodotus, find an 'ultimate explanation' in the divine world (279).

[21] See below, n. 39 with text.

We turn in chapter seven to making the case that Herodotus' narrative invites his readers to appreciate the significance of the Athenians' decision against the background of the negative forces that impede others' action. The final chapters centre upon the *Histories'* two most prominent individuals. The interaction of statements of motives with wider patterns of explanation for Xerxes' failure is examined in chapter eight, where we reflect particularly upon the role of focalization in fashioning motives. Lastly we address Herodotus' presentation of Themistocles' motives (chapter nine), considering the possibility of unreliable narratorial comments, the shifting perspectives offered to readers, and the implied role of later events in the retrospective fashioning of motivation. But let us begin by considering in general terms the nature of the response to be expected on the part of Herodotus' intended audience. Plutarch's insights will allow us to plot Herodotus' strategies for guiding and shaping his readers' response.

## 1.2 PLUTARCH'S RESPONSE

Plutarch was a perceptive reader of the *Histories*, and its first explicit critic—as well as the most disapproving.[22] Driven by frustration at Herodotus' unjust treatment of his hometown Thebes, his *On the Malice of Herodotus (de Malignitate Herodoti)* often strikes us as overblown and mean-spirited. Many of its observations are nonetheless keen. Again, even though Plutarch's second-century AD world, with its culture of reading and return to the classical texts, stands at a significant remove from that of the fifth to fourth centuries BC—culturally and ideologically as well as temporally—his response is closer in time to that of Herodotus' audience than ours is. It exposes us to a refreshingly different perspective. Plutarch's criticisms often miss important aspects, but they still allow us a point of entry into what Herodotus is in fact doing: and indeed they are valuable in sensitizing modern readers to significant aspects of Herodotus' narrative technique. For example, Plutarch responds to, and sensitizes us

---

[22] Dionysius of Halicarnassus and the anonymous author of *On the Sublime* supply more charitable ancient responses to Herodotus' *Histories*.

to, a latent contradiction between Herodotus' claim to preserve *kleos* and his questioning of motives (a tension we introduce below at §1.2.2 and confront in chapter three). With his accusation that Herodotus polarizes questions of motivation into better and worse, emphasizing the latter, Plutarch again puts his finger on something important: his praise-and-blame formulation, if qualified, can at times be appropriate in discussing the *Histories*' presentation of motives (as chapter five suggests). As we hinted above,[23] much hinges in particular on the question of the nature of the response the *Histories* elicits from its readers. In this respect *de Malignitate Herodoti* is especially illuminating. Plutarch himself models one individual's response—that of one far enough removed from ourselves to be enlightening—while at the same time his commentary, with its chosen emphases, illuminates in a more general way the question of the character and range of responses we might reasonably expect on the part of an ancient reader of the *Histories*. To this we now turn, with the aim of establishing the appropriateness to the study of Herodotean narrative of the particular kind of close analysis (informed by Wolfgang Iser's reader response theory[24]) that I pursue over the course of the present work.

### 1.2.1 Subtleties

Plutarch lays particular emphasis on the subtlety of Herodotus' method, which he frames in terms of its deception (ἀπάτη; cf. 854e) and beguilement (cf. 874b) of unwitting readers. Herodotus' gentle style belies the vicious nature of his account: just as with rose beetles on roses, 'one must be on guard against his slanders and insults which are slipped in under smooth and gentle appearances (λείοις καὶ ἁπαλοῖς σχήμασιν ὑποδεδυκυῖαν)' (874b). For rather than expressing his views 'openly and honestly',[25] Herodotus does so obliquely. Plutarch brings to bear several metaphors expressive of the subtlety and deviousness of Herodotean method. Herodotus' *kakoētheia* (malice) works like draughts coming

---

[24] I discuss the *Histories* in relation to reader response theory below (§1.3).
[25] Plutarch determines to sketch out signs of a narrative that is neither καθαρά ('pure', 'open') nor εὐμενής ('well disposed'), but κακοήθης ('malicious', 855b).

through a crack rather than winds in the open (855a). He makes his attacks πλαγίως, treacherously, as if firing from ambush (856c). Further metaphors highlight the sophistication evident in this subtlety. As skilled flatterers season their flattery with mild criticism so as to make it more convincing,[26] Herodotus seasons his criticisms with the occasional word of praise (856d). Like a painter using shadow to bring out bright parts, 'he strengthens his accusations by denials (ταῖς ἀρνήσεσι), and deepens suspicion by ambiguity (ταῖς ἀμφιβολίαις)' (863e).

Plutarch draws attention to several additional specific strategies. One involves Herodotus 'making a charge and then withdrawing' it,[27] with the effect that the account (or, in Plutarch's usual expression, 'accusation') remains in the air for readers to ponder, despite the authorial rejection. The result, in Plutarch's view, is that Herodotus may have his cake and eat it too: include the accusation, yet avoid responsibility for propagating it. Another alleged strategy is yet more devious, entailing Herodotus actually 'saying he does not believe what he very much wants to be believed'.[28] Herodotus' deviousness at times requires perspicacity on the part of readers if they are to see through it, as Plutarch implies by the analogy of the Ethiopian king's recognition of the deceptive nature of Cambyses' gifts: one might equally say, he suggests, as of Cambyses' gifts of Persian perfume and clothes, 'that deceitful are the words and deceitful the forms of Herodotus' *Histories*, "all twisted, nothing that is sound, but all back to front" ' (863d–e).

There is substance in this emphasis on Herodotean subtlety, provided we tone down the praise-and-blame character of Plutarch's formulations (for, I will later argue,[29] Herodotus' method more often *deflects* the rhetoric of blame). For despite his prominent authorial presence,[30] and his frequent expressions of personal opinion, Herodotus is not

---

[26] Cf. Plutarch, *How to tell a Flatterer from a Friend*, 51c–d.

[27] e.g. regarding Herodotus' account of Artaxerxes' reply to the Argive ambassadors to Susa, followed by his refusal to guarantee the story: 'then he withdraws, as usual' (εἶθ' ὑπείκων, ὥσπερ εἴωθε, 863c); cf. Plutarch's remarks on Herodotus' similar presentation of the accusation against the Alcmaeonids (below, §1.4).

[28] Cf. 856c: τῷ φάσκειν ἀπιστεῖν ἃ πάνυ πιστεύεσθαι θέλουσιν.

[29] Esp. in ch. 7.

[30] See esp. Dewald (1987); Marincola (1987). But Darbo-Peschanski (1987), 107–12, emphasizes rather 'la discrétion de l'enquêteur' (108) and the extent to which he gives voice to others, underlining the exceptional nature of Book 2 (which is generally recognized: cf. e.g. Marincola (1987), 123).

always frank in expressing his authorial view. Indeed, at times, far from expressing his opinion openly, he withholds or withdraws it in a strikingly self-conscious manner (as Plutarch observes and as we shall see in the example below). Again, a perspicacious reader may on occasion sense discrepancies between explicit authorial judgements and an alternative reading of the thrust of the wider narrative. Equally, discrepancies at times arise over the course of a particular account as a result of what seems to be a more generally shifting treatment (for example, where changes in the implied perspective are produced). But the obvious nature of many of these suggests a further—and important—qualification to Plutarch's formulation: it invites us to admit the possibility that rather than *deceiving* his readers in this regard, Herodotus *intended* them to notice such discrepancies. The same applies in the case of Herodotus' so-called source citations, which Detlev Fehling interpreted as fabrications intended to deceive his audience into believing fictions: the situation must be more complicated, since Herodotus' presentation *advertises* the doubtful nature of the material.[31]

## 1.2.2 Incongruities and wonders

Indeed a second aspect of Herodotean narrative that Plutarch highlights as characteristic is the presence of the incongruous: of *atopoi,* out-of-place

---

[31] Cf. Erbse (1991), countering Fehling's reading of Herodotus' presentation of the 'Persian' version of the miracle at Delphi as an invention intended to deceive readers: '[d]ie Fiktion soll als solche erkannt werden . . . Herodot teilt mit, was er erfahren hat, aber er arrangiert und ergänzt die Nachrichten so, daß man zum wahren Sachverhalt vordringen kann' ('the fiction should be recognized as such . . . Herodotus recounts what he has heard, but he arranges and completes the material in such a way that one can reach the true facts', 8). Again in opposition to Fehling, Shrimpton and Gillis (1997) present a convincing case for Herodotus' source citations as distancing devices designed to highlight the dubious nature of a report. Luraghi (2001) and (2006) argues that they are not 'source citations' at all but rather '*akoē* statements' reminding readers of the local and collective nature of the knowledge the *Histories* assembles. Dewald (1999) finds in the 'shifting focalizations' of the prologue a warning to readers about the self-interested nature of narrative: the Persian and Phoenician versions (and equally the implied Greek version: (1999), 226) are 'overtly both partial and partisan' (2002), 270. Cobet (1974) recalls the complicated character of the oral traditions available to Herodotus and underlines the unsuitability of Fehling's true/ false framework. The most powerful general critique of Fehling is Fowler's (1996), 80–6 case that Herodotus discovered the *problem* of sources.

elements.³² Plutarch points to numerous instances. One is Herodotus' reporting of Croesus' honouring the gods with rich dedications, yet subsequently presenting the action as ungodly through the inclusion of the tale of their provenance: Croesus' particularly gruesome torture of his half-brother Pantaleon (858d–e). Most serious, of course, and what Plutarch specifically aims at rebutting in detail, is how Herodotus includes 'out-of-place and lying opinions (ἀτόπους καὶ ψευδεῖς . . . δόξας) about the best and greatest of Greek cities and heroes' (874c). Digressions generally, in Plutarch's view, have limited suitability: they belong in *mythoi* (myths) and *archaiologiai* (tales of the distant past), or in *epainoi* (passages of praise) (855c–d). Those that are discreditable are frequently irrelevant and unsuitable to *historia* (cf. 855b–c).

So, too, conjectures about hidden thoughts should not be included if they detract from the account of great deeds (*erga megala*). For just as on the level of events the historian should write what he knows to be true, but in the case of doubt, prefer a better account to a worse (855e), so too particularly when delving into the necessarily more obscure realm of the hidden causes and motives behind those events:

ἐπὶ τῶν ὁμολογουμένων πεπρᾶχθαι, τὴν δ' αἰτίαν ἀφ' ἧς πέπρακται καὶ τὴν διάνοιαν ἐχόντων ἄδηλον, ὁ πρὸς τὸ χεῖρον εἰκάζων δυσμενής ἐστι καὶ κακοήθης . . . εἰ μὲν γάρ τις εὐδοκιμοῦσιν ἔργοις καὶ πράγμασιν ἐπαινουμένοις αἰτίαν φαύλην ὑποτίθησι καὶ κατάγεται ταῖς διαβολαῖς εἰς ὑποψίας ἀτόπους περὶ τῆς ἐν ἀφανεῖ προαιρέσεως τοῦ πράξαντος, αὐτὸ τὸ πεπραγμένον ἐμφανῶς οὐ δυνάμενος ψέγειν . . . , εὔδηλον ὅτι φθόνου καὶ κακοηθείας ὑπερβολὴν οὐ λέλοιπε (855f–856b).

When people agree upon what happened, but the cause and motive are unclear, anyone who guesses the worst is hostile and malicious . . . For if someone conjectures a worthless cause for famous deeds and praised actions, and leads on through slanders to out-of-place suspicions about the hidden purpose of the doer of the deed, because he cannot censure openly the deed itself . . . , he clearly reveals a surplus of envy and malice (855f–856b).

In Plutarch's estimation, the nature of the conjectures Herodotus frequently provides as to the motives of the *Histories'* actors plays a part in undermining the heroism of it all, depriving this tale of *erga*

³² e.g. 855c: the lengthening of an account 'so as to include a misfortune (ἀτύχημα) or an action that is inappropriate (ἄτοπος) or futile (οὐ χρηστή)'.

*megala* accomplished by Greeks of its due dignity. Herodotus' presentation of motives thus represents one variety of his βλασφημία and κακολογία ('defamation and abuse', 874b) that readers must beware (and that the *Malice* seeks to expose).

Plutarch has a point; for there *does* seem to be a pervasive tension within Herodotus' project and purposes, manifest right from the *Histories'* beginning. The project announced in the preface of memorializing heroic human achievement, in epic style—

ὡς μήτε τὰ γενόμενα ἐξ ἀνθρώπων τῷ χρόνῳ ἐξίτηλα γένηται, μήτε ἔργα
μεγάλα τε καὶ θωμαστά, τὰ μὲν Ἕλλησι, τὰ δὲ βαρβάροισι ἀποδεχθέντα,
ἀκλεᾶ γένηται

so that human events do not become effaced in the course of time, nor the *erga megala te kai thōmasta* (great and wondrous deeds) performed by Greeks and non-Greeks become *aklea* (unsung/without fame)

—stands at some variance with the subsequent narrative's persistent scrutiny with a pragmatic eye of the human motives that lie beneath those *erga*.[33] Herodotus' practice when it comes to conjecturing motives seems similar in spirit to his occasional inclination (in accordance with Plutarch's accusation, 855b–c) to foist upon his narrative less reputable versions of events:[34] conjectures are frequently made, and very often in the direction of insisting upon more self-serving motives than readers might otherwise have supposed.[35] Plutarch's anxiety lest this sabotage the project of memorializing Greek achievement is understandable. Herodotus' exposing of human motives will indeed,

---

[33] Although Homer's heroes at times display pragmatic and self-serving motives, the heroic ideal—of *philotimia* (desire for honour) as the prime motivating impulse behind courageous action—stands nonetheless as an ideal, with figures like Odysseus and Paris being in some ways anti-heroic.

[34] e.g. in his account of the Thebans at Thermopylae, whose negative press in the *Histories* was a key reason for Plutarch's defence (864d–865f). Compare also his decision to relate, out of the four different stories he has heard as to Cyrus' end, the one in which the king's head is plunged into a sack of blood (a story that might be felt to demean Cyrus, thereby lessening his status as worthy foe)!

[35] Michael Flower suggests that Herodotus' manner of rooting his analysis of personal motivation in a cynical view of human nature established the practice continued by Thucydides and culminating with Theopompos—who indeed 'is so concerned to discover the moral reason and to unveil all the mysteries of seeming virtue and undetected vice, that he overlooks or disregards the pragmatic element in human decision-making' (1994), esp. 178–81, quote at 171.

on occasion, have the effect of rupturing the narrative's heroic tone, or at least of distracting readers from an exclusive focus on *erga* as traditionally conceived[36]—as we shall find over the course of the Thermopylae narrative.[37] (The work itself will in fact, over its course, develop a far broader definition of what constitute *erga megala te kai thōmasta*.[38])

And yet creating *kleos* is not all that the *Histories*, from the outset, lays claim to be doing: for with the continuation of the opening sentence (. . . *τά τε ἄλλα καὶ δι' ἣν αἰτίην ἐπολέμησαν ἀλλήλοισι*, 'both other things and especially through what cause they warred') there emerges a focus also on *aitiē*, with its range of meaning from 'responsibility' to 'cause'—of which motivation is clearly an important aspect.[39] Human motives are potentially encompassed also by the preface's mention of *γενόμενα ἐξ ἀνθρώπων* ('human events', or more expansively, 'what has come about as the result of human agency'[40]). Herodotus' technique of staging uncertainty surrounding questions of motivation is in keeping with (and reminds readers of) the reality that motivation and psychology are among those areas most hidden from the historian's gaze, and so most requiring his, and readers', conjecture.

## 1.2.3 Cognitive potential?

We have found Plutarch responding to Herodotus' frequent inclusion of incongruous elements in his account, and more broadly to the *Histories'* general multiplicity. The work is indeed filled with elements, including digressions, explanations, and ascriptions of motives, furnishing readers with different perspectives that at times go against the

---

[36] Cf. Plutarch's criticism of Herodotus' failure to do justice to the great battles—most traditional *erga*—of the Persian wars (see esp. 873d–874a).

[37] §3.3 below.

[38] Cf. Immerwahr (1960).

[39] On causal argument in the *Histories*, see esp. Immerwahr (1956); Gould (1989), 63–85; Lateiner (1989), 189–210; Lateiner's discussion (and chart: 206) of the *Histories'* five different levels of explanation exposes the rich variety of causes Herodotus assembles, often complementary (cf. ibid. 208: 'Multiple aetiology is supplementary rather than contradictory'). For the entwining in the *Histories* of various kinds of causal factors and modes of explanation, see also e.g. Cobet (1971); Wood (1972); Hunter (1982).

[40] As Fowler (2006), 31 translates; note Fowler's discussion, ibid. 31–2, of the connection between *aitiē* and *historiē*.

grain of the preceding (or surrounding) narrative. These incongruities in the text invite readerly pause for thought. They provoke surprise and wonder, occasionally shock (as in Plutarch's case), and so draw readers into a process of reflection and re-evaluation, inviting them to reconsider the earlier narrative from a different perspective, even at times (like Plutarch) to challenge the version presented by that narrative. The discordant final chapter on Croesus, for example, just mentioned, exposes an entirely different perspective on the king, which invites readers to reflect back and revise their earlier assessments of his character.[41] Again, readers might well wonder (as Herodotus alleges some already have, 6.43) at the spectacle of Persian nobles in the sixth century conducting a Greek-style debate on constitutional forms, which Herodotus insists actually happened (3.80–2, esp. 3.80.1). This might perhaps destabilize the assumptions of some readers.

Several individuals within the *Histories* demonstrate this cognitive potential of the incongruous or wondrous. The gap between Periander's expectations and Arion's surprising story, for example, causes the tyrant to engage in active inquiry in a bid to determine the truth.[42] Periander's disbelief at the wonder (the θῶμα μέγιστον, 1.23) of Arion's divine rescue, which provokes his further careful inquiry, parallels Herodotus' own response to the story about Arion, as Vivienne Gray observes.[43] Indeed, frequently we sense that astonishment or disbelief has fuelled Herodotus' own additional inquiry or reflection: Readers are invited to respond in a similar way, as they

---

[41] Cf. Ubsdell (1983), 2–5: the example illustrates Herodotus' use of 'instructive paradox'; cf. ibid. 9–77. Compare the similarly surprising final note on Peisistratus, which likewise invites readers to review in retrospect, and with fuller understanding, the preceding account of his career (below, §5.4); and Kurke (1999), 118–21 on Herodotus' closing praise of Polykrates' *megaloprepeia* ('magnificence'): 'For a moment, we glimpse a figure very different from the ruthless pirate portrayed in the earlier narrative' (119).

[42] Gray (2001).

[43] Gray (2001), esp. 15–16 for the several respects in which Periander's inquiry here mirrors Herodotus' (as it does in the related Alyattes story too: 18–19). (Her further suggestion, that as Periander's inquiry confirms his belief in the truth of the wonder, so Herodotus' own belief in the truth of the Arion story may be implied, is an extrapolation I would shy from making.) Cf. de Jong (2004), 113–14; more generally, Hunzinger (1995), 57–8 on the 'séduction intellectuelle' ('intellectual captivation') a *thōma* exercises, stimulating the desire to inquire; Goldhill (2002), 21–6 on wonder as provoking the historian's study of *aitiai*.

confront the gaps that the text opens up between the expected and the actual.[44] Rosaria Munson comments usefully on those occasions when Herodotus speaks specifically of 'wonders':

Whether in the ethnography or in the history, once the metanarrative labels any particular fact a *thoma*, that fact tends to jump out from its narrative context but nevertheless needs a context in which to make sense. It is not explained but demands somehow to be explained and to participate, in its turn, in the text's network of explanations. *It provides an impulse to mental inquiry*, much as, in Aristotle's formulation, wonder provides the impulse to philosophy. *It is an inquiry, however, that the text declines to actualize but implicitly identifies as the task of the recipient.*[45]

These observations might well be applied more broadly to Herodotus' presentation, even without *thōma* terminology, of what appears contradictory, surprising, or wondrous. Wolfgang Iser's notion of the way in which the 'gaps' or 'blanks' in a text invite readers to begin a process of bridging them (by integrating through their reading the variety of different perspectives contained within a narrative text) describes a similar phenomenon.

## 1.2.4 A juridical analogy?

Narrative sites marked by particular dissonance or incongruity are frequently, perhaps most strikingly, produced through the presence of explicitly irreconcilable alternatives.[46] Especially in the absence of straightforward authorial resolution, these alternatives invite readers to engage with the discrepancy by choosing one or the other as the more plausible. Herodotus' adversarial presentation in such instances is a further aspect of his narrative technique that Plutarch's response illuminates, as he brings to bear juridical analogies of

---

[44] We may compare how emotion and cognition were 'inextricably interwoven' in the audience's response to tragic theatre: Lada (1996), 409; cf. Lada (1993).

[45] Munson (2001), 234 (my italics).

[46] e.g. in connection with the accounts arising from different informants, or by means of the common *eite... eite...* formulation. At times such alternatives are not irreconcilable, but together give a similar message, or suggest dual levels of explanation (e.g. divine and human). At times, however, they clearly are. See further below, §5.1.

prosecute and defence in describing the processes of Herodotus'
narrative.[47] In his account of the shield signal following Marathon,[48]
Plutarch describes Herodotus 'pretending to speak in defence
(ἀπολογεῖσθαι) on behalf of the Alcmaeonids against the very charges
(ἐγκλήματα) he had been first to lay against them' (862f). He complains: 'first you prosecute (κατηγορεῖς), then you defend (ἀπολογῇ);
and against famous men you bring false accusations
(γράφεις... διαβολάς), which then you withdraw' (862f–863a).[49]
Plutarch here alights upon a most interesting feature of Herodotus'
presentation. The way in which opposing accounts may be connected
explicitly, by means of source citations, to the versions told to
Herodotus by different groups of informants makes a juridical analogy all the more appropriate.[50]

The nature of the response such an analogy implies (and elicits) is
significant: for in being placed in a position resembling that of jurors
in a *dikastērion* (or of citizens in an *ekklēsia*)—and indeed more
broadly that of audiences of contests of words (*agōnes logōn*) in
general—readers are invited all the more vigorously to judge matters
for themselves. The role was one that Herodotus' fifth-century audience was particularly well equipped to undertake: they were practised

[47] Cf. also Plutarch's general tendency to interpret the *Histories* as promoting
either praise or blame—or rather, as opposing implied Greek stories of praise with
Herodotus' own blame-filled alternative versions. Woodman (1988), 40–4 observes
the general tendency of historians to see their work in terms of praise and blame.
Nagy (1990), 250–73 discusses the *Histories'* juridical aspect. Munson (2001), 217–31
develops Nagy's argument to reveal Herodotus as judicial arbiter of current as well as
past controversy. The judicial stance was regarded as appropriate in historiographical
polemic: Marincola (1997), 218–24.
[48] On which see further below, §1.4.
[49] Cf. Plutarch's descriptions of Herodotean narrative in terms of accusations
(*aitiai*: 858c, 859e, 863c, 871c; *enklēmata*: 863c; *katēgoriai*: 870c) and acquitting
(862e: ἀπολύων... Ἀλκμαιωνίδας ἑτέροις τὴν προδοσίαν ἀνατίθησιν, 'acquitting the
Alcmaeonids he attributes the treason to others').
[50] Fehling (1989) observes how Herodotus has frequently pared down to two
opposing versions the various accounts available to him. Darbo-Peschanski (1987)
underlines the importance of *dikē* in the *Histories* and compares Herodotus' presentation of history to 'une sorte de tribunal informel, où se règlent indéfiniment des
conflits' ('a kind of informal court, where conflicts are settled indefinitely', 72).
Connor (1993) finds the roots of '*histōr*' in the traditional community judge.
Szegedy-Maszak (1987), 173–4 likens the Herodotean narrator to an Athenian
juror. Fowler (2006), 32 with n. 16 notes that Herodotus dramatizes 'judging' in
relation to his own inquiries as well as that of his characters.

in the processes of speakers' debates, in their various contexts—lawcourt, assembly, sophistic *epidexis*, tragic performance, and so forth—and at all levels, public and formal through to private and informal,[51] and accustomed to the need to take a stand and make a judgement. In the case of the Athenian citizen contingent of Herodotus' audience, many were (or had been) jurors, and so were accustomed to listening critically to opposed speeches in a bid to judge the truth particularly about sequences of events and motives. The possibility arises that Herodotus introduced this agonistic framework specifically so as to promote an especially *committed, active* sort of reader response (indeed, a response akin to that of Plutarch), and—so far from 'dancing away the truth'—to underscore the *seriousness* of the responsibility he passes on to his readers. An account of the past, this implies, is not reducible simply (*pace* Darbo-Peschanski's emphasis[52]) to a matter of opinion. Herodotus was working with an audience expectation that a judgement would be made, and one concerning the truth of their recent past: of what happened and why.[53] His original readers came to the text with knowledge of their own about that past, expecting to have their ideas extended, corroborated, challenged. But they certainly expected more than just relative or competing 'truths',[54] especially in view of Herodotus' announced purpose (to publish results of *historiē*, research) and his emphasis throughout the *Histories* on truth finding.[55] His technique obliges readers to work actively in figuring out that meaning, just as characters in his text must.

[51] Thomas (2003) discusses the many varieties of prose performance occurring in the late fifth century, including formal and semi-formal *agōnes logōn* and *antilogiai* ('opposing arguments') on serious subjects (e.g. philosophy, natural philosophy, and medicine); cf. ibid. (2000), 249–69.

[52] Darbo-Peschanski (1985) and (1987).

[53] For all the Athenians' suspicions of rhetoric, they did still believe there was a distinction between true and false; cf. Hesk (2000), esp. 297–8.

[54] *Pace* Darbo-Peschanski (1987), 135–53. I concur rather with Paul Veyne's (1987) rejection of her opposition of opinion v. truth: 'l'opinion est pour Hérodote l'opération implicite du jugement, qui chez un esprit bien fait aboutit à la vérité' ('opinion is for Herodotus the implicit operation of judgement, which in the case of a capable mind ends up at the truth', 10).

[55] Cf. ἀληθείη, 'truth': 1.14.2; 5.88.1; 7.139.1, etc.; cf. τὸ ἐόν: e.g. 1.97.1; 7.209.1; γνώμη, 'opinion', that gets one as close as possible to the truth (cf. above n.): 2.18.1, 2.120; 8.8.3, etc; ἀτρεκείη, 'accuracy': e.g. 5.54.1. See further Marincola (1987); Cartledge and Greenwood (2002); Dewald (2002).

Herodotus' strategy of enfranchising his readers as capable judges seems the reverse of that which Anna Missiou has detected in the oratory of Andocides (as well as Antiphon), which 'encourages submissiveness and passivity in the audience' and even (in the case of *The Spartan Peace*) represents, if Missiou is correct, 'an attack on the democratic behaviour of deliberation and decision-making'.[56] The *Histories* is democratic not simply in giving voice to such a rich variety of perspectives,[57] but also in its *active* promotion of each reader's individual deliberation and response. It may thus be viewed as having *invited* even the vigorous response of Plutarch.

## 1.2.5 Herodotus' sophistic context

The use of varied and even 'sophistic' techniques in 'displaying' knowledge about the past,[58] while alien to Plutarch's experience, seems in keeping with what we know of Herodotus' intellectual milieu. The truth had not yet been categorized; the sophists were engaged in experimenting with manifold ways of attaining and presenting it; everyone claimed to possess it.[59] Though many were aware of the challenges involved in uncovering it, Gorgias was atypical in

---

[56] Missiou (1992), quotations at 176, 182.

[57] Darbo-Peschanski (1985) and (1987), esp. 116 on the *Histories*' 'polyphonie'; Dewald (1999), 221–52; Boedeker (2000), 114: 'Herodotus's new genre reflects in essential ways the politics he explicitly admires. First, his account—like the freedom of speech (ἰσηγορία) that he says made Athens successful (5.78)—gives many different voices their say, even while showing that not all speak with equal veracity and wisdom'. Boedeker (2003), 31 observes that the *Histories* is also dialogic, characterized by a 'profusion of discourses'. Bakker (2002*a*), 13–22 exposes the specifically dialogic semantics of the expression '*histories apodexis*'.

[58] See Thomas (2000), 221–8, 260–4 on the sophistic connotations of *apodexis* ('demonstration, display'), which bears a close relationship with *epidexis*; cf. Bakker (2002*a*). These sit alongside its more traditional, Homeric connotations, underlined by Nagy (1987). Herodotus refers to his work as a *sungraphē* (1.93.1)—which perhaps has connotations of (later) fifth-century sophistic *writtenness*.

[59] Cf. Thomas (2000), 101: 'We are perhaps at a point where ideas about knowledge and truth are on the move, different and competing conceptions coexist of how to get at the truth, the unknown, from the poets, from experience and evidence of experience, to schematic or abstract theories, all with their own plausibility, none quite satisfying or sufficient by itself to jettison all the rest'; Thomas (2000) provides a lively sketch of this background, highlighting the fluidity of disciplinary boundaries.

questioning the essential viability of the task.[60] Herodotus, too, was deeply sensitive to the challenges presented by his project of memorializing the past, and he continually reminds readers of those challenges. Indeed, this constant foregrounding of the difficulties inherent in conducting *historiē* is 'integral to his self-conception and without parallel in the surviving fragments of contemporary writers of history, or in earlier writers of ethnography or geography'.[61] But the project makes no sense unless its aim was to present the truth.

In the ethnographic sections of the *Histories*, as Rosalind Thomas has shown, it is in the challenging places where Herodotus resorts to expressions of current (medical) science and natural philosophy.[62] Perhaps, likewise, it was natural for him to make use of innovative techniques, and specifically of a sophist-like persona,[63] in dealing with the more challenging epistemological problems of the narrative books—such as those requiring conjecture about the hidden workings of people's minds. Indeed, his own narrative stages the constructive use of an unreliable narrator in dealing with difficult epistemological questions in the person of the Egyptian scribe, whose claim to know accurately the sources of the Nile Herodotus recognizes as a jest ('he seemed to me to be joking ($\pi\alpha\acute{\iota}\zeta\epsilon\iota\nu$)...', 2.28.2). Thus Herodotus intimates that the Egyptian was neither mistaken nor deceiving, but rather making his point about the limits of knowledge all the more effectively through the use of irony: for who could possibly know *accurately* ($\grave{\alpha}\tau\rho\epsilon\kappa\acute{\epsilon}\omega\varsigma$) such information as that![64] It seems relevant here that the Egyptians are the *Histories'* historically minded people *par excellence*, whose historical methods Herodotus aligns with his own and whose historical understanding includes awareness of epistemological limits.

---

[60] At least if his treatise *On Not Being* was meant seriously. Gorgias' defence of Helen is placed in an ironic framework by his calling it a *paignion*, 'jest'.

[61] Fowler (2006), 33; cf. Fowler (1996).

[62] Thomas (2000), ch. 6 (on Herodotus' use of deductive argument and proofs) and (2006), esp. 72.

[63] See further ch. 3 below.

[64] It is rare that Herodotus sees someone making fun in this manner; usually an informant is said simply to be wrong or misguided.

Again, Thomas has gestured towards the implications for the rest of the *Histories* of Herodotus' awareness of a theoretical problem of particular significance in late fifth-century science, that of analogy from the visible to the invisible:[65] 'We may wonder about other elements in the *Histories* which are in some sense "invisible": explanations for Greek success against Persia, for instance, knowledge about the gods and *ta theia*' (2.3.2).[66] Conjectures of invisible motivations (from visible signs such as action and speech) were perhaps felt to belong in the same category. Their treatment, likewise, may have invited the use of sophisticated techniques, particularly when the historian came to negotiating the tension between the impulse to present persuasive conjectures and even mimetic re-enactments, while at the same time displaying his awareness of the challenges faced in producing such an account, and of its necessary constraints.

## 1.3 THE *HISTORIES* AND READER RESPONSE THEORY

We have noted Herodotus' tendency in certain narrative contexts to refrain from presenting an overarching judgement or making an overall concluding statement (evidenced most strikingly in the *Histories*' ending, 9.122), but rather to present a range of different perspectives and leave readers to weave together the various threads into their own interpretation. Striking also is the complexity of the *Histories*' narrative twists, including notably (as we shall see) in its presentation of multiple and progressively shifting motivations. This aspect of the *Histories* invites and repays both the reader's close and careful attention, and also a progressive movement through the text, akin to that of a journey.[67] It fits well with Wolfgang Iser's theory of

---

[65] Cf. 2.33.2: συμβάλλομαι τοῖσι ἐμφανέσι τὰ μὴ γινωσκόμενα τεκμαιρόμενος ('I conjecture what is unknown by judging from what is visible'). Corcella (1984), 239–43 points, however, to a contrast between Herodotus and the sophists in the historian's acute sensitivity to the *limits* of human knowledge of the invisible.

[66] Thomas (2000), 211; on such analogy in contemporary science: ibid. 200–11.

[67] The *Histories*' narrative processes may be envisaged in terms of a journey, with Herodotus as guide or traveller (cf. Pohlenz (1937), 43, in his case using the metaphor to comprehend apparently digressive material; Payen (1997), 334–42; Montiglio

reader response. Iser's theory, concerned with describing the interaction between text and reader,[68] may indeed aid us in illuminating
Herodotus' subtle manipulation of his audience's response.[69] The
theory describes techniques that a good storyteller may use naturally
and largely subconsciously. But Herodotus lived in an age of rhetorical awareness: the sophists made their teaching careers from the
fact that the key to political influence resided in the orator's ability to
sway the *dēmos*; experts analysed the workings of persuasion; the
dangers and failures of rhetoric were a contemporary *thōma*.[70] And
the *Histories* itself frequently dramatizes attempts at persuasion.
The fact of the rhetorical awareness of Herodotus' contemporary

(2005), 136–46). Reader response theorists employ the same analogy, envisaging
one's views of the narrative as akin to those from the window of a moving vehicle:
one sees a single view at a time, with views changing progressively as one travels along
and the full picture built up in one's mind modified accordingly.

[68] See particularly his chapter of this title in Iser (1989), 31–41; cf. Iser (1978). Iser
mainly uses fictional works to illustrate his argument, but this (he notes) is because
they 'provide the greatest variety of facets pertinent to an analysis of the act of
reading' (1989), 54.

[69] Reader-response criticism 'no longer exist(s) at the zenith of literary fashion',
but it 'nevertheless continue(s) to operate at the forefront of literary studies' (Davis
and Womack (2002), 156), providing a useful tool for understanding the nature of
reading and the way in which meaning is produced. Although Iser does not provide
the universal model he intended, his system remains worthwhile for illuminating
specific readings; cf. Mailloux's observations in his review of Iser (1989): Mailloux
(1991), 314. Wheeler (1999), 3, for example, finds Iser's principle that literary texts
initiate 'performances' of meaning (Iser (1978), 27) a helpful springboard for establishing a new basis upon which to read the *Metamorphoses*. Foley (1991) builds on
Iser's model in developing his notion of oral poetry's 'implied auditor', whose
memory of prior performances—knowledge of tradition—engenders richer meaning
in any particular performance (e.g. in Homer's text as we have it). The 'certain type of
text and reaction' that Holub (1984), 98–9 identifies as that upon which Iser's model
depends is compatible with the character of Herodotus' *Histories*. Payen (1990)
applies the associated reception theory of H. R. Jauss to the analysis of Herodotus'
second book, with fruitful results.

[70] As Davis and Womack (2002), 52 observe, the reader-response paradigm's
conception 'finds its roots . . . in the ancient Greek and Roman cultures that viewed
literature as a rhetorical device for manipulating a given audience's reactions. The
ancients intuitively recognized that a basic understanding of the rhetorical strategies
inherent in literary works afforded them with the means for registering the impact of
those texts upon their audience of "readers"'. Connor (1984), 17 n. 26 notes that
Iser's main point had been made in antiquity by Theophrastus as quoted by Deme-
trius, *On Style* §222.

audience[71] seems to confirm that a reader-response approach may be a valid and profitable way of analysing the way the text works. We might well, but *need* not, go so far as Plutarch in assuming that much of what is found in Herodotus' text is conscious strategy on the part of the *author*.

Iser's central concern is the way in which a text invites readers to respond to it *actively*—just as skilled orators or storytellers may seek to do, so as to capture and maintain their audience's attention and cause them to engage in a particular way with their words. In Iser's formulation, which draws on psychoanalytic research into interpersonal perception and communication, it is a text's indeterminacy that prompts readers into active interpretation:

it is the gaps, the fundamental asymmetry between text and reader, that give rise to communication in the reading process. . . . What is concealed spurs the reader into action, but this action is also controlled by what is revealed; the explicit in its turn is transformed when the implicit has been brought to light. Whenever the reader bridges the gaps, communication begins. The gaps function as a kind of pivot on which the whole text-reader relationship revolves. Hence, the structured blanks of the text stimulate the process of ideation to be performed by the reader on terms set by the text. . . . The blanks leave open the connection between textual perspectives, and so spur the reader into coordinating these perspectives and patterns (Iser (1989), 33–4).

The different perspectives are both 'marshaled into a graduated sequence' and 'transformed into reciprocal reflectors'.[72] The variety of perspectives that compose a narrative text (and which 'outline the author's view and also provide access to what the reader is meant to visualize')—the main four being those of narrator, characters, plot, and fictitious reader—

---

[71] Recent trends in Herodotean scholarship view the *Histories* as 'rhetorical' both in the general sense of its being fundamentally shaped by literary tradition, (consciously) borrowing literary techniques from poetic predecessors (esp. Homer: cf. ch. 2 n. 2 below), and specifically as reflecting and participating in mid to late fifth-century developments of the art of rhetoric (as employed in the epideictic displays of sophistic rhetoricians and early scientists alike): cf. esp. Thomas (1993); (2000), chs. 7–8. Pelling (2006c) shows Herodotus unmasking travesties of *logos*. Speakers in the *Histories* typically employ 'deflection, circumlocution, or simple deceit' (116)—to which Herodotus' audience is invited to respond critically.

[72] Iser (1989), 36.

may differ in order of importance, [but] none of them on its own is identical with the meaning of the text, which is to be brought about by their constant intertwining through the reader in the reading process (Iser (1989), 35).

These textual perspectives are frequently subdivided (and that naturally leads to an increase in the number of blanks): the narrator's perspective, for example, may be split 'into that of the implied author's set against that of the author as narrator' (35). In accounts of recent history, listeners' pre-existing knowledge of what they think happened perhaps supplies the most powerful of further perspectives that inform their act of contributing to the creation of meaning.[73]

Iser draws an analogy with the fact that nineteenth-century readers often preferred serialized novels to the identical text in book form:[74] an instalment would generally end with a cliffhanger, and while they waited for the next, readers would be drawn into imaginative activity, wondering how the situation might unfold. Their participation in, and consequent satisfaction with, the story would naturally be heightened. The modern TV serial uses the same formula. Iser notes that a common means used in fictional narrative to increase the reader's imaginative activity (a similar technique to that used by the movie preview: 192)

is suddenly to cut to new characters or even to different plotlines, so that the reader is forced to try to find connections between the hitherto familiar story and the new, unforeseeable situations. He is faced with a whole network of possibilities, and thus begins himself to formulate missing links. The temporary withholding of information acts as a stimulus, and this is further intensified by details suggestive of possible solutions. The blanks make the reader bring the story itself to life—he lives with the characters and experiences their activities.[75]

---

[73] In non-fiction as in fiction, Iser suggests, we are given 'something to ideate': the difference is that in the case of fiction, 'the aesthetic object is something that has to be assembled and ideated in the reader's mind and has no exact match in the empirically given world', whereas in non-fiction 'the facts themselves exist independently of our activity of picturing them ... If we have to ideate an existing, though absent, object, we produce certain views of it, but we do not produce the object itself' (55). (The distinction is challenged by Hayden White and others who regard all varieties of narrative as creating reality.)

[74] Iser (1978), 191 Iser (1989), 11.

[75] Iser (1978), 192.

Iser's approach finds its origin in research that examines a situation inherent in *all* communication. Nonetheless, in the theory as he develops and applies it there is room for the author—whether subconsciously or intentionally—to amplify a text's indeterminacy and thus to heighten the consequent effects.[76] In shifting along the spectrum towards contemplating the possibility of deliberate authorial strategy, we may be tempted to compare Iser's notion of the blank with Badian's 'subtle silences': places where Herodotus alerts the reader to a particular interpretation while avoiding explicit comment.[77] These approaches must ultimately be carefully distinguished, for whereas Badian envisages deliberate suppression with a view to making a particular case, for Iser the amplification of indeterminacy is at the service of more general intellectual engagement (and need not be intentional). And yet, Iser's account does nonetheless admit the possibility of authorial guidance in the direction of a particular interpretation: one of a text's given perspectives, for example, might be lent particular emphasis. When it comes to Herodotus' *Histories*, we shall be especially concerned with cases where the narrative techniques under discussion are generally thought-provoking, rather than pressing one particular interpretation. We shall find instances, naturally, where the alert reader is more strongly guided—especially where, for example, a strand of the narrative appears to be challenging readers' assumptions. But the characterization of Herodotus that surfaces is not one of a man with axes to grind. It is rather that of one keenly aware of the challenges involved in recounting the past. Herodotus' narrative techniques alert his readers to the difficulty of knowing and understanding events. The historian's particular idiosyncratic capabilities, and the limited human nature of his knowledge, render his account of the past a matter frequently of possibilities rather than certainties. It remains to some extent provisional, open to his readers' collaboration in extending and modifying it.

---

[76] Note Iser's suggestion that '[w]ith "traditional" texts this process was more or less unconscious, but modern texts frequently exploit it quite deliberately', (1974), 280.
[77] Badian (1994); cf. 318–21 below.

## 1.4 THE ALCMAEONID *THŌMA*

Herodotus' notorious Alcmaeonid excursus begins with the extraordinary rumour about the Alcmaeonid family: that they held up a shield after the battle of Marathon to signal to the Persian fleet that they should now sail around Cape Sunium to Piraeus, in the hope of taking Athens before her soldiers returned to the city (6.115). Plutarch devotes much attention to Herodotus' presentation of the rumour. We may take it as a test case for evaluating the usefulness of a reader-response approach.

In the narration of the shield incident itself we see Herodotus' use of the temporary withholding of information that Iser identifies as a stimulus to reader response: in mentioning the accusation at 6.115 ('there was a charge (αἰτίη) put forth among Athenians...'), but refraining from offering his personal view on the question until 6.121.1—

It is a *thōma* (wonder) to me and I won't accept the assertion (οὐκ ἐνδέκομαι τὸν λόγον) that the Alcmaeonids could ever have held up a shield to the Persians following an agreement (ἐκ συνθήματος), wanting Athens to be subject to non-Greeks and Hippias. After all, they were obviously at least as hating of tyrants (μισοτύραννοι) as Kallias (son of Phainippos, father of Hipponikos), or even more so than he....[78]

—Herodotus leaves readers much opportunity for reflecting upon the matter themselves. The replaying of doubt in readers' minds throughout the several chapters that precede his statement of disbelief in the rumour makes the story more engaging, and also conveys the climate of the times, drawing readers into the atmosphere of rumours and accusations. This purpose goes some way towards explaining the prevalence in the *Histories*, which Plutarch observes,

---

[78] Herodotus reiterates this thought following the Kallias digression: 'it is a wonder (θῶμα), then, to me, and I do not admit the slander (διαβολή) that these people held up a shield: these people who have always consistently fled tyrants (ἔφευγόν τε τὸν πάντα χρόνον τοὺς τυράννους), and through whose contriving the Peisistratids lost the tyranny. And thus they were responsible for freeing Athens more by far even than Harmodios and Aristogeiton, as I judge...' (6.123.1–2).

of τὸ βλασφημεῖν καὶ ψέγειν ('slander and blame', 855d) delivered by people in the text.[79]

Turning to the broader context, we have noted Plutarch's negative response to the *Histories*' tendency to 'seek out digressions', particularly where these seem *atopoi* ('out of place') or otherwise disreputable in effect. Herodotus' strung-along style with its regular digressions does indeed frequently lead to the significant juxtaposition of material or stories, sometimes of quite different periods. While Herodotus gives connections throughout, these frequently seem insufficient as explanations for the full nature of the relationship.[80] It is in this way that he leaves readers to draw out meaning for themselves from the succession of Alcmaeonid tales that are sparked off by his rejection of the accusation of Alcmaeonid treachery and declaration that they have always been strongly *misotyrannoi*, 'hating of tyrants'. These tales document the family's rise to prominence, first with the story of Alcmaeon's enrichment at the hands of a Lydian despot (6.125), then of the next generation's shrewd marital tie with a Greek tyrant's household (6.126–30), rounded off with that of the birth of the latest famous Alcmaeonid—leader in the eyes of some (as Herodotus had no need to point out[81]) of a latter-day tyranny (6.131). Thus again in accordance with Iser's theory, readers' reflections on the accusation are further intensified with the later 'details suggestive of possible solutions' that Herodotus goes on to offer— these stories that hint at Alcmaeonid ties with tyranny, and may be felt to undermine the defence.[82]

---

[79] We might compare the effect of Tacitean *rumores*: see Ryberg (1942).

[80] Cf. e.g. at 5.67: the digression on Cleisthenes of Sicyon's reforms is connected to the previous section by Herodotus' remark that 'in doing these things, this Cleisthenes [of Athens], it seems to me, was imitating his own mother's father, Cleisthenes tyrant of Sicyon': but readers may well look for further levels of connection between the two accounts. See Osborne (2002), 502–4 for Herodotus' use of suggestive juxtaposition to point to a framework of interpretation.

[81] Cf. e.g. the Thucydidean Pericles' final speech (2.63.2). See Thomas (1989), 271 for the possibility that the lion motif at 6.131.2 serves as 'a sinister reference to Pericles' absolute rule within the democracy'; Fornara (1971), 53–4 for the possibility that it refers ominously to Athens' power vis-à-vis the rest of Greece; cf. Gray (1996), 386–7. Brock (2004), 170–1 brings out the expressive ambiguity of the image.

[82] Cf. Strasburger (1955); Hart (1982); Thomas (1989), esp. 264–72; Moles (2002), 40–2.

Indeed, I would suggest, Herodotus guides readers to expand their reflections even further than this, partly through his (twice) labelling the accusation a *thōma*. Rosaria Munson has found 'no implicit retraction of the defence but rather a cheerful reflection on the charge', since

The possibility of the Alcmaeonids' closeness to the Persians is not even taken into consideration. Herodotus rather refutes the charge on the basis of the Alcmaeonids' hostility toward the Peisistratids (6.121–23), a point that the subsequent 'renown' narratives [6.125–31, documenting the family's rise to fame] never undermine.[83]

But as Munson also observes, Herodotus has himself shown his audience over the course of the *Histories* what to do when confronted with *thōmata*: that is, to 'freely associate and reflect, to find a broader context or a different plane of experience where the absurd becomes intelligible and the abnormal meaningful' (265). The '*thōma*' terminology thus invites readers to become all the more alert to potential explanatory connections and wider contexts—and so also, surely, to Herodotus' inclusion in this narrative of *numerous specific allusions* to the earlier Alcmaeonid account that appeared in the *Histories'* first book.[84]

Plutarch made the connection and put it down to 'confusions' (ταραχάς, 863b, with the implication that they result from malicious intentions):

In your defence concerning the Alcmaeonids, you show yourself a false accuser (συκοφάντην). For if the Alcmaeonids 'were obviously at least as hating of tyrants as Kallias (son of Phainippos, father of Hipponikos), or even more so than he', as you write there, how will you account for that conspiracy of theirs, which you wrote down at their first appearance, that in order to make a marriage agreement with Peisistratus they restored him to the tyranny from his flight, and would not have driven him out again, if he had not caused a quarrel with them by sleeping with his wife in an unnatural manner? (863a–b)

---

[83] Munson (2001), 262.
[84] Moles' passing comment—that the account's 'negative implications [are] reinforced by interaction with earlier sections' (2002), 42—suggests his awareness of the significance of these.

More recent commentators have frequently viewed Herodotus as somehow unaware of this contradiction: at the mercy of his sources, he simply repeats, in the later episode, Athenian and Alcmaeonid mythologizing traditions.[85] But such *naïveté* in reproducing without question a single source's version, and ingenuousness in leaving his own account filled with contradictions, would be out of character in a historian as sensitive as Herodotus is in dealing with the difficulties of contradictory sources,[86] and whose narrative sophistication is increasingly being recognized. Furthermore, specific textual pointers in this instance suggest on the contrary that Herodotus is *guiding* his readers to notice and reflect upon the inconsistencies.

To begin with, Herodotus' profession of astonishment that the Alcmaeonids would ever have betrayed Athens 'by agreement' (6.121.1) (or earlier, the rumour that they 'made an agreement with the Persians', 6.115) might well remind readers that an 'agreement' is exactly what Megacles made with Peisistratus at 1.60.2, in marrying off his daughter to the tyrant in return for lending support to his bid to regain power. Moreover, the postscript recounting the dissolution of the contract, as a result of Peisistratus' sexual transgression, made the story all the more memorable. The correlation between Herodotus' statement at 6.121.1 that he refuses to accept the *logos* (θῶμα δέ μοι καὶ **οὐκ ἐνδέκομαι τὸν λόγον**) and the fact that Peisistratus *does* accept Megacles' *logos* at 1.60.3 (**ἐνδεξαμένου δὲ τὸν λόγον** καὶ ὁμολογήσαντος ἐπὶ τούτοισι Πεισιστράτου) may also be expressive. Furthermore, the description in the sixth book of the Alcmaeonids' *removal* of the Peisistratids from power—ἐκ μηχανῆς ('by a contrivance', 6.123.1; cf. μηχανώμενοι, 'contriving', 5.62.2[87])—matches that used in the first to describe the combined Megacles-Peisistratus action in *returning* the tyrant to power (μηχανῶνται δὴ

---

[85] On these, see esp. Lavelle (1993).

[86] Herodotus' frequent presentation of opposed traditions models for audiences the need for healthy scepticism towards sources: cf. Dewald (1987); Erbse (1991). See Thomas (1989) for Herodotus' intelligent use of varied sources. As regards his Alcmaeonid stories, '[h]e seems to have avoided merely repeating any one version. He balanced the Alcmaeonid defence against highly damaging information which he got from wider popular or polis traditions.... He was surely well aware of the pitfalls of the patriotic and family traditions' (282).

[87] Nenci on 6.123.1–5 observes this connection (μηχανώμενοι ∼ ἐκ μηχανῆς).

ἐπὶ τῇ κατόδῳ, 1.60.3): the trick involving Phye.[88] The note at 6.121.2 that Kallias alone dared to buy Peisistratus' possessions 'every time that Peisistratus was driven out of Athens' serves as a further reminder of the earlier narrative, with its focus on Peisistratus' successive banishments and returns.

Again, the Hippias who leads the Persians to Marathon in 490 BC is the very Peisistratid who appeared in the earlier account and was particularly keen that Peisistratus reclaim the tyranny: his active role and the success of his counsel (1.61.3) anticipated his significance in the later narrative.[89] Much as the route towards Athens *via* Marathon, with Hippias dramatically in the lead, is a focus of the later account, so Phye led Peisistratus in a memorable procession into Athens on the occasion of one of his attempts; while on that of another it was *Marathon* that the Peisistratids first occupied on their way towards Athens (1.62). The rumoured 'charge among Athenians' (6.115) regarding the Alcmaeonids seems even to find a parallel in the rumour that came to the ears of the Athenians regarding Phye (1.60.5).

Furthermore, the reference to Marathon, and to 'those who preferred tyranny to freedom' (τοῖσι ἡ τυραννὶς πρὸ ἐλευθερίης ἦν ἀσπαστότερον, 1.62.1), invites readers to expand their frame of reference to a further level, again: to contextualize both sets of events against the broader background of a struggle between freedom and tyranny, with the Persian King coming to represent the relevant 'tyrant'.

Such an accumulation of echoes of the earlier account suggests that there is nothing remotely surprising in the possibility of Alcmaeonid collusion with tyrants again at the time of the battle of Marathon. After all, the Alcmaeonids' eponymous ancestor proved capable of displaying extraordinary opportunism when profit at the hands of an eastern tyrant was to be had (6.125). It works directly against Herodotus' stated opinion that he disbelieves the charge,[90] and counters Munson's notion that '[t]he specific accusation against

---

[88] Compare also Peisistratus' βουλὴ σοφωτάτη ('very clever plan', 1.63.2) that encouraged people to return to their homes at the time of his third occupation of Athens.

[89] Other young sons of tyrants (e.g. Lycophron) likewise prove their intelligence early on: some readers may have been *waiting* for Hippias' reappearance.

[90] Cf. Tacitus' technique of not vouching in his authorial voice for the truth of the *rumores* he reports, but crafting his narrative in such a way as to confirm it: Ryberg (1942).

the Alcmaeonids stands rejected, and [Herodotus] no longer cares' (264). The contradictions and complexities surrounding the case of Alcmaeonids and tyrants/Persians, stretching from the quite distant past right into Herodotus' audience's present, remain a *thōma* good for his readers to think with, and he draws them actively into doing just that.[91] The way in which readers are invited to draw connections even across a space of several books is noteworthy.

Iser's distinction between author and implied narrator opens up the possibility that the assertion of disbelief—'it is a wonder to me and I won't accept the assertion . . .'—represents the perspective of narrator rather than implied author; or, to formulate it differently, that it represents an ironic authorial comment—as Hermann Strasburger proposed many years ago.[92] Readers may not necessarily be intended to share the narrator's view: the authorial persona here may be more like that of the unreliable narrator common in nineteenth-century fiction, than the objective and authoritative voice we expect in narrative history.[93] In that case, the narrator's adoption of an agonistic stance that defies reader expectation and interpretation presents a challenge to readers, provoking their faculty of judgement and causing them to engage more actively with the text. Like the unreliable narrator that Iser finds in certain works of fiction, it seems that 'his "unreliability" possesses a strategic intention, which relates to the steering of the reader in the text':[94] readers are drawn to test

---

[91] Conversely, Raaflaub (2003), taking straightforwardly Herodotus' defence of the Alcmaeonids (67–8) and finding in 'the intensity of [Herodotus'] protest' (68) evidence that liberation from tyranny remained a live issue at Athens in Herodotus' time.

[92] Strasburger (1955); cf. Hart (1982); Moles (2002), 42. The more usual view is that Herodotus' defence is simply (inadvertently) a poor one, e.g. Gillis (1979), 45–58: 'Herodotus answers the charges as best he can' (52); the excursus on Agariste's marriage, etc., is merely diversionary (51).

[93] The *Histories* diverges in several respects from the main characteristics of historical narrative identified by Cohn (1990). See further Payen (1990), who aims 'esquisser . . . les lignes d'une recherche à la frontière de l'histoire et de la littérature *en analysant, à partir de l'oeuvre d'Hérodote, les aspects fictionnels du texte historique, inhérents à l'usage du récit,* et en étudiant comment un discours singulier se glisse dans une syntaxe narrative et l'infléchit en retour' ('to sketch the lines of research at the frontier of history and literature *by analyzing, starting from the work of Herodotus, the fictional aspects of the historical text, which are inherent to the use of the account,* and by studying how a singular discourse slips into a narrative syntax and inflects it on its return', 527, my italics).

[94] Iser (1989), 13 with n. 13.

what he says for themselves, particularly where his comments appear to contradict what they have assumed from the events he has described. Rather than reducing indeterminate areas or 'removing the gaps' through straightforward explanation and objective assessment of the situation, unreliable narratorial comments may 'disconcert, arouse opposition, charm with contradiction, and frequently uncover many unexpected features of the narrative process, which without these clues one might not have noticed' (13).

Herodotus' tendentious narratorial comment thus works against the picture he establishes in the wider narrative. In similar fashion (we suggest in chapter nine) his observation that Themistocles *deceived* the Athenians with his speech at Andros (8.110.1) will be problematized by the wider narrative. The author's stance on such occasions as these, where he obliges readers to weigh up the conflicting strands, is one of deliberate noncommittal.[95] The effects and purposes of the technique mark it as something rather different in character from the simple 'deception' found by Plutarch. Rather, Herodotus' narrative technique appears to *require* attentive and perceptive readers, who may sense the subtleties and complexities of his account, and even develop them; and conversely, it trains its readers to become such, by drawing them into engaging all the more profoundly with difficult historical problems.[96] Even the narrator's occasional ironic or unreliable stance, by enabling readers to get closer to the truth through drawing them into deeper engagement with historical problems, may therefore actually serve to *increase* the authority of the implied author (that is, of the author as constructed in readers' minds)[97]—an apparent tension we shall have occasion to explore further in subsequent chapters.

[95] I thank Mathieu de Bakker for this formulation.

[96] Cf. Erbse (1991), 9: '... Herodot mit einem aufmerksamen, nachdenkenden Leser rechnet, der in der Ausbreitung des Unwahrscheinlichen oder gar Absurden den Spott und die Kritik des Autors aufzufinden weiß' ('Herodotus counts on an attentive, thinking reader, who knows how to find, in the propagation of the improbable or absurd, the author's mockery and criticism'). The pervasive motif of the 'significance of the insignificant' (van der Veen (1996)) is likely to train readers to become more attentive, alert even to minor detail in the expectation that it may prove important.

[97] Cf. Genette (1988), 148, 'everything the text lets us know about the author'. Scodel (2005) confirms the need for the concept even in the case of narratological analysis: 'Often, a primary narrator is for practical purposes identical with the

The use of experimentalist techniques when it came to dealing with the most elusive varieties of historical knowledge—here, a rumoured charge based on no concrete evidence,[98] elsewhere, questions surrounding hidden motives—most likely came naturally to one living in Herodotus' world (as suggested above, §1.2.5). But equally, coming from his quite different intellectual world, where the truth—and a particular variety of moral truth at that[99]—*had* been pinned down more securely, it is small wonder if Plutarch failed to comprehend the impulse behind some of Herodotus' narrative strategies.

implied author, so that discussion of the narrator suffices. But where the primary narrator is unreliable, the reader must construct a hypothetical source of accurate meaning, and I suspect that most of us would prefer not to identify that construct with the historical author, since we can watch ourselves as readers in the act of creating it.'

[98] An unreliable narrator is *not* evident in cases where Herodotus *did* have better evidence—such as in the account of Ephialtes' betrayal of the Thermopylae pass: 7.213–14.

[99] Cf. Fox (1993) on Dionysius.

# 2

## The Homeric background

Herodotus, we have seen, is firmly to be situated against the background of the fifth-century world of the sophists. But at the same time a fascinating and important relationship exists between the historian and his main narrative model, Homer. 'The prose Homer in the realm of history' (τὸν πεζὸν ἐν ἱστορίαισιν Ὅμηρον), as Herodotus is celebrated in an inscription from Halicarnassus,[1] borrowed and adapted for his historiographical purposes a wide range of the poet's narrative techniques.[2] Indeed until Herodotus' time *only* poets had explored the realm of the past; and for the extraordinary breadth and sophisticated narrative structure of what Herodotus hoped to achieve, Homer was the only model available.[3] Equally the expectations and response of Herodotus' audience—themselves steeped in Homer—were doubtless shaped by the familiar contours of the Homeric background. This chapter sets the scene for those that follow by illustrating how the Homeric poems suggestively prefigure the two aspects of Herodotean narrative with which we are principally concerned: the particular, active sort of response it elicits from its readers—how it keeps them alert, undercutting assumptions and

---

[1] Isager (1999).

[2] See particularly Huber (1965b); Strasburger (1972); Lang (1984), 37–51; Erbse (1992), 122–32; de Jong (1999); Boedeker (2002); Marincola (2006); Pelling (2006b). Woodman (1988), 1–5 articulates the disquieting aspect for traditional assumptions about Herodotus' historiography of his 'imitations of Homer', which 'betoken something absolutely fundamental about the nature of his narrative' (4). The implications of this literary/rhetorical aspect of the *Histories* are now coming to be more frequently and directly confronted; however: cf. ch. 1 n. 71 above. Lateiner (1989), 286 n. 7 with text (212) and others underline the *conscious* aspect of Herodotus' art.

[3] Both points well brought out by Romm (1998), 13–18; cf. Herington (1991), comparing Herodotus with Pindar.

expectations, desisting at times from straightforward exposition in a bid to increase readerly engagement—and also its recognition of the crucial importance of the psychological background. This should strengthen our case for employing a reader-response centred approach in interpreting the *Histories*, at the same time as it reveals Homer to be a precursor to Herodotus both in his general interest in opening up questions of motivation and in the complexity of his depictions. The Homeric resonances of Herodotus' *Histories* are likely to have primed his audience to expect points of contact between the poems and this work of a new and as yet indeterminate prose genre. Our focus in this chapter is Homer, although we gesture towards some of these points of contact. More remain implicit, for the sake of avoiding repetition, but readers are invited to bear in mind this significant relationship over the course of subsequent chapters.

One of Herodotus' achievements in depicting motivation is to have struck a balance between including a rich measure of psychology and at the same time confronting and exposing the fact of his limited, human access: that is, the fact of the very real difficulties the historian faces in attempting to pass into this realm of special knowledge, which (as we observed above, 3) is doubly concealed from view, being situated in people's minds and in the past. At times, Herodotus adopts the omniscient style of the Homeric narrator, which leaves the impression of direct access to others' minds (and without even couching it in speech), as in narrating the story of Candaules and his wife (1.8–12). He also includes in his *Histories* numerous speeches, which are akin to the Homeric soliloquies in not only setting forth the available options, but also depicting the speaker's frame of mind.[4] He and his audience presumably took it for granted that this area was one that might involve considerable imaginative reconstruction (an attitude to which Thucydides perhaps responds, and seeks to regulate, in his methodological remarks at 1.22). But more usually, as we shall see in chapter four, what Herodotus presses to the fore in various ways is the *limited* nature of his access to others' minds.

---

[4] Huber (1965*a*) 80–92; Lang (1984), 54. Of course Herodotus' speeches have further functions and effects as well, including rhetorical ones: see Huber (1965*a*), 80–92; Hohti (1976); Heni (1977); de Bakker (2007); and below, esp. §4.2.3 (Maiandrios); §6.2.2 (Aristagoras); chs. 6–7 *passim*; §8.1.1 (Xerxes); §9.3 (Themistocles).

We return in subsequent chapters to the nature of this negotiation Herodotus performs between sketching the psychological, at the same time as he emphasizes the difficulties involved in so doing. Its ramifications are fruitful historiographically—in drawing readers' attention to the problematics of ascribing motivation Herodotus alerts them to important epistemological truths about the limits of historical knowledge—but also in terms of his narrative art, as where it serves, for example, to heighten readerly engagement with his account. It may at first sight seem surprising that Homer's depictions of motivation should prefigure such a negotiation.

## 2.1 AUTHORIAL READINGS: OMNISCIENCE V. READER ENGAGEMENT

Unlike the historian, the Homeric narrator, as well as being omnipresent, is omniscient. Thus he has privileged knowledge of events, including those of future time, of the gods, and of characters' minds.[5] He capitalizes on this third variety of privileged knowledge. He constantly sketches in the psychological landscape, whether, at one end of the spectrum, in the form of his frequent brief observations in passing of a character's attitude or emotion (many of them obvious[6] and so not much dependent upon his authorial omniscience), or, at the other end, of the lengthy monologues that lay out in detail an individual's thought processes in reaching a particular decision. Between these poles we find plenty of (reasonably straightforward and uncomplicated) depictions or evocations of various individuals' motivation at different points in time. Such actorial motivation, as Irene de Jong notes, is 'usually explicit'.[7] More broadly, both poems display subtlety and variety in their characterization of individuals, inviting readings that assume the presence of complex psychology, as Jasper Griffin has amply

[5] See esp. de Jong (1987); Richardson (1990), 109–39.
[6] e.g. 'the old man was seized with fear' (*Il.* 1.33); 'his speech was pleasing to them' (*Od.* 18.290), etc.
[7] De Jong *Comm.* xi.

demonstrated.[8] This is not to say that psychology and character portrayal is of vital interest to Homer *per se*: but rather that it is crucial in conferring importance on and bringing out the character of the events being recounted.[9] Character surfaces through actions and speech, and also through Homer's portrayal of his protagonists' hidden thoughts.[10]

And yet, despite his omniscience, the Homeric narrator does not seek to lay bare everything of his protagonists' minds. Aspects of the character and motivation of some Homeric individuals are not elucidated by the poet, but instead remain partly—in some cases wholly—inscrutable. This is particularly so in the case of several of the females of the *Odyssey*,[11] though also, in some respects, in that of Odysseus himself. In such cases where we are not told explicitly of a character's motivation or psychology, the narrative quite commonly invites the audience to engage in conjecture[12]—*pace* Richardson's statement otherwise, that '[a]mbiguity and conjecture have no place in the Homeric poems. The narrator knows the story and will tell it clearly'.[13] Clarity is indeed a quality of importance to the Homeric

---

[8] Griffin (1980). Ancient commentators on Homer worked on the assumption of complex psychology. Much has been written more recently on the question of whether the people of Homer are real 'individuals' or 'selves', capable of making real decisions; see e.g. Gaskin (1990); Gill (1996), 29–93. See also Rutherford's psychologizing explanation of Odysseus' failure to reveal himself immediately to Laertes, in explanation of which he observes: 'if we reject authorial incompetence as an explanation, then the oddity of Odysseus' behaviour compels us to explore these possibilities' (1986), 161 n. 85; Schadewalt (1959), 234–67 on Achilles' decision; de Jong *Comm.*: 'actorial motivation' features in the glossary, with frequent examples in the commentary.

[9] Griffin (1980), 56.

[10] De Jong (1994).

[11] Cf. Griffin (1980).

[12] See esp. Griffin (1980), 62–5 demonstrating that 'the *Odyssey* contains passages in which the poet explicitly tells us of the psychology which we are to see underlying the words and acts of characters, and also that other passages, where this is not made explicit, come so close to them in nature that we can have no reasonable doubt that there, too, the instinctive response of the audience, to interpret the passages in the light of the psychology of human beings, is sound' (65). Griffin also considers occasions where the *Iliad* deals with similar inwardness. Scodel (2004) well sums up the situation: the narrator 'clearly defines what kind of people the characters are, and invites the audience to imagine that they have psychological complexity. He then leaves many details of motivation opaque, so that the audience must infer or guess (especially in the *Odyssey*)' (51).

[13] Richardson (1990), 157.

narrator, one of obvious value particularly in an oral context; and yet at times it may be cast aside in the interests of different poetic purposes: for example, to heighten audience suspense, or to further a particular character portrayal, as in the case of Odysseus' failure to identify himself to Laertes (discussed below, 43–4). A comparable situation obtains in Odysseus' character narrative, where again motives (his own and others') at times remain inscrutable, although there we may invoke in explanation Odysseus' limited human understanding, along with the rhetorical dimension entailed by the presence of his audience.[14] Of course, Odysseus' narrative is at the same time the product of the Homeric narrator's rhetorical concerns. Odysseus' failure to supply an explanation for identifying himself as Οὖτις, 'nobody', to Polyphemos (9.366–7) must make a first-time audience—and so certainly his internal audience of Phaeacians—wonder about his motivation in so doing, and suspect some significance in the act: for example, that he must be demonstrating foresight.[15] Their suspense is thereby heightened, and with it their engagement with the story. Similarly left unexplained is, for example, Odysseus' bringing of wine with him in exploring the Cyclops' land (9.196 ff.), and anchoring his ship *outside* the harbour of the Laestrygonians (when the others moor inside) (10.95). The presence of oral tradition does complicate the picture, as Homer's external audience will have been familiar with the outline of many of his stories, and this might reduce their puzzlement in some instances.[16]

Again, it may be *largely* the case that

the [Homeric] poems do not depend for their effect on keeping hidden the true interpretations of the actions and circumstances, nor on letting the readers participate by giving them an opportunity to speculate.[17]

[14] On the difference between the Homeric narrator's understanding and that of his characters see, de Jong (1992); and further below, ch. 2 n. 39 with text.

[15] Cf. de Jong *Comm.* ad loc.

[16] Cf. Scodel (1999), 135–9 and (2002b): 'the traditionality of the pattern helps hide any flaws in logic'; Danek (1998) endeavours to reconstruct this 'horizon of expectation' of Homer's original audience.

[17] Richardson (1990), 157. Cf. e.g. Auerbach (2003): 'a continuous rhythmic procession of phenomena passes by, and never is there a form left fragmentary or half-illuminated, never a lacuna, never a gap, never a glimpse of unplumbed depths' (6–7).

But the instances that test this formulation are significant, and raise the possibility that Herodotus' active reader finds a forerunner in Homer. Indeed, these significant exceptions lead some critics to characterize the poems, particularly the *Odyssey*, as fundamentally 'open' in meaning.[18] Simon Goldhill argues convincingly, for example, that the side-by-side, conflicting stories of Helen and Odysseus in Troy told by Helen (4.240–64) and Menelaus (4.269–89) (the one portraying Helen as sympathizer to, the other as near destroyer of, the Greek cause)—which are left wholly unreconciled in the absence of authorial comment—represent an example of juxtaposition serving as 'a source of intriguing openness of meaning, a complex suggestiveness of sense and representation'.[19] Listeners must themselves grapple with the problem of how to evaluate the stories against one another. Similarly in the *Iliad*, Hector and Achilles' conflicting explanations for Hector's not having fought outside the walls (in an episode that preceded the *Iliad*'s opening)—the former claiming he was restrained from doing so (*Il.* 15.721–3), the latter that he did not wish to do so (9.352–4)—are left unresolved, for readers to ponder.

A further such example to which Goldhill draws attention is the disjunction between the primary narrator's account of Penelope and Odysseus' roles in the bow contest (19.572–87: Penelope conceiving the idea as a means of choosing a husband) and that of the suitor Amphimedon in Hades (24.167–9: 'in his great cunning he bade his wife set before the suitors his bow and the grey iron to be a contest for us ill-fated men and the beginning of death'). Goldhill suggests that 'Amphimedon's speech is not only a critical problem but also—in the question of misrecognition in representation—the problem of criticism' (404). We might regard it as encapsulating also the problem of psychological—and historical—interpretation:

---

[18] Cf. Silk (2004), 44: 'The shape, like the scope, of the Odyssean epic enforces its restless, exploratory character: ends are opened, questions raised, alternative voices let loose'; cf. Katz's (1991) emphasis on the indeterminacy of meaning in the *Odyssey*. Ledbetter (2003), 9–39 views Homeric poetics in terms of a 'rhetoric of enchantment' that suppresses interpretation on the audience's part (the theory 'promises divine knowledge and discourages interpretation', 39), but she goes on to show (and here she is clearly correct) how the poems themselves 'would unavoidably seem to invite the very sort of interpretation discouraged by Homeric poetics' (38).

[19] See Goldhill (1999), quote at 422.

Amphimedon's incorrect, though logical, account stages the problem of understanding and narrating people's hidden thoughts. Some of the *Iliad*'s similar discrepancies between the accounts of the primary narrator and those of characters express, in Andersen's view, not merely misreadings, but the fact that 'the past is not fixed but fleeting'—actually *existing* in differing versions.[20]

Irene de Jong's work has brought to the fore the extent to which the Homeric poems are conscious of the effect of different people's *viewing*: how, even within the narrator text (that is, not simply within areas of explicitly reported speech or thought), the Homeric narrator incorporates changing perspectives. Here again, Homer emerges as a precursor to Herodotus—whose narrative is often focalized through the changing gazes of different groups, which may be more or less explicitly signalled, as we will see especially in chapters seven and eight. This, in Homer, might even have a converse reflection back upon the narrative's authority: for the often remarkable *subtlety* of the indicators of 'implicit embedded focalization' de Jong documents[21] might well draw the audience into wondering at the status of—questioning the authority of—any particular account: into pondering whether it represents the (objective and trustworthy) voice of the omniscient narrator, or a (subjective) character opinion. In this area of latent ambivalence we may perhaps detect a strand of 'unreliability' on the part of the Homeric narrator—comparable to the sophistic persona Herodotus occasionally adopts (cf. especially chapter three below)—against which an audience might learn to be on their guard. It would tend to stimulate their active participation. Morrison argues for a narrator of the *Iliad* who, while usually reliable, can indeed at times be manipulative, 'introduc[ing] false and misleading predictions as part of a strategy to mislead the audience' (96); such 'misdirection'

---

[20] Andersen (1990), quote at 29–30, connecting this phenomenon with Homer's oral context—in which the past is embedded exclusively in the present, 'in the minds of the members of the culture', and is 'by nature and necessity adaptive' (42).

[21] See e.g. de Jong (1987), 118–22. On 'implicit embedded focalization' see further below, ch. 7 n. 67 with text. Scodel (2002*b*) highlights some difficulties in applying the concept, e.g. in distinguishing between (realistic) 'inference' of information (on the character's part) and its (unmotivated) 'transference' to the character (by the author, for the narrative's sake).

forces the audience to question the validity of the tradition, as the narrator introduces predictions and events that appear to lead outside the tradition or that contradict what has been foreshadowed elsewhere in the epic (105).

The technique, Morrison suggests, stems from the poet's impulse to engage his audience.[22] More generally it might showcase the Homeric narrator's dexterity, and thus encourage his audience to remain all the more alert.[23]

The notion with regard to oral performance conditions that anything unclear in the plot that prompts conjecture risks causing listeners to lose track of the story[24] is also questionable. Might the effect not be the reverse, such deeper engagement with the material capturing an audience's attention all the more? They might become alert, for instance, to further clues. Indeed, the usual clarity of Homer's style might grant the audience extra leeway in this respect, making it easier for them to follow even while they ponder a particular question. The reaction of an internal audience (themselves shown in the process of wondering at Odysseus' motives, for example) can at times help delineate those areas which we may have reason to regard as problematized. More difficult to evaluate is the significance to be inferred from such an instance as the (at least to modern eyes) enigmatic *Iliad* 8.97, where Odysseus οὐδ᾽ ἐσάκουσε—'did not hear (or listen to)'— Diomedes' call to return to battle (that is, did not hear, or alternatively chose—out of cowardice?—not to heed it) and instead rushed back to the Greek ships, since the internal audience gives no immediate response. Odysseus' bravery is, however, acclaimed over the course of the account that follows,[25] so that perhaps indicates how an external audience might be expected to react.

---

[22] Morrison (1992). For misdirection, see also de Jong *Comm.* xv: 'the **narratees** are emphatically prepared for an event, which in the end does not occur, or takes place later... or differently' (bold in original). Lateiner (2004) emphasizes the *Iliad*'s unexpected elements (2004). Fenik (1974), 105–30 discusses misdirection particularly in the presentation of Arete, but observes also, for instance, how for Nausicaa thoughts of marriage 'are carefully and deliberately aroused, so that the possibility of a romantic attachment between Nausikaa and Odysseus is very strong in the audience's mind' (128)—though nothing is to come of it. On the other hand, the ending of this traditional story, which precludes the possibility of Odysseus' marrying Nausicaa, was probably familiar (cf. n. 16 above with text).

[23] I thank John Marincola for this suggestion.

[24] Cf. e.g. Richardson (1990), 157.        [25] Cf. Stanford (1968), 72.

Thus on those occasions when the narrator refrains from spelling out explicitly his characters' inner thoughts, readers may at times be drawn into a process of conjecturing for themselves. Their response is not always so unguided and apparently 'open' as in Goldhill's examples of juxtaposition. There may be some more obvious 'response-inviting structure' (to borrow Iser's terminology[26]) in any particular case: signals or hints that tend to favour a particular reading. Here again Homer's technique seems comparable to what we will observe of Herodotus', for example in the shifting responses he invites to the question of Maiandrios' motives (§4.2.3), or to that of the Athenians vis-à-vis the Pelasgians or Peisistratus (ch. 5), and others'. In the case of Odysseus' motivation in refraining on several occasions from disclosing his identity, which the Homeric narrator never explains, readers' interpretations are guided by various clues along the way.[27] These interpretations are progressively modified over the course of successive parallel scenes. The element of necessity, for example, that seems to play a part at least in the earlier instances, where the imperative of hiding his identity arises from the need to remain out of danger and to conduct tests of the loyalty of those around him, can no longer be operative in the scene with Laertes. On this occasion—and it is the first on which the poet dramatizes Odysseus' reflections on this matter in an interior monologue, 24.235–40 (there is surely significance in the delay of such revelation until now: Homer allows his audience first to grapple with the question for themselves)—the audience is drawn to revise their earlier assessments. They might for example consider whether Odysseus' conduct at this point marks a development in his behavioural

---

[26] See §1.3 above.

[27] Clues to which modern commentators, too, have responded; e.g. in the Phaeacian context, de Jong *Comm.* finds in Odysseus' parallel refusal at 8.152–7 to participate in the games a clue to interpretation, for '[b]oth acts are untypical of a Homeric hero; as a rule they are proud of their name and eager to show their strength. Odysseus' experiences in the past ten years have undermined his heroic self-confidence and drained his energy. All he wants now is to be left in peace and to be brought home', etc. (171). The narratorial motivation for Odysseus' postponement of disclosing his identity is evident: in particular, it provides a further opportunity for the 'delayed recognition' story pattern; cf. de Jong *Comm.* Again, critics proffer different explanations as to why Odysseus does not let Penelope into his plan; the question is lent emphasis by Amphimedon's assumption from Hades that he *did*.

patterns in response to the need until now to keep his identity secret;[28] or whether it shows that 'secrecy, dissimulation, and restraint are innate, not to say incorrigible, traits of Odysseus' character',[29] in which case his reluctance to disclose his identity may have had a gratuitous aspect to it all along (a reading which his evident pleasure in concocting his elaborate lying tales might seem to confirm).

## 2.2 CHARACTER READINGS: KNOWLEDGE V. LIMITED ACCESS

At the same time as they are drawn into making conjectures, Homer's audience, like Herodotus', are exposed to the acute difficulties involved in reading motivation, difficulties residing not merely in the fact that appearances may deceive[30] (and thus that motives are not always easily determined from behaviour or *ex eventu*, as in the Amphimedon example above: even in retrospect he misinterprets the significance of what he saw of Odysseus and Penelope's behaviour), but also in the way in which individuals, particularly in the *Odyssey*, may *intentionally hide* their real thoughts and feelings. In the *Odyssey deliberately* unspoken thoughts frequently generate

a discrepancy between the knowledge of the reader, who is aware of what is going on in the mind of the character, and that of the other characters in the story, who are not.[31]

Homer exposes a discrepancy, for example, between Circe's words to Odysseus about the possibility of his listening to the Sirens ('if you yourself wish to listen', αὐτὸς ἀκουέμεν αἴ κ' ἐθέλῃσθα, *Od.* 12.49), and his report to his comrades, in which he presents himself as acting under the compulsion of her *instruction* ('me alone she bade listen to their voice', οἶον ἔμ' ἠνώγει ὄπ' ἀκουέμεν, 12.160).[32] The discrepancy allows us to recognize what he hides from his companions: that he is

---

[28] Rutherford (1986), 161: 'he has lived so long with danger and the need for concealment that it has become almost second nature'.
[29] De Jong (1994), 37.
[30] Indeed, deception is one of the *Odyssey*'s key themes.
[31] De Jong (1994), 30.    [32] Cf. Rutherford (1986), 151 n. 38.

in fact motivated by his own curiosity. Indeed, rhetoric is often shown to mask real identity and motives, most conspicuously in Odysseus' lying tales, which are adapted to each of their listeners. But even in his 'true' account of his adventures, Odysseus alters its content depending on his audience, for example tactfully downplaying or revising the role of women when he speaks to Nausicaa or Penelope.³³ Hector in explaining to the army why he must enter the city (*Il.* 6.113–15) shrewdly downplays Helenos' emphasis on the need for calling together the women of Troy to sacrifice specifically to Athene and win her favour (6.86–95). He instead speaks in more general terms of bidding the elders, along with the wives, to pray and offer hecatombs to 'the gods'. J. H. Lesher finds in the *Odyssey* 'a sense of the subtle and potentially deceptive powers of speech, and the corresponding powers of intelligence and ingenuity that is needed to master them'.³⁴ Achilles' condemnation of the man 'who conceals within his mind one thing but says another' (*Il.* 9.313) contains a principle rarely adhered to in this Odyssean world. Homer's acute awareness of the rhetorical dimension again anticipates Herodotus' equal sensitivity, as we shall see particularly in chapter nine below.

In the case of Telemachus' motives in visiting Pylos, we are informed of them by the narrator and so can appreciate the discrepancies between that reality and the motives conjectured by various characters. The reasonable assumption of the suitors (*Od.* 2.325–9),³⁵ and apparently of Peisistratus, in explaining to Menelaus the reason for Telemachus' visit (4.164–7), is that Telemachus' intention is practical: to gain concrete support in terms of manpower so as to return and overthrow the suitors with their help. The particular details of the suitors' conjecture—that he is planning their murder, intending to bring either men to help him, or else poison—reflect far more on their own character than on the reality of Telemachus' aims,

³³ Cf. Odysseus' diplomatic paraphrase of Agamemnon's offer to Achilles, *Il.* 9.260 ff.
³⁴ Lesher (1981), 18. Goldhill (1999), 403 n. 34 notes his preference to downplay the contrast Lesher draws between the two epics in this respect, observing 'an increased emphasis in the *Odyssey*, rather than a lack in the *Iliad*'.
³⁵ The suitors cannot have heard Telemachus' words to Antinous at 2.315–16 expressing his intention to do them harm (the objection of the scholia on 2.325 ff., who note that this supports Aristarchus' rejection of lines 315–16).

for that is presumably what *they* would do in his situation. (Indeed, they are themselves planning Telemachus' murder.) In fact, like his father on several occasions, Telemachus is moved by the simple desire for information (and, of course, by Athene's prompting). (*Athene's* reasons for sending him, on the other hand, are twofold: that he might find out about his father, but also gain *kleos*, 1.94–5.) This is one of the *Odyssey*'s several reminders—which build to a persistent refrain in Herodotus' *Histories*[36]—that 'natural' interpretations of motivation, in accordance with general 'rules of human nature', are not always reliable. Only in the case of Medon, the last person shown in the process of conjecturing about the reason for Telemachus' departure, does a character (without the help of Telemachus' own explanation, *Od.* 4.317–25) alight upon a correct reading of the full situation: of Telemachus' desire for information, and the divine activity behind it (*Od.* 4.712–14).

Characters in Homer are also shown correcting others' reading of their motives, as Paris of Hector's reading of his motives at *Iliad* 6.335–6: not so much anger and indignation, but sadness, he says, has moved him to return to his chamber. Telemachus is vexed by Penelope's failure to welcome her returned husband (*Od.* 23.97–103), but in this he fails to understand her mind and motives as Odysseus does. Even the gods may misunderstand mortals, as Athene seems to do in assuming that the prospect of gifts alone will best placate Achilles (*Il.* 1.213–14) (which *Iliad* 9 will suggest is not the case, for Achilles there rejects Agamemnon's offer of gifts). Presumably the Muses are better at reading mortals than the gods are. If 'natural' interpretations, or interpretations based on appearances, may prove incorrect in the case of humans, that is all the more the case when dealing with inhuman or superhuman figures. The motivation of Circe, or the Laestrygonian Queen, or Aiolos may seem wholly illogical and incomprehensible in human terms.[37] The conduct of the gods may appear similarly capricious.

The limitations of human understanding are especially evident in the contrast between the omniscient Homeric primary narrator,

---

[36] See esp. ch. 4 below.
[37] Griffin (1980), 76–7. Silk (2004) remarks upon the 'behavioural quirkiness of a whole series of [Homer's] characters' (40).

whose correct understanding flows directly from the Muse herself,[38] and the human secondary narrators within the story, whose access to others' thoughts (along with the other forms of privileged knowledge) is severely circumscribed.[39] Over the course of recounting his own lengthy narrative, Odysseus, for example, frequently describes the inner thoughts he *does* have access to—his own—but delves remarkably infrequently into the realm of others'. Where he does, he reduces the complex psychology described by the Homeric narrator to a matter of motives, whether to a single motivation, as when he describes the spirit of Ajax in Hades as standing apart, 'angry on account of the victory (κεχολωμένη εἵνεκα νίκης) that I had won over him ...' (*Od.* 11.544–5), thus stating simply the obvious, basic emotion—in grossly abbreviated form in comparison with what the *Iliad* might have described from Ajax's perspective; or to broad alternatives. In reading Calypso's motivation in ordering him to leave, for example—'either because of some message from Zeus, or because her own mind was turned' (*Od.* 7.263)—Odysseus reduces more complex possibilities to a matter of personal will versus external pressure.[40]

The method seems validated by the way in which the decision-making process as described in the interior monologues *is* frequently reducible to the deliberation upon two main alternatives (or upon three options in cases where the alternatives are rejected and a third course chosen). It nonetheless functions at a far simpler level, one that concedes the fact that the complex reality of human psychology remains partially hidden from any human who seeks to depict it. Even in describing his own past thought processes Odysseus tends to

---

[38] Richardson (1990), for example, considers the Homeric narrator godlike in his omniscience, but perhaps 'seerlike' could better capture the indirect nature of his understanding—cf. Calchas' (below).

[39] De Jong *Comm.* 223–7 helpfully describes Odysseus' narrative style in *Od.* 9–12, bringing out the important differences from that of the Homeric primary narrator.

[40] The audience knows, in this instance, that the first alternative is in fact correct: cf. de Jong (1992), 3. Similarly, Odysseus' conjecture of Polyphemos' reason for moving *all* the flocks inside: 'either from some foreboding or because a god so bade him' (9.339). (In the case of humans being motivated by divine and human sources, these function as equivalents, at least when attributed by the Homeric narrator: cf. Lesky (1961). But since Calypso, and to some extent Polyphemos, belong to the divine community themselves, Odysseus may be understood as conceiving of these options as genuine alternatives.)

simplify it to a matter of motives, as when he recounts that he did not listen to his comrades' advice to return to their ship rather than wait for the Cyclops' return, 'to the end that I might see the man himself, and whether he would give me gifts of entertainment' (*Od.* 9.229).[41] He likewise keeps his psychology simple at 9.102: he bade his comrades embark 'for fear that anyone should eat the lotus and forget his homecoming', and at 10.147: he explored Circe's lands 'in the hope that I might see the works of men, and hear their voice'. (We might draw a contrast with the complexity of the Iliadic warriors' present-time monologues.) Is this a function simply of his storyteller's impulse to keep the narrative moving swiftly, or could it suggest also an acknowledgment of the limitations of human memory, even as regards one's own thoughts? Or does it convey a problem of human communication: the difficulty of conveying *to others* the more complex reality? Similarly, the Homeric primary narrator rarely makes use of indirect discourse (but instead quotes speech directly), whereas his human characters do so readily:[42] presumably they are not regarded as having access to such verbatim records.[43]

A human figure with the understanding of an Odysseus is better placed than the suitors, for instance, to interpret correctly a situation, including the minds of those involved. But even though Odysseus usually seems highly attuned to others' psychology—to Nausicaa's, for example, in making mention, in his opening address to her, of the very subject of marriage that we know is on her mind; in tailoring each of his lying tales to its particular audience; in predicting the Trojan response to the Wooden Horse; and so on—at crucial junctures he falls short in this respect. Nowhere is the limited nature of his vision more clearly expressed than in his terribly ironic, and wholly mistaken, reading of the Phaeacians' character and motives

---

[41] Cf. e.g. Eumaeus on his own motives: he will show the (disguised) Odysseus kindness not for the sake of hearing hopeful lies, 'but from fear of Zeus, the stranger's god, and from pity for yourself' (14.389) (i.e., moved by an external duty plus pity from within).

[42] Richardson (1990), 71.

[43] Occasionally they do. Indeed Odysseus at 10.34–6 reports in direct speech his companions' words in determining to open the Bag of Winds, even though he was asleep at the time.

when he wakes up upon the as yet unrecognized shores of Ithaca
(13.209–16).[44] Again, when it comes to recognizing divine involvement and intentions, like others of the poems' internal human
narrators, he frames his conjectures in terms of 'some god' rather
than naming with certainty a particular god (in the manner of the
primary narrator).[45] The same difference emerges pointedly at the
beginning of the *Iliad* in the contrast between Achilles' incorrect
guess at Apollo's motives in sending the plague ('whether it is because
of a vow that he blames us, or a hecatomb', *Il.* 1.65), and the seer
Calchas' true knowledge (1.93–100: Agamemnon has dishonoured
Apollo's priest in refusing to release his daughter Chryseis). Where
Odysseus *does* include privileged information in his story, he references his source,[46] presumably in the expectation that his (internal)
audience may otherwise doubt the truth of his account. He cites
Calypso, for example, for the account of his men's decision to eat
Helios' cattle (made while he slept) and its aftermath (*Od.* 12.389).
On the rare occasion when he does read the minds of others, an
explanation is usually at hand: hindsight knowledge in the case of his
description of his companions' feelings at seeing him again once they
have been turned back into humans from pigs (10.415–17), since
afterwards they described to him how they had felt (at 10.419–20).[47]
The human narrator's account that comes closest to omniscience in
feel is Menelaus' (at *Od.* 4.351–585), since he makes full use of such
information gathered retrospectively, including all that he has heard
from the infallible (νημερτής) old man of the sea (4.349).[48]

In the main, Herodotus follows the model of the human narrators
of Homer's poems, especially Odysseus. For example, he adopts the
method of the Odysseus narrator of reducing complex psychology to

---

[44] Cf. his failure to anticipate his men's eating of Helios' cattle.

[45] See Jörgensen (1904), 357–82 on the general rules that in the *Odyssey* govern
human speech about the gods.

[46] Human narrators in the *Odyssey* (and *Iliad*: Scodel (2002a), 74) do often cite the
authority behind their story: Olson (1995), 12–13; Scodel (2002a), 65–89 on 'oral
tradition' (what people say) v. 'bardic knowledge' (deriving exclusively from the
gods).

[47] De Jong *Comm.* 224; his reading of Eurylochos' mind at 10.448, by contrast,
remains unexplained: Odysseus' 'desire to expose the abject nature of his companion's thoughts overrules narrative logic' (224).

[48] Cf. de Jong *Comm.* ad loc.

a question of motives (often alternative possibilities, expressed with the *eite ... eite ... formula*[49]), able to be surmised by an outsider. Unlike Odysseus, however, Herodotus is not straightforwardly an actor in his own story, so, when it comes to recounting his narrative of past events, it is *only* others' motives he is concerned to describe. (The ethnographic sections present a rather different picture, for there Herodotus *is* the protagonist, who at times reveals his motives in doing *historiē*.[50]) Nor does he have the advantage of having been present at those events: instead he must negotiate the additional barrier that is entailed by his distance in time and reliance on indirect (and human) reports. His inclusion of the numerous *logoi* of a wide range of informants, with associated source references, reminds us constantly of the fact of his human limitations. He prefers to invite his audience to consider various alternative possibilities, rather than setting forth hard and fast absolutes; his technique recognizes their ability, also, to play a constructive role in evaluating his material. Thus even where he makes use also of the techniques of the Homeric primary narrator, he nonetheless remains always in this persona of *human* first-person narrator with *limited* access. Indeed the radical difference in basic character between this Herodotean narrator and the godlike, omniscient and omnipresent primary narrator of the Homeric poems suggests that de Jong's strategy of working from the framework of the salient characteristics of the Homeric narrator (his externality, omnipresence, and omniscience) in her discussion of the Herodotean narrator, and only subsequently introducing exceptions, perhaps gives a misleading impression.[51] Herodotus' foregrounding

---

[49] See ch. 5 below.

[50] e.g. at 2.44.1, moved by the desire for clearer knowledge. See Marincola (1987) on Herodotus as participant in the narrative in book two (cf. Dewald (2002), 278–9, speaking of the 'quasi-autobiographical "I" '), including as audience to the priests' accounts (whose presentation in long passages of *oratio obliqua* furthers the impression of a conversation: Marincola (1987), 126–7), in contrast with his different, non-participatory presence in the later books.

[51] De Jong (2004). De Jong's earlier article (1999) seems to me to strike a better balance, considering more extensively those significant exceptions (223–7): having discussed the epic qualities of the Herodotean narrator, she opens the following section with the observation that 'En fait la situation est plus complexe. Il y a aussi des différences entre le narrateur hérodotéen et le narrateur homérique qui sont peut-être encore plus importantes et intéressantes que les ressemblances, et qui jusqu' à présent n'ont pas reçu l'attention qu'elles méritent sans doute' ('In fact the situation is more

of so many caveats implies that where he *does* delve into others' minds, he can do so *without* claiming omniscience.

In Homer it is primarily for the sake of his storyteller's art—the desire to engage his audience in his story—that we found (in §2.1) the suggestive negotiation between the omniscient narrator's sketching of his characters' psychology and his refraining from so doing. Herodotus stages a similar negotiation (as we shall see more fully in the chapters that follow), but to epistemological/historiographical ends, and in imitation rather of Homer's human narrators. It comes to serve not only to enhance readerly engagement, but also to stage one of the key challenges involved in reconstructing the past.

## 2.3 FURTHER NARRATIVE EFFECTS OF HOMERIC ASCRIPTIONS OF MOTIVES

Herodotus uses Homeric narrative technique as a model in other ways, too, making requisite changes in keeping with his historiographical purposes.[52] An important instance relates to the presentation of alternatives generally, including those pertaining to questions of motivation: this has a range of narrative functions in Homer that Herodotus makes use of in adapted form.[53] Herodotus shares also Homer's awareness of the various fruitful narrative possibilities opened up by the presentation of motives, which extend far beyond the explanatory function of furthering understanding of an individual's behaviour. Ascriptions of motives in the Homeric poems may have a characterizing effect, for example, not simply in relation to

complex. There are also differences between the Herodotean narrator and the Homeric narrator which are perhaps even more important and interesting than their similarities, and which have not yet received the attention they doubtless deserve.') (223).

[52] Esp. ch. 3 below considers further the nature of these historiographical purposes.

[53] See esp. Gray (2003), 46–8. She demonstrates, for example, that just as the Homeric alternatives of divine versus human motivation represent equivalent sources of motivation that together reinforce the wisdom of those motivated (cf. Lesky (1961)), so in Herodotus the human alternatives of a deed being done αὐτός or ὑπ' ἄλλων (on one's own counsel, or on others' advice) may at times demonstrate equivalences: see below, ch. 5 n. 12 with text.

52 *The Homeric background*

their object, but in relation to the person who makes the ascription (as we saw above, 45–6, in the specific form of the suitors' misreading of Telemachus' reasons for visiting Pylos). Similarly in the *Histories*, the Magians' assumption that Prexaspes will be moved by self-interest (3.74)[54] reflects back upon them, much as Croesus' assumptions about Solon's motivation in visiting Sardis (1.30)[55] reveal more about himself and his priorities than they do about the Athenian. More broadly, even unfounded assumptions of, for instance, negative motives paint a suggestive picture as to 'how the world works'.[56]

In Homer as in Herodotus such ascriptions may also tie into wider patterns or themes. In this way even an incorrect reading may have interesting purchase, serving to open up a different perspective. Amphimedon's broad misconstrual of the events leading up to the slaying of the suitors (including his erroneous statement that Zeus was the god involved, when we know it was Athene), and, in relation to that, his specific misreading of the minds and intentions of Odysseus and Penelope (imagining them to have been plotting together as early as when Penelope suggests the bow contest), under-line the fact of the suitors' delusion.[57] At the same time, however—even while the audience knows it presents a deluded reading, for they have been primed to accept the justice of Odysseus' revenge[58]—his retrospective account, presenting the suitors as those wronged, taps into various strands of what has gone before, hinting that Odysseus' triumph was not without its unsettling aspects.[59] His incomprehen-sion perhaps also sounds a note of pathos. Even though ultimately we reject Amphimedon's perspective, the process invites us to review our

[54] Cf. 84 below.

[55] Cf. ch. 5 n. 20 below.

[56] See e.g. §5.1.1 below.

[57] Cf. Goldhill (1999), 402; Scodel (1999), 63: 'the mistake is mimetically plausible and thematically significant: the suitors still misunderstand the story.'

[58] Especially through the persistent negative characterization of the suitors, shown, for example, devouring Odysseus' property, and through the presence of divine support for Odysseus. Again, Agamemnon's response to Amphimedon (24.192–202) contains only praise for Penelope.

[59] e.g. we have seen certain of the suitors displeased by the actions of their fellows, Odysseus' exaggeration in speaking of their use of force against the maids, etc. As de Jong *Comm.* on 24.121–90 observes, Amphimedon's version is 'largely correct, at times even repeating *verbatim* the narrator's version' (if also marked by 'rhetorical omissions or changes' and so forth: de Jong lists these).

conclusions. Herodotus uses with similar effect the anecdote of 9.122: for though paradoxical and surprising—for it presents a contrast with the earlier depiction of Cyrus at 1.126 *making use* of luxury to inspire his men[60]—it nonetheless guides readers to reflect back upon his (and the Persians'[61]) character from a revised perspective. Again, Odysseus' incorrect *over*-reading of Penelope's conduct in arranging the bow contest—for his smile suggests that he is projecting on to her his own intention of deceiving the suitors, whereas the narrative gives no suggestion that Penelope is not, at this moment, genuinely considering marriage[62]—furthers (in his assumption to that effect) the motif of their two minds working in accord. Or perhaps it is *not* in fact a misreading, in that it displays awareness of the extent of *homophrosunē*—unity of mind and feeling—that does indeed exist between himself and his wife, in contrast to the outsider Amphimedon's ignorance of that state of affairs (which parallels Telemachus' at 23.97–103).[63] Might we even be left with the impression that Odysseus knows Penelope's mind better than she does?

Further points of contact with the Homeric model will become apparent over the course of the chapters that follow. As we have seen, Herodotus appropriates and develops Homeric techniques in representing motivation, in keeping with his various aims in presenting his audience with his project of *historiē* (inquiry). These include the desire both to paint a convincing psychological background that aids readers in interpreting the narrative of *erga*, and to engage them with the challenging nature of the task and the frequently provisional character of its results. Additionally, as in Homer the depiction of psychology may be intricately bound up with other poetic concerns, so in Herodotus it is frequently connected with his broader literary and narrative interests. But the Homeric primary

---

[60] See Pelling (1997).  [61] Fisher (1992), 352.

[62] Cf. de Jong *Comm.* ad loc.

[63] Goldhill (1999), 402–3. In Fenik's view, 'The situation demands that [Odysseus] know his wife's real intentions'; otherwise, '[t]he rich scale of ironies is impossible.... He is therefore simply made to know by the poet who... loses sight of (or willingly ignores) strict motivation in direct proportion to the extent to which he develops his favorite situations with their special emotions and ironies' (1974), 120.

narrator, whose authority and entire account flows from the Muse, by and large presents a contrast with the Herodotean narrator—whose personality is on show, who himself motivates his narrative, and whose personal authority is constantly on the line. In seeking to present the truth, Herodotus troubles over problems of motivation and draws them to his readers' attention. The following chapter considers further Herodotus' characterization of himself, in the hope of uncovering more about the nature of his project. The *Histories* has Homeric aspects alongside those that seem more fifth-century and sophistic (even while the 'sophistic' character of Odysseus must warn us against formulating such a distinction too rigidly). Next we turn to addressing this double character, which proves extremely relevant to our exploration of Herodotus' presentation of questions of motivation.

# 3

## Constructions of motives and
## the historian's persona

### 3.1 A DOUBLE PERSONA?

Plutarch sets up an opposition between 'historian' (ὁ ... ἱστορίαν γράφων) and 'sophist' (σοφιστής) to frame his accusation that Herodotus slides from one category into the other, failing in the historian's duty to declare what he knows to be true (ἃ ... οἶδεν ἀληθῆ ... ἐστι, 855e; cf. 13 above). This seems a response to the doubleness of the persona of the Herodotean narrator, and, accordingly, to that of his implied purposes. The opposition may be felt to be too blunt and slightly anachronistic. It is anachronistic in that the *Histories* precedes the establishment of *historiē* as a genre; and Herodotus probably did conceive of himself as a 'sophist', in the sense of the word as used before Plato.[1] It is the term he chooses to describe Pythagoras (4.95.2) and also Solon (1.29.1),[2] the illustrious Athenian sage and lawgiver whose reputation for wisdom has reached even the ears of the Lydian king Croesus. Indeed the category '*sophistēs*' would itself shift in the later years of the fifth century from denoting the Solon-type figure of wisdom seeking after the truth—with *sophistai*

---

[1] See Thomas (2000), esp. 283–5, noting (283) Alkidamas' suggestive early fourth-century pairing of *sophistai* with *historia*. On Herodotus and the sophists see further Dihle (1962); Ubsdell (1983), 339–99; Corcella (1984), 239–43.

[2] For parallels between Herodotus and Solon: Redfield (1985); Chiasson (1986); cf. Moles (1996) on *sophistai* arriving at Sardis (1.29.1) as analogous to sophists arriving at Athens. Montiglio (2000) suggests an interestingly subversive side that Solon and Herodotus share as wanderers: for this activity had associations of (Odyssean) deviousness and elusive identity. Unlike Odysseus, they wander by choice: for the sake of wisdom *tout court*.

('sophists') being synonymous with *sophoi*, 'wise men': Herodotus was no doubt admired by contemporaries as being such a *sophos*[3]— towards its common fourth-century meaning of teacher of cunning argument.[4] We may even find Herodotus himself reflecting contemporary fluidity between these two constructions of the 'sophist'. In suggesting a dual character to the Herodotean narrator Plutarch's opposition may not, then, be entirely inappropriate.

Plutarch's particular moralism when it comes to his expectations for history writing (as we feel in his response to the *Histories* in the *Malice*, and as he sets forth at *Cimon* 2.4–5[5]) does not find a parallel in the fifth century, but his label 'historian' remains appropriate to the earlier context in its evocation of a category to be contrasted with sophistic trickery. The frequently derogatory aspect *sophistēs* came to have in late fifth- and fourth-century treatments assumes the existence of such a contrasting category: a grouping of practitioners more concerned with truth and accuracy—who strive, Solon-like, to attain wisdom themselves and to educate others—than with using any means to win a case (and attendant profit). Both (in Plutarch's expression) 'sophist' and 'historian' (~ Solon-type *sophos*), as so conceived, may seek to persuade their audiences, but in different ways and to different ends. 'Sophists' employ persuasion of a deceptive sort[6] and lack moral commitment to the truth, focused instead on winning at all costs.[7] 'Historians', on the other hand, provide a straightforward, 'open and honest' (cf. 855a–b) narration (letting great deeds speak for themselves, for example, rather than supplying disreputable extra information as Herodotus does), with the laudable purpose of memorializing.

Thus a contrast equivalent to Plutarch's, framed a little differently, may well be apposite, and useful in clarifying the nature of the Herodotean narrator. Indeed it alights upon a significant tension.

---

[3] Cf. Fowler (1996), 86–7.     [4] See Thomas (2000), 284.

[5] In history writing as in portraiture (so Plutarch suggests at *Cimon* 2.4–5), one should not lay too much stress on a person's faults and weaknesses.

[6] Cf. Plutarch's objection that Herodotus' smooth, gentle style gives an impression that is belied by his underhand, subtle strategies.

[7] Cf. Plutarch's accusation that Herodotus is motivated generally by *kakoētheia* (malice), perhaps, in specific instances, also by bribes (cf. 862a–b); again (as Plutarch implies), that he writes whatever will serve to condemn the Thebans, irresponsibly 'dancing away the truth' in the manner of a Hippocleides, 867b.

For each of these distinct roles, historian and sophist as conceived by Plutarch, maps on to its respective contradictory aspect of the Herodotean narrator, even while Herodotus' *primary* persona remains that of conscientious historian. Usually, whether in composing a narrative of events or in conjecturing underlying causes, Herodotus' primary aim was the straightforward exposition of a *true*, and at the same time *commemorative*,[8] record of the past, with the inclusion of plausible reconstructions for the purpose of enlivening it for readers. That endeavour fits with Plutarch's notion of history as properly concerned with both truth and decorum. At other times, however, Herodotus seems rather (in the style of Plutarch's 'sophists') 'to take up and embellish the worse argument, whether for practice or show' (πρὸς ἐργασίαν ἢ δόξαν . . . τῶν λόγων κοσμεῖν τὸν ἥττονα παραλαμβάνοντ[α], 855e). Again, rather than inevitably aiming to inculcate 'strong belief concerning the matter/ deed' (πίστιν ἰσχυρὰν περὶ τοῦ πράγματος), he seems at times not so far removed from Plutarch's sophists who frequently admit 'that they are working to produce paradox for the sake of the unbelievable' (εἰς τὸ παράδοξον ἐπιχειρεῖν ὑπὲρ τῶν ἀπίστων, 855e).[9] At different times Herodotus appears to be working to achieve quite different sorts of audience impact. Nor, we may note, is persuasion (the prerogative, in different ways, of both 'sophist' and 'historian') the only response that the *Histories* seeks to elicit

---

[8] Herodotus frequently voices his concern for truth (cf. ch. 1 n. 55 above). But his particular focus on a story that deserves *memorialization*—as indicated in the preface (with its concern that human events not become *exitēla*, 'forgotten', and that great deeds not become *aklea*, 'without fame') and in the common criterion of a subject of narration being 'worthy of record, *logos*' (or 'of remembrance, *mnēmē*')—implies that this account of the truth is not to be 'warts and all' but selective—just as any narrative history must be selective, of course.

[9] Note Herodotus' inclusion in the *Histories* of *thōmata/thōmasia* ('wonders', cf. the 'great and *wondrous/remarkable* deeds' specified in the proem)—which may at times be paradoxical or unbelievable: e.g. the surprising speeches of the Debate on Constitutions, which are unbelievable (*apistoi*) to some Greeks, but 'really were said' (3.80.1, cf. above, 16); cf. the extraordinary height to which millet and sesame grows in Babylon, which Herodotus refrains from specifying since what he has said about the corn has already prompted his audience's *apistiē*, 'disbelief' (1.193.4). Ubsdell (1983), esp. 2–77, finds Herodotus 'striving after paradox and surprise' (75) in his depiction of human character.

from its readers[10]—and especially, perhaps, when it comes to questions of hidden motivation.

Indeed, there are many aspects and purposes to Herodotus' narrative technique (including his presentation of motives), not all of them arising from a straightforward concern either to convince readers of what he believes to be the truth, or to preserve the *kleos* of great deeds. The side of the Herodotean narrator that investigates and exposes underlying and often disreputable motives would seem to have more to him of the fifth-century sophist or orator than of Herodotus' predecessors in memorializing great military *erga*, the *Iliad* poet and Simonides.[11] Or, to put it differently, more of the Odysseus about him: of that subverter of the heroic code, who is concerned with *kleos*, though not in the same way as Homer's other heroes are.[12] Indeed the historian, climbing as he does into the minds of others in order to describe their mental processes—whether by means of explicit conjecture, or by focalizing his narrative through them—might be felt to require an analogous facility to Odysseus': so attuned as that hero is to others' psychology (cf. above, 48), and concerned to supply conjectures of it in his own narrative (*Od.* 9–12).[13] Herodotus may even occasionally transform into an unreliable narrator—Odysseus-like[14]—provoking audience scepticism and reconsideration, rather than their belief. Also more akin to sophist

---

[10] *Pace* e.g. Hartog (1988); see Dewald's review (1990), esp. 223: 'It is at least worth asking of the text whether Herodotus has not eschewed the effect of persuasion...in order to use his narrative to struggle with the distance between power and knowledge and with the slippage that often occurs between knowing and doing'. Indeed, to interpret Herodotus' strategies as primarily designed to elicit belief is often to suppress their most interesting features. 'Persuasion' understood more subtly does, however, remain a useful concept in discussing Herodotean narrative: cf. below.

[11] For Simonides' fragmentary poems on the Persian Wars, see Boedeker and Sider (2001). Boedeker (2001) and Flower/Marincola 315–19 bring out the significant points of contrast between Simonides' heroizing Plataea elegy and Herodotus' more complex and critical depiction.

[12] Odysseus concerned with *kleos*: e.g. *Od.* 5.311; 9.20. His unconventional deeds—guile and underhand behaviour—ultimately contribute to his memorialization in poetry, bestowing on him a distinctive sort of *kleos*. On Odysseus 'the untypical hero': Stanford (1968), 66–80.

[13] See above, 47–51 for the conjectures of motivation Odysseus offers in his own narrative and more generally for the Herodotean narrator as following in the manner of Homer's human narrators.

[14] Possibly even Homer-like: see 41–2 above.

than poetic predecessor seems the Herodotus who 'makes a charge and then withdraws', in the manner of an orator;[15] or who shows a persistent interest in the ἐκών/ἀέκων (willing/unwilling) issue, such a live concern of fifth-century discourse; or who, like the fifth-century dramatists, experiments with uses and effects of ascriptions of motives in the service of goals other than simply that of character construction with a view to psychologically plausible explanation;[16] and so on.

And yet it may be that Herodotus' purposes can still be understood in terms of 'persuasion' and 'truth', if in terms of a more subtle persuasion and a more complex truth—a possibility we shall return to below. For his subtle techniques alert readers to the elusive nature of the truth: to just how very difficult it can be to pin down.

The following discussion considers Herodotus' presentation of motives in the light of this double persona, in particular by means of certain figures in the *Histories* whom Herodotus appears to have constructed in the Herodotean narrator's likeness. Our culminating example will be the Spartan king Leonidas, for he is characterized by a similar doubleness, and at times he appears to be imitating, specifically in his approach to the question of others' motivation, the methods and purposes of the narrator (or—if we may admit the historical author—those of Herodotus himself). This in turn enables readers to further their own constructions of the character of Herodotus. But let us begin more generally.

## 3.2 INQUIRERS INTO MOTIVATION

The key importance of the inquiry into human motivation to Herodotus' conception of history is felt from the very outset of the *Histories* in the sheer density of reconstructions of motives and psychology in the Herodotean narrator's own narrative.[17] It is further displayed through Herodotus' portrayal of various actors in the *Histories* whose interest in

---

[15] Cf. above, ch. 1 n. 27 with text.    [16] Cf. e.g. Gibert (1995).
[17] Huber (1965a), 59–99 outlines the varieties of human ('natürlichen') motivation depicted in the *Histories* (focusing on the specifically political).

determining underlying motives appears to parallel his own. Matthew
R. Christ has shown how the methods of Herodotus' inquiring kings—
testing, measuring, mapping the world—invite readers through comparison and contrast to reach a deeper appreciation of the nature of
Herodotus' method and achievement.[18] Again, the many inquiries into
others' hidden thoughts conducted by characters in the text, and the
ramifications of the success or failure of such conjectures, invite readers
to perceive a metatextual dimension.[19]

As in the case of the inquiring kings considered by Christ, Herodotus' portrayal of these inquirers into human psychology (including
those of Christ's kings whose tests concern human objects) delineates
for readers further aspects of his own method and purposes.
The intense curiosity about the world around them displayed by
Herodotean kings is frequently matched by an equal fascination
with the inner world of fellow humans (and of gods). This interest
often has a pragmatic aspect, much as does their curiosity about the
physical world.[20] Xerxes' interest in Spartan psychology, for example
(as in the question of what motivates them to act as they do before
Thermopylae, combing their hair and all), which prompts his inquiries of Demaratus (7.209), has a military derivation: he wishes to
ascertain what it will take to conquer them. Likewise, the interest in
inquiring via an oracle into a god's hidden thoughts, and then in
reading the response correctly, relates to an often quite specific desire
for practical success. At times, however, the interest in psychology
can be purely intellectual. Darius, for example, wonders at Intaphrenes' wife's decision to save the life of her brother over that of her
husband or children, and consequently inquires into the explanation
for her choice. Her paradoxical motivation is a *thōma* ('wonder') in
its own right, and so as worthy of Herodotus' record as of Darius'

[18] Christ (1994).
[19] Compare Dewald (1993) on how, by looking at the way in which people in the
narrative deal with the significant objects they encounter, 'we can more concretely
understand some aspects of Herodotus' conception of his role as a researcher of τὰ
γενόμενα ἐξ ἀνθρώπων and the difficulties and dangers inherent in the task of interpretation' (58). Indeed at several points her discussion could equally well be framed,
as at times it is, in terms of the reading of motives (e.g. those signified by particular
objects) and what that tells us of Herodotean technique.
[20] Cf. Christ (1994).

interest. Cambyses displays a similar interest for its own sake in Psammenitos' psychology, desiring to know why it is that the sight of a beggar draws forth his tears, whereas knowledge of his children's impending fate does not (3.14). It is out of indignation at Apollo, but perhaps with a measure of curiosity too, that Croesus demands an explanation of the god's motives in treating him as he did (1.90)— even once the inquiry could make no practical difference.

Frequently, however, it is not so much the active inquiries of these characters with which Herodotus' narrative is concerned, as their awareness of others' psychology and motives: simply 'taking account' in this respect makes a successful outcome altogether more likely,[21] but in the sense of knowing how to play an audience. Peisistratus demonstrates a clear grasp of Athenian psychology (outdoing even Herodotus, who remains perplexed at the result): the trick involving Phye, where Peisistratus dresses her up as Athene in a chariot to welcome him back to Athens, seems 'extremely silly' (εὐηθέστατον, 1.60.3) to the historian, but elicits from the Athenians the desired response, and thus serves Peisistratus' aim of returning to power. Indeed, all sorts of people in the *Histories* are represented in the process of working to persuade various audiences, and their success or failure in so doing largely depends on their sensitivity or otherwise to the particular psychology of their audience. Aristagoras, for example, correctly appreciates the degree to which Cleomenes may be won over to join the Ionian revolt by the prospect of material advantages (combined with a hint of the public face he could give such an action), but his persuasion is unsuccessful because he fails to appreciate the Spartan attitude to travel so far from the sea (5.49–50). In the case of wise advisers, who frame their advice in accordance with their respective king's degree of enlightenment, persuasion or otherwise seems mostly a function of that enlightenment. Success in this instance may be measured in terms of the extent to which the adviser reads this correctly and so avoids placing himself in personal danger: the greater his sensitivity to kingly psychology in framing his

---

[21] This 'taking account' is of course Herodotean, too. Cf. Dewald (1993): characters in the *Histories* who correctly read the significance of objects (or, I might add in this context, the motives they imply), do so 'by using the same kind of canny general attentiveness that Herodotus himself displays as an investigator' (70).

advice, the lesser the danger he faces. Artemisia is most conspicuous for her skill in this regard, vis-à-vis Xerxes.[22]

The Babylonian Nitokris is another who 'takes account', attuned to the future and to human character. The two are related: it is her understanding of human nature that allows her accurately to predict the future. Correctly anticipating the Median threat (1.185.1), she sets in place what precautions she can, altering the Euphrates' course and excavating a lake to make journeys from Media more difficult, 'in order that the Medes not mix with her people and so learn her plans' (1.185.7)—alert to potential repercussions of such intermingling. Her bridge over the Euphrates is made impassable by night, 'in order that people not cross over at night and steal from one another' (1.186.3)—aware as she is of this likely consequence in view of human nature. Herodotus' culminating story recounts her trick played at the expense of some conjectured future King of Babylon: the building of her tomb and setting it atop the most commonly used city gate, with a graven inscription inviting him to open it should he need the money—but not otherwise. The deception relies upon her expectation of some future ruler's pragmatism and greed. Meanwhile, being situated as it is, the tomb will in any case serve to inconvenience Babylon's future Median rulers,[23] whose arrival Nitokris evidently expects.

The trick catches out Darius: he opens the tomb only to find that it contains no money at all. Nitokris' framing of her response to whosoever should open it—'if you were not greedy (ἄπληστός . . . χρημάτων) and avaricious (αἰσχροκερδής), you would not open the tombs of the dead' (1.187.5)—is a most fitting advance response to this particular king. It suggests that the figure she had in mind was one exactly like him, as depicted in Herodotus' sketch of his mental processes on this occasion,[24] and at greater length in the third book: Darius the shopkeeper (κάπηλος, 3.89.3), who asserts his indifference

---

[22] See Munson (1988), who notes several points of comparison between Artemisia and Themistocles that are suggestive for my discussion below.

[23] As Herodotus' account of Darius' reasoning soon makes explicit: see n. 24 below.

[24] 'Darius resented both not having the use of these gates and not being able to take the money—though it lay there and the writing itself invited him to do so. He could not use the gates at all for the reason that the corpse would be above his head as he rode through' (1.187.3–4).

to the old Persian tradition of truth telling where there is profit (cf. αἰσχροκερδής) to be had (3.72.4–5)—as here he values the prospect of money and practicality (having use of this major gate) over concerns of piety. This instance contravenes Steiner's notion of writing in the *Histories* as oppressive and tyrannical,[25] for Herodotus' account represents this writing as subversive and rebellious: as *challenging* the authority of the anticipated oppressor. Nitokris' writing works at the expense of one future Persian conquering king (much as Themistocles' writing at 8.22.3—the rock-engraved message, cleverly directed at a twofold audience of Ionians and Xerxes—will work at the expense of another, his heir[26]).

In her desire to get the better of Babylon's greedy future conquerors, Nitokris thus brings upon herself the indignity of having her tomb opened. Despite her impulse in other matters to leave behind memorials, she *invites* others to disrespect her tomb in this way—her major and most personal memorial. (Her true and final memorial will however be Herodotus' text: paradoxically, just like Odysseus in Homer, her unconventional behaviour ultimately *contributes* to preserving her *kleos*.[27]) This combination of Nitokris' desire to leave memorials, which seems in keeping with the grandeur and scale of the many *erga* that mark her reign, with her contriving of a clever but undignified deceit,[28] seems peculiarly Herodotean.[29] Herodotus' account, far from expressing disapproval for the queen's

[25] Cf. Steiner (1994), 128: '[t]o write, in the landscape of Herodotus and other contemporary authors, is to enter the world of the tyrant, to set oneself on the side of the autocrat, the oppressor, the enslaver'.

[26] Steiner (1994), 153–4 argues for the exceptional status of Themistocles' writing, contending that the parallels between this episode and Leutychides' later message to Ionians on the coast via a herald (9.98.2–3) 'retroactively restore Themistocles' message to an oral context' (154). I prefer de Bakker's (2007) distinction between *letters*—instruments of secrecy in the Persian empire—and *inscriptions*, which are by contrast a means of publishing words that are to be read by anyone, not just the intended addressee (58–60, 66).

[27] Note Kurke (1999), 84: 'rather than defacing her memory, the opening of her tomb triggers her enduring remembrance through her own words (γράμματα λέγοντα τάδε) and the narrative in which they are embedded (in this case, Herodotus' own account).'

[28] See Steiner (1994), 136–42 for other inscribed messages that subvert the solemnity of funeral monuments.

[29] Cf. Plutarch's charge, that Herodotus' style πολλοὺς ... ἐξηπάτηκε ('has deceived many', 854e).

trick, focuses on the Persian conqueror's greed and comeuppance, presenting it as a climactic and marvellous evocation of her character. Her astuteness seems in itself a *thōma*, and was perhaps the *raison d'être* of Herodotus' account, as we feel in the manner in which he rounds it off: αὕτη μέν νυν ἡ βασίλεια τοιαύτη τις λέγεται γενέσθαι ('and such a woman, it is said, was this queen', 1.187.5).

Thus persuasion entails psychological exploitation: if its aim is to induce action, it seeks to set forth potential motives that may then be claimed as such by its (in-text) listeners. Peisistratus' trick, for example, was intended to imply that he was beloved of Athene, and thus that the Athenians would profit by his rule: it invites them to be motivated by that prospect and so to embrace him as ruler. Nitokris moved Darius to action by holding out the spectre of money. Themistocles is one of the figures in the *Histories* most attuned to his audience's psychology, and therefore most expert at eliciting a particular response—as Herodotus takes care to describe in detail.[30] All these figures work in parallel to Herodotus, whose own skill in this respect, vis-à-vis his readers, is continually being performed.

### 3.3 LEONIDAS AND THERMOPYLAE (7.202–33)

The tension in the historian's purposes between, on the one hand, his desire to confer *kleos* upon *erga apodechthenta* ('deeds performed') and to leave a lasting memorial, and on the other, his intense interest in exploring the underlying human factors at work—factors whose exposure at times risks undermining the glamour and heroism of it all—is one that Herodotus projects onto the Spartan king Leonidas. Leonidas is first introduced into the Thermopylae narrative in heroic vein: singled out among the 'other generals' as 'the one admired most of all (ὁ... θωμαζόμενος μάλιστα) and leader of the whole army (παντὸς τοῦ στρατεύματος ἡγεόμενος)' (7.204), and given his full genealogy right back to Heracles. The Heraclid theme will resurface constantly around Leonidas over the course of the rest of the account

---

[30] Cf. below, ch. 9.

of Thermopylae, accompanied by frequent Homeric resonances, right up until his heroic death as ἀνὴρ γενόμενος ἄριστος ('a man proved most brave', 7.224.1)—over whose body the Greeks fight in Homeric style.³¹ The story of his succession, displaced from a natural position at 5.41 to 7.204, so as to introduce the Thermopylae narrative, is differently idealizing: removing Leonidas from the ranks of the many in the *Histories* we have witnessed wrangling egotistically for power, it presents him as one to whom kingship came unexpectedly (ἐξ ἀπροσδοκήτου, 7.204). This in turn heralds the narrative strand portraying Leonidas as servant of his country, which later culminates with the account of his conscious decision—quite Hector- or Achilles-like—to sacrifice himself, in his case for Sparta's sake.

The narrative register next changes markedly, however, as Herodotus explains the presence of a Theban contingent at Thermopylae by delving into Leonidas' thoughts:

τοῦδε δὲ εἵνεκα τούτους σπουδὴν ἐποιήσατο Λεωνίδης μούνους Ἑλλήνων παραλαβεῖν, ὅτι σφέων μεγάλως κατηγόρητο μηδίζειν· παρεκάλεε ὦν ἐς τὸν πόλεμον θέλων εἰδέναι εἴτε συμπέμψουσι εἴτε καὶ ἀπερέουσι ἐκ τοῦ ἐμφανέος τὴν Ἑλλήνων συμμαχίην. οἱ δὲ ἄλλα φρονέοντες ἔπεμπον (7.205.3).

Leonidas was keen that the Thebans above all other Greeks join the cause, since the charge had been brought against them that they favoured the Medes. Therefore he summoned them to the war because he wished to know whether they would send [troops] along or would instead openly reject the Greek alliance. They sent [troops], but with other thoughts in mind.

Thus Herodotus ascribes to Leonidas an intellectual interest in the question of the Thebans' motives (rather than other possibilities readers might have supposed)—for, as Macan observes, the king is here moved not by the desire to give the Thebans an opportunity to prove themselves in battle (and so purge themselves of the charge), nor by the desire to involve them in the impending disaster: 'he simply wished to know whether the accusation was, or was not true'.³² Leonidas' wish to uncover the truth and his curiosity about

³¹ Leonidas as hero/Heraclid: Munson (1993), 53–4 and (2001), 176–8 (overlooking the less heroic strand that I shall be considering); Boedeker (2003). Leonidas' Homeric death: Munson (1991), 175–8; Boedeker (2003), 34–6; Pelling (2006b), 92–3 with n. 48 (listing the Homeric parallels of the scene).
³² Macan ad loc.

a matter of motivation, which precipitate his personal inquiry by means of a test, seem conspicuously Herodotean, as does the εἴτε . . . εἴτε ('whether . . . or') formula that expresses his focalization of the alternative possible outcomes. The ascription introduces a close-up and human perspective on the king, drawing readers into his mind (and into a thought process, moreover, with a Herodotean familiarity to it, and with which readers may themselves identify, too). This seems quite removed from the preceding heroic and distancing characterization. Moreover, Leonidas' donning here of the role of judge in his interest in the correctness of the *charge* (κατηγορίη), sophistic rather than Homeric, brings him closer to Herodotus' audience in temporal terms, as it represents a move from heroic age into fifth-century present.

A similar effect was achieved in the first book through Herodotus' conjectures of three possible motives for Cyrus' placing Croesus and fourteen Lydian boys on the pyre:

ἐν νόῳ ἔχων εἴτε δὴ ἀκροθίνια ταῦτα καταγιεῖν θεῶν ὅτεῳ δή, εἴτε καὶ εὐχὴν ἐπιτελέσαι θέλων, εἴτε καὶ πυθόμενος τὸν Κροῖσον εἶναι θεοσεβέα τοῦδε εἵνεκεν ἀνεβίβασε ἐπὶ τὴν πυρήν, βουλόμενος εἰδέναι εἴ τίς μιν δαιμόνων ῥύσεται τοῦ μὴ ζῶντα κατακαυθῆναι (1.86.2).

Perhaps he had in mind to burn these as victory offerings to some god or other, perhaps he wanted to fulfil a vow, or perhaps, having learned that Croesus was god-fearing, it was for this reason that he caused him to be put on the pyre, desiring to know whether one of the gods would save him from being burnt alive.

The three options there drew the reader through a spectrum of possibilities, from the grand and dignified—concerns of piety and integrity (suggestive of Cyrus' awareness as regards the divine, and in keeping with the tenor of his portrait up to this point of an attentive, successful man of action whose deeds have been described from a distance[33])—to the far more human and personable—and Herodotean—motive of *curiosity.*[34] It was this third ascription of motive that

---

[33] From Croesus' implicit perspective, in fact: cf. Stahl (2003) (who notes the change at this point, when Cyrus becomes subject).

[34] Unlike the first two, which arise from obligations of sorts, the third motivation represents a purely intellectual interest on Cyrus' part in whether Croesus is really θεοσεβής (god-fearing)—which probably implies his further interest in the underlying explanation for Croesus' conduct and achievement.

the narrative then appropriated and moved on from, for the account that followed did indeed answer Cyrus' question by proving Croesus to be loved by the gods. In tandem with that, a more human perspective on Cyrus began to gain ground at that point, as the narrative conveyed more about his mind and personality. No longer so 'other' (as he had been vis-à-vis Croesus, and as was also conveyed in the exotic flavour of the first of the three alternative motives, with its suggestion of human sacrifice to some unidentifiable god), he was shown able to accept advice—indeed, to reach an immediate understanding of Solonian wisdom—and to have gained an awareness of the humanity he shared with Croesus.

Thus the test arising from Cyrus' curiosity about the gods' attitude towards Croesus gained the historian's implicit sanction, for its outcome as well as Apollo's later reply did indeed confirm Croesus' status as one loved by the gods. However, in Leonidas' case, after evoking the Herodotean quality of the Spartan king's impulse, Herodotus—as he does with many of the investigators considered by Christ—himself trumps Leonidas as inquirer into the Thebans' motives. He signals the limited value of Leonidas' test with his own addition of the enigmatic postscript (οἱ δὲ ἄλλα φρονέοντες ἔπεμπον, 'they sent troops, but with other thoughts in mind'), indicating that the form of the test (the question of whether or not the Thebans come) is inadequate for resolving the question of their guilt or innocence on the charge of medizing. Readers are thus left wondering about those 'other thoughts' as the narrative moves on. And the immediately ensuing narrative again suggests that intentions may not be directly ascertained from resulting action:[35] despite their initial resolve, the Greeks at Thermopylae are moved by fear at the Persians' approach, and their minds turn to the possibility of escape (καταρρωδέοντες ἐβουλεύοντο περὶ ἀπαλλαγῆς, 7.207).[36] Thus the historian emerges in this instance as the real expert in judging questions of motives. Conversely, however, the interest in Herodotean questions displayed by a king of such heroic stature as Leonidas

---

[35] Herodotus' awareness of and focus upon this problem for the historian in working out motives *ex eventu* is explored in ch. 4.

[36] Readers might apply the warning also to Herodotus' own narrative, where the fact of a state's eventual medizing should perhaps not be expected to reveal much about its actual earlier motives. See ch. 7 below.

must also reflect back upon Herodotus' own character and purposes, as I shall suggest further below.

The tension in Leonidas' actions and purposes as depicted by Herodotus (his desire to leave a memorial, and his yearning for *kleos*—but then his disturbing of this idealizing and memorializing impulse with his abrupt refocus on the question of the Thebans' motives) runs in parallel to the historian's own practice through this stretch of narrative. So far from leaving the glorious record of action to speak for itself, right from the beginning Herodotus includes in his account suggestions—at times detailed constructions—of motives that set a rather ambivalent and downbeat tone. The initial chapters are a case in point. Soon after his account turns Greecewards again, opening with the list of Greeks of various nationalities who awaited Xerxes in Trachis, at Thermopylae (7.202), Herodotus sets down a full report of the message with which the Greeks persuaded further allies, Locrians and Phocians, to join them there too. Its main content—to which the Locrians and Phocians do indeed respond (7.203.2)—is platitudes that downplay, with obvious disingenuousness, the danger Xerxes represents. The implication is that these communities joined the Greek cause only after being persuaded of its minimal risk. Next, Herodotus speaks of the commanders, identifying Leonidas in particular. After noting his heroic genealogy and the circumstances of his coming to power, Herodotus moves swiftly (as we have seen) to consider his motives in bringing with him not only Spartans, but also a Theban contingent: to find out the truth of the accusation that the Thebans were medizers. He then observes that the Spartans had sent the men with Leonidas in advance ἵνα τούτους ὁρῶντες οἱ ἄλλοι σύμμαχοι στρατεύωνται μηδὲ καὶ οὗτοι μηδίσωσι, ἢν αὐτοὺς πυνθάνωνται ὑπερβαλλομένους ('in order that the rest of the allies, at seeing these men, would campaign and would not medize like the others, as they would if they learned that the Spartans were holding back', 7.206.1)—a third foray in quick succession into a question of motivation, this time of the Spartans, which again brings to the fore the possibility of Greeks medizing. This stretch of narrative, at least, by showing so many Greeks prepared to medize, works against the thought that surfaces elsewhere (and to which Plutarch responds, 864e) that the Thebans were particularly guilty in this regard.[37]

---

[37] See §7.2 below (§7.2.5 on the Thebans).

Thus Herodotus, in parallel to Leonidas, undercuts the heroic aspect of a situation through his exploration of characters' inner thoughts. A similar combination of discordant registers, in connection with the presentation of motives, also characterizes the later account. In the second stage of the Thermopylae narrative (after Ephialtes' betrayal, which sealed the Greek defeat and precipitated the allies' council and the subsequent departure of the majority of them), Herodotus' initial construction of Leonidas' motivation contributes to the king's idealizing, heroic aspect. Having chosen the version of the story that has the king *order* the Greeks away, Herodotus reflects upon his motives as follows:

λέγεται δὲ <καὶ> ὡς αὐτός σφεας ἀπέπεμψε Λεωνίδης, μὴ ἀπόλωνται κηδόμενος· αὐτῷ δὲ καὶ Σπαρτιητέων τοῖσι παρεοῦσι οὐκ ἔχειν εὐπρεπέως ἐκλιπεῖν τὴν τάξιν ἐς τὴν ἦλθον φυλάξοντες ἀρχήν.³⁸ ταύτῃ καὶ μᾶλλον τὴν γνώμην πλεῖστός εἰμι, Λεωνίδην, ἐπείτε ᾔσθετο τοὺς συμμάχους ἐόντας ἀπροθύμους καὶ οὐκ ἐθέλοντας συνδιακινδυνεύειν, κελεῦσαί σφεας ἀπαλλάσσεσθαι, αὐτῷ δὲ ἀπιέναι οὐ καλῶς ἔχειν· μένοντι δὲ αὐτοῦ κλέος μέγα ἐλείπετο, καὶ ἡ Σπάρτης εὐδαιμονίη οὐκ ἐξηλείφετο. ἐκέχρηστο γὰρ ὑπὸ τῆς Πυθίης τοῖσι Σπαρτιήτῃσι χρεωμένοισι περὶ τοῦ πολέμου τούτου αὐτίκα κατ᾽ ἀρχὰς ἐγειρομένου, ἢ Λακεδαίμονα ἀνάστατον γενέσθαι ὑπὸ τῶν βαρβάρων ἢ τὸν βασιλέα σφέων ἀπολέσθαι.... ταῦτά τε δὴ ἐπιλεγόμενον Λεωνίδην καὶ βουλόμενον κλέος καταθέσθαι μούνων³⁹ Σπαρτιητέων, ἀποπέμψαι τοὺς συμμάχους μᾶλλον ἢ γνώμῃ διενειχθέντας οὕτως ἀκόσμως οἴχεσθαι τοὺς οἰχομένους (7.220).

It is said also that Leonidas himself sent them away, caring that they not be killed; as for him and for those of the Spartiates who were there, it was not fitting to abandon the post they had come at the beginning to defend. To this my opinion too inclines, that Leonidas, when he perceived that the allies were not eager or willing to share in the danger, ordered them to depart, but (said that) it was not right for him to do so. But by remaining there he would leave behind great *kleos* (fame), and the *eudaimonia* (prosperity) of Sparta would not be obliterated. For it had been prophesied to the Spartans by the

³⁸ See Macan on 7.220.2 on the ambiguity here as to whether the clause reports a matter of fact, or Leonidas' view.
³⁹ Reading μούνων (Leonidas wanting *kleos* 'for the Spartiates alone') with Hude, Macan, Legrand (and several translations). Stein and Rosén follow most manuscripts in preferring μοῦνον, which could mean the equivalent, or (Blanco) Leonidas wanting 'to be the only Spartan to win such fame', or again (Blakesley) desiring 'fame alone [i.e. *unmixed* with any discordant incidents', Blakesley ad loc.] for the Spartans'— which would press somewhat less strongly the strand I pursue below.

Pythia, when they consulted it about this war at its very beginning, that either Lacedaimon would be ruined by the barbarian, or their king would be killed . . . .And Leonidas, thinking upon these things and wanting fame to be laid up for the Spartiates alone, sent the allies away, rather than having those who were leaving depart in such disarray after a difference of opinion.

Thus Leonidas is presented as motivated in sending the Greeks away in part by his care for their own safety and for the survival of Spartan *eudaimonia* (in accordance with his awareness of an oracle dating from the very beginning of the war), but particularly—this is the most insistent theme—by his concern for keeping up appearances. He is anxious that the Greeks be seen to have acted on his orders rather than to have departed 'in such disarray' (οὕτως ἀκόσμως);[40] that the Spartans act fittingly (εὐπρεπέως) in not leaving their post, and that they alone of Greeks have the glory (κλέος καταθέσθαι); and that to him, remaining there, 'great fame be left behind' (κλέος μέγα ἐλείπετο). Leonidas, in parallel to Herodotus, is self-consciously monumentalizing *kleos*, even 'writing his own script'.[41] Indeed, in 7.220.2—μένοντι δὲ αὐτοῦ κλέος μέγα ἐλείπετο, καὶ ἡ Σπάρτης εὐδαιμονίη οὐκ ἐξηλείφετο ('remaining there he would win great fame, and the prosperity of Sparta would not be obliterated')—is felt an echo of Herodotus' own preface.[42] (This almost obsessive concern with *kleos* is felt again on the part of Spartans generally in the stage-managed feel of their later preparations 'to slay or be slain', reported to Xerxes. Their pre-battle grooming suggests their self-conscious construction in advance of a memorial for posterity.) Herodotus expands on a further proof that Leonidas did indeed order the allies to depart (7.221), and restates the fact of their departure for this reason (7.222).

[40] There is ambiguity at this point as to whether we are now in Leonidas' mind, or back in Herodotus': Stein inserts <δοκέω> (preceding μᾶλλον ἢ γνώμῃ . . .) to press the latter option, which is favoured e.g. by Waterfield and de Sélincourt/Marincola; I follow Legrand (Leonidas sent the allies away 'plûtot que de voir ceux qui partaient partir en dissentiment avec lui et au mépris de la discipline') and Godley in preferring the former.

[41] Cf. Nagy (1990), 221–7; Munson (2001), 177; Pelling (2006*b*), 93 n. 51, noting (cf. Bakker (2002*b*), 17) a possible allusion to Simonides *PMG* 531. Pelling (2006*b*), 94 for Leonidas and the Spartans as 'almost writing their own script'.

[42] Cf. Bakker (2002*b*), 16.

At this point, however, the narrative's heroic tone, born of the talk of *kleos* and the oracle, is interrupted by Herodotus' surprising explanation for the Thebans' involvement in the Last Stand, which implies a motive on Leonidas' part of an altogether different and less gracious sort than those so far suggested. Herodotus notes that Thebans and Thespians alone stayed at the king's side, the Thespians altogether willingly (ἑκόντες μάλιστα), but the Thebans 'unwillingly and reluctantly (ἀέκοντες . . . καὶ οὐ βουλόμενοι); for indeed Leonidas was keeping them there as hostages' (7.222). Thus at the very moment when Leonidas heroically rewrites the situation—by himself *sending the Greeks away* when the allies' impulse to leave of their own accord threatens to bring dishonour to the Greek cause—he is presented as less than generously insisting that the Thebans remain at his side. (Alert readers might well reflect upon his possible reasons for so doing; the earlier Theban incident suggests the sorts of possibilities they might consider.) That action will in fact precipitate their later open medizing, which in turn threatens to be altogether more damaging to Greek *kleos*.

This hostage explanation for the Thebans' presence even after the dismissal of the rest of the allies is even more peculiar, and unheroic in its effect, than Herodotus' earlier explanation for the Thebans' presence at Leonidas' side. Along with its other contradictory aspects (which Plutarch is at pains to detail, 865b–e)[43] the explanation works strongly against the grain of Herodotus' immediately preceding exploration into Leonidas' mind, in its focus both on his *caring* for the Greeks in sending them away, and on his concern with *decorum*. It offers a different perspective on Leonidas' character from the man as seen earlier (preoccupied with matters grand, heroic, and divine), as one instead closely attentive to the failings of his fellow humans, and indeed intent on exposing them[44] (ungenerously, as Plutarch would say, and also in the style of a Herodotus: in his *Malice* he observes that 'whoever makes a digression out of slander and blame (ὁ δὲ παρενθήκην λόγου τὸ βλασφημεῖν καὶ ψέγειν ποιούμενος) seems

---

[43] See below, ch. 7 n. 29 with text.

[44] In this we see a side of Spartan behaviour that is *not* simply 'utterly conditioned by the divine', Munson (1993), 42, just as there are hints elsewhere in the *Histories*, too (e.g. esp. at 9.8) that other concerns and motivations are frequently operative on the Spartan part.

to incur the curse of tragedy, "for singling out the misfortunes of mortals"', 855d). There *does* seem to be something to Plutarch's accusation as regards the hostage explanation for the Thebans' staying to fight alongside the three hundred:

τὸ δὲ μέγιστον καὶ κάλλιστον ἔργον ἀνελεῖν μὴ δυνηθεὶς ὡς οὐ πραχθὲν αὐτοῖς, αἰτίᾳ φαύλῃ καὶ ὑπονοίᾳ διαλυμαινόμενος ταῦτ᾽ ἔγραφεν . . . (865a).

Being unable to refute the greatest and finest deed by claiming that it hadn't been performed by them, he promoted its undoing through a petty motivation and suspicion in writing this.

Thus with the reappearance of the Theban theme the register again shifts towards the less idealizing and more pragmatic. And yet we might also observe how this hostage explanation focuses readers' attention on a subversive strand that was actually implicit earlier, though in muted form.[45] The shift is only quantitative.

The dualism surrounding Leonidas' character and purposes mirrors the twofold nature of the broader, rival explanations the *Histories* offers for why Thermopylae happened as it did: whether it is more to be explained in terms of Leonidas' personal heroism: his consciously contriving the last stand in the way in which it happened; or whether it was the upshot rather of the Greeks' divided councils and impulse to leave, with the Spartans obliged by circumstance into the particular conduct that would be least damaging to the wider campaign. These explanations are both to be found in the text, whose heroic strand is suggestive of the first, its human strand—emphasizing human frailty and the consequent possibility of flight or medizing—suggestive of the second.

These options mirror the proem's dual paradigms for how things happen: for what sorts of motivating forces are most likely to be operative. They are a mirror (and a reminder) also of the complexity of the past and its traditions. The (implied) Greek view on Helen's theft[46] emphasized the (Homeric, epic) matter of honour: the notion

---

[45] Compare Pelling (2006*b*) on how 'even in the Thermopylae narrative itself there was a hint of the less glorious world that they are living in, the *need* to orchestrate'—which becomes so much more evident in 'the shambles of the Spartan troop-movements at Plataea' (95). Plataea makes us all the more alert to the less than glamorous aspects of Thermopylae, just as the explanation given for the Thebans' remaining does on a more immediate level.

[46] See Dewald (1999), 226 on this absent presence.

of being *duty-bound* to revenge the wrong done, since the woman was symbolic of something far greater. The Persian view, by contrast, displayed a down-to-earth pragmatism, with the notion of women being abducted only if they wished to be (lent reinforcement by the Phoenician story that Io left of her own accord having slept with a ship's captain), and Paris not caring a jot for his reputation— for *kleos* (or *timē*, honour). Rather, like Darius in relation to Nitokris' tomb, working in sophistic fashion from probabilities ('knowing fully that he would not be punished, since the others were not punished', 1.3.1) he jumped at the prospect of gaining a woman for free. It is not so evident that Herodotus' account lends support to one of these motivational paradigms in particular;[47] readers may contemplate both as the *Histories* progresses. In the second book, however, Herodotus comes down on the side of pragmatism, agreeing with the story that Helen was not in Troy at all—since the Trojans would not have sat by and watched their city sacked rather than hand her over!

Similar idealizing versus pragmatic alternatives are staged in the Gyges narrative, which likewise seems programmatic for the rest of the *Histories*: the proverb Gyges tells his master—σκοπέειν τινὰ τὰ ἑωυτοῦ ('one must look at one's own', 1.8.4)—reads two ways. It may be interpreted as being concerned with honour and with correct behaviour in accordance with *nomos* (which is how Gyges there intends it, in relation to the king), or—as it ends up being applicable instead to Gyges—with that quite naked variety of self-interest, one's own survival.[48] For, of the two courses presented to him by Candaules' queen, 'he chose to survive' (αἱρέεται αὐτὸς περιεῖναι, 1.11.4). Thus Gyges chooses the less moral alternative—since a subject ought not to kill a king, as Delphi's response later makes clear (1.91.1)— and gains for himself what (in accordance with the proverb's initial

---

[47] Even if, *methodologically*, Herodotus intends to contrast his own practice with what is staged in the preface in the mouths of Persians and Phoenicians, these different explanatory paradigms can nonetheless remain operative and relevant for readers over the course of the rest of the work.

[48] Pelling (2006a), who translates: ' "Each man should look to his own" (or "to his own interest")', 144–5. σκοπέειν likewise carries a double meaning, 'pay attention to' alongside the more literal and visual 'look to', activated by and contributing to the story's voyeuristic motif: Russo (1997), 53–4.

sense) is not remotely his own:[49] another's wife and kingdom. We might compare the shift in the Thermopylae narrative from honourable to self-interested imperatives (as Herodotus moves into recounting the later stories of Spartan disgrace), with the *survival* motif gradually moving to the fore.

Each of the contending explanations for Thermopylae in turn implies a different purpose on the historian's part. Herodotus' account may on one level be read as intended to preserve the glory of Thermopylae, sustaining Greek, and particularly Spartan, *kleos*—and as thus refiguring as a victory what was in truth a Greek defeat.[50] He records, for example, the 'memorial' left by the *aristos* Deioces in the form of his quip that thanks to the onslaught of Persian arrows he would be fighting in the shade. (This and 'other sayings of such a kind' he was said 'to have left as a memorial', λιπέσθαι μνημόσυνα, 7.226.2). Herodotus also records the Spartan brothers who were next in valour (ἀριστεῦσαι λέγονται...); the Thespian who 'was distinguished most of all' (εὐδοκίμεε μάλιστα, 7.227); and the inscriptions from the concrete memorials to the dead—of Greeks, Spartans, and the seer Megistias (μνῆμα τόδε κλεινοῖο Μεγιστία..., 'this is the memorial of famous Megistias', 7.228.3).

Yet at the same time, Herodotus' narrative drops many *atopous* hints—akin to those to which Plutarch alerts his readers (874b)—of the fact that all the Greeks at Thermopylae did *not* in fact act so heroically: that even some of the Three Hundred Spartiates did not die at Thermopylae but lived on; that heroic patriotism, desire for honour and repute, and so on, were not always powerful enough motives to override self-interest in the form of cowardice and fear.[51] The chapters that conclude the main Thermopylae narrative turn to

---

[49] Indeed, it goes wholly against Gyges' initial understanding of the proverb, for as Delphi states, ἐφόνευσε τὸν δεσπότεα καὶ ἔσχε τὴν ἐκείνου τιμὴν **οὐδέν οἱ προσήκουσαν** ('he killed his master and held his office, **which in no way belonged to him** [i.e. Gyges]', 1.91.1). Thus he ends up acting in accordance with the opposite of τὸ προσῆκον (which is what he had recommended to Candaules).

[50] See Dillery (1996), 217–54 on how Herodotus refigures Thermopylae as a victory by means of the motif of the duel.

[51] This is a part of a broader phenomenon in the *Histories*, as Boedeker (2003) observes: 'More often [than representing heroic deaths in 'poetic' mode], Herodotus seems interested in the various motives, strategies, and behaviors of characters who might have chosen not to fight' (35).

memorializing incidents redolent, rather, of δύσκλεια (*ill* fame). Herodotus tells the story of the Spartan Aristodemos, one of the Three Hundred, who, unlike his braver companion, either used his illness as an excuse for missing the battle (λιποψυχέοντα λειφθῆναι), or else—worse, but in accordance with an alternative account—was away delivering a message and delayed his return. Thus he chose to survive (ὑπομείναντα ἐν τῇ ὁδῷ περιγενέσθαι, 7.230), just like Gyges—and like the helot who led Eurytos into battle then fled (7.229.1)[52]—instead of taking the more honourable path and killing himself. Either way,

ἀπονοστήσας δὲ ἐς Λακεδαίμονα ὁ Ἀριστόδημος ὄνειδός τε εἶχε καὶ ἀτιμίην· πάσχων δὲ τοιάδε ἠτίμωτο· οὔτε οἱ πῦρ οὐδεὶς ἔναυε Σπαρτιητέων οὔτε διελέγετο, ὄνειδός τε εἶχε ὁ τρέσας Ἀριστόδημος καλεόμενος (7.231).

Upon his return to Lacedaemon, Aristodemos suffered reproach and dishonour. He suffered dishonour in that no Spartiate would either light a fire for him or converse with him; and he suffered reproach in being called 'Aristodemos the bolter'.

The extent of his disgrace is especially arresting in light of his name: the same as that of one of the Heraclids earlier listed in Leonidas' heroic pedigree (7.204).[53] Herodotus' mention of his subsequent restoration of his reputation in fighting at Plataea (7.231) invites readers to consider others who survived Thermopylae to fight again in that later battle.[54] Yet another of the three hundred, Pantites—his name bearing an expressive irony (underlining the discrepancy between ideal and reality) if it means 'the all-honouring' or 'all-honourable man'[55]—'carrying a message . . . survived' (ἀποπεμφθέντα ἄγγελον . . . περιγενέσθαι); and 'after returning

---

[52] This mention 'encourages readers to consider the Spartiate survivor as no better than the "inferior classes" at Sparta': Lateiner (2002), 368.

[53] Cf. Macan ad loc., who notes also the reference at 6.52 (Aristodemos the man whom Spartan tradition regarded as having set the Dorians in Sparta). Ironic too is the name's meaning: 'Best of the People', cf. Lateiner (2002), 370.

[54] In the later account, Herodotus will indeed restore Aristodemos' reputation, in the teeth of too-rigid Spartan perspectives on *kleos*: 9.71.2–4 with Lateiner (2002), 370–1.

[55] 'Pantites', if derived from Pan-tites (since the pan- prefix is prominent in Greek nouns of this period, and regarding names it gains some support from Pantimias and Pantimia, though they appear only in the Hellenistic period), denotes 'the all-honouring man' or (so Macan ad loc.) 'the all-honourable man'. But even if derived rather from Pant-ites, since Pant- is a quite common first component in name formation, contemporary readers might have felt the presence of τίω I. (LSJ), 'to honour, revere'. I thank Anna Morpurgo Davies, Mathieu de Bakker, and Nikoletta Kavanou for their assistance.

to Sparta, he was so dishonoured that he hanged himself' (νοστήσ-
αντα... ἐς Σπάρτην, ὡς ἠτίμωτο, ἀπάγξασθαι, 7.232). The indirect
*legetai* construction Herodotus employs in recounting these Spartan
stories evokes the circulation of shameful rumours. Nothing could be
worse than that to the Spartan desire for repute. Moreover, might
these stories of cowardly Spartiate ἄγγελοι (messengers) recall, and
risk contaminating the memory of, the famous inscription in memory of Spartan dead that Herodotus has cited just earlier (ὦ ξεῖν',
ἀγγέλλειν Λακεδαιμονίοις..., 'Stranger, go tell the Spartans...',
7.228.2)? The tales of questionable honour implicating individual
Spartiates are rounded off with the account (now in the direct
discourse suggestive of authorial sanction) of the active medizing
of Thebans as a whole group—which is evidently more shameful
than simply evading battle, but no more surprising than such avoidance of battle by *Spartan equals.*

All this works against the grain of Demaratus' idealizing perspective on Spartan conduct, felt in his statement to Xerxes that 'now you
are up against the finest kingdom of those in Greece, and the most
valiant men' (πρὸς βασιληίην τε καλλίστην τῶν ἐν Ἕλλησι προσφέρεαι
καὶ ἄνδρας ἀρίστους, 7.209.4). It also suggests that his earlier claim
that the Spartans' obedience to law meant that they would never
avoid battle (7.104.4–5) was exaggerated.[56] Thus Demaratus' understanding of the impetus that propels Spartans to fight as they do is
superior to Xerxes' (who responds to Demaratus' opinions on the
matter with laughter or disbelief[57])—as he understands that it is *not*
simply a question of practical factors or numbers; that *to eikos*
(probability) is *not* always sufficient to explain human conduct. But
Herodotus' own understanding trumps even Demaratus', whose

---

[56] The Sphakteria debacle of 425 BC (with so many Spartiates captured *alive*) was
further proof, for Herodotus' readers, of that! Likewise, Demaratus' assertion that Spartans would never accept conditions that bring slavery to Greece (δουλοσύνην...
τῇ Ἑλλάδι) is elsewhere shown to need qualification (since Spartans were ready, at
5.91, to join forces with a Persian-backed tyrant to enslave Athens; and later they will be
unwilling to support Athens and the cause of Greek freedom at Plataea until they have
been prodded to action by the spectre of self-interest, 9.6–11; cf. below, § 7.4). We should
perhaps, however, bear in mind that Demaratus is tailoring his address to Xerxes, framing
it in terms that the Persian King will understand; it may not, in that case, reflect directly his
own belief (but see 176 below for the possibility of Demaratus' nostalgia from afar).

[57] 7.105, cf. 7.209.1, 5. Compare the general Persian misreading of Greek psychology
in assuming (7.218) that no one will fight once the pass has been betrayed.

emphasis on the Spartans' fighting for honour before all pragmatic concerns, and in obedience to their *despotēs nomos*, is too narrow. It does not allow for exceptions, and for the human aspect: for the power, for example, of a deterrent such as fear (which we saw operative in the cases above). Herodotus' account is more nuanced, more alive to the possibility of exceptions. More generally, it demonstrates also that bravery is *not* the only explanatory principle for the initial Spartan success at Thermopylae: it is also through skill and trickery (e.g. at 7.211) that the Spartans outperform the Persians.

But the effect of portraying human frailty in this way is not necessarily what Plutarch supposed. Rather than undermining the heroic record, it may instead augment the status of those *erga* that are nonetheless achieved, since exposing the human aspect—the background of motives, thoughts, fears against which humans act—illuminates the challenge involved. The reputation of the Three Hundred Spartans is perhaps not so much undermined by the record of those who fell short of the ideal, as enhanced through its demonstration of the real difficulties involved: the constant reminders of human weakness that punctuate the Thermopylae narrative as insistently as do the heroic echoes perhaps render the Spartans' achievement all the more marvellous. Nor, indeed, are the worlds of Homer and Herodotus wholly different in this respect: in Pelling's expression, 'perhaps the "heroic" has always gleamed the brighter for its commingling with the ordinary and the messy and the humanly frail'.[58] Those occasions where Homeric heroes weigh up in their own minds the alternatives—never voiced publicly—of fighting or fleeing convey, as Scully observes,

the anxiety of the hero as he moves from indecision to resolution, from fear to courage, from thought to reaffirmation of heroic action. Although the soliloquy calls into question the values of society, it also serves to highlight the particular nature of heroism as conceived in the *Iliad*. Iliadic heroism is not only action, but action born from the consciousness of death and the recognition of the limits of human existence.[59]

The way in which, in the *Histories*, the Thebans with their commander **Leon**tiades come to appear the reverse image of the Spartans under

[58] Pelling (2006*b*), 98.
[59] Scully (1984), quote at 14. Renehan (1987) points to the 'unheroic' quality of Homeric deaths.

Leonidas may offer a reminder of what might have been; of the fact that the Spartans' stance at Thermopylae was *not* inevitable,[60] but chosen, and the result of personal courage. Herodotus perhaps chose the name 'Leontiades' for this very effect, if Plutarch is right that the Theban commander on the occasion was actually Anaxandros (867a). The Lion monument could equally well remind its spectators (and Herodotus' readers) of the medizing Leontiades: a memorial, then, to a man who did not fight, but lived on, branded as a slave. Similarly, the heroism of the Spartan brother who chose to die with the rest becomes all the more conspicuous against the foil provided by his less courageous sibling. Those Greeks who plan to desert make the more apparent the bravery of those (like the Thespians) who determine to stay.[61] The effect seems similar to that of Herodotus' emphasis on the hair's-breadth nature of the wider Greek victory.

The *kleos* that the *Histories* confers (as mentioned in the preface) resides, then, not simply in great and wondrous deeds achieved, but in those deeds as viewed against the background of human actuality. Herodotus' preface brings to the fore the human aspect: the *erga megala* whose fame he preserves are those achieved within the bounds of the human world ('by Greeks and by non-Greeks'). More generally, the *genomena* whose memory his account preserves are those specifically '*ex anthrōpōn*', '(produced) by human beings'. The matrix of thoughts and motivations—which spotlight the challenges involved and the fact that the action might well not have been taken at all—allows us to appreciate the magnitude of the achievement all the more.

## 3.4 SELF-CHARACTERIZATION AND NARRATIVE AUTHORITY

The way in which Herodotus has Leonidas and other figures in the *Histories* imitating his own interest in and sensitivity to the question of determining people's underlying motives underlines

---

[60] Cf. Herodotus' entertaining at 7.139 the possibility that the Spartans might have medized.

[61] Likewise the medizing *poleis* will supply the foil against which Athens at 8.144 (and 9.11) may be judged: cf. ch. 7 below.

the key importance to his conception of history of the inquiry into human motivation. It represents a crucial complement to the record of *erga*. These in-text inquirers may allow readers to sense something of Herodotus' *manner* of inquiring into this sort of question: his own keen and urgent interest, reflected, perhaps, in the way Leonidas 'was keen' (σπουδὴν ἐποιήσατο) to conduct his testing of the Thebans' motives. Plutarch remarks upon Herodotus' evident similar *zest* in this regard, in the context of the Alcmaeonid accusation (τί γὰρ ἐσπούδακας..., 'for why are you so keen...', 862f).

All these layers of the reading of others' motives and purposes in the text—Herodotus reading Nitokris' reading of Darius' motives—encourage *readers* to do it vis-à-vis *Herodotus*, too. For part of its effect (as it was in the case of Nitokris and Leonidas) is the construction of character: it furthers readers' understanding also of Herodotus' own character and purposes, as one who is at times moved by a serious memorializing impulse, duty-bound accurately to record the past;[62] but at times moved by a more personal curiosity, or by the occasional impulse even to *test* his readers—as Leonidas tests the Thebans, or even as Nitokris tests future conquerors of Babylon.

Much as in the parallel the preface draws between 'deeds displayed' in battle and in the writing of history, Herodotus' self-construction in the likeness of figures like Cyrus or Leonidas must potentially enhance his own heroic stature. The spectacle of kings of the *Histories* struggling with multiple *logoi* and variant explanations lends strength to the historian's self-presentation (as Dewald has described it) as being himself engaged in an heroic *agōn* of *logoi*.[63] Again, the interest that such a king as Leonidas—'the perfect embodiment of the Spartan model'[64]—can display in the question of the human thoughts and motivations that lie behind the *erga* suggests that they, too, may be a significant part of the record (and may actually—*pace*

---

[62] As we may sense in Herodotus' occasional statement that he is 'constrained' in some way, e.g. 7.139.1: ἀναγκαίη ἐξέργομαι γνώμην ἀποδέξασθαι ἐπίφθονον ('I am constrained by necessity to give an opinion that will arouse jealousy'). Cf. Munson (2001), 272 on how he is politically free, but morally constrained; Marincola (1997), 175–9 and (2006), 18–19 on how Herodotus, like all ancient authors, is careful in the matter of praise.

[63] Dewald (1987), 147. See Connor (1993), 12 n. 33 on the different metaphors Herodotus applies to his task, including engaging in a battle.

[64] Munson (1993), 44.

Plutarch—*enhance* that record). It hints that there may be a heroic aspect even to this side of Herodotus' project—in which case his character and purposes are not so polarized after all. Part of Herodotus' achievement resides in his poignant depiction of the heroism involved in rising above the limits imposed by the human condition.

However, just as in this positive respect the affinities between kings and Herodotus as investigators do *not* only (*pace* Christ) invite readers 'to compare, and ultimately distinguish between, his approach and theirs',[65] but also hint at possible similarities, so with the more negative. For the Herodotean narrator, too, may perhaps have some vested interest; may at any rate not always be entirely straightforward and reliable in presenting his views (as we suggested in chapter one in connection with his presentation of the rumour that the Alcmaeonids signalled to the Persians after Marathon). He, too, may at times have a more subversive aspect to him. Though most often he presents himself as a Solon-type truth seeker, at times we catch him making use of techniques that would seem to be more in the province of the late fifth-century sophist. This, however, serves ultimately, I suggest, to *strengthen* the authority of the implied author, who in adopting this particular narrator persona—whose opinions may be set against other strands of the text—may be recognized as engaging his readers in processes that will enable them to come closer to understanding the truth. We have seen that Herodotus' text assumes perspicacious readers, and suggested that it even *trains* its readers to become such[66]—and that seems to be the case also on the level of conjecturing motives: for the text furnishes readers with examples of how to do it for themselves. The narrative's staging of successful and failed readings of motives guides readers in moulding their own interpretative methodology, to be used especially on those occasions when no motives are ascribed, or when Herodotus suggests several possible options. But equally, it equips readers on occasion to challenge the Herodotean interpretation.

It serves also to expose the manifold *difficulties* involved in reading motives or intentions, whether those of the gods, such as Apollo's, or of humans, such as Cyrus': Croesus miscalculates in assuming Cyrus will not act so swiftly after the first engagement (1.77). Carolyn

---

[65] Christ (1994), 175.        [66] Ch. 1 n. 96 with text.

Dewald has illuminated ways in which Herodotus does generally expose the challenging nature of his task as historian. Even in the mode of 'critic' his is 'only partially a rhetoric of assurance, authority, and control'; he emphasizes the limitations of his data, his efforts in evaluating it.[67] This seems especially so as regards questions of motives. Not even the historian is envisaged as always capable of reading motivation accurately: Croesus' difficulties in interpreting Cyrus' intentions find a parallel in Herodotus' inability to pinpoint Cyrus' reasons for putting Croesus on the pyre. Much, Herodotus warns his readers—when it comes to motives that are doubly hidden, in people's minds and in the past—must inevitably remain obscure.

The following chapter turns to considering how his narrative exposes the particular challenges involved in reading motivation. We shift at this point back again into the late fifth century, and into the realm of history, in seeking our primary touchstone; for the practice of Herodotus' near contemporary Thucydides may illuminate the distinctiveness of his method in this regard.

---

[67] Dewald (1987), quote at 160 (note however that Dewald (2002), 277 redefines the categories of (1987) as representing interlinked parts of a single authorial register, which she describes as the '*histōr*'); cf. Dewald (2002), 279.

# 4

## Problematized motivation in the Samian and Persian *logoi* (Book III)

### 4.1 THUCYDIDES AND THE LOGIC OF ASCRIBING MOTIVES

Thucydides frequently attributes to his actors motives that stretch far beyond what he might have known from evidence. All historians, moderns included, at times guess at and supply the motives behind actions to make their narratives readable and coherent. But Thucydides goes rather further: many of his motivation statements are remarkable in both their length and detail, and in their strange congruence with the action that ensues, a congruence that literary echoes draw attention to. Many scholars are drawn to the conclusion that Thucydides invented, or rather conjectured, likely motivations, either reasoning backwards from what actually happened,[1] or using 'character evidence': making inferences from his knowledge of the character of the individuals involved as to their likely reasons for

---

[1] Cf. Hunter (1973), 17: Thucydides 2.20 'consists entirely of thoughts in the mind of Archidamos *or what his thoughts would have had to be in order to make this move a purposeful one in view of the results*' (her italics). Hunter overstates the formulation, however; cf. Pelling (1991), discussing this very case. See generally Thompson (1969); Hunter (1973); Schneider (1974). Note that Hans-Peter Stahl's (2003, orig. 1966) important study represents a qualification of the *communis opinio* I here set forth. Thucydides, on Stahl's view, exposes the *fallibility* of human projections, and in this and in other ways is far more closely aligned with Herodotus on my interpretation in this and the following chapters. Connor (1984) and (1985) brings out how Thucydides, especially through his difficult style and use of multiple viewpoints, gives a feeling for the complexity of motives and events. He documents a 'bleak progression' through Thucydides' *Histories* 'from confidence in prediction and rational analysis to a growing awareness of the power of the unexpected and unpredictable' (1984), 246.

action.[2] (The view is sometimes pressed too far: Thucydides will undoubtedly have used oral evidence where it was available, as we are reminded by Simon Hornblower—who points to the likelihood that his northern exile gave him the opportunity to talk to Brasidas, for example.[3]) The technique assumes consistency in human character and response. Hornblower summarizes succinctly:

The generalisations in [Thucydides'] narrative about human nature or the human condition ... imply that although human behaviour changes according to changes in attendant circumstances, the 'nature of men' can be made the basis for predictions. The assumption behind all this is that people are rational and act according to their own interests—a Socratic view—so that outsiders can infer motive from action.[4]

Where humans do not act in accordance with their own interests, error or ignorance can be assumed to be at play.[5]

Doubtless Herodotus, too, used the 'it *must* have been so' ($\tau \grave{o} \ \epsilon \grave{\iota} \kappa \acute{o}s$) criterion[6] in satisfying his audience's desire for explanations, and regularly inferred motives from what he knew of an individual's character,[7] or from what had actually resulted.[8] But he seems to have done so in a far less systematic or detailed fashion than Thucydides. The keynote of his narrative is not the Thucydidean pattern of congruence (in the absence of human ignorance or error) between human intention and resulting action, where the way *logoi* predicting human behaviour are confirmed by *erga* lends the work its 'aura of inevitability',[9] but rather the disjunction between those. The reader is drawn to confront the gaps that open up between motivations (whether explicitly stated by the narrator or alleged by sources, or implied by the narrative) and the ensuing action, and thus to appreciate the unpredictability of actions and their frequent remoteness from intentions. In this process emotion—a far less predictable yardstick than self-interest—proves to

---

[2] Pearson (1947).    [3] Hornblower (1987), 79; cf. Westlake (1989).
[4] Hornblower (1987), 76–7.    [5] Schneider (1974), e.g. 87; Edmunds (1975).
[6] On Herodotus' use of arguments from probability see Lloyd (1975), 162–3; Müller (1981), 307–11; Thomas (2000), 168–90, observing (190 n. 51) that $o \grave{\iota} \kappa \acute{o}s$ (the Ionic form of $\epsilon \grave{\iota} \kappa \acute{o}s$) occurs forty times in the *Histories*.
[7] Cf. Pearson (1941), 351–5.
[8] Hohti (1976) calls attention to the *ex eventu* nature of Herodotean speeches (but overstates the situation, in my view, e.g. at 142).
[9] Hunter (1973), 180.

be a wild card. Strange, paradoxical, or impulsive motivations, ones no one could reasonably predict, at times steal the limelight. Predictions about human behaviour as often as not are shown to have been incorrect, or at least turn out only in an off-key sort of a way.[10] Herodotus' Darius enunciates the (Thucydidean) view that it is consideration of personal advantage, κέρδος, that motivates people in determining whether to lie or tell the truth (3.72.4–5). But Prexaspes' subsequent behaviour reveals the inadequacy of the generalization, for he gains no personal advantage in choosing to leap to his death rather than tell a further lie, after he has revealed that the Magians, not Cambyses' brother, are now ruling Persia (3.75). The attitude expressed by Darius (and demonstrated by the Magians—for they use logic like Darius' in determining to confide in Prexaspes, 3.74) is also in clear opposition to Herodotus' emphasis on Persian aversion to lying. Indeed, the *Histories* more often than not undermines simple generalizations about human character—whether concerning East/West stereotyping,[11] or the characteristics of certain peoples, or anything else. Equally, readers are shown that the character of individuals is unstable and liable to change—affected by the exercise of absolute power,[12] or the ravages of illness,[13] with the same or similar conditions not necessarily resulting in the same or similar behaviour.[14] While absolute rulers may in a general way be expected to be motivated by

---

[10] Pelling (2002) has shown how the predictions/generalizations contained within the debate on constitutions (which in some ways function rather like Thucydides' *logoi*) are realized only in an off-key sort of a way: the opinions on a tyrant's behaviour in the debate are not altogether mirrored by the practical examples of tyranny. But van der Veen (1996) emphasizes *too* absolutely the contrast Herodotus sets forth between theory and practice; see n. 56 below.

[11] Cf. Pelling (1997) and further below.

[12] Cf. Otanes' formulation at 3.80.3–4.

[13] Cf. the narrator's comment (with regard to Cambyses) at 3.33: οὔ νύν τοι ἀεικὲς οὐδὲν ἦν τοῦ σώματος νοῦσον μεγάλην νοσέοντος μηδὲ τὰς φρένας ὑγιαίνειν ('now it is in no way improbable, if the body is seriously ill, that neither should the mind be healthy').

[14] Compare Schneider on Thucydides: 'Die Fähigkeit zur Voraussicht beruht auf dem Wissen, daß der Geist der Menschen abhängig ist von den Bedingungen der äußeren Welt. Wenn dies Prinzip allgemein gilt, dann läßt sich aus ihm auch der Satz begründen, daß *gleiche oder ähnliche Verhältnisse gleiche oder ähnliche Verhaltensweisen zur Folge haben*' (1974), 121 (my italics; 'The ability of foresight is based on the knowledge that the mind of man is dependent upon the conditions of the outside world. If the principle is universally valid, then so too is substantiated the statement that *the same or similar conditions have as a consequence the same or similar patterns of behaviour*').

*hybris* and *phthonos* (the twin motivating factors Otanes associates with tyrants, 3.80), their most pronounced trait is the *unpredictability* of their mental processes and subsequent behaviour.[15] The implication of all this seems to be that Herodotus, unlike Thucydides, did not believe that character evidence or actual deeds were a reliable guide as to motivation. His narrative implies a rather more complex and ambiguous view of the relationship between (expressed) intent and character or action.[16] Thus it exposes the fact of the historian's *limited* access to people's minds:[17] of the challenging nature of his task.

A further contrast with Thucydides may be felt in the *Histories'* characteristic *multiplicity*, including in relation to questions of character and motivation. Thucydides' usual technique in dealing with such questions, as with the wider narrative of events, was to further one strong interpretation: when it came to questions of explanation including motivation, he generally focused all attention on what he considered to be the *single* 'truest' cause.[18] 8.87, where he reflects on several possible motives for Tissaphernes' actions in relation to Aspendos, is unusual;[19] and there is but a single instance of the *eite… eite…* ('either… or…') formulation applied to a question of motives (5.65.3),[20] which Rood suggests is expressively Herodotean.[21] 'Thucydides sometimes… acknowledges mixed motive or causation, and [in such cases] *indicates clearly where in his view the preponderance lies'.*[22] Similar restriction of the range of motives open to the audience's reflection was characteristic also of forensic oratory: such an orator's interest lay in driving home the single interpretation of motives that best suited a particular client.

Herodotus' third book is a fascinating site of ascriptions of motivation that work either to destabilize assumptions of a straightforward

---

[15] See below, §4.3.4 (Cambyses).

[16] See below, esp. §4.2.3 (Maiandrios).

[17] Compare Darbo-Peschanski (1987) on Herodotus' (ostentatious) exposure of his limited access to another form of 'special knowledge', that concerning the gods: '[l]e silence que s'impose l'enquêteur est alors à la fois rigoureux et ostentatoire: il s'agit de le souligner, de le dramatiser' ('the silence imposed upon himself by the enquirer is therefore both rigorous and ostentatious: it must be emphasized, dramatized') (42).

[18] Cf. Thuc. 1.23.6; 6.6.1; and Pelling (1991), 142.

[19] See Lateiner (1976); cf. Connor (1985), esp. 12 n. 9 with text.

[20] There is only one further instance of the formulation (6.60.2).

[21] Rood (1998), 106 with n. 100 and (2004), 119; Hornblower (2004), 300 concurs.

[22] Hornblower (2004), 300, my italics.

connection between genuine intentions and outcome; or to emphasize the dissonance between the rhetorical stance that alleges a particular (lofty) intention and the *Realpolitik* that characterizes actual behaviour. In the case of Maiandrios it will not be altogether clear which we are dealing with. Darius' pronouncement in planning the conspiracy on the disjunction between words and deeds (3.72.2) might prepare readers to notice ways in which the formal *logoi* of the constitution debate, for example, are undermined by the surrounding action: the actions of men may be better judges of their motivations than what they say.[23] Over against the truth/lie polarity that is a pervasive theme of this stretch of the *Histories* (in the Persian storyline, which is intertwined with the Samian)[24] is set a more graduated framework, one that admits degrees of adequacy and truthfulness in statements and explanations given, recognizing a distinction between the misleading and the false. As we shall see, the narrative showcases motivations that are paradoxical, inadequate, misleading, or false: the 'Persian' truth/lie opposition serves as a foil to what is a far more nuanced reality. Careful—at times somewhat forced[25]—chronological connections, along with simple juxtapositions, interrelate the different storylines and so guide the reader to draw comparisons: as Immerwahr recognized, the three Samian stories form a unity in themselves—'one unit in a series of three'—but each is also intricately bound to its context in the Persian narrative.[26]

The third book may well be significant in a programmatic sense because it steers the reader back to the trunk storyline (and associated themes) following the ethnographic excursus on Egypt of the preceding narrative. The opening discussion of Cambyses' reasons for invading Egypt, with its three versions pressing the themes of female involvement, personal grudges, and disproportionate response, mirrors the wider framework of motivation of the Persian campaign against Greece. In similar fashion the opening lines of the third and final of the Samian *logoi*, which usher in the tale of Darius' conquest of Samos, are reminiscent of the opening of the *Histories*: Μετὰ δὲ ταῦτα Σάμον βασιλεὺς Δαρεῖος αἱρέει, πολίων πασέων πρώτην Ἑλληνίδων καὶ βαρβάρων, διὰ

---

[23] See Pelling (2002), 130–1 on ways in which the debate of the conspirators (3.70–3) foreshadows the constitution debate (3.80–2).
[24] For this polarity see Benardete (1969), 69–98; Asheri (1990), xix–xx.
[25] Cf. Pelling (2002), 131.
[26] Immerwahr (1957), 320.

τοιήνδε τινὰ αἰτίην ('After this King Darius captured Samos, the first of all the cities of Greeks and non-Greeks (he captured), through the following cause', 3.139.1). May we expect, then, to find themes played out here that match or illuminate those of the whole?

## 4.2 MOTIVATION IN THE SAMIAN *LOGOI*

Herodotus introduces the first Samian *logos* with the mention of the Spartan war against Samos and its tyrant Polykrates, then delves back in time to tell of Polykrates' rise to power, friendship with Amasis, and the famous ring story that explains Amasis' dissolution of the friendship: 'he did this for the following reason: in order that he should not grieve in his soul as for a friend, if a great and terrible occurrence should seize Polykrates' (3.43.2). Thus directly the reader is confronted with a paradoxical motivation, Solonian in sentiment but neither natural nor plausible on the human level[27] (for Amasis will now grieve at a friend's loss prematurely!). It is a fitting introduction to a narrative that will prove to be laced with instances of problematic motivation.

Readers next hear of Polykrates asking Cambyses to request a Samian contribution of troops for his Egyptian expedition, so that he may rid his island of certain dissidents. A harsh juxtaposition thus surfaces between the fairytale story that led to a broken-off friendship, and the concrete military aid against Egypt—forty triremes—that Polykrates goes out of his way to offer, that would help to ensure Egypt's conquest by Persia.[28] The story of the ring is

---

[27] By contrast, the motivation and related denouement *is* logical on a higher (superhuman) level, since the broader patterns suggest that Polykrates has failed to follow Amasis' advice, either (van der Veen (1996), 6–22) in not throwing away an item of such value to himself as Amasis meant, i.e. his power; or (Kurke (1999), 105) in not respecting distinctions (e.g. of divine/human, good luck/bad luck). Kurke expresses the latter in terms of the individual's psychology—'Amasis comes to realize that Polykrates' fortune is irredeemable, so he imposes the only kind of discrimination possible—between himself and Polykrates' (105)—but it seems to me that it is more a matter of broad patterns.

[28] Of course in the event, they will not arrive. It is perhaps for the sake of this juxtaposition that Herodotus suppresses the likely historical explanation: Polykrates' desire to signal his support of Persia (which will have been at least as important a concern as expelling the dissidents): Tölle-Kastenbein (1976), 25–6.

causal:[29] it is not simply in order to get rid of the dissidents that Polykrates sends to Cambyses, but also because Amasis has renounced the alliance; but Polykrates' response seems nevertheless disproportionate. The Samian dissenters escape, however (and the various versions of this Herodotus offers—including the possibility aired but rejected that the returning exiles actually defeated Polykrates—remind readers that the ensuing account may contain much uncertainty, too). They successfully petition Sparta for help against their tyrant (3.46.2).

### 4.2.1 The Spartan Campaign against Samos (3.39–60)

It is this Spartan campaign, whose synchronicity with Cambyses' Egyptian invasion is underlined from its first mention (at 3.39.1), that binds together the various strands of the first Samian *logos* (3.39–60), providing the lynchpin for digressions that stretch both backwards and forwards in time from that point.[30] The chronological parallelism will prime readers throughout the account to notice points of comparison between the two expeditions, perhaps to wonder whether the Greek attack really had much more justification than Cambyses'—a question brought to the fore at 3.56, when the Spartan campaign is envisaged as a first move eastwards that balances the first move westwards by the Persian reconnoitring expedition that Democedes headed.[31]

---

[29] This was recognized by Immerwahr (1957), 315: Polykrates sends his enemies to join Cambyses' attack on Egypt, 'not only in order to rid himself of the Samian opposition, but also because Amasis was no longer his friend. The second reason is not specifically mentioned by Herodotus, but must, I believe, be understood. If this is correct, the famous ring story becomes a direct motivating factor of the Spartan campaign and the whole logos has chronological, as well as causal, unity'. In similar fashion the Libyan digression on customs, geography, etc. (4.168–99) becomes a direct motivating factor of that expedition.

[30] e.g. backwards in time: mention of the Spartan expedition at 3.39.1 (as occurring 'while Cambyses was attacking Egypt') leads into the narrative of Polykrates' earlier rise to power and his relations with Amasis; the mention at 3.44 leads into the background of Cambyses' raising of an army and Polykrates' opportunistic expulsion of the dissenters. At 3.47 the expedition itself takes place. Forwards in time: 3.55 leads Herodotus forward to his own time, to tell of the grandson of one of those Spartans who fought.

[31] This balance is recognized by Immerwahr (1957), 315.

Herodotus sets down the outcome that flowed from the Spartan decision to help the Samians, and two accounts of the motivation that precipitated that outcome:

καὶ ἔπειτα παρασκευασάμενοι ἐστρατεύοντο Λακεδαιμόνιοι ἐπὶ Σάμον, ὡς μὲν Σάμιοι λέγουσι, εὐεργεσίας ἐκτίνοντες, ὅτι σφι πρότεροι αὐτοὶ νηυσὶ ἐβοήθησαν ἐπὶ Μεσσηνίους, ὡς δὲ Λακεδαιμόνιοι λέγουσι, οὐκ οὕτω τιμωρῆσαι δεομένοισι Σαμίοισι ἐστρατεύοντο ὡς τίσασθαι βουλόμενοι τοῦ κρητῆρος τῆς ἁρπαγῆς, τὸν ἦγον Κροίσῳ, καὶ τοῦ θώρηκος, τὸν αὐτοῖσι Ἄμασις ὁ Αἰγύπτου βασιλεὺς ἔπεμψε δῶρον (3.47.1).

And then, after making preparations, the Lacedaemonians campaigned against Samos. The Samians say that they made the expedition in repayment of a favour, since the Samians had earlier given them aid with ships against the Messenians. But the Lacedaemonians say that they campaigned not so as to help the Samians and at their request, but rather because they wanted to punish them for the theft of the mixing bowl, which the Spartans had been taking to Croesus, and of the breastplate, which Amasis king of Egypt had been sending to them as a gift.

Much here is perplexing. The alternative motivations sit oddly after the self-contained tale that had already recorded the Samian request for help and Spartan decision to oblige. The motivations are left unresolved, and are puzzling: why, Plutarch reasonably asks, would the Spartans deny an honourable and just explanation (τὴν καλλίστην καὶ δικαιοτάτην . . . πρόφασιν) for their campaign, to claim instead that petty vindictiveness (μνησικακίαν καὶ μικρολογίαν) was actually what drove them to it (859d–e)? This is the reverse of Fehling's 'party bias' principle:[32] it is the Samians who provide the Spartans with a respectable motive. How, Plutarch objects again, could Herodotus have the Spartans deny having come to help or free the Samians, despite the fact no other polis was as φιλότιμος (loving of honour) or μισοτύραννος (tyrant-hating) as theirs (859c)? 'What sort of a breastplate or what sort of a mixing bowl was it that made [the Spartans] expel the Cypselids from Corinth and Ambracia, Lygdamis from Naxos, the sons of Peisistratus from Athens . . . ?' (859d). It is certainly ironic that the Spartans, held by tradition to

---

[32] Fehling (1989), 105–8.

have been extremely anti-tyrannical (cf. Thuc. 1.18.1[33]), should propose a quite unrelated explanation for this expedition.[34]

But Plutarch's questions seem very much the sort Herodotus intended to provoke in his readers. It *is* on account of 'remembering past wrongs' that his narrative (especially in the opening chapters of the work as a whole, and of the third book) has shown people commonly act: readers have seen political and military action motivated by personal grudges, indeed even specifically 'by a small word'[35] (cf. Plutarch's διὰ μνησικακίαν καὶ μικρολογίαν, above). Very little has been seen of fine or just *prophaseis* (explanations/ justifications). The account of motivation also seems intended to destabilize the Spartan reputation Plutarch refers to. Plutarch's use of μισοτύραννος brings to mind the passages for which Herodotus apparently coined the term,[36] on another occasion where his narrative destabilizes accepted tradition: the defence of the Alcmaeonids as μισοτύραννοι, 'tyrant-hating', which is in tension with the narrative that follows.[37] The truth about the attitudes to tyranny of either Spartans or Alcmaeonids is not so simple. Further ironies on this same theme will surface in the subsequent account of Corinthian motivation in assisting the attack on Samos—angered that the Samians had prevented their tyrant from executing his barbarous purpose!

Herodotus' refraining from expressing explicitly his own opinion on the question of Spartan motivation and simply setting the two versions side by side has the effect of drawing his audience further into their individual process of (source) evaluation. The sense of perplexity noted above arouses curiosity that engages readers further,

---

[33] Note also Soklees' expression of surprise at Sparta's plan to reinstall tyrants at Athens (5.92*a*).

[34] Cartledge (1982), 256 argues convincingly (*pace* e.g. Tölle-Kastenbein (1976), 26) that the notion of 'revenge' for Samian piracy may be historically correct: the items were intrinsically precious and of high sentimental value, while revenge carried positive moral associations. My suggestion is that Herodotus' presentation problematizes its sufficiency as cause of the Spartan campaign a generation later.

[35] e.g. Cambyses' mother's word provokes Cambyses' later desire (3.3); a Samian citizen's rebuke prompts Maiandrios to retain power (3.142.5–143.1): cf. Benardete (1969), 97. Even accounts that provoke Herodotus' scepticism as to their truth value (e.g. 3.3, the proem) may contribute to this explanatory texture (cf. ch. 3 n. 47 for the proem).

[36] 6.121, 123; cf. Bowen on *Malice* 859c.

[37] See above, §1.4.

as do the hints in the text that one or other of the alleged motivations is to be favoured. The narrative that precedes the record of alternative possible motivations favours the Samian interpretation: the narratorial voice, in first mentioning the Spartans' expedition, noted that they were 'invited' by the Samians (3.44.1); then after the story of the sack, that they resolved to 'give assistance' to the Samians (3.46.2). But the subsequent narrative tilts the balance the other way: Herodotus notes, with no intimation of doubt, that the Corinthians also helped in the expedition ἐπὶ Σάμον ('against Samos'), 'for they too had been treated insolently by the Samians a generation before this expedition, about the time of the robbery of the bowl' (3.48.1).[38] The alleged thefts by the Samians lead Herodotus into an account of the Corinthians' involvement and of the background of that expedition—including the story of the three hundred Corcyrean boys sent by the tyrant to be eunuchs at Alyattes' Lydian court. The Corinthians' *anger* towards the Samians was thus motivated by the Samians' *rescue* of boys about to be castrated by the Corinthian tyrant Periander—which implies their ancestors' support of their tyrant in the planning of that act.

Plutarch again objects:

As for the *polis* of the Corinthians—though in that location it was far from his course—nonetheless embracing the detour, as they say, he added in a terrible accusation and a most wicked slander (πάρεργον ἀνέπλησεν αἰτίας δεινῆς καὶ μοχθηροτάτης διαβολῆς) . . . . And in inflicting this reproach upon the Corinthians he thus represents the *polis* as more wicked than the tyrant (ἀποφαίνει τοῦ τυράννου μοχθηροτέραν τὴν πόλιν, 859e–f);

for, as Herodotus only later reveals, Periander at least had reasonable grounds for revenge in the murder of his son. Part of Herodotus' point, however, seems to be precisely that the tyrant/citizen polarity is a problematic one. It is thus 'the tyrant' who initiates the action: 'Periander the son of Cypselus' sends the boys to Alyattes (much as tyrants of the *Histories* do frequently collaborate with one another, without the knowledge of, or to the detriment of, their people:

---

[38] Cf. Cartledge (1982), 247, adding that 'it cannot automatically be inferred that [Herodotus] also preferred his Spartan informants' version of Spartan motives in 525 . . .'. I suggest that for a reader, authorial agreement on that question of motives might well seem to be implied.

cf. Periander and Thrasybulus, 5.92ζ; Histiaeus and Darius, 4.137 and §6.4.1 below). But next we find 'the Corinthians' charged with the mission going to all lengths to execute it successfully, attempting to drag the boys from their temple refuge, and even to starve them out; and they seem to persevere for some time.[39] Only after telling the whole story does Herodotus register the inadequacy of the justification it provides for the Corinthians' participation in the expedition—a narrative delay that has allowed reflection on the adequacy of the reason professed:

εἰ μέν νυν Περιάνδρου τελευτήσαντος τοῖσι Κορινθίοισι φίλια ἦν πρὸς τοὺς Κερκυραίους, οἱ δὲ οὐκ ἂν συνελάβοντο τοῦ στρατεύματος τοῦ ἐπὶ Σάμον ταύτης εἵνεκεν τῆς αἰτίης (3.49.1).

Now if, upon Periander's death, friendship had existed between the Corinthians and the Corcyreans, the Corinthians would not have assisted in the campaign against Samos for reason of this *aitiē* (cause/charge).

An old quarrel with their colony Corcyra explains the Corinthians' grudge against the Samians for the saving of the boys.

The account of the Corinthians' motivation introduces a digression on the background to Periander's sending the boys for castration: only at this point, two chapters after the deed was described, are we told that it was done 'in vengeance' (3.53.7) for the Corcyreans' terrible crime against him. It therefore represents not so much a tyrant's impulsive, barbaric gift to a fellow autocrat, as readers are likely to have assumed, as behaviour explicable in more acceptable traditional Greek terms. During the course of the tale of Lycophron, which is next recounted, readers' initial condemnation of the tyrant is softened: 'Ne emerge la figura tragica di un padre e di un tiranno che invano cerca una soluzione alla propria crisi dinastica, e arriva a eccessi di crudeltà vendicativa'.[40] Periander's murder of Melissa and Lycophron's fate are glossed as *sumphorai* (accidents) that have befallen him (3.50.1).[41] It is

[39] Cf. ὅσον χρόνον ἱκέτευον οἱ παῖδες... (3.48.3), ἐς τοῦτο δὲ τόδε ἐγίνετο, ἐς ὅ...(3.48.4).
[40] Asheri on 3.48–53 ('From this emerges the tragic figure of a father and tyrant who seeks in vain a solution to his own dynastic crisis, and reaches excesses of vindictive cruelty'); cf. on 3.50.1: '[l]'eroe tragico è evidentemente Periandro'.
[41] Before the tale of Lycophron the wife murder was mentioned in passing, perhaps as necessary background information. Herodotus saves the details until book five, in which the tyrant is far more negatively portrayed (cf. Asheri on 3.45–53). The irony of

Lycophron who appears harsh, inflexible in his attitude towards an ageing and remorseful father,[42] and the Corcyreans' action that appears most disproportionate, when they murder a son for fear of his father inhabiting their island. Periander's capture of Epidauros and imprisonment of its ruler Prokles (his sons' maternal grandfather, who hinted at their mother's fate) 'on the grounds that he was most responsible (ὡς . . . ἐόντα αἰτιώτατον) for his present troubles' (3.52.7) makes clear his deep self-delusion (for he himself killed Prokles' daughter, after all!) and invites reflection on the warped nature of such a view of causality. It is a further instance of the personal justifying the political. But the preceding account has built up a psychological and emotional profile of a man genuinely aggrieved, that allows readers at the same time to understand his reaction in human terms.

The digression may be read as a study in the adequacy and complexity of motivations. Whereas at its outset 'the Corinthians' (3.48.1) desired vengeance following their hubristic treatment by the Samians, at its close Periander alone is mentioned before we return to the main storyline: the expedition against Samos. Concerning this, the views of some readers, at least, have shifted. They have seen the perversity of the claim, being made by contemporary Corinthians, that their ancestors' participation in the Samian war was partly motivated by their tyrant's desire to be avenged on those who prevented him from punishing his son's murderers—especially since the Samians' only involvement was indirect. The juxtaposition of Periander's personal desire for vengeance (3.53.7) with the Spartan's arrival 'with a great host' to besiege Samos (3.54.1) expresses again the contrast between slippery rhetorical justifications and the harsh reality of a military response.

The narrative of this campaign, like that recounting the Corinthians' motivation, destabilizes the notion of a straightforward tyrant/people dichotomy, complicating further the questions surrounding its motivation. The Spartan expedition is initially pictured as one directed against a tyrant (3.39.1: ἐπὶ Σάμον τε καὶ Πολυκράτεα . . ., 'against Samos and Polykrates', 3.44.1) and at the invitation of a group of

such brief coverage becomes apparent when the details of the Corcyreans' crime emerge, since that too was a killing.

[42] Cf. Gray (1996), 371–2, 375–6.

Samians (3.44.2–45.2). In sending to Cambyses 'unknown to the Samians' to contrive the removal of certain citizens (3.44.1), and taking
hostages to be burned if the men desert to the returning exiles
(3.45.4),[43] Polykrates in the following chapters displays conventional
tyrant characteristics. The subsequent references, by contrast, describe
the expedition as 'against Samos' (ἐπὶ Σάμον, 3.47.1, 48.1, 49.1; cf. 54)
*tout court*, and as motivated by the alleged actions of 'the Samians':
their benefits given, or their thefts of bowl and breastplate, or their
hubristic behaviour. Not only Polykrates and the foreign mercenaries,
but also many of the Samians (3.54.2), resist the invaders for a short
time, before fleeing back pursued and slain by the Spartans.

The war of Spartans and dissident Samians against the tyrant
Polykrates thus evolves into an external war, Spartans fighting and
killing Samian citizens. No war of 'liberation', it is now an international
conflict. Plutarch clung to the fact of the Spartan Archias' tomb at
Samos having been erected δημοσίῃ, 'at public expense' (3.55.2; cf.
*Malice* 860c), as an indication that the Spartan war was recognized by
Samians as an act of liberation. But as Herodotus' readers will have
known, such a public funeral could not have taken place without the
tyrant's support. Thus here again the narrative works to collapse the
tyrant/*polis* divide.[44] Herodotus' extremely unusual reference at this
point to a personal meeting with a descendent[45]—Archias' grandson
Archias, who explained his grandfather's reason for honouring the

---

[43] Arkesilaos punished his opponents by sending some away (to be slain) and
burning others (4.164), as Polykrates threatens here.

[44] Asheri on 3.48–53 suggests apropos Plutarch's objection to the notion that
Corinthians might have retained grudges from the era of tyranny that 'le alleanze e le
inimicizie tra città resistono in genere ai mutamenti costituzionali interni delle città
stesse. A parte questo, la campagna del 525 non era diretta contro i «Sami» in generale,
come giustamente osservava anche Plutarco, ma contro Policrate, il cui rovesciamento
era nell'interesse delle potenze marittime rivali' ('alliances and enmities between cities
generally withstand constitutional changes internal to the same cities. Besides this, the
campaign of 525 was not directed against the 'Samians' in general, as Plutarch, too,
rightly observed, but against Polykrates, whose overthrow was in the interest of his
powerful maritime rivals'). But Herodotus' narrative expressly blurs this distinction.
The blurring of tyrant/people and tyrant/*polis* dichotomies was a feature also of the
Archaic period, and precisely the reason tyrants could come to power and remain there
in the first place, as Rosalind Thomas points out to me.

[45] Herodotus mentions only three such personal meetings with individual informants over the course of the *Histories* (cf. 4.76.6; 9.16.1). He inquires in person
with groups of informants at 2.54.2, 91.5, 104.1.

Samians—adds to the sense of shifting perspectives, reminding readers of the many different sources and traditions which must have been at Herodotus' disposal.

The problematics of 'liberation' rhetoric, on the part of Sparta, will resurface in Herodotus' later account of the Spartan desire to reimpose Athenian tyranny once it no longer suits their purposes (5.90–1; the Corinthians, represented by Soklees, will oppose them). As the Corinthians found in their history an insolent action (ὕβρισμα, 3.48.1) of the Samians that could serve as a justification for revenge, so there the Spartans will find an extra justification in the Athenian *dēmos*' hubristic expulsion (περιυβρίσας ἐξέβαλε, 5.91.2) of their king. Past *hybris* comes to seem an easy *prophasis*, and glosses over the moral complexities that come into play when tyranny is concerned.

The injustice of the Spartan campaign against Samos is highlighted by the way in which the narrative has gradually brought to the fore the Greekness of the island, which will culminate at 3.60.1 with Herodotus' statement that he has dwelt upon the Samians 'because they built the three greatest works achieved by any Greeks' (ὅτι σφι τρία ἐστὶ μέγιστα ἀπάντων Ἑλλήνων ἐξεργασμένα). No mention here of Polykrates: the '(oriental) tyrant' dimension of earlier has been suppressed in all its aspects, for whereas the account of Samos began with his seizing power and sharing it with his two brothers, subsequently executing one and banishing the other,[46] and maintaining eastern royal and satrapal connections (3.39.2), it concludes with reference to the Samians alone, as exemplary Greeks.

At the same time, the Samian exiles, in the stretch of narrative that follows the failure of the expedition to which they had invited the Spartans, are painted in increasingly negative light, their intentions shown to be far from honourable. They demand money of the Siphnians, and at their refusal ravage their lands, confront them in battle, and exact a hundred talents (3.58). They next seize Hydrea from its citizens, gifting it to the men of Troezen (3.59.1; such shifting of populations will later be seen to be characteristic of the

---

[46] Killing without trial is typically tyrannical (cf. Otanes at 3.80.5). For such execution specifically of a brother, cf. Cambyses' of Smerdis (3.30.1, 65.3) and Xerxes' of Masistes (9.113.2). Polykrates seems also to demonstrate the tyrant trait of 'failure to distinguish', in robbing 'all alike' (ἔφερε δὲ καὶ ἦγε πάντας διακρίνων οὐδένα, 3.39.4): see below, n. 64 with text.

tyrant Darius); and then go to Crete to drive the Zakynthians out—
only *ending up* settling there, though that had not been their intent:
αὐτοὶ δὲ Κυδωνίην τὴν ἐν Κρήτῃ ἔκτισαν οὐκ ἐπὶ τοῦτο πλέοντες, ἀλλὰ
Ζακυνθίους ἐξελῶντες ἐκ τῆς νήσου ('these men founded Kydonia in
Crete, though not sailing with this intention, but in order to drive
the Zakynthians out of the island', 3.59.1). Herodotus thus ascribes
to the Samians an ignoble motivation, denying outright the more
reasonable explanation that he might have conjectured *ex eventu* (i.e.
conjecturing from the fact that they settled on Crete that that had
been their intention in visiting). The effect is to shed light upon the
exiles' earlier actions (in fomenting the Spartan expedition), to
prompt reflection again on the justice of that campaign: were these
aggressors motivated any differently then? No mention is made of
divine sanction for the Cretan colony; the fact that five years down
the track they are defeated and enslaved hints rather at the possibility
of divine displeasure. Thus the wandering viewpoint (to use Iser's
expression) has indeed shifted radically from the first appearance of
these Samians. Conversely, Polykrates—whose return to centre stage
is heralded by the *logos* recounting his murder—will come to be seen
increasingly more positively, in contrast with the despicable Oroites.

## 4.2.2  Oroites' murder of Polykrates (3.120–6)

In the second Samian *logos* (3.120–6) a close tie is again maintained
with the Persian plotline, this time through the synchronicity of
Cambyses' illness and death with the expectation then realization of
Polykrates' (3.120.1; 3.125.4–126.1). The narrative has left hanging
the anticipated deaths of both rulers.[47]

The *logos* opens with a statement of Oroites' desire, followed by the
explanations suggested by two groups:

οὗτος ἐπεθύμησε πρήγματος οὐκ ὁσίου· οὔτε γάρ τι παθὼν οὔτε ἀκούσας
μάταιον ἔπος πρὸς Πολυκράτεος τοῦ Σαμίου οὐδὲ ἰδὼν πρότερον ἐπεθύμεε
λαβὼν αὐτὸν ἀπολέσαι, ὡς μὲν οἱ πλεῦνες λέγουσι, διὰ τοιήνδε τινὰ αἰτίην....
οἱ δὲ ἐλάσσονες λέγουσι... (3.120.1–121.1).

47  Immerwahr (1957), 317.

Oroites conceived a desire to do an impious deed. Not having suffered anything nor heard an insulting word from Polykrates of Samos, nor even having seen him before, he desired to catch him and kill him, as the majority say, through such a cause as this: . . . But the minority say . . .

Oroites' desire is strange and unreasonable, for he has had nothing to do with Polykrates before this.[48] Its unexpected and precipitate character seems comparable to Candaules' impulse to show Gyges his wife naked (1.8: might the mention of a Gyges at 3.122.1 point to this connection?). According to 'the most part', Mitrobates the satrap of Daskyleion, and Oroites, satrap of Sardis, had fallen to arguing and comparing their achievements. Mitrobates taunted Oroites for lacking *aretē*, since he had failed to conquer Samos for the King, although the island lay close to his province and a native (Polykrates) had gained control of it with such ease.

οἱ μὲν δή μίν φασι τοῦτο ἀκούσαντα καὶ ἀλγήσαντα τῷ ὀνείδεϊ ἐπιθυμῆσαι οὐκ οὕτω τὸν εἴπαντα ταῦτα τείσασθαι ὡς Πολυκράτεα πάντως ἀπολέσαι, δι' ὄντινα κακῶς ἤκουσε (3.120.4).

Some say that after hearing this and being stung by the reproach, Oroites conceived a desire not to punish the person who said it, but rather to destroy Polykrates for causing him to be insulted.

The strange *misdirection* of Oroites' vengeance is thus underlined (misdirection reminiscent of the way in which Candaules' wife's first thought upon seeing Gyges in her chamber was that her *husband* was to blame: she was correct, though that reaction was surely not the most natural).[49] No one could have reasoned *ex eventu*, from the action taken, that it was Mitrobates who precipitated the original offence.

The version of 'the few', who recount Polykrates' failure to respond to Oroites' herald, underlines this time the fact of the satrap's *overreaction* to a situation that could easily be interpreted innocently in the symposium context sketched. For, of the alternative explanations for Polykrates' remaining turned to the wall when the herald entered and

---

[48] By contrast, in the cosmic scheme the sequence of events is logical, if Oroites may be viewed as the gods' instrument in punishing Polykrates (cf. Darbo-Peschanski (1987), 66), just as Darius would serve as a means for the supernatural to punish Oroites: 'Ορότεα τὸν Πέρσην Πολυκράτεος τοῦ Σαμίου τίσιες μετῆλθον ('the powers that avenged Polykrates of Samos overtook Oroites the Persian', 3.128.5).

[49] Cf. Amestris' anger at 9.110, misdirected against the chaste Masistes' wife rather than her less chaste daughter Artaÿnte.

addressed him as he lay in the dining room in the company of Anacreon of Teos (εἴτε ἐκ προνοίης αὐτὸν κατηλογέοντα τὰ 'Οροίτεω πρήγματα, εἴτε καὶ συντυχίη τις τοιαύτη ἐπεγένετο, 'whether deliberately he made small account of Oroites' affairs, or whether some chance occurrence happened', 3.121.2), the second points to a range of possibilities, most obviously that he was simply drunk or asleep. The pair of double unresolved motivations suggest that an instant assumption of *pronoia* (intention), as Oroites presumably made, was precipitate (even if it matches Herodotus' own practice of assuming the worst).

Readers are left to choose which of these explanations they prefer: 'These are the two reasons given for Polykrates' death, and one may be persuaded by whichever one prefers' (αἰτίαι μὲν δὴ αὗται διφάσιαι λέγονται τοῦ θανάτου τοῦ Πολυκράτεος γενέσθαι, πάρεστι δὲ πείθεσθαι ὁκοτέρῃ τις βούλεται αὐτέων, 3.122.1). Either way, it is a personal snub that motivates the satrap, and his reaction is disproportionate—as is emphasized by the subsequent account of the lengths to which Oroites goes in planning Polykrates' death and the killing itself in some way 'not fit to be told'. No one could have guessed from the vengeance taken its trivial cause.[50] Fehling (1989) lists the passage among those in which Herodotus can be seen '[a]dducing several versions', in a subgroup of the cases where 'a variant on a single point is adduced for no discernible reason' (108): the detail of whether it was his knee or his thigh that Militiades injured (6.134.2), for example,

is almost certainly intended to provide additional confirmation. Such slight variation is tantamount to the agreement of two separate sources and at the same time serves to demonstrate the author's painstaking accuracy (108–9).

But in this case the double unresolved motivations suggest rather the difficulty of conjecturing the motives of one whose psychology is abnormal.

The framing of the double unresolved cause of Polykrates' behaviour within the account of Oroites' double unresolved motivation emphasizes further the great uncertainties involved in reconstructing mental processes. It is far from evident that the version of 'the many'

---

[50] Cf. Kurke (1999), 113: 'Herodotus is at pains to suggest the obscurity of motive and the preponderance of randomness'.

represents a Samian source patriotic and sympathetic to the tyrant, and one that Herodotus prefers, 'the few' another Samian source, hostile to Polykrates.[51] The first story seems too closely tied in thematic terms to the narrative that follows, pre-playing Atossa's bedroom advice to Darius (3.134) that to prove a man he should be adding to his dominions,[52] or Charilaos' double-pronged chiding of Maiandrios for not daring to avenge himself even though the Persians would be easy ($\epsilon \dot{v} \pi \epsilon \tau \acute{\epsilon} a \varsigma$) to master (3.145.2).[53] At 3.126.2 Mitrobates, another victim of Oroites, appears as 'Mitrobates . . . who reproached him in regard to Polykrates' affairs ($\delta \varsigma$ οἱ ὠνείδισε τὰ ἐς Πολυκράτεα ἔχοντα)'—which seems to take as definitive the version of 'the many'. Such planting of post-hints that favour one of the motivations earlier offered is familiar. Here the brief mention might seem simply a pleasing transitional and integrative device—until one recalls that the phraseology only shows that Mitrobates had heard what was said (not that he necessarily considered it true and was moved to action by it).

In the account of the murder itself, misleading explanations of motivation are the theme. Oroites exploits Polykrates' twin desires for wealth and conquest so as to seduce him with an offer of financial support. His allegation that Cambyses is plotting his death, and that he himself will therefore profit in being removed together with the money, presents a plausible explanation for his behaviour: the appearance of acting from self-interest keeps Polykrates off the scent of the real nature of the deception taking place. Thus the self-interest factor works in the service of *misleading* motivations, as it will again in Atossa's bedroom speech to Darius: her claim of being motivated by a personal desire for Greek handmaids hides the fact that she is

---

[51] Cf. Asheri on 3.120.5–6, 121.1. Mitchell (1975) argues for the presence throughout Herodotus' Samian stories of Samian aristocratic, anti-Persian bias, which suppresses Polykrates' connections with Persia.

[52] Stein on 3.120.12 notes the parallel.

[53] Cf. Mitrobates' words to Oroites: Σὺ γὰρ **ἐν ἀνδρῶν λόγῳ**, ὃς βασιλέϊ νῆσον Σάμον πρὸς τῷ σῷ νομῷ προσκειμένην **οὐ προσεκτήσαο**, ὧδε δή τι ἐοῦσαν **εὐπετέα** χειρωθῆναι, τὴν τῶν τις ἐπιχωρίων πεντεκαίδεκα ὁπλίτῃσι ἐπαναστὰς ἔσχε καὶ νῦν αὐτῆς τυραννεύει ('For how are you to be **accounted a man**, you who **have not acquired in addition** the island Samos for the King, though it lies close to your province and is so **easy** to conquer that a local rose and took it with the help of fifteen hoplites and now holds it, ruling as tyrant', 3.120.3).

actually speaking as she does because of her debt to Democedes, and speaking in his interest rather than her own.[54] The fact that motivations deriving from self-interest strike their in-text audiences as plausible indicates that conjecturing motivation in that way is a reasonable method: but Herodotus seems more interested in the cases that challenge such a straightforward equation.

### 4.2.3 The Persian Campaign against Samos (3.139–49)

The third of the Samian *logoi* (3.139–49) opens with the statement of Darius' conquest of Samos, and then reverts to tell its story, which begins with Syloson. He is the link, this time, between Persian and Samian stories, being Polykrates' banished brother who came to Egypt along with other Greeks at the time of Cambyses' invasion. He also represents a connection between the old regime and the new, for at the earlier period he granted one of the royal guards, Darius, a favour, and now approaches the new king to ask a favour in return.[55] Declining Darius' offer of an abundance of gold and silver, he asks instead for support in winning back Samos (3.140.5). The king sends an army with Otanes to command it, under instructions to perform all Syloson's will. The motif of a favour demanded whose giving ushers in terrible consequences will reappear in the *Histories*, but already here, in the very specificity of the terms Syloson lays down ('without bloodshed or enslavement', 3.140.5) and of Darius' instruction to Otanes ('to do all that Syloson requested': ὅσων ἐδεήθη ὁ Συλοσῶν, ταῦτά οἱ ποιέειν ἐπιτελέα, 3.141), may be felt an ominous indication that all may not turn out as expected. In historical terms, the story of the cloak is unnecessary to explain why Syloson should be the Persians' choice for governor of Samos, being brother of the former ruler. But as well as planting seeds of significant themes, the story provides another serious juxtaposition of a fable-like, personal

---

[54] Compare, in the narrative that follows upon the final Samian *logos*, the ease with which the Babylonians are persuaded by Zopyros' claim that having been wronged by the King he desires revenge for himself (3.155–7).

[55] Van der Veen (1996), 56–66 discusses the occurrence of the unexpected in this story, bringing out the contrast between the insignificance of Syloson's gift of his cloak, and its major consequences.

cause and the harsh reality of military invasion it precipitates, encouraging reflection once again upon the dissonance between explanation and outcome—a central theme in the subsequent narrative. The focus now turns to Samos, ruled by Maiandrios, Polykrates' former secretary (3.123.1) now become deputy. Directly Herodotus calls attention to the integrity of his intentions: 'though he desired to be the most just of men, he did not succeed' (τῷ δικαιοτάτῳ ἀνδρῶν βουλομένῳ γενέσθαι οὐκ ἐξεγένετο, 3.142.1). At Polykrates' death, Maiandrios sets up an altar to Zeus the Liberator and assembles the townsfolk to make a proclamation. After first observing that it is in his power to continue to rule, he declares:

ἐγὼ δὲ τὰ τῷ πέλας ἐπιπλήσσω, αὐτὸς κατὰ δύναμιν οὐ ποιήσω· οὔτε γάρ μοι Πολυκράτης ἤρεσκε δεσπόζων ἀνδρῶν ὁμοίων ἑωυτῷ οὔτε ἄλλος ὅστις τοιαῦτα ποιέει. Πολυκράτης μέν νυν ἐξέπλησε μοῖραν τὴν ἑωυτοῦ, ἐγὼ δὲ ἐς μέσον τὴν ἀρχὴν τιθεὶς ἰσονομίην ὑμῖν προαγορεύω (3.142.3).

I, however, as far as it is in my power, will not do that which I criticize in another. For neither did it please me that Polykrates ruled over men who were his equals, nor would it please me if anyone else should do this. So, Polykrates has fulfilled his fate, whereas I set the rule into the hands of all [literally, 'into the middle'] and proclaim *isonomiē* ('equality before the law') for you.

Claiming for himself and his descendants certain privileges (six talents of Polykrates' wealth, the priesthood of Zeus the Liberator), he concludes: 'I bestow freedom on you' (3.142.4). The narrator underlines the fact of the promise made: 'And he indeed promised these things to the Samians' (3.142.5).

At this point one of the town's reputable citizens challenges the authority of such a lowly man to rule, and suggests he should rather account for his expenditures. Maiandrios instantly performs a volte-face, resolving to cling on to the tyranny after all rather than let it fall to another.[56] Thus the *men-de* contrast his speech drew between

---

[56] In my view the narrative does *not* imply that it was in good faith, 'per salvare la patria dalla tirannide di un altro' (Asheri on 3.139–49; cf. van der Veen (1996), 60), that Maiandrios decided after all to become tyrant himself. Nor is it evident that Telesarchos' arrogance transforms Maiandrios 'from well-meaning democrat to vindictive oligarch', Kurke (1999), 126. Rather, the nature of his initial frame of mind and intentions remains largely inscrutable (as I suggest further below). It is not clear, *pace* van der Veen (1996), 58–61, that the 'theory' was genuine, just undermined in practice: van der Veen's analysis downplays the complications entailed by the rhetorical dimension of Maiandrios' initial statement.

Polykrates and himself—Polykrates' deserved fate for having ruled as an autocrat, and his own aspirations democratically to share the power[57]—is immediately undermined. Whereas in the first Samian *logos* the Polykrates-Samians divide was progressively collapsed, here the reverse is the case, with Maiandrios pictured increasingly as a tyrant standing in opposition to his subjects. He next employs a deception reminiscent of Polykrates' of the Samian dissenters, in withdrawing and summoning the dissidents individually, as if intending to account for money spent but actually in order to imprison them. When he falls ill (a hint of divine disapproval?), his brother Lykaretos, hoping to increase his chances of seizing power in the case of Maiandrios' death, has the prisoners killed.

The narrator rounds off the tale with what appears to be irony: the Samian people 'did not, it seems (ὡς οἴκασι), want to be free' (3.143.2)—thus opening up various possible strands of questioning. Were the Samians themselves to be held somehow responsible for this outcome, in not being *ready* for freedom?—in being unprepared to risk the absolute commitment that freedom requires? That notion goes against the grain of the account thus far, with its focus on the prominent individuals and their responsibility.

None resist when the Persians bring Syloson back to Samos (in an indication, perhaps, that the Samians in general welcomed the brother of Polykrates?). Otanes accepts Maiandrios' offer to depart from the island under a treaty (3.144). It is ratified with libations. But the next two chapters document its treacherous and impious contravention by Maiandrios, who displays utter disregard for anyone's security other than his own, and indeed knowingly brings harm upon the citizens of Samos. The genuineness of his initial gesture towards freedom is brought progressively further into question. First, in a travesty of the wise-adviser scenario, he allows himself to be persuaded by his 'half-mad' (ὑπομαργότερος, 3.145.1: as of Cambyses at 3.29.1) brother Charilaos to hand over to him his mercenaries (ἐπίκουροι) so that he may punish the Persians while Maiandrios escapes safely away. (The presence of such *epikouroi* underscores his

---

[57] The combination of setting the rule *es meson* with the proclamation of *isonomiē* has democratic overtones, cf. e.g. Vlastos (1953); Ostwald (1969), 107–9. Steiner (1994), 174 describes Maiandrios' action as 'impeccably democratic'.

increasingly tyrannical aspect, for they are a typical tyrant attribute, and Polykrates had them too.[58] Maiandrios accepted Charilaos' advice, Herodotus conjectures (ὡς μὲν ἐγὼ δοκέω), in a lengthy passage of interior monologue,

οὐκ ἐς τοῦτο ἀφροσύνης ἀπικόμενος ὡς δόξαι τὴν ἑωυτοῦ δύναμιν περιέσεσθαι τῆς βασιλέος, ἀλλὰ φθονήσας μᾶλλον Συλοσῶντι εἰ ἀπονητὶ ἔμελλε ἀπολάμψεσθαι ἀκέραιον τὴν πόλιν. ἐρεθίσας ὦν τοὺς Πέρσας ἤθελε ὡς ἀσθενέστατα ποιῆσαι τὰ Σάμια πρήγματα καὶ οὕτω παραδιδόναι, εὖ ἐξεπιστάμενος ὡς παθόντες οἱ Πέρσαι κακῶς προσεμπικρανέεσθαι ἔμελλον τοῖσι Σαμίοισι, εἰδώς τε ἑωυτῷ ἀσφαλέα ἔκδυσιν ἐοῦσαν ἐκ τῆς νήσου τότε ἐπεὰν αὐτὸς βούληται· ἐπεποίητο γάρ οἱ κρυπτὴ διῶρυξ ἐκ τῆς ἀκροπόλιος φέρουσα ἐπὶ θάλασσαν (3.146.1–2).

not because he was so stupid as to think that his force would be superior to that of the King, but rather being jealous at the prospect of Syloson effortlessly recovering the city unharmed. So, he desired to anger the Persians in order to make Samos as weak as possible before handing it over, for he knew very well that if the Persians were badly treated they would be bitterly angry with the Samians. And he knew that for him there was a safe way off the island should he ever need it; for he had built a secret tunnel leading from the acropolis to the sea.

Thus Herodotus denies Maiandrios any possibly high-minded (if deluded) motivation in acting as he does, rejecting the possibility that he might have believed himself strong enough to vanquish the King (and thus have acted from a desire that the Samians not be subject to Persia). Rather, the initially self-proclaiming democrat is envisaged as spurred on by the *phthonos* of a tyrant (or possibly that of an oligarch[59]): by selfish, personal motivations. Where Croesus took thought for his subjects and contrived that the captured Sardis not suffer harm, and Syloson demanded of Darius assurances to this

---

[58] Xenophon, *Hiero* 6.10–11, 10.3–4 on the tyrant's hired guards; Polykrates' *epikouroi* at 3.45.3.

[59] Cf. Kurke (1999), 126: here 'Maiandrios, still perhaps trying to be the most just of men, suddenly snaps into oligarchic spite (φθονήσας): in the competition of the *dokimoi*, he would rather see the city devastated than safely in the hands of another'. I prefer to regard the tyrant aspect as primary in view of the Polykrates-role Maiandrios has adopted, the tyrant/people opposition that pervades these chapters (and that at least in Athens was the dominant ideological polarity in Herodotus' day: Raaflaub (2003)), and the comparison between Maiandrios and king Cleomenes that 3.148 will invite (see below).

end concerning Samos, Maiandrios—once his own safe passage is assured—considers how most effectively to bring Persian wrath upon the Samians so as to weaken the city before handing it over. The madness of Charilaos ensures that Maiandrios bears full responsibility for what ensues.[60]

Thus Maiandrios sets sail from Samos, while Charilaos' guards attack the Persians unawares, killing many even of the highest rank— for all are secure in the belief that a full agreement has been reached. At seeing what the Persians have suffered, Otanes puts from his mind Darius' instructions and commands his army to kill indiscriminately. On this occasion, the expectations of a Herodotean character have indeed prefigured exactly the outcome, as is reinforced (in Thucydidean fashion) through linguistic parallels[61]—but this serves only to underline again, on the broader scheme, the *dissonance* between Maiandrios' earlier professed motivations and this result. Such precise anticipation of the Persian reaction underscores his cynicism and callousness, qualities quite removed from those implied by his earlier act.[62] Likewise his impiety here presents a harsh contrast with his first appearance making a generous dedication in the Heraion (3.123.1). Otanes' behaviour, too, is ironic on the part of the one who has argued for democracy (3.80), for now it is he who 'deliberately forgot' ($\mu\epsilon\mu\nu\eta\mu\acute{\epsilon}\nu os$ $\dot{\epsilon}\pi\epsilon\lambda\alpha\nu\theta\acute{\alpha}\nu\epsilon\tau o$)[63] the *monarch's* instructions to neither kill nor enslave Samians but return the island safe, and chooses instead to command his army 'to kill anyone they found, man and child alike' ($\pi\acute{\alpha}\nu\tau\alpha$ $\tau\grave{o}\nu$ $\mathring{a}\nu$ $\lambda\acute{\alpha}\beta\omega\sigma\iota$, $\kappa\alpha\grave{\iota}$ $\mathring{a}\nu\delta\rho\alpha$ $\kappa\alpha\grave{\iota}$ $\pi\alpha\hat{\iota}\delta\alpha$, $\dot{o}\mu o\acute{\iota}\omega s$ $\kappa\tau\epsilon\acute{\iota}\nu\epsilon\iota\nu$, 3.147.1). Herodotus' addition of $\mu\epsilon\mu\nu\eta\mu\acute{\epsilon}\nu os$ ('deliberately/mindfully') presses the more negative reading of Otanes' behaviour: rather than forgetting in his fury Darius' orders (an easily conjectured explanation), Otanes makes a deliberate decision to flout them. Might $\dot{o}\mu o\acute{\iota}\omega s$ (alike/undistinguishing) ($\kappa\tau\epsilon\acute{\iota}\nu\epsilon\iota\nu$) here be

[60] Contra Asheri on 3.146.2, for whom Maiandrios is only 'corresponsabile del massacro' ('jointly responsible for the massacre').
[61] 'Ο$\tau\acute{\alpha}\nu\eta s$... $i\delta\grave{\omega}\nu$ **$\pi\acute{\alpha}\theta os$ $\mu\acute{\epsilon}\gamma\alpha$ $\Pi\acute{\epsilon}\rho\sigma\alpha s$ $\pi\epsilon\pi o\nu\theta\acute{o}\tau\alpha s$** (3.147.1) commanded the slaughter; Maiandrios $\epsilon\mathring{v}$ $\dot{\epsilon}\xi\epsilon\pi\iota\sigma\tau\acute{\alpha}\mu\epsilon\nu os$ $\dot{\omega}s$ **$\pi\alpha\theta\acute{o}\nu\tau\epsilon s$ οἱ $\Pi\acute{\epsilon}\rho\sigma\alpha\iota$** $\kappa\alpha\kappa\grave{\omega}s$ $\pi\rho o\sigma\epsilon\mu\pi\iota\kappa\rho\alpha$-$\nu\acute{\epsilon}\epsilon\sigma\theta\alpha\iota$ $\acute{\epsilon}\mu\epsilon\lambda\lambda o\nu$... (3.146.2).
[62] Cf. Asheri on 3.142.2: 'Per Erodoto la rinuncia alla tirannide è un atto rarissimo di «giustizia» esemplare' ('Renouncing tyranny is for Herodotus a most rare act of exemplary justice').
[63] Cf. van der Veen (1996), 59.

reminiscent of his own earlier characterization of tyrants as those who put to death the ἀκρίτους ('untried', 3.80.5)?[64] Some of the Persians next besiege the acropolis; others 'killed anyone (πάντα) in the way, inside the temple precinct and outside of it alike (ὁμοίως ἔν τε ἱρῷ καὶ ἔξω ἱροῦ)' (3.147.2). The repetition of πάντα (cf. above, 3.147.1) underscores the indiscriminate nature of the killing, which has stretched beyond the brutal to the impious.

Next, juxtaposed with the scene of the terrible fate of the Samians, is a sketch of Maiandrios' arrival safe at Sparta along with all his treasures—in a contrast that crystallizes the tyrant/ citizen divide— and his attempt to bribe the Spartan king. But in the face of Maiandrios' several offers of expensive cups Cleomenes 'proved most just (δικαιότατος) of men, for he did not think it right (οὐκ ἐδικαίου) to take the gifts' (3.148.2), and instead has him expelled. The justice of Cleomenes' decision perhaps hints at a contrast with the earlier collective decision of the Spartans to assist the Samian exiles, looking forward to Herodotus' witty, memorable remark about how much easier it is to deceive many people than an individual (5.97.2: another occasion when Cleomenes makes a correct decision, in choosing not to offer military support to the Ionian rebels). With this description of Cleomenes as *dikaiotatos*, strong in refusing to be motivated by bribes, readers are brought full circle. Was this same Maiandrios really deserving of the epithet *dikaiotatos* at 3.142?[65] Or was that authorial verdict intended to be ironic? Maiandrios may only have been *trying* to act justly at 3.142, but the rapidity with which he abandoned his attempt leaves the impression that he could at least have tried harder.

---

[64] LSJ: ἄκριτος, ον: I. *undistinguishable, confused*; II.1. *undecided, doubtful*; II.2. *unjudged, untried, without trial* (Hdt. 3.80); cf. Waterfield, de Sélincourt/Marincola; but Godley prefers 'high and low alike'. Kurke's interpretation finds even greater irony: Otanes 'horribly reinstates Maiandrios's vision of all the Samians as *homoioi*— in death (1999), 126.

[65] Asheri's suggestion (on 3.142.2–3) that the ironic phrase perhaps reveals a serious judgement on Maiandrios, as an 'eroe tragico, pieno di ottime intenzioni, ma travolto dalla realtà politica' ('tragic hero, full of excellent intentions but over- come by the political reality'), overlooks the fact that Maiandrios has also been shown to be carried away throughout by his own selfish concerns. Asheri ad loc.; van der Veen (1995), 139–40; and Kurke (1999), 127 observe this echo.

The reader has certainly been prompted to change perspective over the course of the narrative, with the expectations engendered by Maiandrios' initial description left entirely unfulfilled. Did Herodotus choose to open his story of Maiandrios in that way so as to shock readers, through the subsequent contrast, into reflecting more actively on the man's initial intentions: to reflect upon whether they might have been genuine, but then tested by the stress of circumstance, or discarded once he himself had been corrupted by absolute power (as Otanes had envisaged)? (Polykrates made no such illusory show of lofty motivations: he openly—with the result that Oroites heard of it—'aimed at mastery of the sea ($\theta a\lambda a\sigma\sigma\sigma\kappa\rho a\tau\acute{\epsilon}\epsilon\iota\nu$ $\acute{\epsilon}\pi\epsilon\nu o\acute{\eta}\theta\eta$)...and had great hopes ($\acute{\epsilon}\lambda\pi\acute{\iota}\delta a s$ $\pi o\lambda\lambda\grave{a}s$ $\acute{\epsilon}\chi\omega\nu$) of ruling Ionia and the islands', 3.122.2.) An explanation in terms of Maiandrios' realization of the impossibility of laying down tyranny safely (in consequence of the people's proverbial hatred of it)[66] seems less plausible, since he has scarcely touched the rule at this point. Alternatively, is Herodotus inviting readers to challenge that authorial opinion? Was Maiandrios' behaviour really cynically self-serving all along? Perhaps he hoped that his lofty professions might secure his bid for power, rather as Deioces contrived through just and virtuous posturing to have tyranny thrust upon him (1.96–8). Perhaps he guessed that the Samians would anyway reject his humble authority and prefer that of one—a brother, say!—who could better match Polykrates' splendour (which Herodotus will emphasize on the occasion of Polykrates' death, 3.125.2).

The conclusion to the final Samian story is the scene of the island being swept clear of men and delivered to Syloson. Otanes, we hear, will later be moved by a dream to repopulate it, having suffered a sickness of the genitals. That may seem to indicate that the gods hold him responsible for the emptying of the island—the very man who desired to wait for *greater* numbers before deliberating on the question of Persian succession,[67] and went on to assert in his speech that $\acute{\epsilon}\nu\ldots\tau\hat{\omega}$ $\pi o\lambda\lambda\hat{\omega}$ $\acute{\epsilon}\nu\iota$ $\tau\grave{a}$ $\pi\acute{a}\nu\tau a$ ('everything is in the many', 3.80.6).[68]

---

[66] Cf. Raaflaub (1987), 226.

[67] I agree with Asheri on 3.71.12 that this can be read as an early hint of Otanes' democratic tendencies, though Pelling (2002), 130 n. 24 is sceptical.

[68] Wood (1972), 85 observes this irony. See Pelling (2002), 134 n. 29 on the various translations of this.

Such an outcome might cast a shadow over readers' attitudes to his earlier intentions in arguing for *isonomiē* in the Constitution debate—even if already at that point, his sentiments (like those of the other conspirators) were rather self-focused;[69] but again, readers might wonder whether it was a matter of the collapse of good intentions under the pressure of circumstance. The narrative points to a comparison between Otanes and Maiandrios—Persian and Greek—in several respects.

## 4.3 MOTIVATION IN THE PERSIAN *LOGOI*

### 4.3.1 The limits of *nomos*

Virginia Hunter observes that in Thucydides,

Past *erga*, what happened, can serve as a model for the future. What mediates in the present is the *logos* or διδαχή, in human terms, the man who has learned from experience and so can make predictions about the future.[70]

Herodotus, by contrast, shows how difficult it is to work from generalizations to predictions. Events rarely happen as people predict; human character is not always stable; people's intentions do not always match their actions, or else change as the situation develops— as we have found in the Samian *logoi*. The frequently suspected or exposed dissonance between expressed intent and reality lends further complication. A major Herodotean rule is that you cannot assume developments: the programmatic principle cited at 1.5.3, often assumed to express the inevitability of rise followed by fall—

τὰ … τὸ πάλαι μεγάλα [ἄστεα] ἦν, τὰ πολλὰ σμικρὰ αὐτῶν γέγονε, τὰ δὲ ἐπ᾽ ἐμεῦ ἦν μεγάλα, πρότερον ἦν σμικρά. τὴν ἀνθρωπηίην ὦν ἐπιστάμενος

---

[69] Pelling (2002), 139–40.
[70] Hunter (1973), 55; cf. Thuc. 1.22.4: his work aspires to be judged useful by those who βουλήσονται τῶν τε γενομένων τὸ σαφὲς σκοπεῖν καὶ τῶν μελλόντων ποτὲ αὖθις κατὰ τὸ ἀνθρώπινον τοιούτων καὶ παραπλησίων ἔσεσθαι ('will want to have a clear picture of events that have happened and of events that are going to happen again at some time in the future, in the same way or similarly, in accordance with *to anthrōpinon* (the human condition)'). Stahl (2003) challenges this reading of Thucydides: see n. 1 above.

108	*Problematized motivation*

εὐδαιμονίην οὐδαμὰ ἐν τὠυτῷ μένουσαν ἐπιμνήσομαι ἀμφοτέρων ὁμοίως (1.5.4)

Of cities that were great, the majority have become small, and those that in my time were great had once been small. Knowing, then, that human prosperity never remains in the same place, I will mention both kinds equally

—seems intended (like Solon's observation that πᾶν ἐστι ἄνθρωπος συμφορή, 'everything human is a matter of chance', 1.32.4) rather to warn *against* predictions of any sort of stability in human affairs, than to promise accurate forecasts that disaster is impending. The principle also deals in probabilities rather than certainties: not all but 'many' states once great are now small. Again, it implies nothing as to the specifications (for example of extent, or timescale) of outcome: Gyges' transgressive rise to power will indeed be paid for, as readers expect, but not until five generations down the track.[71] Herodotus seems to have regarded the correlation between human motivation and resulting behaviour as similarly uncertain. His treatment of motivation implies that an action or outcome is not inevitably proportionate to, or even related to, the intention that inspired it; nor can an individual's motivation be reliably determined from wider patterns of behaviour (whether those of the same individual, or of others), even if frequently the historian has little choice but to do so.

The Persian *logoi* test the difficulty of conjecturing an individual's motivation from the general principles that underpin the behaviour of his group. A major theme of this stretch of the *Histories* is the role of *nomos* in determining human attitudes and behaviour. Darius' comparison of Persian and Indian funerary customs illustrates Pindar's notion that '*nomos* is king of all' (3.38). Cambyses is pronounced mad because his actions contravene the customs of his own community; his failure to respect other communities' *nomoi* shows that to be all the more the case. And yet it is not only in the account of Cambyses that we encounter tension between the dictates of *nomos* and the reality of an individual's idiosyncrasy.

---

[71] This principle of rise and fall thus gives no indication of timescale that might allow a 'warning' any sort of immediacy for current perpetrators of wrong, e.g. one aimed at Athenian imperialists regarding the fall of their empire: Herodotus' readers may well have found allusions at the close of the *Histories* to the great Athenian empire of their day, but to read the ending as a specific warning that it is soon to dissolve, e.g. Moles (1996), robs his text of some of its most studied indeterminacy.

Even greater difficulty surrounds the attempt to apply general principles of motivation / outcome across different groups. Later in the *Histories* Greeks and Persians respectively set forth opposing theories—one assuming autocratic rule, the other *isonomiē*—to explain (or predict) the same behaviour on the battlefield (7.103–4). The Greeks fail to act as the Persians expect: the criterion of numerical strength, upon which Xerxes bases his prediction that the Greeks will flee without offering battle, is overridden by less tangible factors such as personal courage and freedom. And yet at the same time we see that Xerxes' prediction was rational, and could easily have come true.[72]

Human behaviour that is inexplicable or contrary to others' expectations (whether disproportionate or paradoxical) is a *thōma* of sorts, interesting per se and belonging to Herodotus' favourite subject matter (*thōmasta*, wondrous things[73]), but it also presents a serious challenge to the historian and his audience who seek to comprehend the motivation behind it. Cambyses' psychological experiment on the captured Psammenitos suggests how very strange human responses may seem, and how easily the motivation that underlies them may be misinterpreted. Cambyses is astonished that the king fails to cry out in response to his children's fate (as do the Egyptian nobles to theirs), but does so upon recognizing a past companion reduced to beggary, thereby seeming to honour the old man above his own children. Further inquiries uncover Psammenitos' explanation: his private grief was too great for tears, but he could weep for the misfortune of his friend, 'who, on the threshold of old age, has lost his wealth and good fortune and has been reduced to beggary' (3.14.10). (Conversely, showy displays of grief, like the noble Persians' at Cambyses' deathbed address, may be artificial, 3.66.1.) Christ (1994) notes that '[t]he extraordinary means [Herodotean kings] possess and the power they exert over others ... allow them to conduct inquiries that the historian could not hope to carry out' (168). The falsity of Cambyses' initial assumptions about Psammenitos' motives might serve as a reminder that Herodotus will not always have had the means to test so vigorously his own initial conjectures about people's motives. The difficulty of reading kingly motives will be staged most vividly at 8.97, where 'all the others',

---

[72] See ch. 8 below.    [73] Cf. ch. 3 n. 9 above.

110     *Problematized motivation*

πάντες οἱ ἄλλοι (Greeks and Persians understood, cf. 8.97.1) are deceived by Xerxes' show of military preparation; Mardonios alone—'as he was more acquainted than anyone with his mind' (μάλιστα ἔμπειρον... τῆς ἐκείνου διανοίης)—is not deceived.

Unexpected or paradoxical-seeming behaviour prompted by inscrutable motivations is not confined to royalty. Intaphrenes' wife's choice (3.119) appears astonishing, until, at Darius' command, she provides an explanation for her reasoning. (Again, such a demand is within the power of a ruler to make; it might be less within that of a historian.) Nor is it the mark exclusively of the non-Greek 'other'. Particularly from Cambyses' time onwards Greeks begin appearing in the Persian *logoi*, who provide a point of comparison for Herodotus' audience that as often as not serves to destabilize easy assumptions of Persian otherness.

### 4.3.2 Cambyses' Egyptian campaign (3.1–15)

The opening chapters of book three describe the nexus of personal, trivial causes, arising from different parties' selfish grievances, that allegedly induced Cambyses to invade Egypt. The juxtaposition of personal causes with a serious military effort aimed at conquest underlines the disproportionate nature of the response. The emphasis on causation (δι' αἰτίην τοιήνδε, 3.1.1) recalls the opening chapters of the *Histories*, where Herodotus delineated the mythological tales explaining Graeco-barbarian conflict from the real-world causes that a historian should try to identify (he will indicate 'the man I myself know (τὸν δὲ οἶδα αὐτὸς) was the first to begin committing unjust acts against the Greeks', 1.5.3). Here we find no such explicit indication as Herodotus moves smoothly from the fourth fairy-tale-like (and in his view least believable) explanation—the tale of Cambyses' boyhood promise to turn Egypt upside down for his mother—on to a more realistic and contemporary plane, and one that implicates Greeks, with the introduction of Phanes:

Another incident also occurred (συνήνεικε δὲ καὶ ἄλλο τι τοιόνδε πρῆγμα) that tended towards this expedition. For among Amasis' *epikouroi* (mercenaries) was a man Halicarnassian by race, whose name was Phanes... (3.4.1)

We nonetheless remain in the realm of personal grievances, for it is some private grudge against Amasis (μεμφόμενός κού τι Ἀμάσι, 3.4.2) that motivates Phanes to flee to Cambyses and reveal to him the Egyptian situation and a plan for crossing the desert. By the time Cambyses reaches Egypt, however, Psammenitos has replaced Amasis on the throne. Cambyses' persistence with a campaign that has until now been directed at Amasis himself, whose death might have been expected to dispel Cambyses' rage, calls into doubt the status of the earlier recounted grievances.[74] Were they merely convenient *prophaseis* (justifications) for a campaign which had after all been contemplated much earlier by Cambyses' Median predecessor on the throne, Cyaxares (1.105)? The expansionist narrative patterning, too, suggests that Persian expansionism may be inevitable.

The grim postscript to Phanes' story indicates that Greeks no less than royal Persians are capable of disproportionate or incongruous responses:

> The Egyptian king's *epikouroi*, who were men both Greek and Carian, blamed Phanes because he had led a foreign army against Egypt (μεμφόμενοι τῷ Φάνῃ ὅτι στρατὸν ἤγαγε ἐπ᾽ Αἴγυπτον ἀλλόθροον) and so contrived against him the following incident (πρῆγμα) (3.11.1).

Standing a large mixing bowl between the two armies, they—within Phanes' sight—cut the throats of his sons over it, add wine and water, and all drink from it. The foreignness of Egypt vis-à-vis Greece as already described in the Egyptian *logos* (the Egyptians' customs entirely contrary to those of the Greeks, their climate and river peculiar, and so on: 3.35–7) hints at a degree of hypocrisy on the part of these Greeks, who are themselves serving in a foreign land.[75] The form their vengeance takes displays barbarism that Herodotus' Greek audience might have associated with Persia.[76] The choice of punishment for Phanes is even crueller, however, than the one chosen by Cambyses which follows

---

[74] As always, my discussion concerns the account as presented by Herodotus, rather than the historical event. Herodotus' portrait of Cambyses in Egypt is different in various respects from the historical Cambyses as reconstructed by means of Egyptian epigraphy. See e.g. Asheri on 3.1–38.

[75] Godley's translation of both instances here of the term *epikouroi* as 'foreign soldiery' captures nicely the hypocrisy that this group should be angry at another's leading a 'foreign' or 'stranger' army into Egypt.

[76] See How/Wells ad loc. on the barbarism of human sacrifice in the eyes of fifth-century Greeks. Herodotus does not condemn this deed explicitly, whereas the cannibalism at 3.25.6 will be described as a δεινὸν ἔργον ('terrible deed').

on its tail (at 3.14), for he parades children before their fathers but conducts the executions elsewhere. Cambyses does subsequently murder Prexaspes' son before his eyes, but in anger ($\dot{o}\rho\gamma\hat{\eta}$, 3.35.1) and out of madness: the Greeks' behaviour is no *crime de passion* (punishment is not exacted until several months after the crime), and they, unlike Cambyses, are not clinically mad. Moreover, although we are never told the nature of Phanes' grievance, the parallel (his 'blaming' Amasis as the Greeks 'blame' him) raises for the attentive reader the possibility that it may have had as much substance as the Greeks'. In any case, the Helen story (2.112–20) has already called into question Greek moral superiority: Paris' 'impious deed' ($\dot{a}\nu\acute{o}\sigma\iota o\nu$ $\ddot{\epsilon}\rho\gamma o\nu$) in abducting the wife of his host was trumped by Menelaus' 'unholy affair' ($\pi\rho\hat{\eta}\gamma\mu a$ $o\dot{v}\kappa$ $\ddot{o}\sigma\iota o\nu$, 2.119.2) in the barbaric killing of two children of local Egyptian men—even after his hospitable reception in Egypt, which included the return of his wife and possessions!

Greeks (and Carians) serving on the Egyptian side will be implicated in a further barbaric act that follows the Persian victory, for some must be imagined to have been driven into Memphis along with the Egyptians, and thus part of the general sally ('streaming out of the city walls all at once ($\dot{a}\lambda\acute{\epsilon}\epsilon s$)', 3.13.2) responsible for the massacre of the Mytilenean crew aboard the herald ship sent by Cambyses. The Persian response, for its part, is equally excessive: two thousand Egyptian boys killed, 'to pay the penalty for the Mytileneans who had been destroyed in Memphis together with their ship' (3.14.5)—the royal judges having determined that each man's death be paid for by the life of ten noble Egyptians. The equation is not proportionate but arbitrary and exponential (as again Darius' will be in impaling 3000 Babylonians, at 3.159.1).

### 4.3.3 The Ethiopian campaign and the lie (3.17–25)

Cambyses captures Memphis and mutilates Amasis' corpse at Sais, apparently venting his anger of old, and then 'he planned three campaigns, against the Carthaginians, the Ammonians, and the long-lived Ethiopians' (3.17.1). Taking advice ($\beta o\upsilon\lambda\epsilon\upsilon o\mu\acute{\epsilon}\nu\omega$), he resolves to mount traditional campaigns against the Carthaginians and Ammonians, but to send spies in the first place ($\pi\rho\hat{\omega}\tau o\nu$) against the Ethiopians,

ὀψομένους τε τὴν ἐν τούτοισι τοῖσι Αἰθίοψι λεγομένην εἶναι ἡλίου τράπεζαν εἰ
ἔστι ἀληθέως, καὶ πρὸς ταύτῃ τὰ ἄλλα κατοψομένους, δῶρα δὲ τῷ λόγῳ
φέροντας τῷ βασιλέϊ αὐτῶν (3.17.2).

to see whether the Table of the Sun, said to be amongst these Ethiopians,
truly existed, and in addition to this, to spy out all the rest (τὰ ἄλλα
κατοψομένους), under the pretext of bearing gifts to their king.

Thus Cambyses' intent with respect to Ethiopia differs only in form,
not object, from the other campaigns: the implication of πρῶτον is
that a military campaign is to follow in due course. The concern for
the truthfulness of the Table of the Sun is aired only after the campaign
has been decided upon, apparently in consequence of advice received:
might it be felt to represent useful rhetoric rather than the king's
genuine interest? Cambyses' interest in the *truth* status of the table is
juxtaposed uneasily (within the same sentence) with his own deceptive
behaviour in conducting his researches 'under the pretext' (τῷ λόγῳ)
of offering gifts to the Ethiopian king. Would such cover be necessary
if he were moved solely by interest in the table? Rather, together with
καὶ πρὸς ταύτῃ τὰ ἄλλα κατοψομένους imperialistic interests are
implied.[77] The motif of spies being sent to reconnoitre as an overture
to conquest is one we find again in the pages of the *Histories*. The
Ethiopian king recognizes at once the reality of the situation: Cambyses does not value his friendship, nor is he *dikaios* (in desiring to
enslave another country), and the messengers have come as spies. He
indicates also the inherently deceptive (δολεροὺς) nature of the Persian
gifts. Commentators note the irony that Cambyses, with his (Zoroas-
trian) abhorrence of the Lie, is here caught out himself,[78] but how
easily can his 'lotta contro la menzogna' seem genuine to readers,
directly in the wake of its employment (at 3.17, above) as a useful
rhetorical stance that furnished a *prophasis* for spying out Ethiopia?

But the reader's thoughts as regards Cambyses' motives are next
tilted in the opposite direction. When the spies return to Cambyses
with tales of the rejuvenating pond, the Table of the Sun, alabaster
coffins that display bodies in the likeness of the living, and so on,

---

[77] See Christ (1994) on the way in which ethnographic interests are often a
precursor to conquest; cf. Harrison (2003), 148.
[78] e.g. Asheri on 3.21.9-10: 'Cambise, sempre in lotta contro la menzogna, qui è
accusato di frode' ('Cambyses, always fighting falsehood, is here accused of deceit').
For the Persian abhorrence of lying, see Herodotus 1.138; for Cambyses', 3.1.

Cambyses was enraged and immediately set out to attack the Ethiopians (αὐτίκα ... ὀργὴν ποιησάμενος ἐστρατεύετο ἐπὶ τοὺς Αἰθίοπας), although he had not ordered any preparation of supplies, nor considered (οὔτε λόγον ἑωυτῷ δούς) that he was about to march to the far ends of the earth. But inasmuch as he was mad and not sound of mind (οἷα δὲ ἐμμανής τε ἐὼν καὶ οὐ φρενήρης), as soon as he heard from the Fish Eaters, he set out.... (3.25.1–2).

This strange, precipitate (αὐτίκα) anger (rather like Oroites' toward Polykrates)—apparently provoked by the Ethiopian King's derogatory comments about the Persians and Cambyses' intentions, or by the deceptive nature of the coffins (or the table)[79] (and in that case blatantly hypocritical, since Cambyses' whole expedition has occurred under the cover of a false explanation)—seems genuine. For were it merely a *prophasis* for conquest, systematic attention would be expected to have been paid to planning that conquest. Thus an odd contradiction arises between the fact that Cambyses intended the campaign right from the start and was readying for it in a rational manner (taking advice, sending spies, and so on), and his total unpreparedness at this point for that very campaign,[80] which is now embarked upon at breakneck speed and as a consequence of mental instability. Here we find the first explicit note of Cambyses' madness. His mental processes were still quite rational at 3.19.3, when his reasoning on two levels, moral and practical respectively,[81] impelled him to refrain from attacking the Carthaginians without Phoenician compliance: 'he did not think it right (οὐκ ἐδικαίου) to use force against the Phoenicians, since they had surrendered to the Persians of their own accord, and the whole fleet was dependent on them'. Herodotus thus guides the reader's judgement to wander from one extreme to the other: from a standpoint that regards Cambyses'

[79] Readers might recall Cambyses' great anger at Amasis' deceiving him by sending him Nitetis in the place of his own daughter, which according to the Persian story incited him to invade Egypt (3.1). Cf. Benardete (1969), 71: 'it was the way Amasis lied that enraged him. It was not a spoken but a silent lie.... Telling the truth and the truth must coalesce among the Persians.'

[80] Cf. Asheri on 3.25.3–4: 'la notizia contraddice non solo il resoconto dettagliato dell'esplorazione e dello spionaggio (capp. 20–4), ma anche quello sui preparativi dello stesso Cambise per l'attraversamento del deserto' ('the information contradicts not only the detailed account of the reconnaissance and espionage (chs. 20–4) but also that of the preparations of Cambyses himself for crossing the desert').

[81] Cf. Asheri ad loc.

truth/lie discourse as convenient rhetoric employed by one proceeding rationally, to one that views him as genuinely enraged (and
moved to action) by the falsity he detects, explaining the intemper-
ance of his reaction as stemming from insanity.

This second strain now persists. Before the army has completed
even a fifth of its journey to Ethiopia, provisions are at an end and
the troops have consumed the transport animals and begun eating
grass, but still Cambyses perseveres: 'taking no account (οὐδένα λόγον
ποιεύμενος), he went ever farther (αἰεὶ ἐς τὸ πρόσω)' (3.25.5: in
intentional contrast with the more reflective nature of Herodotus'
own progress through his *Histories* ἐς τὸ πρόσω τοῦ λόγου, 'to the
farthest point of the account', 1.5.3?). Only after his men resort to
cannibalism does Cambyses withdraw, having lost a good portion of
his army. His parallel expedition against the Ammonians, though it
too had been planned well in advance (3.17), is an even greater
disaster (3.26). The mysterious disappearance of the entire division,
according to one account buried in sand by a violent wind, hints at
divine displeasure provoked presumably by Cambyses' sacrilegious
command to burn the oracle of Zeus (3.25.3). Thus Cambyses is
shown to be gradually losing his wits, in a process that will be
delineated more explicitly as the account continues (and he is described as 'half-mad', then 'mad', and so on), perhaps as he is
corrupted by power along the lines Otanes will set out at 3.80.

### 4.3.4 Madness v. Persian kingly custom
### (3.15–16, 27–30, 65–66)

At the close of the account of the capture of Memphis, Herodotus
reasoned that Cambyses would have made Psammenitos governor of
Egypt, rather than executing him as actually happened, if only he had
refrained from fomenting trouble,

since the Persians are accustomed to honour the sons of kings (ἐπεὶ τιμᾶν
ἐώθασι Πέρσαι τῶν βασιλέων τοὺς παῖδας). For even if they revolt against
them, nonetheless they give the rule back to their sons. One may judge by
many instances that they hold it as a custom so to do (ὅτι τοῦτο οὕτω
νενομίκασι ποιέειν) ... (3.15.2–3).

116     *Problematized motivation*

Following that statement came the description of Cambyses' treatment of Amasis (3.16), which strikingly displayed his utter disregard for Persian practice.[82] Herodotus detailed Persian and Egyptian *nomoi* concerning the dead so as to emphasize that in ordering that Amasis' corpse be burnt, οὐδετέροισι νομιζόμενα ἐνετέλλετο ποιέειν ὁ Καμβύσης ('Cambyses commanded that what was customary to neither of the two peoples be done', 3.16.4). Here began the series of anecdotes that proved Cambyses' madness, parading his deliberate perversion of *nomoi* at every turn, and concluding with Herodotus' judgement that unless Cambyses had been mad he would never have so derided religion and customs (3.38.1). It is at this point that Herodotus includes his most striking articulation of his own respect for *nomoi*, in the story of Darius' experiment comparing funeral customs of Greeks and Indians—each of whom is horrified at the other people's burning or eating, respectively, of their dead. Herodotus tells the story to prove the strength of belief in one's own *nomoi*, and makes use of Pindar's authority in concluding emphatically that '*nomos* is king' (3.38.4).[83] The clash between Cambyses' behaviour and this affirmation of respect for *nomoi* is thus powerfully depicted. The juxtaposition at 3.15–16—of the general rule that enables Herodotus to contextualize Cambyses' treatment of Psammenitos within a wider pattern of Persian kingly behaviour, with the implication (supported by lengthy demonstration) that such rules do not in the least influence Cambyses' behaviour—is conspicuous.[84]

Herodotus thus exposes the difficulties faced by the historian seeking to understand motivation, in reconciling general with particular: in

[82] '*Nomos*' and its derivatives recur: νομίζουσι, οὐδαμῶς ἐν νόμῳ οὐδετέροισι, νενόμισται, οὐκ ... νόμος οὐδαμῶς, οὐδετέροισι νομιζόμενα (3.16.2–4).

[83] Recent discussion underlines the importance of *nomos* to Herodotus' thought and regards him as engaging with the contemporary sophistic debate on *nomos/physis*—most clearly in this passage (on which see esp. Thomas (2000) and (2006); Rood (2006), 298–300).

[84] The juxtaposition is lent emphasis through the syntactical reflection of 3.15.3: πολλοῖσι μέν νυν καὶ ἄλλοισι ἔστι σταθμώσασθαι ὅτι τοῦτο οὕτω νενομίκασι ποιέειν, ἐν δὲ καὶ τῷ τε ... (demonstrating Persian custom) in 3.38.2: ὡς δὲ οὕτω νενομίκασι τὰ περὶ τοὺς νόμους οἱ πάντες ἄνθρωποι, πολλοῖσί τε καὶ ἄλλοισι τεκμηρίοισι πάρεστι σταθμώσασθαι, ἐν δὲ δὴ καὶ τῷδε (demonstrating human custom, and so proving the extent of Cambyses' madness in contravening it). Nor is Darius altogether respectful of custom, however: his play with others' *nomoi* demonstrates a failure to appreciate that *nomos* is in fact *king*: Christ (1994), 188–9.

merging opposed strategies, one concerned with the practice of the wider group, the other with individuals in all their idiosyncrasy. While the behaviour of individuals at times, for example, mirrors that of their state,[85] such reflection is not inevitable. Obvious tension emerges also between 'Persian' and 'royal' practice, for, as has become apparent, to be kingly is by definition to be unpredictable.[86]

Cambyses' behaviour cannot be predicted, or in retrospect comprehended, by the dictates of Persian custom; and moreover his actions are not straightforwardly or inevitably—*predictably*—contrary to such *nomoi*. Nor can underlying rules be found in his own earlier conduct to aid in the comprehension of his action and motivation, for that is above all inconsistent. He is at times motivated by impulsive emotion, at times by illogical reasoning, and at times acts for no reason at all (as well as occasionally being motivated in a more ordinary way)—all of which underlines the difficulty of conjecturing *ex eventu*, from his actions, their cause. His dealings with the Apis bull are a case in point. The purely coincidental relation of his own arrival at Memphis with the Egyptians' celebrating the revelation of Apis is in Cambyses' mind transformed into a causal one: seeing the Egyptians celebrating, 'he firmly believed (πάγχυ ... καταδόξας) that they were rejoicing in this way because he had failed' (3.27.2). Thus his paranoid, self-focused psychology leads to misinterpretation of his *opsis* and a warped ascription of motive for the Egyptians' behaviour, giving their religious act a personal explanation. Cambyses summons the governors of Memphis to explain, and they reiterate the authorial explanation—which he rejects. The narrative thus points to the way in which kingly inquiry is apt to be infected by a paranoid or narcissistic state of mind (assuming a personal role for the king in the causal chain), and quick to reject divergent explanations. Not only, it seems, is an absolute ruler διαβολὰς ... ἄριστος ἐνδέκεσθαι, 'best—at accepting slanders' (as in Otanes' formulation at 3.80.4); he is quick to interpret any situation in an analogous way, even in the face of clarification to the contrary.

---

[85] Huber (1965a), 169–72.

[86] Cf. Otanes' description of an absolute ruler as ἀναρμοστότατον δὲ πάντων ('most erratic of all men', 3.80.5). 'Persian' practice seems also to be envisaged as rather unstable and difficult to define, since 'the Persians adopt foreign customs (ξεινικὰ ... νόμαια ... προσίενται) most of all men' (1.135).

Herodotus underscores with ὡς the subjective nature of Cambyses' opinion of the governors' account: 'upon hearing this Cambyses accused them of lying, and he punished them with death on those grounds (ὡς ψευδομένους)' (3.27.3). His response seems excessive, and the accusation of lying is employed all too readily. Readers might reflect that the removal of these governors of Memphis was also convenient—especially in view of the fact that the priests, whose opinion Cambyses next asks, give the same account but are flogged rather than executed. The priests' punishment, he tells them, is not for lying, but for ridiculing him (3.29.2).

The self-absorbed and arbitrary nature of Cambyses' reasoning is again brought to the fore in his interpretation of his dream about 'Smerdis' (3.30), which causes Cambyses—'fearing for himself, lest his brother should kill him and rule' (3.30.3)—to have his brother Smerdis killed. But when later on his deathbed Cambyses recapitulates the dream and his response, he says that his fear in the wake of the dream was that his brother would seize his sovereignty (3.65.3): a fear for his power not his life; and he admits that he acted 'with more haste than wisdom' (ταχύτερα ἢ σοφώτερα). In his enlightened state he sheds the paranoia that drove his earlier logic.[87] A degree of self-justification perhaps already accompanied the earlier delusion, however, since prior to the killing Cambyses had sent Smerdis from Egypt out of jealousy (φθόνῳ, 3.30.1): present close at hand in the narrative, the same emotion may well be felt to have played a contributory role in inciting Cambyses to murder. Thus the narrative sets forth various possible interpretations of Cambyses' motives, and stages the difficulty involved in reading them—including, in Cambyses' case, in reading his own.

The subsequent narrative presents further instances of problematic motivation on Cambyses' part, from the illogical reasoning that moves him to murder Prexaspes' son (3.34–5)[88] and to put to death the servants that have pleased him by saving Croesus' life (3.36.6), to his failure to act on any reason at all in having twelve of the noblest Persians executed, ἐπ' οὐδεμιῇ αἰτίῃ ἀξιοχρέῳ ('on no adequate charge', 3.35.5: he thus contravenes the Persian *nomos* that Herodotus

---

[87] Cf. Immerwahr (1957), 316: 'now, having regained his senses, he treats the murder as a ruler's excessive and futile precaution.'

[88] Cf. below, 271.

praised, 1.137.1). By the moment of his enlightenment, Cambyses' in-text audience of Persian nobles can only interpret his final speech (3.65) against the background of his past behaviour, and thus they remain suspicious of his intentions, even as Herodotus' readers are this time aware that he is telling the truth. (The Themistocles situation will be the converse, for there the Athenians are persuaded but readers are brought to question Themistocles' intent;[89] here readers know that the nobles' assumption of sinister motivation is unfounded, even if it does fit with Cambyses' earlier character.) Only the accumulation of further evidence dispels their disbelief.

A broader argument could be developed from this point, as to how far, and simply *how*, Persian tyrants come to fit both a general pattern of human behaviour, representing an extreme example of how life works for anyone, as well as a more specific pattern of Persian kingly *nomoi*. The Solonian echoes that punctuate the account of Cambyses present the possibility that although he in some respects represents a special case, the model of irrational motivation and behaviour he exemplifies may to some extent apply to human beings in general.[90] The absence of firm knowledge that characterizes the human condition perhaps entails that truly rational conduct is unattainable. At the best, one may work from probabilities in resolving upon a particular course of action; and one is liable even then to miss the mark in doing so.[91] Reading the mind and motives that underlie human behaviour therefore presents chal-lenges. What emerges is a rather less straightforward and predictable picture than Harrison envisages in maintaining that most actions in the *Histories* 'would appear to be performed as a result of the automatic, almost robotic, fulfilment of human customs or *nomoi*'.[92] Herodotus

---

[89] 8.109–10 with ch. 9 below.

[90] Braund (1998), 173 argues in parallel vein that Herodotus presents Cambyses' madness as an extreme form of the dysfunction that frequently characterizes cross-cultural interaction. Ubsdell (1983), 15–16 considers tyrants in the *Histories* in their capacity of ordinary humanity writ large.

[91] Cf. Croesus in his interpretation of the dream about his son, and subsequent action, which ironically hastens the course of fate.

[92] Harrison (2003), 144–5. See rather Huber (1965a), 184–6, observing the im-portance of *nomos* to Herodotus' depiction of political motivation, while at the same time emphasizing that it 'konstituiert keine Notwendigkeit und berechtigt nicht, Geschichte als einen zwangsläufigen Prozeß zu sehen' ('constitutes no necessity and does not entitle one to view history as an inevitable process', 186).

seems more interested in exploring the extent to which *nomoi* do *not* determine human behaviour; he considers, for example, how, even where custom is strong, humans may have a determining role, choosing to transgress them.

Again, the narrative as it progresses into Darius' reign invites readers to consider the degree to which Cambyses is really so singular among Persian monarchs. It turns to underlining areas of continuity and similarity. Darius' responses come to seem as excessive and precipitate as those of his predecessor, Cambyses' paranoid psychology and harsh ($\chi\alpha\lambda\epsilon\pi\delta\varsigma$) and contemptuous ($\delta\lambda\delta\gamma\omega\rho\rho\varsigma$) nature (3.89.3) less idiosyncratic. Darius' dealings with Democedes, for example, will seem rather sinister and manipulative, like Cambyses' with the Ethiopian King: whether or not the king really is making trial of him in his seemingly generous offer of gifts for the doctor's Crotoniate family, which Herodotus relates directly after Darius' stern order to his men not to let him escape 'but at all costs to bring him back' (3.135.1), Democedes fears as much (3.135.3).

The broader patterns too sound a familiar note. Darius will soon be sending 'spies' into Greece, as Cambyses did into Ethiopia. The profit-driven reality, when it comes to motives, remains cloaked in, or accompanied by, elevated rhetoric: Darius succumbs to Atossa's appeal to tradition (the Persian *nomos* of expansion[93]) in combination with directly self-serving factors. Personal, frivolous interests continue to usher in devastating military action: Syloson's request triggers the conquest of Samos, Atossa's ( *via* Democedes' equally self-regarding request), the conquest of Greece. The narrative portrays individuals with an eye to personal gain seeking the aid of the King, who himself also has a vested interest. The Persian King exploits as *prophaseis* for conquest the invitations of such individuals,[94] who frequently (as expelled outsiders) have little authority to extend an invitation. Gillos, for example, will ask to be restored to Taras in return for restoring Darius' men (3.138), as did Syloson to Samos in

---

[93] Atossa speaks not of '*nomos*' but of what is οἰκός, 'fitting' (from her Persian perspective) for a young man to do; Persian tradition, or *nomos*, may be understood from the way her sentiments parallel those uttered elsewhere, especially 7.8α.1–2 (where Xerxes formulates the idea explicitly into a *nomos*: cf. §8.1.1 below).

[94] Immerwahr (1956), 269–72; Huber (1965a), 93. Austin (1990) documents the historical phenomenon of individual Greeks approaching Persian rulers, especially from Darius' time onwards.

return for the gift of a cloak. Gillos' care in ensuring that a στόλος μέγας ('great expedition') *not* be sent on his behalf, so that wider Hellas not be disrupted, serves as a foil to what is the more selfish norm, and displays his (extraordinary) awareness of the way in which even small beginnings may (be exploited by others in such a way that they) usher in far greater consequences. Readers may well ask whether Darius' efforts at conquest are any more justified than those of the mad Cambyses, or whether they stem from equally inadequate *prophaseis*.

But readers must reflect also upon the fact that similar patterns have emerged on the Greek side. The Spartans' campaign against Samos allowed the Corinthians to get their own back for an old (and irrelevant) grudge. Exactly as Darius sent an army against Samos at the ousted Syloson's request, so the Spartans did upon hearing the Samian exiles' request. Herodotus' narrative destabilizes any complacent or easy assumptions of rock-solid justification on either side. The leitmotiv of the third book seems to be not so much 'il conflitto, metafisico e morale, tra menzogna e verità',[95] as the deconstruction of that polarity through the revelation of its inadequacy. Equally important, since interpretation so often depends on one's point of view, is the fact of persuasion, a point underscored by Darius' claim that those who lie hope 'to gain profit **through persuading** by means of their lies' (τοῖσι ψεύδεσι **πείσαντες** κερδήσεσθαι', 3.72.4). A lie is of use only if it persuades—for that is when it enters the world of action—and is only discovered if it does not. Herodotus' Persian and Samian *logoi* illuminate the complex and nuanced character of human motivation, in its sometime murky relationship with ensuing action.

Explicating such complexities surrounding human character and action demands nuanced and sophisticated narrative techniques on the historian's part. Next we turn to considering more closely one important and pervasive category of such techniques, involving the staging of alternatives—a category whose double character strangely mirrors that of Herodotus' own narrator persona (as we saw in chapter three), and proves highly effective in its capacity to engage readers.

---

[95] Asheri (1990), xix ('the metaphysical and moral conflict between falsehood and truth').

# 5

## For better, for worse . . . : motivation in the Athenian *logoi* (Books I, V, and VI)

### 5.1 ALTERNATIVE CONSTRUCTIONS OF MOTIVES

We noted earlier how Plutarch's response illuminates the at times *adversarial* nature of Herodotus' general presentation.[1] Likewise, in framing his discussion of Herodotus' ascription of motives in terms of better or worse alternative readings—thus assuming the presence of *two* possible interpretations, one positive, the other negative[2]—Plutarch alights upon Herodotus' tendency in this particular area to employ a polarizing technique of presentation.[3] While (a version of) Plutarch's particular positive versus negative, praise-and-blame formulation can at times seem appropriate in discussing the *Histories'*

---

[1] §1.2.4.

[2] 855 f–856a (e.g. ὁ πρὸς τὸ χεῖρον εἰκάζων . . ., 'whoever guesses the worst . . . '); cf. his more general remark: τῶν δ᾽ ἀδήλων [δίκαιός ἐστι] τὰ βελτίονα δοκεῖν ἀληθῶς λέγεσθαι μᾶλλον ἢ τὰ χείρονα ('in cases of doubt, it is right that the better account be declared true, rather than the worse'), 855e.

[3] The general tendency to see things in terms of opposites seems particularly Greek: see Lloyd (1966). It is prevalent in the *Histories* (cf. Cartledge and Greenwood (2002)) in e.g. its basic premise of Greek/barbarian opposition; its structural and explanatory antitheses: see Flory (1987) on those of logic/accident, truth/fiction, nature/culture, discipline/freedom; and Immerwahr (1966), 50–1 on the 'inner antithesis' that pervades the *Histories* 'in the juxtaposition of autonomous members of a chain, often with the implication that they should be compared with each other by the reader' (51); its tendency to offer *two* opposing accounts, a phenomenon that may represent 'difference' rather than 'polarity' on a strict definition, since the two accounts may not be *wholly* mutually exclusive (cf. Cartledge and Greenwood's definition (2002), 363–4), but nonetheless tends the same way; etc. Simple oppositions are generally deconstructed, however, as the text moves along, as in the case of the truth/lies polarizing framework considered in the previous chapter.

presentation of motives, more often the Herodotean alternatives are of a rather different nature, and not easily reducible to such moralizing opposites. They come in a variety of forms, working to different effects at different times. Again, some ascriptions of alternative motives would seem to lie purely within the province of the storyteller, as a form of 'spurious *akribeia*'[4]—for example in relation to Megacles' daughter ('she told her mother—whether bidden or not, I cannot say', 1.61.2)[5]—and so are to be distinguished from those that point to actual competing explanations suggested by the historian (and often arising from variant traditions or informants). And yet these 'storytelling' instances may nonetheless have some bearing on readers' interpretation of historical explanation, as we shall see. The following discussion will review some of the forms of Herodotean alternatives, mainly of the 'historical' variety, before considering the phenomenon in detail in the context of two significant Athenian *logoi*—two cases which confirm the gist of Plutarch's observation (for there can indeed be a better/worse polarizing aspect to Herodotus' presentation), while exposing the need for important qualifications.

Donald Lateiner has observed the remarkable extent to which Herodotus includes in his narrative alternative versions,[6] some of which pertain to questions of motivation. His illuminating chapter, subtitled 'The Reader's Autonomy', examines three broad categories: 'simple imprecision (a necessary vagueness) or those occasions when Herodotus chooses to avoid a misleading and unjustified precision' (78); places where Herodotus' own analysis produces an alternative account by disputing that of others; and—Lateiner's main focus, and also most suggestive for our present discussion—alternatives that arise from Herodotus' inclusion of his informants' discrepant reports.[7] Lateiner

---

[4] Cf. Wiseman (1983), 21; in Herodotus, for example, the detail that Io and the other maidens came down to the shore of Argos 'on the fifth or sixth day', 1.1.

[5] See further below, n. 87 with text.

[6] Lateiner (1989), 76–90, including a list; cf. Shrimpton and Gillis (1997), 249–50. Herodotus includes alternative versions on more than 125 occasions, Lateiner (78) specifies!

[7] On Herodotus' alternative versions generally, see also Flory (1987), 49–79, arguing that an alternative is often included more for its thematic or artistic significance—which may illuminate, for example, characters or motives: 77 (cf. 52–3 on Herodotus' inclusion of fictional anecdotes that 'illuminate the psychology of individuals', 53)—than for its literal truth value; Gray (2003); and (less satisfactorily) Groten (1963).

considers Herodotus' means of indicating the varying levels of credibility of alternatives of this last sort, both explicit and implicit (e.g.
through the use of 'intrusive oblique infinitives or optatives in ὅτι and
ὡς constructions in primary sequence' to 'express . . . irony, scepticism,
or disbelief without explicitly rejecting the alternative version' (80);
through the inclusion of a source's office, name, ethnic origin (83);
etc.). He refuses to find their *raison d'être* in simple curiosity,[8] or to take
at face value Herodotus' profession simply to λέγειν τὰ λεγόμενα ('to
report what is said', 7.152.3).[9] He instead confirms Hignett's conclusion
that such alternatives arise either from '"genuine inability to choose
between the variants or a desire to stress the superiority" of one'.[10]
Lateiner suggests that on those occasions when Herodotus 'knows no
more than his audience, he leaves open the process and option of
determining the truth, or admits that the evidence is insufficient even
for a confident suggestion' (80); Herodotus'

largesse in offering an organization of opinions invites the audience's active
participation, intervention, even disbelief. In his distrust of revealed, eternal
truths, he considers all issues discussable, his own version merely the best
working hypothesis, and other accounts not merely prejudices to be reduced
in presentation or dismissed (84).

### 5.1.1 Alternatives in form only

Stewart Flory's discussion invites qualification of this emphasis Lateiner lays upon 'the reader's autonomy' by showing how the presentation
of alternatives may in fact *limit* the reader's autonomy in important
respects—particularly by closing down other possible interpretations
by reinforcing one.[11] And indeed, as with alternative versions generally

---

[8] 'Far from being the victim of childish curiosity, [Herodotus] directs his
narrative' (82).
[9] 79, 82–3; cf. Thomas (2000), 188 n. 47 with text, 213–14; Moles (1993), esp. 95–6;
Erbse (1991), esp. 5–7: e.g. the source citations concerning the route of Sesostris'
conquests (2.104) 'sind . . . nicht ernst gemeinte Beglaubigungen eines sagenhaften
Zusammenhangs, sondern sichtbare Zeichen des Mißtrauens gegen unverbürgte Über-
treibungen' ('are . . . not seriously meant authentications of a fabulous connection, but
visible signs of distrust of unconfirmed exaggerations', 7).
[10] Hignett (1963), 32 quoted by Lateiner (1989) at 83.
[11] Flory (1987), 70–9. Gray reviews the discussions of both Lateiner and Flory and
then herself moves to explore the narrative functions of alternative accounts, and

about how an event has unfolded, so in the case of a question of motives, the common thrust of both accounts is at times more significant and arresting than their particular differences. The contending Persian and Phoenician accounts in the proem of Io's move from Greece to Phoenicia, for example, *agree* in assuming that this is to be explained in rational and human (not divine) terms (whether she was abducted by the sailors, or went willingly (ἐθελοντήν, 1.5.2), ashamed to face her parents after her affair with the captain)—and this concurrence must have seemed the most striking point to contemporary readers familiar with the usual Greek story. The differences nonetheless remain significant, in this case, for they bring to bear the alternatives on the woman's part of compulsion or free will—which are also of wider thematic interest to Herodotus' narrative. At times the alternatives may suggest wholesale *equivalences* (and here again it seems a matter of narrative art rather than of genuine variants). For example, the alternatives 'advised by someone/thought it himself' may together (in Homeric fashion) reinforce the wisdom of a decision, as Vivienne Gray observes. Alyattes, for example, sent to Delphi to inquire of the oracle 'whether because someone advised him, or because he himself thought it a good idea to send to the god and inquire about his illness' (εἴτε δὴ συμβουλεύσαντός τευ, εἴτε καὶ αὐτῷ ἔδοξε πέμψαντα τὸν θεὸν ἐπειρέσθαι περὶ τῆς νούσου, 1.19.2).[12] But even in such a case the

especially further ways in which they may reinforce a central point. Much of her discussion concerns instances specifically of alternative motives, most usefully illuminating their various narrative effects. See also Lang (1984), 73–9, who lists instances of double unresolved motivations in the *Histories* (73) and focuses particularly on the narrative functions of Herodotus' presentation of motivation (esp. as a transitional device).

[12] Gray (2003), 46–8. See Bischoff (1932), 8–11 and 26 ff. on the Herodotean topos that being advised by others or counselling oneself are equivalents; Immerwahr (1966), 74 n. 78 observes how in the *Histories* 'counselors sometimes address their audience as if the latter were taking counsel with themselves'. The single instance in Thucydides of the *eite . . . eite . . .* formula expressing alternative possible motives is of this form (5.65.3); cf. above, ch. 4 n. 20 with text. It presumably has the usual effect, i.e. of reinforcing the wisdom of Agis' decision. Gray (2003) offers further examples of the production of equivalences. The alternative motivation for the traitor Lycides, for example—εἴτε δὴ δεδεγμένος χρήματα παρὰ Μαρδονίου, εἴτε καὶ ταῦτά οἱ ἑάνδανε ('whether because he had been bribed by Mardonios, or because these proposals were pleasing/pleasurable to him', 9.5.2)—gives 'two equivalent sources of corruption, for the pursuit of money is one particular form of the pursuit of pleasure, which Greeks generally found to be a source of corruption' (48).

alternatives may bear an additional expressive power (as I shall argue below, in the context of Megacles' daughter's motives in confiding in her mother—'whether or not her mother had inquired'—about her abnormal sleeping arrangements with Peisistratus, 1.61.2)—or at least create a pause in the narrative that lends emphasis to what comes next.

Again, the two explanations may not represent true alternatives if they are to be regarded as *both* being operative, as in the case of divine and human double motivation (as also in Homer[13]): Xerxes' invasion of Greece, like the Greeks' success in warding off the attack, is to be explained in terms of (simultaneous) divine and human causes. In other sorts of instances of double motivation too, readers frequently suspect that the alternatives are not mutually exclusive, but rather that each of the two has played some part in precipitating the outcome, even though the narrative presents them as alternatives. We might note, for example, the *cumulative* psychologizing interpretation some have read into the triple ascription of motives for Cyrus' placing Croesus on the pyre (1.86.2, quoted above at 66).[14] Similarly, the alternatives may together construct a particular view of an individual's character. For example, the alternatives at 2.181.1 concerning Amasis' motives in marrying a woman of Cyrene ('whether (εἴτε) because he desired a Greek wife, or whether (εἴτε) for the sake of friendship with the Cyreneans') capture once again the *dual* nature, common versus kingly, of Amasis' character, 'since his desire for a wife is a common affair, but his friendship with Cyrene involves him as a king'.[15]

---

[13] The technique of presenting alternative motivations, usually in the form of divine v. human, is found in the *Odyssey* and *Iliad*: Homer 'seems through their differences to produce equivalences that reinforce the wisdom and authority of those who are motivated.... To alternate human motivation with a god's instruction and leave it unresolved is to present it as good thinking', Gray (2003), 46–7; Lesky (1961) formulated the principle. In parallel, the story told by the Homeric narrator gains authority through stemming both from the Muses and from human knowledge: de Jong (1987), 51–2.

[14] e.g. Stahl (1975), 31–2; Flory (1987), 76: 'Herodotus wants us to accept all three possibilities: that Cyrus had vowed to some god that if he were victorious he would sacrifice Croesus as part of his *akrothinia* (the first two alternatives), but then, seeing Croesus on the pyre and learning his reputation, the thought occurred to Cyrus to test the loyalty of Croesus' god'.

[15] Gray (2003), 55–6 (quote at 56); cf. Herodotus' construction of Athenian character through the alternative accounts of their expulsion of the Pelasgians: Gray (2003), 57–9 (and below, §5.3).

In any case, even a rejected possibility may serve to convey a richer impression of how things *might* happen in another similar instance.[16] We saw a similar phenomenon in Homer, in the case of certain characters' (mis)readings of others' motives.[17] The tale that Cassandane's expression of anger in the presence of the child Cambyses about her husband's favouring an Egyptian concubine motivated Cambyses to conquer Egypt in later life is disbelieved by Herodotus (3.3), but nonetheless models the way in which Cambyses, along with others in the *Histories*, *is* at times moved to respond disproportionately.[18] It also furthers the Herodotean theme of 'the significance of the insignificant'.[19] Atossa's claim that she is moved to urge Darius to the conquest of Greece on a personal, self-focused whim (a desire for Greek handmaids, 3.134.5) is untrue—she in fact makes her request for Democedes' sake—but in convincing her in-text audience it indicates the *plausibility* of such a motive, as well as its vast potential impact. Croesus' limited understanding of Solon's intended meaning and motivation in speaking to him as he did at 1.30–2 (for he assumes that Solon has come *only* for the sake of *theōria*,[20] and narrows down his message in paraphrasing it to Cyrus at 1.86) makes a point about Croesus' own character, but also exposes the limits more generally of human understanding—a fact of great importance elsewhere in the *Histories*.[21]

---

[16] See Flory (1987), esp. 49–79, on fiction at the service of more general truths; Moles (1993); Lateiner (1989), 77, and 80 on motivation in particular (Herodotus' inclusion of '"[l]ogical possibilities" concerning personal motives').

[17] Above, §2.3.

[18] Cf. §4.3.2 above.

[19] Cf. van der Veen (1996).

[20] Readers know he has come *also* for the sake of wisdom (in addition to the political reason of his voluntary exile from Athens: 1.29). Alternatively, Croesus assumes that Solon has come merely for *theōria* in a particular, restricted sense; cf. Long (1987), 66–7: Solon intends to 'inspect' something more profound than the material realm (i.e. the treasure chambers), which is Croesus' concern. In Montiglio's expression (2005), 132, Croesus mistakes Solon's *theōria* (1.30.1) for the less involved and intelligent *theasthai* (1.86.5, i.e. 'watching' as opposed to 'contemplating'; cf. Konstan (1987), 65–9).

[21] On the elusiveness of wisdom as a theme in the *Histories* see e.g. Dewald (1985), (1987), and (1993); Pelling (2006*a*).

## 5.1.2  Genuine alternatives

Where they represent more genuinely contending options, Herodotean
alternative motives are frequently of a sort that implies no obvious
moral or ethical judgement attaching to a particular choice, but simply
provides readers with a broader background of potential explanation:
for example, that of inner impulse versus impetus from without.[22] The
three possible motives ascribed to Cyrus for placing Croesus on the
pyre fall into a polarity of this kind: external duty, to fulfil a sacrifice (in
thanks for victory) to a god or a prayer/vow (to a god/man), as against
Cyrus' personal impulse (curiosity). Here, as so often, beyond the
broad polarity produced, there are additional levels of significance in
this presentation: the resulting spectrum of perspectives on Cyrus is
fruitful,[23] and together these portray Cyrus, once again, as a figure who
gives rise to a range of different stories and explanations.[24] They also
enhance Cyrus' identification with Croesus in the earlier part of the
story, 'prov(ing) the point that the lesson [about the transience of
happiness] will apply to him as well as Croesus'.[25] Again, in the case
of these ascriptions of various motives to Cyrus we see clearly how even
alternatives that remain unactivated in the subsequent (or wider)
narrative (which here responds only to the third option, proceeding
to answer Cyrus' question by proving Croesus loved by the gods) may
nonetheless be included to interesting effect. Leonidas' motives in the
Thermopylae narrative fall into a similar polarity: outward-regarding
(moved by thoughts of future fame for himself and Sparta: that is, by

---

[22] Though this form—self-motivation versus motivation by others—can also be
used to produce equivalences, cf. Gray (2003); e.g. in the case discussed above of a
person acting on his own impulse/on someone else's advice. Lang (1984), 74–5
discusses Herodotus' presentation of internal and external motivations, viewing
both as satisfying 'Herodotus' need as both inveterate inquirer and audience-pacifier
to find answers and explain', with external motivation having an additional narrative
function as a transitional device (75).

[23] Cf. n. 14 above with text.

[24] Cf. Pelling (2006*a*).

[25] Gray (2003), 50–1: the motives establish Cyrus' resemblance to Croesus in his
current happiness (making a victory offering, piety, and testing of the gods (Flory
(1987), 76 observed the last two points of resemblance); cf. also Pelling (2006*a*), 156.
Gray notes that '[o]ther obvious motives for the attempted immolation, such as
revenge, would not have produced such an effect, since the message about happiness
does not encompass revenge' (51).

concern for others' opinion) versus inward-focussed (driven by his personal curiosity).[26]

Another form of this polarity (external pressure/internal impulse) is that considered above, of one's own resolution as opposed to advice from without. In this case, where the second alternative (the 'impetus from without') tends towards a matter of compulsion we may no longer be dealing with a question of positive 'motivation': the options may together map onto the ἑκών/ἀέκων (willing/unwilling) scheme, with 'motives' at issue only in the case of the first option. For example, the first of the alternatives 'advised from without/thought it oneself' may shade into a matter of compulsion if the advice from without comes in the form of an order. The Prexaspes story presents a sensational illustration: drawn between the external pressure applied by the Magi to lie to the Persians, and his own desire to expose the truth, Prexaspes jumps to his death from the tower (3.74–5). In the case of Xerxes' decision to make a sacrifice on the Athenian acropolis—'whether because he had seen some vision in sleep, or whether because it weighed on his mind that he had burned the temple' (εἴτε δὴ ὧν ὄψιν τινὰ ἰδὼν ἐνυπνίου..., εἴτε καὶ ἐνθύμιόν οἱ ἐγένετο ἐμπρήσαντι τὸ ἱρόν, 8.54)—the dream might well be considered a force of compulsion, its advice impossible to ignore, particularly if readers bear in mind its counterpart of 7.12–18. We may be dealing with a matter of compulsion also if positive *intention* is simply absent, as when Polykrates fails to respond to Oroites' herald (to turn to a different form again of internal/external alternatives), 'whether deliberately..., or whether some chance occurrence happened' (εἴτε ἐκ προνοίης..., εἴτε καὶ συντυχίη τις τοιαύτη ἐπεγένετο, 3.121.2). Here the second alternative suggests an accident over which Polykrates had no control.[27] However, as the *kai* in the two preceding

[26] See above, §3.3. Cf. also Nitokris, in her outward-looking desire for memorialization into the future (i.e., for continuing fame in the eyes of others) v. her more personal impulse to play a trick on a future conqueror (see above, ch. 3 n. 28 with text).

[27] Powerful emotions are perhaps similarly understood in Herodotus, as overcoming an individual as an insuperable force from *outside* (rather as love commonly is in poetry, striking in the form of Aphrodite's/Eros' arrows)—e.g. potentially of Amasis in his desire to marry a Cyrenean wife (2.181.1; cf. above, n. 15 with text), either overwhelmed by the emotion (emanating from outside), or making his own rational decision.

examples suggests,[28] it frequently seems a matter of a *combination* of external pressure and internal desire: an individual must usually find advice appealing before he or she will determine to act upon it,[29] as Polykrates καὶ νόῳ λαβὼν ὥς οἱ εὖ ὑπετίθετο Ἄμασις ('because he also thought that Amasis had advised him well', 3.41.1), resolved to take Amasis' advice.[30] And again, even determining the bounds of what is done willingly versus unwillingly may be a challenging task, as Herodotus' choice of alternative explanations for Arkesileos' behaviour seems to imply: 'So then Arkesileos, whether he did so willingly or unwillingly (εἴτε ἑκὼν εἴτε ἀέκων), fulfilled his destiny by missing the meaning of the oracle' (4.164.4).[31] By thus closing an account that up to this point has seemed to rule out any possibility that Arkesileos fulfilled the oracle 'willingly', Herodotus frustrates—and complicates—our reading.

### 5.1.3 Morally weighted alternatives

We have considered instances, then, where Herodotean alternatives are not genuinely in contention, but instead produce equivalences, or are to be understood as working concurrently; and instances again where (more genuine) alternatives produce various effects but without entailing ethical judgement in the choice of one over the other. At times, however, Herodotus' presentation of alternative motives *does* more readily invite a morally laden interpretation, for example when the alternatives tend towards idealistic (and other-regarding) over against self-seeking. Christopher Gill argues that the emphasis of recent ancient philosophical study on the ideal of altruism (versus egoism) is anachronistic, since the ancient Greeks took for granted an expectation of mutual benefit. We may compare, in the *Histories*, Themistocles' achievement in benefiting the city and himself *at the*

---

[28] For the *kai* in the Xerxes example as implying options that are not mutually exclusive see 286 below.

[29] The 'no-choice' presented to Gyges seems a clear exception.

[30] Cf. Gray (2003), 48.

[31] The sentence is bracketed by Rosén, but not by Stein, Legrand, Medaglia (in Corcella).

*same time.*[32] In the *Histories* we do, however, find a related, if less absolute, polarity, of other-benefiting (frequently with some degree of simultaneous self-benefit assumed) versus *exclusively* self-benefiting. That similar distinctions can be made about results as well as motives seems evident in the case of a figure like Peisistratus, whose motives are mainly concerned with self-benefit (i.e., gaining power for himself), but the upshot of whose actions, at least, is partly other-benefiting at the same time, as we shall see below—and this distinguishes him from a more blackly tyrannical figure like Cambyses.

In the context of such instances—and they are important ones, for they elicit an especially committed response on the reader's part— Plutarch's response comes to seem more reasonable. In fact, it alerts us to a significant feature of Herodotean technique, even if we must take particular care in this matter to avoid anachronism (whether that produced by Plutarch's distance from Herodotus' fifth-century readers or by our own). For central to many of the *Histories'* narratives is the polarity between, on the one hand, idealistic motives of various sorts (including *philotimia*, just revenge, friendship, desire for freedom, etc.)—that is, the sorts of motives often central to the rhetoric (as well as the reality) of reciprocity,[33] those with evident moral justification, those at times even imbued with a certain heroic quality—and on the other hand, the powerful motivating force of κέρδος ('profit') *tout court.*[34] Gyges' interpretation of the proverb 'look to your own' wavers between two such alternatives.[35] Paris, in the (programmatic) proem, is driven by *kerdos* in abducting Helen (*not* by the justice of an abduction that answers all those earlier abductions), expecting simply that he will thereby gain a woman for free.[36] Herodotus remarks in his Egyptian *logos* that even if Helen had been the woman of Priam

---

[32] Gill (1998). And yet the rhetoric of Athenian public trials did separate the two: individuals suppressed personal motives so as to appear to be acting rather for the sake of the *polis*: Kurihara (2003). Christ (2006) brings out just how pervasive and expected was self-interest as a motive in Athenian ideology. For Themistocles, see ch. 9 below.

[33] Cf. Gould (1989) and (1991) on reciprocity as a fundamental structuring device in the *Histories*.

[34] Plato (e.g. in the *Republic*) shifted the polarity, placing 'desire for justice' as the ideal over against self-regarding motivations—in which camp he includes desire for honour. Herodotus—even if, in the Leonidas sequence, we see how desire for honour can have an artificial quality (cf. above, ch. 3 n. 41 with text)—continues by and large with the 'common-sense' understanding usual in fifth-century thought.

[35] Above, ch. 3 n. 48 with text.      [36] Above, 73.

himself, he would have given her back (if she had really been in Troy), 'so as to be released from the present evils' (μέλλοντά γε δὴ τῶν παρεόντων κακῶν ἀπαλλαγήσεσθαι, 2.120.3)—countering the possibility that he could have made a choice to prioritize his personal honour over his men's lives. Herodotus makes explicit the moral judgement that may be attached to the choice of a noble course of action over a pragmatic one in his account of the Kimmerians' deliberations in response to the impending Scythian invasion:

τὰς γνώμας σφέων κεχωρισμένας, ἐντόνους μὲν ἀμφοτέρας, ἀμείνω δὲ τὴν τῶν βασιλέων· τὴν μὲν γὰρ δὴ τοῦ δήμου φέρειν γνώμην ὡς ἀπαλλάσσεσθαι πρῆγμα εἴη μηδὲ πρὸς πολλοὺς δεόμενον κινδυνεύειν, τὴν δὲ τῶν βασιλέων διαμάχεσθαι περὶ τῆς χώρης τοῖσι ἐπιοῦσι (4.11.2).

There were two opposed opinions, and while each of them was championed vehemently, that of the kings was **better**. For the people held the opinion that the best course was to depart and not risk a battle against so many;[37] but the kings held the opinion that they should fight for their country against the invaders.

The Kimmerian people save their skins by fleeing without a fight, 'surrendering (παραδόντας) their country to the invaders' (4.11.3); their kings remain and die in their own land.

In cases such as these, Plutarch's 'better' and 'worse' formulation is not wholly inappropriate. We shall next consider in more detail polarized constructions of motivation of this sort, which invite a somewhat moralizing response. Even in such cases, however (as the final section of this chapter will argue), the initially staged opposites may be partially deconstructed in the ensuing or wider narrative, thus diminishing the possibility of a harshly moralizing judgement.

## 5.2 IDEALISTIC V. SELF-SEEKING MOTIVES

Plutarch, as we have seen (§1.2.2), remarked upon Herodotus' inclination to favour a more negative interpretation of motives when more than one appears to have been available to him. This inclination finds

---

[37] Emending the text at this point to read μηδὲ πρὸ σποδοῦ δὴ μένοντας κινδυνεύειν (Stein, Bredovius, Waterfield), 'and not run the risk of staying for the sake of dust', strengthens the opposition between land as simple earth, and land as important symbolically.

expression in various forms. At times the version Herodotus tells contradicts what may seem the more natural interpretation implied by the event itself. For example, in his account of the Spartans' expedition against the Samian tyrant, as Plutarch observes, Herodotus has the Spartans declare that they had done this 'not to help the Samians nor to free them, but so as to be avenged upon them' (οὐ βοηθοῦντες οὐδ' ἐλευθεροῦντες, ἀλλὰ τιμωρούμενοι Σαμίους, 859c), and thus denying 'the finest and most just *prophasis* (explanation/justification) for the expedition' (859d–e, cf. 89 above). This is indeed a most striking instance; more often it is a matter of people claiming lofty motives that Herodotus declares or implies are untrue—or at least not the full story, and therefore misleading. For example, the specific claim to be acting out of a desire to 'free (others or oneself) from tyranny' is frequently made by actors in the *Histories*, as by the Athenians in their speech at 8.144, and almost as frequently is brought into question by the surrounding context or authorial comment. And the interlocked nature of the *Histories* makes the ramifications of this significant (a factor that perhaps helps us understand the depth of Plutarch's indignation): for readers are constantly prompted to draw connections between different levels of the narrative. Thus themes that surface, for example, in the account of the Ionian Revolt (which might have furnished Plutarch with many more examples of Herodotus conjecturing disreputable motives) have purchase on the later parallel bid for 'freedom from (Persian) tyranny' as much as they do on the tale of Athens' freedom from Peisistratid tyranny (more directly linked with the Ionian narrative by means of a digression).[38] They therefore contribute to what Plutarch in his *Malice*[39] sees as a downbeat reading of the Greeks' achievement in the Persian wars.

This Herodotean tendency 'to go for the worst interpretation' riled Plutarch, who scoffs, in relation to Herodotus' notorious analysis of Phocian motives in not medizing (that they abstained from medizing

[38] Chs. 6 and 7 will consider further these themes. For the Athenians' freedom from Peisistratid tyranny see below, §5.4.

[39] Plutarch takes a rather different view, however, in his *Epicurus makes even a pleasant life impossible* 1093b–c; cf. Pelling (unpublished paper), who discusses the variation in Plutarch's mindset and stated principles depending on the genre he is working in, and concludes: 'in Plutarch we have a spectrum of different attitudes to Herodotus, a very negative one in *Malice*, a more measured and more selectively critical one in the *Life* [of Themistocles], a very positive one in the Epicurus essay' (22).

simply because their hated neighbours medized): 'he should have
declared the proofs by which he was persuaded that men who
achieved deeds identical to those of heroes (τοὺς ὅμοια πράττοντας
τοῖς ἀρίστοις) had in mind the same thoughts as the most cowardly
(τὰ αὐτὰ τοῖς φαυλοτάτοις διανοηθῆναι)' (868e). Often Herodotus
explicitly contradicts the positive interpretation of motives he expects his readers to have reached—in commenting, for example, that
'it *wasn't* due to *eunoia* (goodwill)...'[40]—and supplies instead a
negative explanation (in terms of fear, hatred, jealousy, and so on):
as he does in the case of the Spartans' advice to the Plataeans to seek
an alliance with Athens rather than themselves: 'the Spartans gave
this advice not so much out of goodwill for the Plataeans, as because
they wanted the Athenians to have troubles through coming into
conflict with the Boeotians (οὐ κατὰ εὐνοίην οὕτω τῶν Πλαταιέων ὡς
βουλόμενοι τοὺς Ἀθηναίους ἔχειν πόνους συνεστεῶτας Βοιωτοῖσι)'
(6.108.3; Plutarch once again protests: 861d–e). The narrator's practice of countering reader expectation in this way[41] (by means, again,
of a *thōma* of sorts) attunes readers to the likelihood that their initial
impressions may be mistaken, and so guides them to examine more
carefully and sceptically the motives people claim. Alternatively
Herodotus adopts a subtler and more expansive version of the
same technique, in implying an ideal motivation, only to undercut
it over the course of the narrative that follows. In this case readers
may be drawn to wonder whether this is a case of an initial attitude
changing under the pressure of circumstance, or one that never in
fact existed to begin with. We have seen an extended instance of this
with Maiandrios of Samos.[42] The movement is usually from a more

[40] Cf. Nenci on 6.108.14: 'l'εὔνοια è la motivazione ideale dalla quale Erodoto al
solito mette in guardia' ('goodwill is the ideal motivation which Herodotus usually
cautions against').
[41] De Jong (1987), 67–8 discusses the Homeric narrator's similar practice, noting
that '[t]he NF₁ [primary narrator-focalizer] uses negative statements *in interaction with*
his addressee, the NeFe₁ [primary narratee-focalizee], contradicting the latter's expectations (based on contextual knowledge, general knowledge of the world, 'historical'
knowledge, or knowledge of the heroic code) and/or creating expectations (suspense).
Sometimes the negative statement contradicts expectations of characters in the story'
(my italics). Cf. Hornblower (1994a), 158–9 on counterfactuals in Thucydides.
[42] §4.2.3 above. The same question surfaces in relation to the Samians: see §6.4.4.

idealistic construction of motivation in the direction of one that is more exclusively self-seeking.

Herodotus dramatizes characters in the *Histories* working from negative assumptions that match his own: we are told, for example, of Athens' assumption that Aegina is siding with Persia out of hatred of *her* (6.49.2). These assumptions are significant not only in shaping future behaviour (at the level of narrative and history: seen in this case in Athens' proactive seizure of Aegina's apparent motivation as a *prophasis* for involving Sparta), but also in reiterating to readers the sort of motives they should be expecting to find elsewhere. Herodotus' suspicions about characters' motives re-enact for readers the suspicions he finds pervasive in the history of the period, and places them in the position of engaging with and evaluating them. Moreover, even his authorial ascriptions of motivation can at times seem equivalent to *prophaseis*—justifications, explanations—on behalf of actors in the text. Rawlings observes that the 'attempt to persuade is fundamental to the meaning of *prophasis*; it is the *raison d'être* for even offering a *prophasis*' ((1975), 28): though justifications may be true, they are of their nature more likely to be false, or at least misleading or inadequate, being unnecessary where explanations are self-evident. We may compare *prophasis* for Pindar, which cloaks virtue in shame (fr. 228). Herodotus' frequent addition of explanations or justifications where they seemed self-evident—often ones that challenge those that readers have assumed—has the effect of engendering his readers' questioning, alerting them to the fact of being persuaded. (By the same token—and this is a theme we shall pursue further in chapter nine—they may alert readers to the possibility of their being misled even by 'authorial' statements.)

Frequently, however, Herodotus' method is less straightforward than simply favouring the more negative reading of motives, and he chooses instead to mould an account in such a way as to keep different possible motives in play over its course. This is an aspect of his wider technique of setting forth contrasting perspectives, and is perhaps in part what Plutarch is responding to when he comments on Herodotus' practice of 'mingling praise with blame': in his ninth book, for example, 'not knowing how to deal with the Athenians, at times he exalts the city, at times he abuses it, **ever shifting his treatment upwards and downwards** (⟨ποτὲ μὲν αἴρει⟩ ποτὲ δὲ καταβάλλει τὴν πόλιν *ἄνω καὶ κάτω μεταφέρων*)' (872a). The narrative as it progresses may then invite shifting responses on the part of readers as different factors are brought to their attention.[43] Once again the various possible motives frequently fall into a polarized scheme, as Plutarch's praise-and-blame formulation reflects, with a more ideal motive (or collection of motives) set against a more pragmatic.[44] Of course Herodotus does at times simply accumulate an assortment of motives of a similar pragmatic kind; and the occasional exceptional individual will act in what seems a wholly noble and selfless way;[45] but where ideal motives are brought in, the polarized schema is often apparent. Again, Herodotus' presentation of (alternative) motives does not always fit so easily into a black-and-white pattern, as the foregoing chapter has already indicated, but I shall begin with simpler cases of ideal~pragmatic, just~unjust motivation. Subsequent chapters will examine more complicated instances that map rather less readily on to Plutarch's schema.

## 5.3 ATHENIANS AND PELASGIANS: JUST OR UNJUST MOTIVES? (6.137–9)

The conflict between positive and negative readings of motives may be attached to conflicting sources (for example, an 'opinion generally held' versus Herodotus' personal view, but frequently involving more specific groups of informants, e.g. the Samians' interpretation versus the Spartans', and so on[46]), as is the case in the exposition of alternative

[43] Cf. Munson (2001), 175 on 7.139: with the hypothesis that even the Spartans might have made terms with Persia 'Herodotus slightly corrects the impression just conveyed about the intransigent courage of Sperthias and Boulis' (7.134–6); such 'instability of evaluation is typical of Herodotus' interpretative technique in his account of Greek city-states in the Persian Wars'.

[44] Cf. Nenci's formulation (on 5.24.8–9): 'doppia motivazione' in the *Histories* is typical, frequently consisting of 'una motivazione ideale e una motivazione materialistica'.

[45] Cf. Kadmos in giving over tyranny (7.164); Prexaspes in the circumstances of his suicide (3.75).

[46] I sidestep here the question of whether these informants may be genuinely historically derived or more literary, for example Hecataeus in espousing the negative view of the Pelasgians' motives in the tale below, who in his appearances in Egypt and in the Ionian Revolt narrative seems to be a literary construction: cf. West (1991). It *is*

and strongly contrasting interpretations of motivation ('just' versus 'unjust') in the account of the expulsion of the Pelasgians (6.137–9). This is a significant tale that seems in various respects programmatic,[47] and in providing an expanded (and explicit) version of the sort of thing readers find elsewhere in more skeletal form it may guide them in interpreting those other instances:[48] that is, where Herodotus sets forth two contrasting ascriptions of motivation, followed by an outcome that guides the reader's response to those ascriptions. We might compare Pindar *Pythian* 11.22–5, where alternative possible motives, revenge or lust, are given for Clytemnestra's killing of Agamemnon: Pindar 'strictly refuses to adjudicate, and puts the matter in interrogative form', but readers may nonetheless infer from Pindar's presentation his preference for the second option.[49]

After recounting Miltiades' trial in the aftermath of the Marathon campaign, during which his supporters made reference to his earlier conquest of Lemnos and punishment of the Pelasgians, Herodotus pauses to delve into the background of this episode. He begins by noting that at some early point in Athens' history the Pelasgians had been expelled from Attica by the Athenians, εἴτε ὦν δὴ δικαίως εἴτε ἀδίκως· τοῦτο γὰρ οὐκ ἔχω φράσαι, πλὴν τὰ λεγόμενα ('whether justly or unjustly, I cannot say; I can only report what is said', 6.137.1); and then he expands on each of the two interpretations of the Athenians' action given by his informants. 'Hecataeus the son of Hegesander, on the one hand, said in his account that they had acted unjustly (ἀδίκως)': it was upon seeing the now desirable condition of the land they had earlier given the Pelasgians in payment for building the Acropolis wall that the Athenians drove them out:

difficult to imagine fifth-century Spartans claiming on the part of their ancestors the motives they do for the Samian expedition.

[47] Cf. below, 143–4.

[48] Immerwahr (1966) underlined the need to recognize thought patterns in analysing the *Histories*: 'it is necessary to be aware of... the full form in each instance, for the narrative of Herodotus is often elliptic, and a short story or phrase may be unintelligible without reference to the complete pattern' (75).

[49] Hornblower (2004), 296–300, quotation at 300; cf. Gildersleeve (1899), 360. Pindar's 'response-inviting structures' in this case seem rather less explicit than many of Herodotus'.

ταύτην [τὴν χώρην] ὡς ἰδεῖν τοὺς Ἀθηναίους ἐξεργασμένην εὖ, τὴν πρότερον
εἶναι κακήν τε καὶ τοῦ μηδενὸς ἀξίην, λαβεῖν **φθόνον τε καὶ ἵμερον τῆς γῆς**, καὶ
οὕτως ἐξελαύνειν αὐτοὺς οὐδεμίαν ἄλλην πρόφασιν προϊσχομένους τοὺς
Ἀθηναίους (6.137.2).

When the Athenians saw that this land—which formerly had been in a bad
condition and worthless—was now well tilled, they were seized with **envy
and desire for land**, and thus they drove the Pelasgians out, putting forward
no other excuse (*prophasis*).

But according to another version, 'as the Athenians themselves say, they
drove out the Pelasgians justly (δικαίως)': for the Pelasgians were acting
criminally (ἀδικέειν), assaulting the Athenians' daughters[50] out of
arrogance and contempt (ὑπὸ ὕβριός τε καὶ ὀλιγωρίης βιᾶσθαι σφέας,
6.137.3) whenever they came to collect water at the spring, and were
eventually caught in the act of plotting to attack Athens. The Athenians'
response was thus one of self-defence, and represented a most moderate
punishment:

ἑωυτοὺς δὲ γενέσθαι τοσούτῳ ἐκείνων ἄνδρας ἀμείνονας, ὅσῳ παρεὸν αὐτοῖσι
ἀποκτεῖναι τοὺς Πελασγούς, ἐπεί σφεας ἔλαβον ἐπιβουλεύοντας, οὐκ ἐθελῆσαι,
ἀλλά σφι προειπεῖν ἐκ τῆς γῆς ἐξιέναι. τοὺς δὲ οὕτω δὴ ἐκχωρήσαντας ἄλλα τε
σχεῖν χωρία καὶ δὴ καὶ Λῆμνον (6.137.4).

They themselves proved far better men than the others, in that although they
could have put the Pelasgians to death when they caught them plotting, they
refused to do so, but instead ordered them to leave the country. So the
Pelasgians left and took possession of other lands, including Lemnos.

Herodotus rounds off his narrative of these alternative versions—
ἐκεῖνα μὲν δὴ Ἑκαταῖος ἔλεξε, ταῦτα δὲ Ἀθηναῖοι λέγουσι ('Hecataeus
said the former, whereas the Athenians say the latter')—before turning
to recount the aftermath of the Pelasgians' expulsion, which, along with
the narrative context that precedes the digression, in fact plays a significant role in guiding readers' assessment of the Athenians' motives—
despite Herodotus' gesture at 6.137.1 of refraining (τοῦτο . . . οὐκ ἔχω
φράσαι . . .) from offering his own opinion. The chapters preceding the
digression predispose readers to accept Hecataeus' account of the story

---

[50] Deleting τε καὶ τοὺς παῖδας (6.137.3) with Hude (cf. Stein, Legrand; Rosén and
Nenci retain it), since without this the pattern created is more effective; cf. below (in
chiming with the later motif of women subjected to *bia*, and also with the *Histories'*
wider theme of the abduction of women—which this section also feeds back into).

and the reading of the Athenians' motives implicated in it. Readers have witnessed the ease with which Miltiades was able to use the promise of gold to dissolve any potential Athenian concern about the hazy morality of his expedition (which was obvious from the fact he refused to disclose the land he intended to march against: readers might well recall the similarly underhand methods of Cleomenes, in refusing to inform his Peloponnesian allies of *his* corrupt objective: the re-establishment of tyranny at Athens, 5.74.1).[51] For Miltiades there demanded seventy ships, an army, and money,

οὐ φράσας σφι ἐπ' ἣν ἐπιστρατεύσεται χώρην, ἀλλὰ φὰς αὐτοὺς **καταπλουτιεῖν** ἤν οἱ ἕπωνται· ἐπὶ γὰρ χώρην τοιαύτην δή τινα ἄξειν ὅθεν **χρυσὸν εὐπετέως ἄφθονον** οἴσονται (6.132);

not relating to them which land it was that he would campaign against, but merely saying that they **would become rich** if they followed him; for he would lead them against some such land from which they would **easily** carry away **boundless gold**;

and the Athenians, 'excited by this prospect' (τούτοισι ἐπαρθέντες), obliged. Further, the narrative implies that it is not for the injustice of his actions (which is underscored by means of the alternative conjectured motives[52] for his entering the temple of Demeter—herself the *lawgiver*, θεσμοφόρος, 6.134.2) that Miltiades finds the Athenians unsympathetic when he returns. Rather, 'he sailed back φλαύρως ἔχων ('in a sorry state/doing badly': not just because of his leg, but because of his failure), **neither bringing money for the Athenians nor having acquired possession of Paros** (οὔτε χρήματα Ἀθηναίοισι ἄγων οὔτε Πάρον προσκτησάμενος)...' (6.135.1). Only at *this* point is he impeached on the charge of deceiving the people, when in fact the Athenians were complicit from a far earlier stage.[53] The Athenians'

---

[51] But compare, for a later example which is *not* categorically negative, Xenophon's presentation of Cyrus' concealing the goal of his expedition, *Anabasis* 1: in Xenophon's eyes it is clearly compatible with being an admirable person. Herodotus' narrative, too, I suggest below, comes to evoke a less than wholly negative picture.

[52] εἴτε κινήσοντά τι τῶν ἀκινήτων εἴτε ὅ τι δή κοτε πρήξοντα ('whether intending to move one of the inviolate sacred objects, or to do something else', 6.134.2): as Gray (2003), 59 notes, '[t]he alternative..., in refusing to become specific, makes him indescribably impious and ambitious, leaving this to the reader's imagination.'

[53] At 6.140 the movement is in the opposite direction: 'Miltiades the son of Kimon' the key player at 6.140.1, but 'Athenians and Miltiades' by 6.140.2; cf. Wood (1972), 143. The Athenians' involvement together with Miltiades in that act of conquest again points to the likelihood of their involvement in the earlier Parian expedition.

avarice seems underscored finally in the fact that they acquit him of
this particular offence in choosing not to sentence him to death,[54]
but nevertheless exact in punishment—κατὰ τὴν ἀδικίην—the large
fine of fifty talents!

Athenian ἵμερος τῆς γῆς ('desire for land') provides the story's *raison
d'être*, since Miltiades' supporters know that a reminder of his *successful*
conquest for Athens of Lemnos will be well received—and it is with the
account of this that the whole digression will culminate (at 6.140). And
of course particularly significant in the successful conquest of Lemnos
is the fact of Athens' recent acquisition of territory in the Chersonese
(which is lent additional narrative space through the account of the
Myrinaians' disagreement about this, at 6.140.2). The same greedy,
land-hungry Athenian character has thus been on show as readers
find in the Hecataean version, as has the same propensity (especially
on the part of their commander) for acting unjustly—as Herodotus'
construction of Miltiades' hidden motives makes even more clear. For
while acting on the pretext (πρόφασιν ἔχων) that the Athenians' strike
was in retaliation for Parian medizing, this was merely an excuse (τοῦτο
μὲν δὴ πρόσχημα λόγου ἦν, 6.133.1): he was in fact motivated by
a personal grudge (ἔγκοτον) against the Parians after one of their
number turned the Persian commander Hydarnes against him.

The aftermath of the story, on the other hand, tends to shift readers'
sympathies instead towards the Athenians' version, for the Pelasgians
come to appear of the sort of character that *would* act in such a way.
Their seizure of many of the Athenian women festival-goers, taking
them back to Lemnos to be concubines, matches their alleged acts of
violence stemming from *hybris* against the Athenians' daughters. Such
treatment of Artemis' worshippers parallels Miltiades' sacrilegious behaviour in Demeter's shrine.[55] Next, we find the Pelasgians taking
counsel together (βουλευομένοισι, 6.138.3) against the Athenian
mothers and their now grown sons, rather as they were alleged by the
Athenians to have been plotting (ἐπιβουλεύοντας) against the Athenian
state. Their *bia* against the women (cf. βιᾶσθαι above) is escalated when

[54] The charge of *apatē*—of deceiving the people—was punishable with death.
[55] Nor is this the first hint that the roles of Athenians and Pelasgians may be
reversed: for the Athenians' note (at the end of their account, and with more of an
appearance of neutral fact) that the Pelasgians took possession of several other lands
in addition to Lemnos (6.137.4) shows them too demonstrating land hunger.

they gratuitously murder them in addition (προσαπολλύουσι... καὶ τὰς μητέρας, 'they killed **besides**... **also** the mothers') to the sons who pose the threat. The horror of this is brought home by Herodotus' comment that it provides part of the explanation for the use of the expression 'Lemnian' throughout Greece for describing all savage deeds (6.138.4). The Pelasgians' act of violence contrasts sharply with the Athenians' earlier decision to expel rather than slay the Pelasgians, lending conviction through the comparison to the Athenians' claim that they acted compassionately. Further, the Pythia renders the Athenians arbiters of justice when she proclaims them the appropriate judges of the penalty to be paid by the Pelasgians.

And yet, in the Athenians' choice of punishment the motif of land hunger is again brought to the fore:

Ἀθηναῖοι δὲ ἐν τῷ πρυτανηίῳ κλίνην στρώσαντες ὡς εἶχον **κάλλιστα** καὶ τράπεζαν **ἐπιπλέην ἀγαθῶν πάντων** παραθέντες ἐκέλευον τοὺς Πελασγοὺς τὴν χώρην σφίσι παραδιδόναι οὕτως ἔχουσαν (6.139.3).

The Athenians set out in their town hall a couch adorned **most finely** and placed beside it a table **covered with all sorts of good things**, and bid the Pelasgians to hand over to them the land in a similar condition.

This scenario recalls Hecataeus' version, according to which the Pelasgians were made to turn over to the Athenians their finely worked land.[56] However, by this stage readerly concern with the texture of the Athenians' earlier motives has diminished in response to the Pelasgians' cruelty: changing circumstances have shifted readers' interest from evaluating the justice of the Athenians' motives (which has now paled to lesser significance), to reflecting upon the blatantly unjust nature of the Pelasgians' deed. And in any case, Hecataeus' notion of land hunger pure and simple (οὐδεμίαν ἄλλην πρόφασιν..., 'no other excuse...', 6.137.2) on the Athenians' part has been qualified, for there seem to be entirely adequate grounds for desiring retribution against a people who could behave in such a way. By the same token, the Athenians' motives in demanding Lemnos now come to seem a mixture of justified vengeance (in greater proportion, perhaps, since the Pelasgians' demonstration of brutality

---

[56] Cf. Gray (2003), 58; but she suggests it reveals also the leniency of which the Athenians in their version had boasted, for they restrict their demand to land rather than deaths in return.

still governs readerly imagination at this point) and greed for land
(which has remained a simmering theme): the combination represents a middle of the road between the two versions of their motivation in expelling the Pelasgians in the earlier incident. Thus
Herodotus' citing of specific informants whose accounts are reported
in indirect speech preserves the subjectivity of each of those versions,
by keeping readers alert to the source derivation of each: for each
group *would* give that story. It strengthens the notion that history is
full of such plausible contestabilities,[57] thus underlining the likelihood that neither account should be taken as wholly authoritative;
but at the same time Herodotus' narrative, as we have seen, does
guide readerly opinion. It may be a matter of guiding readers to
favour one source and account over the other, or of guiding them to
distrust both—an issue on which the wider account may have some
bearing.[58] Often the ultimate effect is not so much definitively to
prove one or other conjecture correct,[59] as to open up a range of
possibilities as to how one or other might be supported. The choice
between the two versions is *not* simply (in Lateiner's expression) left
up to 'the reader's autonomy'.

The Pelasgian digression thus exposes how ascriptions of double
unresolved motives in the context of alternative accounts may have
far more elaborate effects and purposes than simply reiterating the
same basic information. Indeed, Herodotean alternative versions do
frequently have more interesting functions than simply persuading
readers of the truth of a common core (in this case, of the fact that
the Pelasgians were expelled from Athens and went to Lemnos; or—
on the level of motives—of land hunger as the force that drives the
Athenians). Although frequently in cases of alternative accounts
there is a degree of congruence on the level of *what* happened,
what seems particularly expressive and interesting is often the way
each may imply rather *different* interpretations surrounding the
possible reasons for *why*: that is, regarding the motives involved on
a human level, whether these are stated explicitly or implied. Gray

[57] I owe this expression to Chris Pelling.
[58] See below, 144–7, for consideration of the wider account.
[59] Cf. Hunter's argument (1973) that in Thucydides the subsequent *erga* (in the
absence of explicit authorial evaluation) guide reader responses to his speakers'
opposed *logoi*, proving one or other of them the stronger argument.

has observed how, in the story of Amasis and the shrine (2.175.3–5), the unresolved alternatives for the fact that the shrine remains outside the temple (either because a man died during its construction; or because Amasis told them to stop work) together emphasize the enormous *size* of the shrine.[60] But these alternatives *also* offer *contrasting* perspectives on Amasis' character, one positive, the other not (*pace* van der Veen's wholly positive interpretation[61]): either as capable of listening to his chief builder and taking pity on the workers, or as persisting (tyrannically) in an excessive and dangerous project that risks the life of his workers and possibly, in light of the outcome, lacked divine approval. In the Pelasgian story, the alternative readings of Athenian motivation set forth contrasting perspectives on the Athenians' behaviour and character, which integrate with the surrounding account, as we have seen, but also with the wider work (to which we now turn).

For the Pelasgian digression is significant, even programmatic. Its textual location so soon after the Marathon sequence is striking. In stemming from the account of Miltiades' conquest of Lemnos (which Herodotus displaces to this point, though it occurred probably in the time of Miltiades' exile,[62] and might have been told earlier)—which prefigures later fifth-century Athenian conquests and thus draws a narrative link between Athens' success in the Persian Wars and her later imperialistic conquest in *Greece*—it becomes expressive as regards that whole sweep of Athenian action. We might expect such a story of early Athenian behaviour to be of particular significance in depicting Athenian character, particularly one concerning her relations with a people from whom, in some versions, she was derived. The picture it paints of Athenian character and motives does indeed parallel, and encapsulate in more explicit form, the same sort of polarized combinations found elsewhere in relation to Athenians in the *Histories*—for example, in Miltiades' and Themistocles' trajectories from heroes acting justly in defence of their homelands to bullies motivated simply by the desire to exploit powerless victims in the hope of gain.[63] Again, the 'home and away' character of the

---

[60] Gray (2003), 53.    [61] van der Veen (1996), 119.
[62] Marincola (1996), 584: *c*.511–496 BC.
[63] Miltiades extorting from Parians (6.133); Themistocles extorting from Andrians, Karystians, and Parians (8.111–12). Of course, in neither case is the

Pelasgians—who are both Athenian and not, the Athenians' ancestors
(cf. 1.57) and outsiders[64]—might potentially evoke the later relationship
between Athens and the (especially Ionian) *poleis* subjected to her rule.[65]

The digression is entwined closely and subtly into the broader
texture of the *Histories*, by means of the Pelasgian wall imagery. The
wall built by the Pelasgians around the Athenian acropolis is significant, in being a literal foundation stone of Athenian history, and
one implicated with the present. It links also into the *Histories'*
broader walls imagery, which has become strongly evocative by the
end of the work, and whose reverberations stretch also into the
future, past the bounds of Herodotus' text. Interestingly, this network of imagery seems often to be found at narrative sites where the
same questions as those raised in the Pelasgian digression are again
strongly at issue (e.g., whether an action should be explained in terms
of noble or more selfish motives; or as inescapable (for reasons of
self-preservation) or chosen). It may be expressive, for example, that
it was at the Pelasgian wall that Cleomenes and 'the Athenians who
wanted to be free' pinned the Peisistratid tyrants (5.64)—not long
before the story turned from portraying Cleomenes freeing Athenians from tyranny, to instead becoming a promoter in his own
interests of the would-be replacement tyrant Isagoras. Another
Athenian acropolis 'wall' will prove significant (7.142.1) in the debate
Herodotus recounts in the lead-up to the Salamis narrative, over the
meaning of Athens' 'wooden wall', ξύλινον τεῖχος (7.141–3): significant to Athens' choice of her future identity, as seafaring state and
consequently saviour of herself and Greece—or not. The 'great and
powerful walls' (τείχεα μεγάλα τε καὶ καρτερά, 1.98.3) of Agbatana,

movement absolutely cut and dried, but rather seeds of the men's later characters are
evident earlier, cf. Ubsdell (1983); for example, in Miltiades' speech persuading
Kallimachos before Marathon, we find hints again of *Athens'* constant desire to be
*first* (cf. below, ch. 6 n. 79 with text).

[64] Sourvinou-Inwood (2003) explores the complex doubleness of the Greeks'
conception of Pelasgians, and how, in 'ethnicity discourses' like Herodotus', it
could be used to 'articulate the barbarian as both other and significantly comparable
to the self' (144).

[65] Gray (2003) observes how the two versions of the Athenians' motives 'point to a
character that establishes a setting for the subsequent history of their relations with
their empire' (57): that is, 'as land-grabbers who are nevertheless merciful' (58); she
compares Thuc. 1.76.3.

in their seven concentric circles, symbolize—and effect—Media's move from the autonomous rule of townships to Deioces' centralized tyranny (1.96–9).

Perhaps similarly evocative, the Kimmerian walls (*Κιμμέρια τείχεα*) that survive in Scythia down to Herodotus' day (4.12.1) are mentioned directly after the story of the Kimmerians' dispute about whether to flee the country before the Scythians' advance, or honourably to stay and die (4.11; cf. above, 132). They serve as a reminder of that episode, which forms part of the version of the Scythians' arrival in Scythia to which Herodotus most inclines (4.11.1). The rise of a further wall—across the Isthmus—gives the Spartans confidence (if unwarranted: cf. 7.139) in their own security, tempting them to dispel any cares for the rest of Greece in the run-up to the battle of Plataea. The hair's-breadth nature of the Greek victory is there underlined; identity issues, too, are once more at stake. Past the confines of Herodotus' text, but probably familiar to most readers, is Athens' shrewd rebuilding of her city wall, overseen by Themistocles, after its destruction by the Persians (cf. Thuc. 1.90.3–91.7). This was to play as significant a role as did the Isthmus wall in defining Athens' relationship with Sparta: for although she had played second fiddle to Sparta throughout earlier history, as the *Histories* has underlined, from the moment of the wall's rebuilding forward—in the wake of her efforts in the Persian War—the relationship would be one of *equals*.[66] And like the Pelasgian wall, Athens' city wall had deep, indeed literal, links with an earlier layer of Athenian history: cf. Thuc. 1.93 (*still* in Thucydides' day signs were visible of its having been built in haste;[67] and it incorporated various sorts of material of the day, such as columns from grave monuments).

The responses to the questions brought into play at these historical (and narrative) junctures seem crucial in establishing the character and identity of a people at that moment in time, or in evaluating the nature of that identity retrospectively. It is this that perhaps explains the associated walls imagery: for walls are the defence that secure a city's survival, preserving its identity. A Roman example may be

---

[66] Cf. Themistocles' insistence: Thuc. 1.91.7.

[67] Indeed even today, Mathieu de Bakker points out to me, it is evident that the wall was built under circumstances different from those of the building of later walls.

suggestive: in jumping the city wall (or moat)[68] Remus presented a twofold challenge to the identity of newly founded Rome: a symbolic challenge to his brother's foundation, in recalling the original possibility of the city being named Remuria, after Remus (with the contrasting character that that would entail),[69] and a more practical one, in indicating that future enemies would likewise be able to breach the city's defences (and thus transform its nature through conquest). Parallel incidents surface in Greek mythology, from which the Roman tale probably derived.[70] A similar combination of practical and symbolic perhaps produces the particular urgency with which Homer's Achaeans (as depicted in *Iliad* 12) seek to protect their wall—'a defence ($\epsilon\hat{\iota}\lambda\alpha\rho$) for their ships and for themselves' (7.437; cf. 12.7–8)—and then the fevered nature of the battle that follows the Trojan success in breaching it (12.438). The Achaeans are driven in rout (12.470–1) and lose heart (cf. 13.85–7). The rupturing of the Achaean wall appears to carry a significance beyond simply the practical, indicating that wider Greek victory or defeat, along with the contrasting implications of each for future Greek identity, is at this moment on the line.[71] As well as being bound up with defence, however, walls are also perceived as fulfilling an important memorializing function—an aspect powerfully evoked in the *Iliad*, where a *god* (Poseidon) is anxious that the fame of the Achaean wall may eclipse that of his own: 'Surely its fame ($\kappa\lambda\acute{\epsilon}os$) will reach as far as the dawn spreads, and men will forget the wall that I and Phoebus toiled over building for the hero Laomedon' (*Il.* 7.451–3). Zeus suggests

---

[68] Wall: Dionysius of Halicarnassus *Ant. Rom.* 1.87.4; Livy 1.7.2; trench: Diodorus Siculus 8.6.1–3. Walls and moats are equivalent in purpose. From earliest times they could be used in conjunction: cf. Homer *Il.* 7.449–50.

[69] For Remuria, see Dionysius of Halicarnassus *Ant. Rom.* 1.85.6, 87.3; Plutarch *Romulus* 9.4, 11.1; *Origo Gentis Romanae* 23.1; Wiseman (1995), 102, 110–17 ('Remuria'). Wiseman's discussion illuminates the matter of the opposite potential identities for the city implied by (strong and vigorous) 'Romulus' v. (delaying) 'Remus'.

[70] Cf. Plutarch *Greek Questions* 299c–d: Poemander fortified ($\dot{\epsilon}\tau\epsilon\acute{\iota}\chi\iota\sigma\epsilon$) Poemandria; his master builder Polycrithus 'belittled the fortifications and, laughing scornfully, jumped over the moat'; enraged, Poemander threw a stone at him that instead slew his son Leucippus, etc.; Apollodorus *Library* 1.8.1: Oeneus, king of Calydon, 'begat Toxeus, whom he killed with his own hands because he leaped over the moat'. Cf. Ogilvie on Livy 1.6.3–7.3.

[71] Cf. the metaphor of taking a city as being like rape (e.g. in Aristophanes' *Lysistrata*: cf. Foley (1982), 7), which presses the notion that its capture risks, in a further sense, compromising a city's identity. The tyrant's violation of women's bodily 'boundary' parallels his violation of territorial boundaries: cf. e.g. Dewald (1981).

that he destroy this μέγα τεῖχος ('great wall') once the Achaeans have returned home (7.459–63); a dramatic prolepsis subsequently describes the three gods working together to that end (12.10–33). The Pelasgian wall too, as we noted above, has this memorializing aspect.

The Pelasgian digression thus invites readers to bring in a far wider subtext as they consider the significance of the question of the justice or not of the Athenians' motives.[72] And in turn that discussion of motivation may inform other instances too, having a bearing on readings of the Athenians' motives elsewhere (for example, in representing an explicit reminder of how very different motives may look from different perspectives). It exposes the interlocking effect that ascriptions of motivation may have, reverberating elsewhere in the text through the associations lent by imagery. It is significant too in rearticulating the sorts of motives readers should be expecting to be operative: most often positive desires for profit, power, vengeance, along with (negative) fear (e.g. in the Athenians' version of the Pelasgians' expulsion, about the safety of their daughters). We found a just and reasonable motivation being claimed by the Athenians, but one that nevertheless arose from anxiety for self-preservation and security. Are readers left with the sense that it may be only to this limited degree that people usually attain to ideal reasons for action?

The sense that ideal motives have a limited role to play in the *Histories*' conception of human behaviour is reinforced by the primacy in the work of the opposite principle: *kerdos*—advantage, profit—as the driving force of individuals (as well as communities). *Kerdos* is an especially dominant principle in Herodotus' account of the Ionian Revolt. There, but also in the wider work, with which it is intertwined, we shall indeed find remarkably little room for high ideals—for acting out of reverence for the notions of freedom and Greek unity claimed by the Athenians at 8.144, for example—if ever any prospect of *kerdos* enters the equation.[73] But despite this apparent impotence, such motives remain an oddly pervasive presence in the rhetoric, with appeals that others act (or rather, *seem* or *be seen* to

[72] My argument suggests that to describe the incident as portrayed by Herodotus as a 'clear case... of envy motivating [the Athenians'] action', cf. Harrison (2003), 150, risks reductionism.

[73] See esp. ch. 6.

act[74]) in accordance with such ideals expected to be effective in helping to persuade them to a certain course of action.

The *kerdos* principle is enunciated by Darius, and we see it operating in Persian affairs, particularly in Herodotus' account of the conspiracy of the Seven, the Constitution Debate, and Darius' accession.[75] But it is as applicable, perhaps even more applicable, on the Greek side, possibly because democracy unleashes greater potential for the individual to find profit for himself (cf. 5.78: αὐτὸς ἕκαστος ἑωυτῷ προεθυμέετο κατεργάζεσθαι, 'each individual was eager to achieve for himself'[76]), rather than having to gain benefit solely through the King's favour—though that too is a recurrent theme, even—especially?—on the part of Greeks. For the Greeks' possession of freedom entails the possibility of choosing to forfeit it, at least on the part of those high-placed individuals who are in a position to do so. Such people (including Syloson, Megacles and the Alcmaeonid family as a whole, Hippias, Democedes, etc.) may find appealing the personal benefits to be gained from forfeiting their *polis*' internal freedom to a tyrant at home, or its external freedom to the Great King.[77] The means so to choose are out of the reach of most ordinary citizens, however. In that case the alternatives of serving the cause of freedom versus collaborating with tyranny (whether internal or external) are not so easily delineated, as we shall see in the following section.

## 5.4 ATHENIANS, ALCMAEONIDS, PEISISTRATIDS: FREEDOM-LOVING OR COLLABORATING WITH TYRANNY? (1.59–64; 5.55–65)

We earlier considered the subtlety with which Herodotus engages his readers' response over the course of his account of the accusation against the Alcmaeonids of treacherously signalling to the Persians

---

[74] Cf. Aristagoras giving Spartans and Athenians public reasons for action (5.49 and 5.97; cf. §6.2.2 below); Miltiades similarly to Kallimachos (6.109; cf. 170–1 and ch. 6 n. 79 with text).

[75] See esp. Pelling (2002).

[76] Compare also e.g. Themistocles' rhetorical strategy at 8.60β, urging Eurybiades that in so acting χρηστὰ εὑρήσεις ('you will find profit').

[77] Democedes' case presents a less extreme instance: he prioritizes his own escape from Darius over the danger of attracting Persian attention to Greece.

after Marathon (chapter one). But already within the account of the Peisistratids of the first book, Herodotus employs equally subtle strategies to engage readers in confronting the complex question of Athenian and Alcmaeonid attitudes to the Athenian tyranny, and to guide them towards adopting a sceptical stance in particular towards the Alcmaeonid 'freedom' rhetoric of the later books. Particularly notable is his strategy of progressively presenting gradually changing perspectives—through 1.59–64, and again when he returns to the material in later books—which bear upon the question of the sorts of motives operative in each camp. These changing perspectives draw readers continually to re-evaluate their earlier conclusions. The broad alternative constructions of motivation on the part of Athenians and Alcmaeonids that the narrative keeps in play—desire for freedom, over against willingness to accept or even cooperate with tyranny for one's own immediate benefit—give way ultimately (as this section aims to demonstrate) to a more nuanced picture. Such polarized views of motivation ('freedom-loving' versus 'tyrannical') are prevalent in rhetorical contexts; they may even be good for the reader to think with; but, as the *Histories* constantly reminds us, they do not map directly on to more complex realities.[78]

The beginning of Herodotus' account of the Peisistratid tyranny probably aroused expectations in his audience that he would tell a tale in keeping with their negative presumptions about tyranny generally. It probably left the Athenian contingent with the impression that his story would tie in with their mythologizing tradition: that it would portray the Athenians as hating their tyrant but ineffective before his irresistible power.[79] Peisistratus' father, a private

---

[78] The attraction to and use of such polarizing schemata, in company with a (stronger) impulse to move past them so as to accommodate less schematic realities, parallels the tension in Herodotus' treatment of the physical world 'between the traditional desire for symmetry, or the demands of theories such as that of environmental determinism, and the messier realities of world geography which are revealed both by his experience and by others': Thomas (2000), 101; cf. also below, ch. 8 n. 4.

[79] For tyranny in archaic literature as negative/sinister/fearful, see Giorgini (1993), 69–105; de Libero (1996). For fifth-century perceptions of tyranny, see particularly Lanza (1977), discussing the fifth-century ideological representation of the tyrant on the Athenian stage as a scapegoat figure embodying all that the (Greek, but esp. Athenian democratic) *polis* repudiates (e.g. the irrational, fearful, foreign...); and Giorgini (1993). Raaflaub (2003) argues for a uniformly negative *official* view of tyranny in Athens; Kallet (2003) suggests that the *popular* view could fluctuate. For fifth-century

citizen (ἰδιώτης),[80] travels to Olympia, where the marvel (τέρας) of a cauldron boiling without fire prompts Chilon to warn him not to marry; to leave his wife; or at the very least to disown any child born to him. Hippokrates disregards the advice—and this strikes an ominous chord in the ears of an audience familiar with Herodotus' wise adviser theme—and μετὰ ταῦτα, 'after these things', Peisistratus is born (1.59.1–3). The supernatural omen suggests the sinister and irresistible qualities of the tyrant to be, a figure who (in the usual story pattern) arises inexplicably from the margins—in this case, from ordinary parentage (for the narrative has revealed nothing, as yet, of the family's aristocratic credentials)—to wield absolute power.[81] Next, the adult Peisistratus is shown taking advantage of a period of stasis to raise a third faction of his own, already at this point 'aiming at tyranny' (καταφρονήσας τὴν τυραννίδα, 1.59.3): the advance ascription of motivation pushes the narrative forward to what seems its inevitable conclusion. The choice of καταφρονέω, besides its basic sense in this context of 'aiming at',[82] seems to

Athenian mythologizing traditions regarding the Peisistratids, see Lavelle (1993). A negative template of tyranny (including the motif of the tyrant's irresistible power) also emerges later over the course of the *Histories* itself: cf. Dewald (2003), esp. 27–32; Lateiner's chart of 'The Characteristics of Autocrats...' in the *Histories*, (1989), 171–9; but note also Gray's (1996) emphasis on the differences that surface within Herodotus' 'patterns' of tyranny. The *Histories* may be used with caution to uncover strands of earlier tradition. Forsdyke argues that the anecdote about Thrasyboulos' advice to Periander, for instance, probably reflects 'a widespread, even Panhellenic tradition about the dangers of tyranny' (2002), 542 with Forsdyke (1999) (arguing specifically for its reflection of *Athenian democratic* tradition; cf. Forsdyke (2001)).

   [80] The *idiōtēs-tyrannos* polarity that is central to Herodotus' first book is likely to suggest to readers that *idiōtēs* here is to be understood as private citizen as contrasted with 'tyrant' / 'ruler', rather than as contrasted with 'religious envoy'. Gray (1997), n. 60 observes further: 'Hippocrates is described as *idiotes* to contrast him with the *tyrannos* his son became (as Amasis is also, before his tyrannical coup: 2.174), not because he had held no public office. His description as an "*idiotes* seeing the sights of (*theoreonti*) the Olympic Festival" contrasts with the tyrant's inability to travel to festivals for fear of loss of security: Xen., *Hiero* 1.11–12, Plato, *Rep.* 571–9.'

   [81] e.g. in the *Histories* Perdikkas, whose loaves rise to double the height of those of his two brothers, returns from exile to take over the power of Macedon (8.137–8); Cyrus, brought up in the mountains by the herdsman and his wife, returns to seize power over all of Asia—as predicted in Astyages' dreams about the urine and the vine (1.107–8); cf. the widely familiar story pattern of the exposed king-child (Oedipus, Moses, etc.) who returns to rule.

   [82] Cf. the frequent Homeric and occasional Herodotean usage of the preposition κατά + accus. with this meaning (cf. LSJ s.v. κατά B. III.)

indicate again Peisistratus' superiority/ascendancy (over the people of Athens), whether the *kata-* prefix introduces a supplementary notion of his looking down from above (recalling the Herodotean use of the same verb to mean 'to look down upon/despise', cf. 4.134.9), or simply intensifies the sense of φρονέω[83] and so underlines the fact of his intellectual prowess. As champion of the hill men merely τῷ λόγῳ ('in word'), Peisistratus contrives (μηχανᾶται) to wound himself, pretending it is the work of his enemies, in order that the *dēmos* are deceived (ἐξαπατηθεὶς, 1.59.5) into granting him a bodyguard. And with that he seizes the acropolis.

At this point the narrative veers in a rather different direction, however, from the sort of tyrant tale its opening has implied,[84] with Herodotus' observation that:

ἔνθα δὴ ὁ Πεισίστρατος ἦρχε Ἀθηναίων, οὔτε τιμὰς τὰς ἐούσας συνταράξας οὔτε θέσμια μεταλλάξας, ἐπί τε τοῖσι κατεστεῶσι ἔνεμε τὴν πόλιν κοσμέων καλῶς τε καὶ εὖ (1.59.6).

After that, Peisistratus ruled the Athenians. Neither disturbing the existing structure of offices nor changing the laws, he administered the *polis* constitutionally and organized its affairs properly and well.

Moreover, if Lisa Kallet's attractive suggestion is correct, and we may translate that last phrase with 'adorned the city beautifully and finely', then Herodotus gestures towards Peisistratus' impressive *erga*,[85] worthy of the historian's record. One's initial impression of Peisistratus' menacing aspect begins to be undercut in another direction, too: for the other faction leaders are coming to appear equally focused on their own advantage as Peisistratus was in aiming at tyranny, and equally unconcerned with anyone else's interests— let alone with removing tyranny for the sake of the *dēmos'* freedom. Megacles and Lycurgus, τὠυτὸ φρονήσαντες[86] ('having in mind the

---

[83] Cf. LSJ s.v. κατά E. (in compos.) IV.

[84] This incongruity prompts Frost (1999), 11–12 to find an explanation in the possibility that the divine omen was in fact *positive*, aimed at Athenians: just as the oracle to Aigeus, ignored, allowed Theseus to be born, so this omen, luckily ignored, allowed Peisistratus to be born! (His n. 13, however, allows that Herodotus left his audience to interpret the ambiguous terms.) Differently, Gray (1997), likening Peisistratus here (at 1.59.6) to Deioces' *seeming* constitutional at first.

[85] Kallet (2003), 125.

[86] Recalling Peisistratus' καταφρονήσας τὴν τυραννίδα?—the sinister/tyrannical potential of *phronēsis* appears to unite them all. Note also the suggestive linguistic

same goal')—the expulsion of Peisistratus—unite their supporters so as to drive him out, but soon fall to feuding once again (αὖτις ἐκ νέης ἐπ' ἀλλήλοισι ἐστασίασαν, 1.60.1). Finding himself 'driven around by faction' (περιελαυνόμενος δὲ τῇ στάσι), Megacles makes an offer to Peisistratus 'to have his daughter as wife, and the tyranny too' (τὴν θυγατέρα ἔχειν γυναῖκα ἐπὶ τῇ τυραννίδι, 1.60.2), thus showing no qualms at all about forging a close permanent alliance with the tyrant. Megacles' formulation recalls that of Candaules' wife earlier in the book, when she made Gyges choose between his own death, or killing Candaules and 'having her and the kingdom of the Lydians' (ἐμέ τε καὶ τὴν βασιληίην ἔχε τὴν Λυδῶν, 1.11.2). Thus it draws into the reader's mind disquieting connotations of eastern tyranny and powerful women. Together the two men contrive (μηχανῶνται, 1.60.3—as Peisistratus did with his self-wounding earlier) to return Peisistratus to power *via* the trick of the Athene lookalike Phye.

But Peisistratus, Herodotus explains,

inasmuch as he already had young children, and the Alcmaeonids were said to be accursed, did not wish to have children from his newly married wife. So he slept with her **not in the usual way** (ἐμίσγετό οἱ **οὐ κατὰ νόμον**) (1.61.1).

At this point Herodotus turns to focalizing the narrative through the gaze of the girl, who hid the matter initially, but then—εἴτε ἱστορεύσῃ εἴτε καὶ οὔ ('whether her mother had inquired about it or not', 1.61.2)—she told her mother who told her husband. The mention of this intriguing unresolved motivation slows the narrative down slightly, allowing the reader pause for thought; it presents the outcome as a product of wisdom;[87] and with this 'single sentence', as Stewart Flory remarks, 'Herodotus implies a whole series of embarrassing, intimate scenes'.[88] Perhaps more to the point, however, is the way in which Herodotus thus underlines the fact that *this* is the

mirroring in 1.61.1 between καταλλάσσετο (τὴν ἔχθρην) in relation to Megacles and ἀπαλλάσσετο of Peisistratus; cf. Powell (1937), using this as an example of places where '[a] slight irony is sometimes produced by the repetition of the same stem with different prefixes' (105).

[87] Gray (2003), 48: 'For the mother to make an inquiry makes the outcome as much a product of wisdom as to recognize the importance of the information and give it unasked, since investigation has special importance for Herodotus as the source of knowledge'.

[88] Flory (1987), 45.

extent of Peisistratus' lawlessness: the contravention of a deal made with another power-hungry aristocrat—whereas concerning the *polis*, he has changed no laws (θέσμια, 1.59.6) at all. Readers may generally expect such sexual transgression to be an affront in itself, but at the same time emblematic also of greater transgression in relation to the wider community—as it is in Cambyses' case, for his *oikēia kaka* ('private/domestic wrongs', cf. 3.33: ταῦτα μὲν ἐς τοὺς οἰκηίους[89] ὁ Καμβύσης ἐξεμάνη..., 'these were Cambyses' mad acts towards his household...'), evident particularly in his violence towards women,[90] parallel his treatment of the rest of Persia (cf. 3.34.1: τάδε δ᾽ ἐς τοὺς ἄλλους Πέρσας ἐξεμάνη, 'these were his mad acts towards the rest of the Persians'). The violation of women in the *Histories* can symbolize the violation of what they stand for: respect for culture and the constraints of *nomoi*.[91] In this case, however, the point is precisely that no deeper symbolism is to be found. Furthermore, Herodotus' explanation of Peisistratus' motives (1.61.1) has shown them to be practical and reasonable.

In avoiding an elevated reading of the affair—in terms of a juxtaposition of noble proto-democratic impulses with the evils of tyranny—Herodotus' presentation of the episode seems comparable to Thucydides' account of the Peisistratid Hipparchos' insult to Harmodios' sister (following his failure to seduce Harmodios), in preventing her from participating in the Panathenaic procession. This, according to Thucydides, is what precipitated the tyrannicides' killing of Hipparchos: an offence against a woman so very *slight* in comparison with the sort of *bia* usually to be expected of a tyrant—which indeed Aristogeiton fears may be employed against his lover Harmodios (ὁ δὲ ἐρωτικῶς περιαλγήσας καὶ **φοβηθεὶς τὴν** Ἱππάρχου **δύναμιν μὴ βίᾳ προσαγάγηται αὐτόν**..., 'he was greatly pained in his desire and **feared Hipparchos' power, lest he use force against him**', 6.54.3). But Aristogeiton's expectation that Hipparchos

---

[89] I read οἰκηίους with Rosén and Medaglia (in Asheri) for the more attractive parallel produced with ἄλλους at 3.34.1; Hude reads οἰκηιοτάτους.

[90] The violence expected of a tyrant, who, according to Otanes (3.80.5) βιᾶται γυναῖκας ('violates women'); cf. Periander's violence against Melissa (3.50; 5.92η.3). On the motif of the tyrant's sexual transgression in Herodotus and Greek literature more generally, see Holt (1998).

[91] Cf. Dewald (1981). Herodotus' women are not *always* the champions of culture, however: see Gray (1995).

may resort to force proves wholly mistaken (in fact, the expression ἐρωτικῶς περιαλγήσας—'greatly pained in his desire'—suggests it originates in love-struck delusion), as Thucydides highlights both through the detail that the Peisistratid 'wished to do nothing violent' (βίαιον . . . οὐδὲν ἐβούλετο δρᾶν, 6.54.4) and through his sketch of the virtuous character of the tyranny (6.54.5–6).

It is the *tyrannicides* who worsen the situation by bringing force to bear in assassinating Hipparchos[92] (ironically at the very moment at which he is 'setting in order (διακοσμοῦντι)' the Panathenaic procession, 1.20.2), thus causing the previously mild regime to become χαλεπωτέρα ('more cruel', 6.59.2) under the now fearful Hippias. The whole account demonstrates that the tyrannicides' deed arose 'because of a chance love affair' (δι' ἐρωτικὴν ξυντυχίαν, 6.54.1; cf. 6.59.1: δι' ἐρωτικὴν λύπην, 'because of lovers' grief'): it was an entirely personal incident, in no way originating in opposition to tyranny *per se*. (This reality is only made all the more evident by the freedom-speak that surfaces in the tyrannicides' last-minute hope—which anyhow fails to eventuate—that other Athenians, witnessing events unfolding, 'would wish to join in setting themselves free', ἐθελήσειν σφᾶς αὐτοὺς ξυνελευθεροῦν, 6.56.3.) Thucydides uses the account to exemplify his assertion that 'neither the other Greeks, nor the Athenians themselves, say anything accurate about their own tyrants or about this event' (οὔτε τοὺς ἄλλους οὔτε αὐτοὺς Ἀθηναίους περὶ τῶν σφετέρων τυράννων οὐδὲ περὶ τοῦ γενομένου ἀκριβὲς οὐδὲν λέγοντας, 6.54.1). Herodotus' point seems much the same.

To return to the *Histories*, the above reading of this passage is lent emphasis by the humorous tone that Flory observes,[93] and by the additional expressiveness of the alternative motives ascribed to the girl. For the glimpse here allowed of the close family dynamic—mother still in a position to question the daughter in this way even after the marriage (as Plutarch's domesticating paraphrase—ὦ μαμμίδιον . . . ('O mummy', 858c)—actually underlines)—reminds readers of the *link* between

---

[92] Rather, indeed, as the Greeks of Herodotus' proem escalate matters by responding to Paris' theft of Helen with military force! See the excellent analysis of Stahl (2003), 1–13, which makes this point (that the *tyrannicides* are responsible for worsening the situation), and generally runs in parallel to the discussion presented here.

[93] Cf. Dewald and Kitzinger (2006), 151: the story 'probably counted as political humour in the world of fifth-century Athens'.

households that this is all about. They might recall the famous match of an earlier Megacles with Agariste daughter of the tyrant Cleisthenes of Sicyon, which had given the Alcmaeonids their famous reputation (6.126–31). Thus in his brief aside Herodotus has conjured up a wider network of family ties and influential women, and so underlined the fact that Athens is still very aristocratic in texture, and perhaps hinted at an explanatory principle: this Athens does *not* seem yet to be ready for democracy.

Angered at the insult (τὸν δὲ δεινόν τι ἔσχε ἀτιμάζεσθαι πρὸς Πεισιστράτου. ὀργῇ δὲ..., 1.61.2), Megacles again made up his quarrel with the other faction, and at hearing this news the Peisistratids again left Athens. (Thus even at this point Herodotus does not see the situation quite in terms of Megacles 'driving him out', as in Plutarch's paraphrase, 858c.) But the preceding narrative invites readers to suspect that Megacles' anger is motivated less by the dishonour—in Plutarch's interpretation of Herodotus' account, by his and other Alcmaeonids' 'indignation at his abnormal behaviour' (τῷ παρανομήματι σχετλιάσαντας, 858c)—than by concerns of *Realpolitik*: at the dissolution of the possibility of a tyrant offspring for his own family. The specifics leave no room for belief in an Alcmaeonid claim of constant noble anti-tyrannical motivation, for Megacles in this account (as Plutarch bemoaned in returning to the episode for a second time, 863b) would have remained content with the match if Peisistratus had treated his daughter as a real wife. Megacles was willing to use his daughter as a pawn to cement this tyrant match, concerned, no doubt, with her honour as well as that of the whole family; it can hardly be just a question of fatherly emotional sympathy.[94] His motives become loftier, at least in appearance, only once circumstances have removed the possibility of personal profit.

The details underscore the irony that it is the Alcmaeonids who will contrive the final removal of the Peisistratid tyrant (and indeed their manner in so doing—bribing the Oracle—is similarly ambiguous). Plutarch is as indignant about Herodotus' representation of this as he is about the account of the Spartans' denial that they made

[94] Contrast the concerned father Otanes, who cannot bear the thought of his daughter in the harem of a usurper. Moreover, as Gray (1997) observes, it was *Peisistratus* who put an end to the alliance by his action.

their expedition to Samos to help the *dēmos* rid themselves of their tyrant, claiming instead the motive of vengeance for the theft of a mixing-bowl.[95] But what both instances go to show is the way Herodotus' world works: people do *not* on the whole act out of high and mighty motives; their concerns are personal and generally selfish. While the reciprocity model (of action in return: in gratitude, vengeance, etc.) is of central importance in the *Histories*,[96] people may also exploit it as an excuse for an action that is *not* in fact motivated by it. This is not to downgrade the importance of the concept, however. Lendon's formulation is instructive:

Vengeance also regularly appears in ancient authors as a dishonest pretext. . . . It is then very easy to dismiss references to vengeance as self-justifying persiflage concealing 'real'—more familiar—motives. In fact the regular use of vengeance as a pretext argues powerfully for its ideological legitimacy and so its historical importance as a real cause of real wars.[97]

Darius, for example, employs reciprocity rhetoric in returning Syloson to power—though the action seems motivated by a desire not so much to return Syloson's favour of the cloak as to gain a friendly toehold on Samos.[98] Here, likewise, while Megacles' response implies that he views his daughter's treatment as emblematic of something bigger, and as an insult both to her and her natal family, readers might equally feel that he is here representing as righteous an action primarily motivated by more pragmatic and self-interested concerns. The failure at 1.61.2 to specify the source of his sense of dishonour allows readers either to share Plutarch's interpretation (which emphasizes the indignation felt by the Alcmaeonid family at the tyrant's

---

[95]   859b–c; cf. above, ch. 4 n. 34 with text.

[96]   Cf. Gould (1989) and (1991); Braund (1998).

[97]   Lendon (2000), 2 (referencing Dawson (1996), 65). I am not persuaded by Harrison's view that the ubiquity of reciprocal action in the *Histories* invites an emphasis on the degree to which its action is 'merely, and mechanically, reactive' (2003), 145: rather, Herodotus *foregrounds* the fact that people exploit actively the justifications etc. supplied by reciprocity rhetoric. Indeed, in my view, Herodotus invites a quite different emphasis from Harrison's, rather on the notion of reciprocity as exploited *actively* by individuals. Evans (1991), 16–22 discusses vengeance as *alleged* cause.

[98]   Cf. the wider practice of Persian monarchs of responding to inside invitations as an excuse for conquest, from people who frequently lack the authority to make such an invitation: above, ch. 4 n. 94 with text.

transgressive conduct regarding the girl), or alternatively to regard the dishonour as arising primarily from Peisistratus' refusal fully to share power with Megacles and his line. In combination, the first reading may be felt to convey the public face given to the incident by the Alcmaeonids; the second, Herodotus' plausible conjecture about Megacles' personal motives.

Nor, however, are the Athenians entirely wedded to the idea of freedom, but apathetic and complacent. When Peisistratus returns for the third time, and for the long haul, he receives support from the city of 'those valuing tyranny above freedom' (τοῖσι ἡ τυραννὶς πρὸ ἐλευθερίης ἦν ἀσπαστότερον, 1.62.1). The Athenians 'take no account' (λόγον οὐδένα εἶχον, 1.62.2) of his raising money or taking Marathon (and readers might well linger on the phrase, which is expressive in the *Histories*[99]), and oppose him only once he is actually marching on the city. Even then, by the time he makes his attack they have turned to other pursuits, and thus are easily put to flight. The keynote here is Peisistratus' *avoidance* of full military force (much as his offence against the girl was not the tyrant's typical *bia*), devising a 'very clever plan' (βουλὴν ... σοφωτάτην, 1.63.2) to make the Athenians return to their homes. 'And the Athenians were persuaded' (πειθομένων δὲ τῶν Ἀθηναίων, 1.64.1)—again! And this despite the fact that Herodotus has made so much of Athenian cleverness in telling the story of Phye: they of all people, 'said to be first, with respect to wisdom (σοφίην), of all Greeks' (1.60.3), should have be able to see through this *boulē sophōtatē*. This triple deceit/persuasion of such a clever people may point to the irresistible nature of the tyrant's power, but it might reflect back on the Athenians too: are they really all that reluctant to accept Peisistratus' rule? It is perhaps expressive that the 'deceit' at 1.59.5 has softened into 'persuasion' in the following episodes: has the Athenians' realization that recurring stasis is the inevitable default option[100] warmed them to the prospect of Peisistratus' leadership? Aristocratic faction fighting will continue, in Herodotus' account, to characterize Athenian politics even after the final removal of the tyrants: it will be only Cleisthenes' use of the people's support to further his own faction's strength—and on the

---

[99] Cf. ch. 3 n. 21 above.
[100] Note the *stasis* words in relation to Megacles (emboldened above, 152).

model of his tyrant grandfather's practice! (5.67.1)—that will pave the way for democracy at Athens.

And perhaps, as another strand of the narrative has suggested, Peisistratus was not such a bad choice under the circumstances. The *dēmos* granted him a bodyguard only after it had taken into account his virtuous past actions, including his role in taking Nisaea, and the fact that 'he had performed other great deeds' (ἄλλα ἀποδεξάμενος μεγάλα ἔργα, 1.59.4)—and this is high praise, with its implication that his deeds compare with the 'great deeds performed' (ἔργα μεγάλα . . . ἀποδεχθέντα) of Herodotus' own preface. The final glimpse of the Peisistratids at 5.65 will cast events in a different light again, encouraging readers to think back and reflect: for his sinister initial presentation, with ominous signs heralding a rise from obscurity, gives way to an entirely different perspective. Herodotus strikes an almost nostalgic note, delving back into the Peisistratids' illustrious ancestry: their family were descendants of Neleos the king of Pylos, from the same stock as Kodros and Melanthos, kings of Athens—which was why Hippokrates had called his son Peisistratus, to recall (ἀπεμνημόνευσε, 5.65.4) Peisistratus son of Nestor. (The mention of Hippokrates harks back to the earlier tale of Peisistratus' background.) In this light his rise to power comes to seem less inexplicable, as does the fact of his good and constitutional rule—for he has constitutional kingship in his bloodline. The Athenians were perhaps not so very silly after all in allowing themselves to be tricked.[101]

At the very least, Herodotus' account suggests that the desire for 'freedom' as an alternative to tyranny is rather meaningless, if the realization of that desire issues in terrible *stasis* and self-serving aristocratic factionalism.[102] His comment that in their third attempt the Peisistratids received the support of 'those valuing tyranny above freedom' (1.62.1) only underlines the difficulty: the polarity certainly

---

[101] Compare, on a historical level, Connor's reading of the Phye episode as reflecting a communal drama in which Peisistratus enacts his divinely championed return to protect the city, and the sixth-century Athenians—'not naive bumpkins taken in by the leader's manipulation, but participants in a theatricality whose rules and roles they understand and enjoy' (1987, 46)—express their acceptance of his leadership; cf. Sinos (1993); Ferrari (1994/5), 225.

[102] Cf. Fornara and Samons (1991), 14–15, 145–7. The prospect of aristocratic factionalism is one of Darius' arguments against oligarchy (3.82).

stands as an ideal—freedom in Herodotus' mind is altogether superior to tyranny (at least, in the case of the later Athenian democracy, from the perspective of the democracy itself[103])—but these seem not to be the alternatives operating here. The Athenians by and large would prefer to dine and play dice than risk their lives fighting for the meagre sort of 'freedom' that is on offer.[104] Thus in Herodotus' account, rather than 'painful truths' about the tyranny emerging, in Lavelle's words, only 'obliquely and, many times, as a result of imperfect revisions' from beneath the misinformation of the historian's narratives,[105] Herodotus is making a *point* about the paradoxes involved: about the gulf between Alcmaeonid/Athenian revisionist traditions and the reality of motivation at the time. The book-one narrative primes readers to suspect authorial irony when Herodotus later speaks of noble motivation on the Alcmaeonids' part—just as it exposes the ambivalent nature of the Athenians' attitude to their tyrants at that time.

The gulf between noble rhetoric and base reality is indeed a theme that Herodotus presses elsewhere in his *Histories*. But it is not a matter simply of allocating praise and blame (as Plutarch in the *Malice* takes it to be). Rather, Herodotus' emphasis is on demonstrating the inadequacy of simple slogans to do justice to the reality of a complex piece of history and complex motivations, and on engaging readers in thinking about these dilemmas and in bringing together for themselves the contradictory strands. Thus readers may arrive at a reasonably coherent view of the past, one not so much characterized by good/bad contrast. We shall explore further this phenomenon, and Herodotus' approach to the problem of reconciling rhetoric with the reality of people's motives, over the course of the following two chapters.

---

[103] §6.4.5 below considers Herodotus' treatment of the paradox, sharpened by Thucydides, of the connection between democracy at home and tyranny abroad (i.e., freedom *to* . . . ).

[104] The situation will be different, however, by 490 BC: cf. Gray (1997).

[105] Lavelle (1993), 13.

# 6

## 'For freedom's sake …': motivation in the Ionian Revolt (Books V–VI)

### 6.1 ATHENIAN IDEALS: 8.144

The Athenians at 8.144, in the presence of Alexander of Macedon (come to persuade them to medize), deliver a famous speech to the Spartans setting out their motives in refusing to contemplate taking the Persian part. Having underlined to Alexander their devotion to freedom ('we so strive after freedom that we will defend ourselves however we can', 8.143.1), and instructed him to pass on to Mardonios a similar message ('as long as the sun keeps to its present course, we will never make terms with Xerxes…', 8.143.2), they turn to addressing the Spartan ambassadors. It is shameful, they say, for the Spartans—knowing the Athenian temperament—even to fear that they would do such a thing,

ὅτι οὔτε χρυσός ἐστι γῆς οὐδαμόθι τοσοῦτος οὔτε χώρη κάλλεϊ καὶ ἀρετῇ μέγα ὑπερφέρουσα, τὰ ἡμεῖς δεξάμενοι ἐθέλοιμεν ἂν μηδίσαντες καταδουλῶσαι τὴν Ἑλλάδα. πολλά τε γὰρ καὶ μεγάλα ἐστὶ τὰ διακωλύοντα ταῦτα μὴ ποιέειν μηδ' ἢν ἐθέλωμεν, πρῶτα μὲν καὶ μέγιστα τῶν θεῶν τὰ ἀγάλματα καὶ τὰ οἰκήματα ἐμπεπρησμένα τε καὶ συγκεχωσμένα, τοῖσι ἡμέας ἀναγκαίως ἔχει τιμωρέειν ἐς τὰ μέγιστα μᾶλλον ἤ περ ὁμολογέειν τῷ ταῦτα ἐργασαμένῳ, αὖτις δὲ τὸ Ἑλληνικόν, ἐὸν ὅμαιμόν τε καὶ ὁμόγλωσσον, καὶ θεῶν ἱδρύματά τε κοινὰ καὶ θυσίαι ἤθεά τε ὁμότροπα, τῶν προδότας γενέσθαι Ἀθηναίους οὐκ ἂν εὖ ἔχοι (8.144.1–2).

for there is not anywhere in the world a large enough quantity of gold, nor a country so exceptional in its beauty and fertility, that we would accept it in return for medizing and enslaving Greece. Many and great are the things that would prevent us from so doing, even should we wish to. First and most important are the statues and temples of our gods, which have been burned and demolished: on this account we are compelled to exact retribution to the greatest degree, rather than make terms with the one who carried out such actions. Next, there is the fact of our Greek identity (*to Hellēnikon*): our sharing the same blood and the same language, and having temples of the gods and sacrifices in common, and shared customs. It would not be good for the Athenians to become traitors of all of this.

This is a powerful speech indeed, one that—along with Demaratus' on the Spartans' devotion to freedom under the law (7.104), or the Spartan ambassadors' assertion that the taste of freedom causes a man to fight for it to the bitter end (7.135.3)—has influenced many readers of the *Histories* to find in the Greeks' commitment to the (twinned) ideals of freedom and Greek identity (*to Hellēnikon*) the primary explanation for their success in the Persian Wars.[1]

The Athenians' speech represents a dramatic and memorable highpoint of the *Histories*: it occurs soon after the account of Salamis, in which the Athenians have played a decisive role, and which Herodotus introduced with his opinion (expressed proleptically at 7.139) that the outcome of the Persian Wars hinged wholly on this choice faced by the Athenians as to whether to take the Persian part. But readers recalling earlier dimensions of the work are unlikely to accept unreservedly the Athenians' sentiments, ignoring their rhetorical aspect, since the prior narrative has scrutinized with scepticism the likelihood that such

---

[1] Cf., for a recent example, Duff (2003), 19–21, esp. 20: 'If the Greeks could beat the Persians, though overwhelmingly outnumbered what made them so special?... [B]y describing cultures so different to the Greeks, Herodotos gives to his readers a reverse image of what they themselves are, a standard against which to measure themselves. The Persians, once they have achieved their conquests, are luxury-loving and all, even the greatest of them, are slaves to a single master. The Greeks by contrast are, in Herodotos' ideal projection, frugal, the hard products of a hard, unforgiving land; they serve no master but law itself'. Many scholars and textbooks accept the Athenians' words at face value, e.g. Walbank (2002): 'These are clear, unambiguous words—common blood, common tongue, common religion, and a common way of life' (249). But note Macan's more careful formulation (on 8.144.14): 'under each of the four great tests, or factors, of Hellenism here propounded, history has significant exceptions and contrary instances to notice. Blood, Dialect, Religion, Ethos, were dividing lines'; cf. Stadter (2006), 249: the Athenians' vision is utopian. See also Thomas (2000), 121–2: Herodotus' declaration about Athenians not speaking Greek (1.57.3) suggests irony in such a claim of Hellenism based on language; and (2001), 213–15, locating the appeal to τὸ Ἑλληνικόν in the context of flexible and politically motivated definitions of Hellenism. Cf. more generally Malkin (2001) for definitions of Hellenism as inevitably contentious.

abstract ideals should function as genuinely motivating forces. The relative status of noble and altruistic versus more egotistical motives in explaining the behaviour under various circumstances of individuals and states has been subjected to constant and often explicit interrogation. More often than not, abstract concepts have come to seem relevant only on the level of rhetoric; or they have featured in close company with more pragmatic and immediate concerns. There seems some substance, in fact, to Plutarch's objection to the way praise in the *Histories* of certain people's actions and intentions can serve to highlight the *less* honourable nature of others';[2] perhaps even to the further objection that in the *Histories* malice (*to kakoēthes*) (in mirror opposition to the practice of flatterers) 'throws out some advance praise so as to heighten belief in its criticisms' (εἰς πίστιν ὧν ψέγει προαποτίθεται τὸν ἔπαινον, 856c–d; cf. 11 above). Herodotus has led readers by example in tending to disbelieve easily made claims of noble motives, and—in cases where intentions (as often) remained unclear—to assume the worst. Plutarch's complaint in this regard (855 f–856b; cf. §1.2.2 above) is founded upon observation of what is indeed a pronounced feature of Herodotean historiography, even if its *raison d'être* is not what he supposes: Herodotus' own jealousy (*phthonos*) and malice (*kakoētheia*).

Specifically, the Athenians' expression of resolute commitment to the particular ideals they espouse at 8.144 stands in surprising contrast to various aspects of Athens' earlier history as described by Herodotus, as also to the apparent volte-face readers are soon to confront when they threaten medism at 9.11.1–2,[3] and to the role (all too familiar to the *Histories*' contemporary audience) that she would play in the later years of the fifth century. The ironies that emerge over the course of Herodotus' narrative in connection with freedom and democracy and Greek unity no doubt struck a particular chord with all those living under the Athenian Empire and at the beginning of the Peloponnesian War.

The foregoing discussion has considered in general terms the status of ascriptions of principled or ideal motivation in the *Histories* (§5.1.3 and §5.2). This chapter will focus on the two specific motives (beyond the broad desire for vengeance in the name of the gods:

---

[2] *Malice* 864a–b on the Athenians as saviours; 869a–c on the praise of Demokritos.
[3] See §7.5.

8.144.2) that are claimed by the Athenians at 8.144, particularly in the context of their treatment in the Ionian Revolt narrative. The aim, over the course of this chapter and the next, is to illuminate Herodotean strategy in this and in other such instances where more pragmatic readings of motivation are introduced that challenge the ideal interpretation championed in the rhetoric. We may well find a textual explanation—perhaps even a 'motive' on the historian's part—other than the *kakoētheia* posited by Plutarch.

## 6.2 THE IONIAN REVOLT

As an earlier bid on the part of Greeks acting in unison for 'freedom from tyranny', and one that foreshadowed in several respects the main Persian Wars campaign as well as being causally connected to it, the Ionian Revolt no doubt struck Herodotus as a useful site for exploring the sorts of factors that motivate people in taking such an action— particularly one that in retrospect seemed not to have been worth it. His account of the revolt is closely allied to the later narrative, and predisposes readers' responses to the motives that will there be uncovered or alleged. Aristagoras' arrival at Sparta and then at Athens provides the occasion for expressive analepses recounting the early Spartan colonizing expeditions to Libya and Sicily, in connection with Dorieus' inability to endure losing regent status,[4] and the story—held back until this point—of how Athens was freed from her tyranny. Herodotus thus skilfully suggests connections on several levels, encouraging readers to compare the situations and motives at work in each of these bids to remove tyranny: the Athenians' bid in ousting Peisistratid tyranny, the Ionians' bid in ousting Persian tyranny, and the Greek *poleis'* bid in ousting the Persian tyrant and (implied) the new tyrant—Athens, the tyrant city itself. In doing so he engages readers in confronting the problem of how ideal motives—those so commonly espoused in the rhetoric—interact with motives that seem more pragmatic and self-serving. The Ionian Revolt narrative may thus prove a useful touchstone for evaluating the Athenians' sentiments at 8.144.

---

[4] Hornblower (2004), 306 n. 55 (with text) underlines how very closely this account is intertwined with the wider revolt narrative.

The account of this first stage of Greek resistance to Persia sets the scene for readers' understanding of the factors most likely to be at work in the later Persian campaign. Commentators have frequently underlined the importance of the revolt in the structure of the *Histories*,[5] though generally it is the *contrast* between it and the later Greek defence that is lent most emphasis. It is certainly the case, as Dewald writes, that

the implications of the story H[erodotus] tells here—the consequences of disorganization and treachery, seen in the ruthless punishment Persians mete out afterwards to rebels—help organize our readerly perception of what the Greeks do right later and how acute the danger facing them in 481 BCE really was.[6]

Modern accounts have sought to explain Herodotus' apparently more idealistic view of the later defence. Murray notes the differences between oral narratives of defeat versus those of victory.[7] Stadter views the Samian revolt (440 BC and following) as a key factor influencing Herodotus' negative presentation of the Ionian Revolt.[8] Mitchell suggests that Samian sources, hostile to their rival Milesians, underlie the Ionian account.[9] And yet this characterization of the *Histories* has perhaps been overstated. There are many points of contact between the two accounts, and the later defence as presented by Herodotus constantly appears at risk of falling into the same Ionian pattern: the difference in its outcome was indeed 'only just', in large part because the very same motivational dynamics were at

[5] e.g. Fowler (2003), esp. 315.

[6] Dewald *Comm.* on 5.30–6.33.

[7] 'The Persian Wars themselves were a story of co-operative effort (however imperfect) and success; the tale had a natural coherence which could only improve with time, as for later Greeks it became a symbol of a national identity and a lost unity. Inevitably the tradition presented the action as more coherent and the Greeks as more united than they actually were, and local variants disappeared. The oral traditions of a defeated people behave quite differently from those of a victorious one. No unity presents itself, memory is fragmented into individual episodes of folly, treachery or heroism; self-justification and accusation become primary reasons for remembrance', Murray (1988), 471. Cf. Lang (1968): failure of the revolt accentuated elements explaining failure, rather than positive traditions.

[8] Stadter (1992), 802–8.

[9] Mitchell (1975), 88–91. But note Thomas' (2004) recent emphasis on the extremely varied nature of the oral traditions of the revolt with which Herodotus was working, including East Greek accounts underlining Ionian resistance and courage.

play. One difference perhaps is that in the later defence Greek *communities* have generally appropriated the self-serving role that in the Ionian narrative was more a prerogative of *individuals*.[10] In Herodotus' conception, states do by and large appear to be motivated similarly to individuals. Even when crowd psychology takes over and 30,000 are more easily persuaded than one (5.97.2), that psychology seems simply to accentuate aspects of individual psychology: Aristagoras' wild evocations of *kerdos* become even more irresistible.

## 6.2.1 Dorieus and Theras (5.42–8; 4.147–65)

The tale of Dorieus, being closely entwined (as noted above) with the Ionian Revolt narrative, gives a preliminary indication of the sorts of motives that can be expected to be in play. Where the digression on the Peisistratid tyranny at Athens emphasized that the choices open to people may be severely circumscribed, and include little possibility of action in accordance with idealist principles,[11] the Spartan story implies that less ideal motives may be extremely influential. Particularly expressive is the way the story of Dorieus links back to a previous narrative of early Spartan history (much as later Athenian history is intertwined with the Pelasgian sequence[12]), a narrative whose primal nature perhaps renders it similarly revelatory of Spartan character as the Pelasgian digression was of Athenian.

At the prospect of Cleomenes' becoming king in his place, Dorieus, 'considering it a terrible thing (δεινόν . . . ποιεύμενος), and refusing to be ruled (οὐκ ἀξιῶν . . . βασιλεύεσθαι) by Cleomenes' (5.42.2), heads the Spartan colonizing expedition to Libya (later redirected to Sicily)— with men of *Thera* to guide him. It is a 'most beautiful land' (*chōron*

---

[10] I am speaking of *Herodotus'* emphasis on individuals (which again exposes his particular interest in human psychology on the personal level; cf. Huber (1965a), 166–73); modern scholars find different explanations for the historical revolt, on which see esp. Tozzi (1978); Lateiner (1982); Murray (1988); and most recently Scott (2005), 37–73. Thomas (2004) views the emphasis on the individual instigators as arising from traditions seeking to explain the revolt's failure. But Forrest (1979) warns against downplaying Herodotus' emphasis ('Herodotos was writing of, if not in, a period when individuals did matter more than historians now think they matter or mattered at any time', 313).
[11] Above, §5.4.
[12] Above, ch. 5 n. 65 with text.

*kalliston*) that he chooses first to settle (5.42.3). In the earlier Minyan tale, Theras—who had been regent in Sparta until his nephews were old enough to rule—likewise 'considering it a terrible thing to be ruled (δεινὸν ποιεύμενος ἄρχεσθαι) by others, once he had tasted rule (ἐπείτε ἐγεύσατο ἀρχῆς), said that he would not remain in Lacedaemon but would sail away to his relatives' (4.147.3): to Thera, which until this point had been named Kallistē ('Most beautiful (land)', 4.147.4).[13] He presumably becomes king, as his descendant Grinnos does (4.150.2). Herodotus observes that Kadmos had earlier put in at Thera—'either because the land pleased him (εἴτε δή οἱ ἡ χώρη ἤρεσε), or because for some other reason he desired to do so' (4.147.4)—leaving behind Phoenicians, including Theras' ancestor. At a later point the Minyan Battos is instructed by Delphi to send a colony to Libya. Locals lead these Greeks from their initial settlement to Cyrene by night, 'in order that the Greeks should pass through the most beautiful of their lands (τὸν κάλλιστον τῶν χώρων)'—Irasa, Herodotus specifies—'without seeing it' (4.158.2): for they might be expected then to desire to claim it for themselves. Subsequently more Greeks arrive, and seize from the locals 'much land' (γῆν πολλήν, 4.159.4). A battle ensues, in which the Cyreneans defeat Libyans and Egyptians, and so claim Irasa after all (4.159.5). The story's postscript recounts the wrangling for kingship and vengeance that marks the succeeding generations of Battoses and Arkesileoses, ending with Pheretime's invitation to the Persian satrap of Egypt to help her gain vengeance on the people of Barca for her son Arkesileos' assassination (4.165).

The tales of Dorieus and Theras foreground the twin desires for personal power and beautiful land as motivating forces potent enough to determine Spartan action. Thera's ancient name, Kallistē, lends her the symbolic status of archetypal target of conquest. The promise of *kalē chōrē* (beautiful land) and *archē* (power) continually resurfaces in the *Histories* as a powerful temptation (including and especially in Mardonios' speech at 7.9). It is powerful enough, in-deed, to override a community's or individual's initial principled intentions, as we shall find in the case of the Samians[14] (who have

---

[13] Theras' expression strikingly mirrors in reverse—and potentially problem-atizes?—the later assertion of the Spartan ambassadors to Hydarnes, 7.135.3.
[14] Below, §6.4.4.

in fact played an important role in the middle of the Theras story, at 4.152). The digression primes readers to sense that the idealist strand of Aristagoras' rhetoric, following on its tail, may not be the one that is most seductive.

## 6.2.2 Aristagoras' persuasive strategies (5.49, 97)

Aristagoras' speeches to Cleomenes and the Athenians, urging them to support the Ionian Revolt, set forth explicitly at the outset what (Herodotus was told by sources or conjectured) Aristagoras expects will prove effective inducements to action: he presents a range of potential motives in the hope that they may be claimed as such by his listeners. He begins his speech to Cleomenes with an appeal to the same pair of ideal motives as the Athenians later claim for themselves, i.e., regarding Greekness and freedom. Irony is directly engendered, for he comes as a tyrant himself,[15] and indeed was earlier depicted trying to persuade the satrap Artaphrenes of Naxos' wealth and prime location as stepping stone for further *Persian* conquest in *Greece*! (5.31). Cleomenes ought not to be surprised at his zeal in coming, Aristagoras asserts,

For the present situation is as follows. That the children of the Ionians should be slaves rather than free (δούλους εἶναι ἀντ' ἐλευθέρων) is a disgrace and the greatest grief for us, but also for you in particular out of the other Greeks, in that you are the champions of Greece (ὅσῳ προέστατε τῆς Ἑλλάδος). Now, then, by the gods of the Greeks (πρὸς θεῶν τῶν Ἑλληνίων), rescue the Ionians—men with whom you share the same blood—from slavery! (ῥύσασθε Ἴωνας ἐκ δουλοσύνης, ἄνδρας ὁμαίμονας) (5.49.2–3).

But from this moment forth, space is devoted instead to extensive evocations of the very two factors that the Athenians at 8.144 will deny could ever entice them to medize—*money* (and other material goods) and *land*—along with an emphasis on the *ease* of the task.[16] When Herodotus comes to briefly recapping this speech, noting that Aristagoras said much the same things to the Athenians, these features

---

[15] Nenci on 5.49.1 notes the negative effect of Herodotus' specification ὁ Μιλήτου τύραννος.

[16] Cf. Solmsen (1943), 199.

alone are mentioned: 'he said the same things as in Sparta, about the good things in Asia (περὶ τῶν ἀγαθῶν τῶν ἐν τῇ Ἀσίῃ) and, on the subject of warfare, that the Persians would be easy to conquer (εὐπετέες . . . χειρωθῆναι) since they used neither shields nor long spears' (5.97.1). This clearly represents the essence of the speech: what Aristagoras expects most likely to persuade. His additional line of argument, tailored to the Athenians, includes what seems an expressive ambiguity inviting readers to reflect again on the ironies inherent in his double motivational strategies: 'He also said the following, that the Milesians were colonists from Athens, and it was *oikos* (right/reasonable) to rescue them, being very powerful (οἰκός σφεας εἴη ῥύεσθαι δυναμένους μέγα)' (5.97.2). A shift thus occurs mid-sentence from the further '(Athenian) Unity' line of the first clause, to the more subversive possibility opened up in the alternative possible reading of the second. That is, *dunamenous mega* ('being very powerful') refers (most naturally) to the Athenians, who being so powerful ought to help out; but it might potentially refer instead to the Milesians, who being so powerful would prove a worthwhile asset for Athens if she helps them out.[17] The suggestion of righteous reasons for joining in with the revolt is in any case overshadowed by the self-serving arguments that follow. Does Aristagoras' talk of ideal motives therefore represent little more than a decorous surface to help disguise a self-interested substance, while also hinting at how his Athenian listeners might portray their action to the wider world? Or is there any sense that they might have some persuasive value in themselves?

Cleomenes is nearly persuaded; the Athenians (ἀναπεισθέντες, 5.97.3) are completely. The Spartan king's decision hinges on his concern for Spartan interests and security: he refuses to lead his army so far from the sea; and it is presumably for equally self-regarding reasons that Athens belatedly extricates herself from the war (at 5.103.1, once the Ionians have been caught by the Persians at Ephesus and severely defeated), no doubt regretting having risked her safety over what was clearly *not* after all going to be an easy task. Other *poleis* likewise join in the revolt only once success seems assured. The

---

[17] Godley's translation captures the ambiguity: '(Aristagoras added) that the Milesians were settlers from Athens, and it was but right to save them, being a very wealthy people.'

Ionians' capture of Sardis, in particular, persuades many that this is so[18]—ironically, since Herodotus' account indicates that this impression of strength was misleading. The sack was more a matter of chance, and an incident not followed up; indeed, the allies fled at the first sign of Persian resistance (5.101.3). Thus in no respect was this freedom drive on the part of the Ionian cities *unconditional*: there was always an equation to be made as to whether it would be worth it in the end—and wholly understandably, considering the fate of such a city as Miletus (6.18–20). The revolt gained momentum through a deceptive appeal to the self-interest of a larger city— Athens—whose involvement gave other smaller and more vulnerable states the impression that the venture would be worth the risk, but who, unlike them, was in a position to remove herself from the proceedings when the situation degenerated. By contrast, as Herodotus underlines, the Ionian states did not have that option:

μετὰ δὲ Ἀθηναῖοι μὲν τὸ παράπαν ἀπολιπόντες τοὺς Ἴωνας ἐπικαλεομένου σφέας πολλὰ δι' ἀγγέλων Ἀρισταγόρεω οὐκ ἔφασαν τιμωρήσειν σφι.[19] Ἴωνες δὲ τῆς Ἀθηναίων συμμαχίης στερηθέντες (οὕτω γάρ σφι ὑπῆρχε πεποιημένα ἐς Δαρεῖον) οὐδὲν δὴ ἧσσον τὸν πρὸς βασιλέα πόλεμον ἐσκευάζοντο (5.103.1).

Afterwards **the Athenians, on the one hand**, entirely abandoned the Ionians and refused to lend them assistance (although Aristagoras called on them to do so many times through messengers). **The Ionians, on the other hand**, although deprived of the Athenians' support, kept on making ready for war against the King: for they were already so far implicated in what had been done to Darius.

(The mention of Aristagoras recalls his earlier deceptive argumentation.[20]) These circumstances may go some way towards explaining Herodotus' negative attitude towards the Ionian Revolt generally, which has surprised many commentators in an author 'usually so favourable to such aspirations'.[21] Herodotus was perhaps struck by

[18] Cf. e.g. 'even Kaunos', 5.103.2.

[19] Following Hude, Stein, Legrand, Nenci. Rosén's reading, ἐπικαλεομένους ... σφίσι ('although the Ionians called on them to do so . . .'), seems to me to diminish the contrast.

[20] Note too how he, like Athens, bowed out safely at 5.99.2, choosing to remain at Miletus rather than advancing with the army.

[21] Murray (1988), 474, finding an explanation in the ambivalent connotations of *isonomiē* for mid fifth-century Ionians (including Herodotus). Solmsen (1943) represents an exception (cf. e.g. 204: 'the revolt was in [Herodotus'] opinion not an admirable fight for liberty but an unfortunate and ill-judged undertaking').

the irony that whereas the cities on the whole entered into it frankly with their own security as a top priority, rather than in (genuine, or even pretended) deference to idealist principles, their calculations were based on misleading perceptions and so mistaken. Athens' 'sending of ships' was an *archē kakōn* ('beginning of evils', 5.97.3) not only in that it would provide Darius with a useful pretext for extending the reach of his campaign, but also in offering a misleading gesture to the Greeks of Ionia, one that implied a degree of Athenian support which would not eventuate.

Thus we discover ironies on two fronts, in *Aristagoras'* use of such rhetoric, though he has no loyalty whatsoever for Greece: we know that his every action has been *entirely* self-serving, and that he lacks any commitment to either of these ideals; and in how Athens and Sparta, as well as most of the Ionian cities, seem to respond to his rhetoric only in so far as it appears to be in their own interests. The fact that 'Freedom' and 'Greek Unity' should be made use of so persuasively by such a cynical and self-serving individual—who has no concern at all for Ionian wellbeing, as Herodotus emphasizes in his pointed comment concerning Aristagoras' motives in coming up with the plan of encouraging the Paeonians to return to Ionia (5.98.1: 'he came up with a plan from which no benefit at all would come to the Ionians—nor, indeed, was that his purpose in adopting it, but rather that he might vex King Darius')—arouses suspicion as to whether we may expect to read other such statements of ideal motives straightforwardly either. Moreover, we have already seen Aristagoras using very similar lines of argument—emphasizing ease and money—in his speech to Artaphrenes pressing the allurements of conquest in *Greece* (cf. above, 167).[22]

And yet while Aristagoras' rhetorical strategies are obviously disingenuous, and his listeners' responses seem transparently self-serving, similar rhetorical appeals in the mouths of others—like Miltiades' urging Kallimachos to vote for battle at Marathon—are not so easy to read. That appeal is to the twin prospects (to be embraced by his listener as motives) of Kallimachos' freeing Athens and—more egotistically—of 'leaving behind for all future generations a memorial such as not even

---

[22] Solmsen (1943) observes the conspicuous and expressive similarities between these two speeches.

Harmodios and Aristogeiton left' (6.109.3): Kallimachos may himself expect to be mythologized epic hero-/ tyrannicide-[23]/ Herodotean-style! The narrative of the aftermath, however—where Kallimachos, unnamed (now described simply as ὁ πολέμαρχος, 'the War Archon'), is slain alongside 'many other famous Athenians' (6.114)[24]—shifts the reader's focus to the selflessness of the outcome rather than the partly self-regarding motives to which Miltiades had appealed.

We now turn to focus more closely on Herodotus' treatment of the two most prominent of ideal motives claimed by Greeks in the *Histories*, in the work as a whole, but particularly from the point at which he turns his focus to the Greek world at 5.28. We shall consider to what extent the broader narrative implies that they might in truth be operative forces. That in turn will provide a base from which to evaluate (in the following chapter) the *Histories'* presentation of the motives of the Greek *poleis* in determining to medize or not in the face of Xerxes' advance, and particularly the Athenians' speech at 8.144.

## 6.3 GREEK UNITY?

So far from regularly finding in the *Histories* sketches of Greeks moved to behave in a certain way by their commitment to an idea of Greek unity—or even the emergence of this as a less obvious theme, even as a principle within the narrative—throughout the work there is in fact a preponderance of the opposite attributes of *phthonos* (jealousy) and *echthrē* (hatred), especially between Greeks. Most notorious (but also representative) is Herodotus' explanation for the Phocians' not medizing:

οἱ ... Φωκέες μοῦνοι τῶν ταύτῃ ἀνθρώπων οὐκ ἐμήδιζον, κατ' ἄλλο μὲν οὐδέν, ὡς ἐγὼ συμβαλλόμενος εὑρίσκω, κατὰ δὲ τὸ ἔχθος τὸ Θεσσαλῶν. εἰ δὲ Θεσσαλοὶ τὰ Ἑλλήνων ηὖξον, ὡς ἐμοὶ δοκέειν, ἐμήδιζον ἂν οἱ Φωκέες (8.30).

---

[23] This appeal may be expected to be especially effective since Kallimachos came from the tyrannicides' deme, Aphidna: 5.55; cf. Dewald *Comm.* on 6.109. The extraordinary material rewards given the tyrannicides' descendants, quite apart from the fame, will have made the possibility all the more seductive in the eyes of Herodotus' readers.

[24] See Loraux (1986), esp. 278, for the emphasis in Classical Athenian ideology on the anonymity of death in hoplite battle.

The Phocians alone of the people of that region did not medize, for no other reason, as I find through conjecturing [/as I suppose and conclude], than their hatred of the Thessalians. And if the Thessalians had supported the Greek campaign, it seems to me that the Phocians would have medized.

Herodotus thus lays emphasis on motivational principles that run completely counter to the possibility of commitment to Greek unity being an effective determinant of action. Indeed his whole project frequently appears on the brink of fragmentation, at every level, as Greek conflicts threaten to appropriate the space set aside in his preface for exploring the *aitiē* of the Greeks' war with the *barbaroi*. From the moment when his focus (in step with the Persian advance) turns to Greece—with the account of the beginnings of the Ionian revolt, but even more so with that of the lead up to Darius' and then Xerxes' mainland Greece campaigns (6.46 ff.)—his project threatens to transform into the Thucydidean (late fifth-century) one: a narrative of inter-Greek wars. On a structural level, the overarching Greek-Persian framework of the *Histories* is constantly challenged by the Greek-versus-Greek, *polis*-versus-*polis* reality he depicts, whose conflict is mirrored in his conflicting sources.[25]

Whereas the Ionian Revolt narrative (to which we return below[26]) was largely a story of individuals' willingness to betray their own communities in the hope of personal profit from the Great King, the lead-up to the later campaigns is more frequently marked by the conflicts between whole communities. (There remains room for individuals, and for individuals interacting with communities; but we have moved along the spectrum nonetheless in the direction of the community.) Such conflicts risk driving one party to turn outside Greece for assistance. This changed texture is foreshadowed by the surprising postscript to the Ionian Revolt, when Herodotus notes how Persian hostilities were replaced by 'extremely beneficial developments (χρήσιμα κάρτα) for the Ionians':

---

[25] Munson (2001), 218–31 develops this parallel between Herodotus' depiction (in the 'narrative') of instances of historical *stasis* between the Greek states, and his inclusion (in the 'metanarrative') of conflicting traditions ('verbal and ideological quarrels' (231) between his informants, i.e. the descendants of those involved)—by means of which Herodotus points to continuity with contemporary (late fifth-century) military conflicts. See also ch. 9 n. 16 below on the motif of Greek disunity.

[26] At §6.4.2.

Artaphrenes the governor of Sardis summoned messengers from the cities and compelled the Ionians to negotiate agreements among themselves, in order that they would submit to arbitration rather than raiding and plundering each other. . . . And these measures encouraged peace for the Ionians (καὶ σφι ταῦτα μὲν εἰρηναῖα ἦν) (6.42–43.1).[27]

On show even more strongly from this moment, so far from expression of commitment to any abstract notion of *to Hellēnikon*, are demonstrations of disloyalty (slanders, accusations, betrayals) proliferating on all levels. In the year after Mardonios' brief and abortive first mission against Eretria and Athens (6.43–5), Darius takes charge, his first reported act being to send an order of compliance to the Thasians 'who had been falsely informed against by their neighbours (διαβληθέντας ὑπὸ τῶν ἀστυγειτόνων) on the grounds of planning revolt' (6.46.1). Next he demands earth and water of the Greek cities so as to learn what they intend: whether to make war against him, or to surrender (6.48.1). Most of the mainlanders oblige, and all of the islanders—including in particular the Aeginetans, who thereby appear to the Athenians

to have given [earth and water] out of enmity to themselves (ἐπὶ σφίσι ἔχοντας . . . δεδωκέναι), in order that together with the Persian they might campaign against them (ὡς ἅμα τῷ Πέρσῃ ἐπὶ σφέας στρατεύωνται) (6.49.2).

Gladly seizing upon this *prophasis*, the Athenians accuse the Aeginetans at Sparta of being traitors to Hellas (6.49.2); and from this point until 6.94 the narrative is structured around this trunk story line of Cleomenes' visit to Aegina and attempt to prevent the Aeginetans from medizing.

This stretch of narrative dramatizes Greek *diaphorē* (division, conflict) on the level both of the *polis*, in Athens' quarrel with Aegina, which is given extensive narrative coverage, and of the *oikos* (family), in the rivalry of Cleomenes and Demaratus.[28] To turn to the latter, the Spartans' account of the history of their dual kingship finds the origins

---

[27] Cf. the authorial comment at 8.3.1: στάσις . . . ἔμφυλος πολέμου ὁμοφρονέοντος τοσούτῳ κάκιόν ἐστι ὅσῳ πόλεμος εἰρήνης ('civil strife is worse than united war to the same degree as war is worse than peace'). Thomas (2004), 38 observes the puzzling aspect of this 'rather generous settlement of Ionia' on the heels of narratives recounting the destruction of Ionian cities, netting of islands, etc.

[28] See Boedeker (1987) on duality and division in this and other stories of Demaratus.

of its discord in the sons of Aristodemos and Argeia, who were constantly at feud (διαφόρους, 6.52.8). Their mention of Argeia's descent from Polyneices (6.52.2) conjures up the brothers of myth who destroyed their family and city through conflict. The tale underscores the strength of the hostility between Cleomenes and Demaratus, but also implies that the blood relation only makes the enmity stronger. Indeed, so far from being moved by thoughts for the best interests of Greece, Demaratus acts simply out of jealousy and malice towards his fellow king:

> Demaratus slandered Cleomenes, who was in Aegina and working on behalf of Greece at achieving collective benefits (κοινὰ τῇ Ἑλλάδι ἀγαθὰ προεργαζόμενον). Demaratus did this not so much out of care for the Aeginetans, as out of envy and malice (οὐκ Αἰγινητέων οὕτω κηδόμενος ὡς φθόνῳ καὶ ἄγῃ χρεώμενος) (6.61.1).

Thus an alternative possibility, that he might have been motivated by (positive) care for Aegina, is carefully closed down. These strong emotions, reminiscent of the 'strong personal hatreds' (ἔχθεα ἴδια ἰσχυρά) Darius saw operating in oligarchies (only Demaratus is not even working ἐς τὸ κοινόν, 'for the common (good)', 3.82.3), override any other potential concerns, including for the good of Greece: Demaratus goes so far as actively to lend advice to Krios the Aeginetan, much as later he will advise Xerxes, after being turned against Sparta (cf. 7.239.2) by his exile.

We might well recall Otanes' bleak formulation, according to which φθόνος ... ἀρχῆθεν ἐμφύεται ἀνθρώπῳ ('jealousy (*phthonos*) is ingrained in human nature', 3.80.3)—particularly since Herodotus has chosen to include at this point an ethnography of Spartan kingship that makes several specific comparisons with the Persian (6.56–60). In the case specifically of a man—even the best of men—holding absolute power, that circumstance simply increases his *hybris* and also (so far from lessening it: cf. 3.80.4) his *phthonos*; and 'in having these two things, he possesses every evil (πᾶσαν κακότητα): for through being sated with *hybris* on the one hand, and with *phthonos* on the other, he commits many acts of savage violence' (3.80.4). Achaimenes at a later point expresses his fear that Demaratus, in advising Xerxes, 'is jealous at your success (φθονέει τοι εὖ πρήσσοντι) or even a traitor to your cause (προδιδοῖ πρήγματα τὰ σά)'; such behaviour, in his view, is particularly characteristic of Greeks ('the Greeks relish such ways as these: they are jealous of success (τοῦ... εὐτυχέειν φθονέουσι) and hate what is stronger (τὸ κρέσσον στυγέουσι)', 7.236.1). The motif of *phthonos* overriding the interests of Greece surfaces elsewhere, for example in relation to the Athenians' achievement in the Persian Wars and to Themistocles' at Salamis. So far from celebrating the Athenians, as does Herodotus, as 'saviours of Greece' (7.139.5), such a notion, the historian says, would be invidious (ἐπίφθονος) to most (Greeks); while the *stratēgoi* at Salamis each claim the *aristeia* for themselves, though mostly allotting Themistocles second place, and out of jealousy (φθόνῳ) the Greeks refuse to pass judgement on the question of who really deserves it (8.124.1). Themistocles turns to Sparta for acknowledgment ('since despite winning the vote he had not been honoured by those who fought at Salamis' (8.124.2): doubtless largely Athenians, who represented a considerable proportion of those who fought: 8.1.1). Readers might wonder whether the lack of adequate recognition at home played a part in his later defection to Persia. Timodemos' nasty accusation, made in jealousy (φθόνῳ, 8.125.1), upon Themistocles' return from Sparta to Athens, presses yet again the same theme.

Consequently, even if Greeks are indeed ὁμαίμονες ('sharing the same blood')[29] in accordance with the Athenians' definition of *to Hellēnikon* (8.144.2), it does not follow that they will be moved by a sense of loyalty to fellow countrymen or to a more abstract notion of common identity. Even an *ancestral* or even more intimate *fraternal* blood tie is no guarantee of that, but may rather have a reverse effect, arousing hatreds and jealousies that are all the more intense.

This picture tends to corroborate the model Xerxes sets forth, in defence of Demaratus' good intentions towards himself and qualifying Achaimenes' model as applying to Greeks *at home*, according to which people feel more warmly towards those at a distance from them:

A citizen is jealous of a successful fellow citizen and shows his hostility in silence (πολιήτης μὲν πολιήτῃ εὖ πρήσσοντι φθονέει καὶ ἔστι δυσμενὴς τῇ σιγῇ), and even if his own townsman should ask his advice he would not

---

[29] Cf. 5.49 (Ionians kinfolk of Athenians); 1.151 (Lesbians enslaved by their kinfolk!). However, Herodotus' first book to some extent challenged this notion, as does 6.53, tracing Dorians back to Egyptians.

give what seemed to him the best advice.... A *xeinos* [foreigner/guest-friend], on the other hand, is most well disposed of all people to a successful *xeinos* (ξεῖνος δὲ ξείνῳ εὖ πρήσσοντί ἐστι εὐμενέστατον πάντων), and if the latter should ask his advice he would give the very best. (7.237.2–3)[30]

Demaratus himself provides an exemplum of this, for he gives the Great King greater benefit through his advice[31] than he ever gave back in Sparta, where instead he was preoccupied with jealousy of his fellow king. Further proof again is felt in the change in his perspective on Greece that comes about from afar, turning rose-tinted, as in his powerful speech to Xerxes on Greek and Spartan devotion to freedom: 'through *aretē* (valour) Greece defends herself from poverty and despotism' (7.102.1); and as for the Spartans, 'it is not possible that they should ever accept proposals from you that bring slavery upon Greece...' (7.102.2). His own commitment to freedom was not a great priority while he remained at home in Sparta, as was evident in his undermining Cleomenes' efforts against those who were threatening Greek freedom by medizing.[32] Moreover, we are invited to draw this parallel between Spartan ex-king and Spartiate citizens by the like parallel drawn by Xerxes (7.103.1–2) in response to Demaratus' speech. Demaratus' newfound concern from a distance (despite his defensive claim to Xerxes at 7.104.2: 'you know what love I bear them...') perhaps explains his warning Sparta of Xerxes' resolve (7.239)[33]—which Herodotus provokes readers to ponder carefully through his inclusion of alternative possible motives.

Throughout the *Histories* we continue to find examples of individuals willing to court the favour of or even actively aid distant foreigners, thus harming their own country, if there is a prospect of gaining vengeance upon a close enemy (as in Demaratus' case regarding Aegina)—for Herodotus' world was distant from the one Plutarch imagined in scoffing at the 'silliness of mutual enmities'

[30] This suggests an odd parallel with Thucydides' Pericles at 2.45.1 on how there is no *phthonos* of the dead because they are removed from one's path; so only *eunoia* (good will).

[31] Esp. at 7.235.

[32] Compare how the account of Greeks at the Olympics contending for crowns (∼ *aretē*) rather than material gain is found on the lips of Arcadian *deserters* seeking (financial) betterment of their situation in Xerxes' employ!

[33] The chapter is regarded by many as an interpolation; it is retained by e.g. Stein (with the exception of the first sentence), Legrand, Hude, Rosén.

(868e)³⁴—or profit in the form of power or money. The Paeonian brothers, for example, 'wishing to rule as tyrants over the Paeonians' (αὐτοὶ ἐθέλοντες Παιόνων τυραννεύειν, 5.12.1), are willing to subject the Paeonian population to a forced migration and Persian rule, to which end they stage the show at Sardis with their sister that attracts Darius' attention. This conduct feeds into patterns throughout the *Histories* of people betraying their cities in the hope of personal gain: at any moment, the King can rely on individuals willing to play the traitor in the expectation of marvellous recompense.³⁵ Likewise factions within Greek states commonly betray them to Greek outsiders, as the democratic Aeginetans led by Nikodromos, for instance, seek military assistance from the Athenians (6.88–91). Treachery is what most often causes cities to fall.

A further pervasive pattern is that of Greeks actively *attracting the attention* of the Persian invader. There is a strong sense in the lead-up to the Marathon narrative that the rest of Greece reads Athens' behaviour in these terms. Like the Scythians' neighbours as regards the parallel Scythian request for assistance (4.119), they prefer to distance themselves from the notion that the *whole* nation is in this together (and thus should support Athens at Marathon), since in their view she has brought Darius' ire upon herself. And to some extent this perspective gains textual support. It was Athens that turned Darius' attention to regions west of the Hellespont when she sent her twenty ships to help the Ionians (even if their participation was ultimately of limited value, and it was as a *prophasis* (excuse) that Darius exploited it). Much is made in Herodotus' account of Athens' responsibility, with Artaphrenes and then Darius asking who the Athenians are, followed by the memorable anecdote of Darius vowing revenge and asking to be reminded of the Athenians at his every meal (5.105; cf. 6.94.1). But

---

³⁴ The prevalence of *phthonos* (jealousy) as a motive predisposes readers to favour the view, which the narrator makes what seems an ironic show of rejecting (cf. §1.4), that the Alcmaeonids τι ἐπιμεμφόμενοι Ἀθηναίων τῷ δήμῳ προεδίδοσαν τὴν πατρίδα ('betrayed their native land **because they bore some grudge against** the Athenian people', 6.124.1). Harrison (2003) suggests that 'Envy... is arguably for Herodotus the primary motor of historical action' (157). Marincola (1994) observes that Herodotus probably *did* seem to Plutarch 'the dissonant voice' among (eulogizing) local historians—whom Plutarch probably assumed to have *preceded* Herodotus—'with his narrative of inter-state rivalries and jealousies' (202).
³⁵ The wider pattern includes figures like Alcmaeon (6.125).

the most dramatic instance of 'Greeks attracting/inviting the foreign invader' is perhaps the one that remains hypothetical: the allegation that Argos *invited* Xerxes into Greece following her defeat at Sparta's hands at Sepeia (7.152.3, discussed below, §7.2.1).[36] This sense that some Greeks would prefer to distance themselves altogether from appeals to Greek unity vis-à-vis the Persian threat makes all the more problematic the idealizing 'unity' rhetoric.

## 6.4 FREEDOM?

Thus patterns in Herodotus' text work against the possibility that the idea of *to Hellēnikon* should prove a powerful motive. In similar vein, the *Histories* foregrounds patterns and principles that fly in the face of the likelihood (or possibility) that individuals and communities should be genuinely motivated by abstract and noble concerns with 'freedom', as the Athenians claim to be at 8.144. If it is true that Herodotus understands the desire for freedom (for oneself and one's community) to be a basic force at play in communities,[37] his text also underlines the equally dominant counter-principle, that states and individuals are driven above all by their desire for *power* (over others). We have this formulated most strikingly on the Persian side, in the '*nomos* of expansion', but it is equally pervasive and visible on the Greek, most notably perhaps, for contemporary readers, in the way in which the *Histories* at its end recalls Athens' move to replace the Persian empire with her own.[38] Herodotus observes that evils (κακά) came to Greece in the three generations of Darius, Xerxes, and his son Artaxerxes, 'some coming from the Persians, but others coming from their own leading states warring **about power** (ἀπ' αὐτῶν τῶν κορυφαίων περὶ τῆς ἀρχῆς πολεμεόντων)' (6.98.2). He perhaps even includes a powerfully expressive, deliberate

---

[36] Cf. also the Cyrene/Barca narrative: see Dewald *Comm.* on 4.145–205; the Pisistratids (6.94.1; 7.6) and Aleuadai (7.6) at the Persian court, inviting Xerxes into Greece; Syloson inviting Darius into Samos (3.140.5).

[37] Cf. e.g. Marincola (1996), 579: 'the extent of [Herodotus' depiction of] political motivation is the natural expectation that states wish to be free'.

[38] Cf. Dewald (1997); Moles (1996), etc.

anachronism, in having the Spartans throw at the Athenians the accusation that the war began 'for the sake of your empire' (περὶ τῆς ὑμετέρης ἀρχῆς, 8.142.2)—if with Gilula we may trust in the consensus of all codices, in the teeth of modern emendations.[39]

The pervasiveness of this counter-principle—the desire for power—frequently brings into doubt the genuineness of claims that one is motivated by the desire for freedom per se. Herodotus' text at times also contests the pairing that emerges on the level of rhetoric, but is also a polarity of some substance in the *Histories*, of love of freedom and being Hellene: for the former is shown in no way inevitably to be predicated upon the latter. The *Histories*' numerous accounts of *Greek* tyrannies leave this impression, as does—from the opposite direction—the account of the Constitution debate, which presents freedom under democracy as a *choice* that was open to Persia at a point in the past,[40] and the fact (lent authorial emphasis) of Mardonios' establishment of democracies in the wake of the Ionian Revolt (6.43.3). Even Demaratus' lofty assertion that with *aretē* (valour) 'the Greeks' defend themselves from tyranny (7.102.1) is qualified not only by the facts of his own career (as we saw above), but also by the fact that we have just witnessed Ionians and Aeolians (thus *divisions* of Greeks) serving as slaves in Xerxes' army.

### 6.4.1 Motives of the tyrants (4.128–43)

Herodotus' juxtaposition at the Ister River of subservient Ionian tyrants with freedom-loving Scythians (who baulk at the mere word slavery: 4.128.1) provides a memorable instance of the same principle, and one that is expressively linked to the later narrative through the figure of Histiaeus (who first appears here, and goes on—thanks in part to this very episode—to become the key player in the Ionian Revolt). Herodotus on this occasion dramatizes a striking misreading of the Greeks' motives by the Scythians, which again sounds a precautionary note to readers: for in their approach and address to the Ionian tyrants guarding Darius' bridges, the Scythians

---

[39] Gilula (2003), 85–7.
[40] Fowler (2003), 309 n. 12 on the striking aspect of this.

work on the assumption that everyone is motivated by as powerful a
desire for freedom as are they.[41] After their initial request (accompanied by heartfelt proclamation: 'we have come bringing you freedom', 4.133.2) that the Ionians destroy Darius' bridges once the
agreed sixty days have passed has met with no response, the Scythians
return a second time and say:

Ionians, the numbered days have passed, and you do not act justly in still
remaining. But since previously you remained because of fear ($\epsilon\pi\epsilon\grave{\iota}\ \pi\rho\acute{o}\tau\epsilon\rho o\nu$
$\delta\epsilon\iota\mu\alpha\acute{\iota}\nu o\nu\tau\epsilon\varsigma\ \acute{\epsilon}\mu\acute{\epsilon}\nu\epsilon\tau\epsilon$), do now break up the bridge as quickly as possible and
depart, rejoicing at being free men ($\chi\alpha\acute{\iota}\rho o\nu\tau\epsilon\varsigma\ \acute{\epsilon}\lambda\epsilon\acute{\upsilon}\theta\epsilon\rho o\iota$), and thanking the
gods and the Scythians. As for your former master, we will inflict such a defeat
on him that he will never again campaign against any other men (4.136.3–4).

Thus they imagine that fear alone could have delayed the Greeks
from acting in defence of freedom.

But the debate among the tyrants that ensues showcases a rather
different ranking of priorities. The dramatization of their change of
mind makes clear that it is a question of ranked motivations rather
than of cut-and-dried absolutes; not that the noble motive has no
bite at all. 'Freedom' does indeed have a pleasing ring, and the other
tyrants are initially persuaded by Miltiades' opinion that they should
follow the Scythians' advice and free Ionia ($\pi\epsilon\acute{\iota}\theta\epsilon\sigma\theta\alpha\iota\ \Sigma\kappa\acute{\upsilon}\theta\eta\sigma\iota$
$\kappa\alpha\grave{\iota}\ \acute{\epsilon}\lambda\epsilon\upsilon\theta\epsilon\rho o\hat{\upsilon}\nu\ \mathit{'}I\omega\nu\acute{\iota}\eta\nu$, 4.137.1). And yet Histiaeus' speech pointing
out that their own personal power is dependent on Darius'—since
the cities would prefer to be democracies rather than tyrannies
($\delta\eta\mu o\kappa\rho\alpha\tau\acute{\epsilon}\epsilon\sigma\theta\alpha\iota\ \mu\hat{\alpha}\lambda\lambda o\nu\ \mathring{\eta}\ \tau\upsilon\rho\alpha\nu\nu\epsilon\acute{\upsilon}\epsilon\sigma\theta\alpha\iota$, 4.137.2)—soon changes
their minds: 'immediately all inclined towards this opinion, although
previously they had been in favour of Miltiades' proposal' (4.137.3).
Thus the ideal that seemed appealing in principle is overridden by a
more immediate concern with hanging on to personal power. (And
in any case, and significantly, rule can in itself have a certain 'freedom' about it.[42]) The tyrants choose to do all they can to hide the
truth from the Scythians, destroying the bridges at the Scythian end
so as to be able to claim: 'as you see, we are dismantling the bridge,
and we will exert ourselves to the full in our desire to be free' ($\dot{\omega}\varsigma\ \gamma\grave{\alpha}\rho$

---

[41] Cf. above, §5.2 on the Herodotean pattern of expectations of positive motives
being undermined.

[42] Cf. Raaflaub (1984) and below, §6.4.5.

ὁρᾶτε, καὶ λύομεν τὸν πόρον καὶ προθυμίην πᾶσαν ἕξομεν θέλοντες εἶναι ἐλεύθεροι, 4.139.2). In this way they *exploit* the Scythians' mistaken assumptions about their motives so as to elicit their further (false) belief.

The Scythians are taken in; Histiaeus responds instantly ('at the first command', 4.141)—subserviently—to Darius' call; and the Ionian tyrants thus become responsible for the Persians' escape (cf. 4.142). Herodotus rounds off the story with his report of the Scythians' blistering judgement of the Ionians:

τοῦτο μέν, ὡς ἐόντας Ἴωνας ἐλευθέρους, κακίστους τε καὶ ἀνανδροτάτους κρίνουσι εἶναι ἀπάντων ἀνθρώπων, τοῦτο δέ, ὡς δούλων Ἰώνων τὸν λόγον ποιεύμενοι, ἀνδράποδα φιλοδέσποτά φασι εἶναι καὶ ἄδρηστα μάλιστα (4.142).

If they were to regard the Ionians as free men, they judge them to be the most cowardly and least courageous of all mankind. But if they were to take account of the Ionians as slaves, they say that they are the most master-loving of captives and least likely to run away.[43]

The Scythians' perspective here is limited: for we have heard Histiaeus' view that the Ionian *people* would in fact prefer to be free. Thus the Scythians, like others in the *Histories*,[44] assume that a subject population shares their rulers' attitudes and motives. That assumption is challenged in the *Histories* from various directions: the question of whether responsibility rests with individual leaders or with the whole community, for example, is frequently raised.[45] Again, according to Otanes' formulation in the debate of the seven conspirators, absolute rule 'would cause even the best of all men to abandon his customary thoughts (ἐκτὸς τῶν ἐωθότων νοημάτων

[43] Corcella on 4.142.2–6—'Erodoto si fa volentieri portavoce del parere degli Sciti, dato il suo giudizio generalmente negativo sugli Ioni' ('Herodotus gladly is a mouthpiece of the Scythians' opinion, given his generally negative judgement of the Ionians')—oversimplifies, since only the Ionian *tyrants* (whose attitude has been explicitly contrasted to that of their subjects) are at this stage under discussion, and it is more a matter of their desiring rule than of preferring slavery to freedom (which they *did* indeed find appealing at the outset, as we have seen): Herodotus' point is perhaps not that the Ionian tyrants are naturally slavish (that is the *Scythians'* point), but rather that all else became irrelevant compared with their personal interest in ruling (and see n. 42 above with text).
[44] e.g. Xerxes, in assuming that the Thessalians share their leaders' attitude towards him (7.130).
[45] Note how some narratives shift from having an individual as their subject, to the individual as well as his community, e.g. in the case of Miltiades (see above, ch. 5 n. 53 with text) and Themistocles (see below, 316–18).

στήσειε)' (3.80.3): on which view a tyrant's thought processes (come to) differ qualitatively from those of his subjects. And yet, as we shall see, the gap between the Scythians' view and actuality will indeed diminish in the coming account as the Ionians' attitude towards freedom—when it comes to the hard work necessary for retaining it— begins to appear less absolute than had been implied by the tyrant's unqualified statement of the *dēmos*' preference (δημοκρατέεσθαι μᾶλλον ἢ τυραννεύεσθαι, 'to be under democracy rather than tyranny', 4.137.2). But Histiaeus' comment may also be read more in terms of its rhetorical force: in part he said all he could to alarm his tyrant contemporaries into voting in the way that would best secure for himself Darius' future favour.

The narrative that follows further evokes the tempting inducements to be expected from the King that—beyond their basic desire for power—must have persuaded the Ionian tyrants to rank their priorities as they did (e.g. the listing at 4.138 of those of them 'highly esteemed with the king'). For in recounting how Darius on his way back eastwards set Megabyzus to the task of conquering the Hellespont cities, Herodotus digresses to tell of how to him 'Darius once (κοτε) had given an honour (γέρας)' (4.143.1), flattering him in the presence of Persians (with his remark that he should rather have as many men like Megabyzus as seeds in a pomegranate than conquer Greece!); while now (τότε) he made him *stratēgos* over an army of eighty thousand, matching the intangible honour with concrete reward. Histiaeus is indeed soon rewarded for his good service at the Ister (5.11): Darius invites him to Sardis along with the Milesian Coes (in return for his good council), so as to grant each of them whatever reward they should choose. Herodotus' presentation of this choice lends emphasis again to the fact that desire for tyranny—for personal power—is a major default motivation of individuals (unless, that is, they happen already to be tyrants):

ὁ μὲν δὴ Ἱστιαῖος, **ἅτε τυραννεύων τῆς Μιλήτου, τυραννίδος μὲν οὐδεμιῆς προσεχρήιζε,** αἰτέει δὲ Μύρκινον τὴν Ἠδωνῶν, βουλόμενος ἐν αὐτῇ πόλιν κτίσαι. οὗτος μὲν δὴ ταύτην αἱρέεται, ὁ δὲ Κώης, **οἷά τε οὐ τύραννος δημότης δὲ ἐών,** αἰτέει Μυτιλήνης τυραννεῦσαι (5.11.2).

Histiaios, **since he was already tyrant of Miletus, desired no additional tyranny besides that**. He asked instead for Myrkinos in Edonia, as he wished to found a city there. So he asked for this, whereas Coes, **inasmuch as he was not a tyrant but a private citizen**, asked to be tyrant of Mytilene.

This is a fitting precursor to the Ionian Revolt narrative and the presentation of motives there: for indeed the desire for personal power on the part of individuals—so far from any sincere concern for the freedom of their states!—will be a leitmotiv.

### 6.4.2 Motives of the instigators (5.35–7, 5.102–6.18)

It is largely around the motives and consequent actions of individuals (Histiaeus, Aristagoras, Megabates, Artaphrenes—all of them desirous of personal influence) that the initial stages of the Ionian Revolt narrative are described as unfolding. Ironies thus abound. For example, a significant contributory cause of this revolt in the name of Greek freedom is the tyrant Histiaeus' choice of Myrkinos as a further power base for himself. Darius, advised by Megabyzus—who had become apprehensive about Histiaeus' increasing power in such a prime location, and in an area under his control—invited Histiaeus to live at his court at Susa (5.23–4); Aristagoras took over his rule at Miletus; and Histiaeus—whose reasoning Herodotus recounts precisely (5.35.4–36.1)—fomented revolt in Ionia in order to be sent home to deal with it. Paradoxical, too, are the motives that induce Aristagoras on his side to become a key instigator: for again they are not merely far removed from, but antithetical to, concerns with freedom per se, and also *negative* (in the sense of potentially *inhibiting* action)—as Herodotus' detailed construction of his thought processes again makes clear. **Unable** to fulfil his promise to Artaphrenes (to subject easily Naxos and neighbouring islands to the King), **pressured** by the army's expenses, and **afraid** as a result both of the military failure and of his quarrel with Megabates,[46]

---

[46] Cf. Nenci on 5.35.5–6: 'la rivolta ionica che Aristagora presenterà presto agli Ioni come frutto di sue scelte ideali, come la libertà dei Greci dal giogo persiano, è vista da Erodoto come una scelta dominata da motivazioni non nobili...' ('the Ionian Revolt, which Aristagoras will soon present to the Ionians as the outcome of his idealistic choices, as the freedom of the Greeks from the Persian yoke, is viewed by Herodotus as a choice dominated by ignoble motivations'); Flower (1994), 178–9.

he thought it likely that he would be deprived of the rule of Miletus (ἐδόκεέ τε τὴν βασιληίην τῆς Μιλήτου ἀπαιρεθήσεσθαι). Driven by all these fears (ἀρρωδέων δὲ τούτων ἕκαστα), he began to plan revolt. For it also happened that the man with the tattooed head had arrived from Susa, from Histiaeus, signalling that Aristagoras should revolt from the King (5.35.1–2).

Aristagoras was earlier pictured assisting the Naxian exiles only because—with perverse logic—he thought he would thus become their ruler (5.30.3). The Naxian exiles had in mind a similar outcome for themselves: rule of Naxos and the neighbouring islands (5.30.6); as indeed, of course, did Artaphrenes, on behalf of the King. Similarly, though on a personal level, Megabates' subsequent betrayal of the Naxian plot (whose failure would have such significant repercussions) was motivated by anger at Aristagoras' assertion that he belonged within his sphere of influence and so must obey him, and not vice versa (5.33.4). Thus the key triggers of the revolt at each juncture lie wholly in the power-hungry motives of these individuals. Unlike the later Greek defence, it is presented as having been avoidable at several stages.[47]

Once the Ionian Revolt is underway, 'freedom' rhetoric is put to explicit pragmatic and political purposes. After arranging the seizure of some of the other Ionian tyrants, Aristagoras revolts openly, 'contriving everything possible against Darius' (πᾶν ἐπὶ Δαρείῳ μηχανώμενος, 5.37.1; thus here again, we are left with the impression that his greatest concern is to harm the King!):

καὶ πρῶτα μὲν λόγῳ μετεὶς τὴν τυραννίδα ἰσονομίην ἐποίεε τῇ Μιλήτῳ, **ὡς ἂν ἑκόντες αὐτῷ οἱ Μιλήσιοι συναπισταίατο**, μετὰ δὲ καὶ ἐν τῇ ἄλλῃ Ἰωνίῃ τὠυτὸ τοῦτο ἐποίεε, τοὺς μὲν ἐξελαύνων τῶν τυράννων, τοὺς δ' ἔλαβε τυράννους ἀπὸ τῶν νεῶν τῶν συμπλευσασέων ἐπὶ Νάξον, τούτους δὲ **φίλα βουλόμενος ποιέεσθαι** τῇσι πόλισι ἐξεδίδου, κτλ (5.37.2).

First of all relinquishing his tyranny **merely in word**, he established *isonomiē* (equality before the law) for Miletus **so that the Milesians would voluntarily join him in his revolt**. Next, he did the same in the rest of Ionia too. Some of the tyrants he expelled from their cities, but those he seized from aboard the ships that had sailed together with him against Naxos he handed over to their respective cities **because he wanted the cities to be well-disposed towards him**.

---

[47] Solsmen (1943), 204–5; Hornblower (2004), 301–6 observes the strong sense of contingency in Herodotus' account.

The *epi* repetition—ἐπὶ Νάξον ('against Naxos') then, as ἐπὶ Δαρείῳ ('against Darius') now—as well as συμπλευσασέων ('that had sailed together with (him)') emphasizes again the fact of Aristagoras' turncoat character, with his motives dictated by expediency alone and without ethical foundation. It is simply because his project requires the Milesians' support that he gives Miletus *isonomiē*, exactly as Cleisthenes of Athens ἑσσούμενος... τὸν δῆμον προσεταιρίζεται ('since he was on the losing side... made the *dēmos* his friend/ *hetairos*', 5.66.2—the aristocratic nature of the word bringing home the reality), in a move Herodotus thinks mimicked that of his tyrant grandfather.[48] And again, he hands over the tyrants to their respective cities simply to please the cities and get them on side, rather than for any deeper reason. In similar fashion at a later stage, Aristagoras, Herodotus notes, 'who had set Ionia in confusion and concocted great troubles, at seeing what he had done, began to contemplate flight. Moreover it seemed to him impossible to outdo King Darius' (5.124.1). Thus he gathers together his supporters so as to secure a place of refuge for himself—with no thought for the fate of the people of Miletus, just as Maiandrios secured safety for himself with no thought for the people of Samos, or as Athens extricated herself from the Ionian Revolt leaving the Ionians in the lurch. Readers well know (and are soon to be told) the terrible fate he is letting Miletus in for. They will again be reminded of his involvement by Herodotus' choice of chronological marker when the capture of Miletus occurs.[49] The sordid, needless nature of Aristagoras' death— for he and his army are slain by Thracians while he lays siege unnecessarily to a Thracian town: πόλιν περικατήμενος καὶ βουλομένων τῶν Θρηίκων ὑποσπόνδων ἐξιέναι ('while investing the town even though the Thracians were willing to depart from it under truce', 5.126.2)— casts a grim shadow over the Ionian Revolt, hinting perhaps at its similar futility.

---

[48] On this interpretation Herodotus' comparison of Cleisthenes of Athens to his tyrant ancestor comes to appear less strange than readers have often supposed; cf. Munson (2001), 53–6 (noting further points of comparison between the two figures).

[49] 6.18: ἕκτῳ ἔτεϊ ἀπὸ τῆς ἀποστάσιος τῆς Ἀρισταγόρεω ('in the sixth year after Aristagoras' revolt').

### 6.4.3  Motives of the people

Rhetoric cannot neglect its *audience*'s wishes, however, and the free-dom line is used because it has bite. In the hints even early on that the attitudes of subject peoples (including the Ionian) may not concur with those of their rulers, and in the wider pattern in the *Histories* of communities seeking freedom, readers may find an alternative ex-planation of the Ionian Revolt's origins. At this point Herodotus refrains from expressing it explicitly, however, presumably so as to focus attention on the salient ironies that surround the individuals' involvement. In the later stages of the revolt narrative he does indeed shift the focus to the Ionian communities' desire for freedom—and here, ironies again surface, but this time in the highly *qualified* nature of that desire. The sketch of the Ionian tyrants at the Ister provided an appropriate introduction (as we saw above, §6.4.1) to the notion that motives are dictated by people's shifting priorities, and tend to change as different factors come into view. The same pattern marks the *Histories'* depiction of the Ionians' attitude to freedom: their initial commitment proves easily sidelined once the prospect surfaces of the hard work necessary for maintaining it.[50]

At first the Ionians work zealously in the cause of Ionian freedom. Despite their defeat at Ephesus (5.102.2) and the Athenians' abandon-ment of their cause (5.103.1), they gain control of Byzantium as well as all the other Hellespontine cities (5.103.2), and acquire the greater part of Caria as an ally—'including even Kaunos', at which point the Cyprians too join their cause willingly (with the exception of the Amathusians, whose city Onesilos of Cyprian Salamis lays under siege, 5.104). Called upon to come to the aid of Onesilos, after he has heard rumour of the impending Persian attack on Cyprus, 'the Ionians, without much deliberation (οὐκ ἐς μακρὴν βουλευσάμενοι), came with a great army (πολλῷ στόλῳ)' (5.108.2). They respond in kind to the Cyprians' freedom rhetoric (urging them to act 'in such a way that—so far as the responsibility lies with you—Ionia and Cyprus may be free', 5.109.2), valiantly embracing their duty to fight the Phoenicians on sea:

---

[50] On Herodotus' presentation of the attitude of the Ionian people see e.g. Evans (1976); Lateiner (1982); Murray (1988); Stadter (1992), 803–8; and most recently Thomas (2004) (highlighting more positive elements of the depiction than are usually recognized).

We, then, will try to make ourselves useful in fighting in the place where we have been stationed (ἡμεῖς μέν νυν ἐπ᾽ οὗ ἐτάχθημεν, ταύτῃ πειρησόμεθα εἶναι χρηστοί). As for you, it is right that you remember what you suffered as slaves at the hands of the Medes, and prove yourselves brave men (5.109.3).

Indeed they live up to this: they vanquish the Phoenicians, 'proving themselves excellent fighters' (ἄκροι γενόμενοι); the Samians in particular 'gained the highest distinction' (ἠρίστευσαν, 5.112.1). Only through an individual's treachery do the Persians ultimately defeat the Cyprians (5.113.1) and quash their revolt. Subsequently the Ionians (here 'the Milesians and their allies', 5.120) come to the aid of the revolted Carians, who are fighting on despite their recent defeat (which occurred simply διὰ πλῆθος, 'on account of (lesser) numbers', 5.119.1). A heavy defeat results, and the Milesians especially are stricken. And yet with the Persians next moving to attack Miletus and the rest of Ionia, the Ionians are again prepared to fight, resolving to defend Miletus by sea at Lade (with Milesians and Samians taking the wings).

But at this point the narrative's perspective on the Ionians changes subtly, with Herodotus' observation that those to whom the Persian *stratēgoi* promised gentle treatment if they ceased their revolt immediately, and threatened with a terrible fate otherwise, 'displayed *agnōmosunē* (inflexibility, obstinacy) (ἀγνωμοσύνῃ τε διεχρέωντο) and did not agree to the betrayal' (6.10). This charged explanation of the Ionians' behaviour at this point is perhaps related to, and foreshadows, the final outcome (at Lade),[51] which is already in view and will suggest that the Ionians were less committed to their cause than their posture in 'not accepting treachery' implied. (The additional note that each was under the false impression that he alone had been approached hints, moreover, that otherwise there might indeed have been some response to the Persian overtures.) For in retrospect—with knowledge that the Ionians would indeed cave in later on—this show of commitment doubtless appeared a sort of senseless obstinacy,[52] as this seems to have been a final

---

[51] Cf. Evans' (1976) more general emphasis on the way in which Herodotus treats the failure of the revolt as a foregone conclusion.

[52] Most translations of 6.10 register this negative tone, e.g. Nenci: 'si comportavano con stoltezza e non accettavano il tradimento'; Legrand: 'persistèrent dans leur manque de jugement...'; Godley: 'were stubborn...'; though not e.g. Waterfield; de Sélincourt/Marincola.

moment at which the Ionians might have chosen to bow out of the revolt unharmed. The same motivation was ascribed some chapters earlier, again in relation to a decision to revolt, to the Aeginetans, who 'building ships and displaying *agnōmosunē* (ἀγνωμοσύνῃ χρησάμενοι) revolted from the Epidaurians' (5.83.1). There it underlined the rather gratuitous nature of an action that unsettled what had been a time-honoured (cf. 'still throughout this time as well as earlier...') and reasonable state of affairs (with the Aeginetans 'crossing over to Epidaurus to settle the lawsuits that arose among themselves', 5.83.1), pointlessly—or at least without deep reason, particularly in view of the outcome—issuing in destruction and conflict on all sides.

And yet even earlier Herodotus' wording (above: οὐκ ἐς μακρὴν βουλευσάμενοι, 'without much deliberation', they helped the Cyprians) had hinted in the same direction, that had the Ionians reflected more fully they might not have acted as they did. The outcome, soon to be described, could well lead to the conclusion that the Ionians' initial enthusiasm *must have been* unthinking. Readers may well sense the *ex eventu* nature of Herodotus' conjectures,[53] which is drawing them on towards the final key sequence. For it is at this point that Herodotus recounts Dionysius' impassioned speech in the name of freedom at Lade, in which he is open-eyed about the necessary effort but convinced it will pay off in the end (6.11.2); the Ionians' seven-day endurance of his tough but necessary training programme; and their subsequent about-turn and decision that freedom is not a worthwhile goal after all if it demands so much work. As they finish up by complaining:

πρό τε τούτων τῶν κακῶν ἡμῖν γε κρέσσον καὶ ὅ τι ὦν ἄλλο παθεῖν ἐστι καὶ τὴν **μέλλουσαν δουληίην ὑπομεῖναι τις ἔσται**, μᾶλλον ἢ τῇ παρεούσῃ συνέχεσθαι (6.12.3).

Better than this misery would be for us to suffer anything else at all, and **even to endure the coming slavery, whatever it may be,** rather than to be oppressed by that of the present.

From this moment they refuse to obey Dionysius, building themselves tents on land οἷα στρατιὴ, 'like an army' (thus abandoning

---

[53] Evans (1976) likewise proposes that Herodotus judged the revolt by its outcome and (at 37) draws a connection with Solon's 'look to the end'.

their earlier voiced commitment to the sea), and no longer board their ships or continue training. Their quick collapse presents a stark contrast with the extremely persistent—*non*-Greek—Carian effort (which included three spirited returns to the fray on the heels of disaster) that was on display in the preceding narrative (5.119–22). Upon witnessing the Ionians' conduct the Samian generals resolve to desert, as indeed most of their captains do in the battle that follows. The Lesbians follow suit; and likewise does the greater part (οἱ πλεῦνες) of the Ionians (6.14.3). After defeating the Ionians by sea, the Persians lay siege to Miletus, capture it, and bring the enslaved inhabitants to Susa. Readers might reflect that the Ionians, like the Samians at 3.143.2, 'did not, it seems, want to be free' (οὐ ... δή, ὡς οἴκασι, ἐβούλοντο εἶναι ἐλεύθεροι).[54]

## 6.4.4 Motives of the Samians (6.22–4)

The story that follows upon Miletus' capture likewise documents changing motives in response to changing circumstances: Herodotus again stages a mid-narrative shift from ideal to self-regarding. After the sea battle the subset of wealthy Samians, being not at all (οὐδαμῶς) pleased with their generals' conduct towards the Persians (ἐς τοὺς Μήδους), resolve 'to sail away on a colonizing expedition before the tyrant Aiakes should arrive in their country, and not to remain to be slaves to the Medes and Aiakes (μηδὲ μένοντας Μήδοισί τε καὶ Αἰάκεϊ δουλεύειν)' (6.22.1). Thus high-mindedly they forsake their country rather than submit to slavery to a tyrant or Persia. This course of action was open to them thanks to an invitation made to Ionians about this time from the Zancleans of Sicily, inviting (ἐπεκαλέοντο) them to come to Sicily's *Kalē Aktē* ('Fair Cape') and there found an Ionian *polis*. So—'with these people inviting (them)' (τούτων ... ἐπικαλεομένων: the invitation aspect thus underlined)—the Samians, along with those of the Milesians who had escaped (6.22.2), set out.

---

[54] Stadter (1992), esp. 807–8 presses this reading, relating it to the similar situation of 440–425 BC. Cf. Evans (1976), 37: 'although Herodotus does not deny the Ionians' courage, they failed to muster enough unity or purpose during the Revolt to make a decision and abide by it'. Differently, Thomas (2004), highlighting narrative strands indicative rather of Ionian achievement.

In the course of their journey, however, a chance incident occurs (τι συνήνεικε γενέσθαι) that disrupts their noble intentions: Anaxileos, tyrant of Rhegium, being at feud with the Zancleans and learning of their besieging another Sicilian city at the time, persuades the Samians to forget Kalē Aktē and instead set their sights on Zancle: indeed, 'to seize Zancle, while it was empty of men' (τὴν δὲ Ζάγκλην σχεῖν, ἐοῦσαν ἔρημον ἀνδρῶν, 6.23.2). Persuaded, the Samians do just that. The initial sincere invitation narrative—for the Zancleans made their invitation without malicious ulterior motive—thus transforms into a mixture of two of a sort with which readers are more familiar: an invitation made with a view to harming one's personal enemy, and an invitation accepted with a view to one's own gain; indeed, more specifically, as a licence to transform into the aggressor. Only here it is Greeks exploiting the tyrant's invitation, rather than the more common reverse formula (as we find in the narrative of Aryandes responding to a Greek invitation to meddle in Cyrenean affairs, 4.165–7).[55] Zancle lay in a glaringly profitable location: across from Rhegium on the other side of the all-important straits of Messine. The irony that Milesians, themselves having narrowly escaped slavery, should be involved in this exploitation of a city 'emptied of men' (ἔρημον ἀνδρῶν), whose inhabitants are soon to be enslaved, is felt in the echo of 6.22.1 (Μίλητος μέν νυν Μιλησίων ἠρήμωτο, 'Miletus, then, was **emptied** of Milesians'). This once again breaks down the sort of ethnic distinction that the rhetoric of 8.144, twinning freedom with Greek identity, seems to demand.

The Zancleans called upon (ἐπεκαλέοντο) their ally Hippokrates tyrant of Gela to come and help, and he 'came with his army **to give help** (βοηθέων)' (6.23.4)—but so far from doing that, he threw the *basileus* (king) and his brother into chains for losing the town and betrayed the Zanclean people, handing them over to the Samians in return for a generous reward. Thus again in Hippokrates' case a gulf is exposed between intentions and resultant actions. The echo felt in ἐπεκαλέοντο ('they called upon/invited', cf. ἐπεκαλέοντο above, 6.22.2) suggests a parallel between the Samians' earlier betrayal of

<hr />

[55] See Munson's discussion of the episode (2006), 262–3 in terms of the confrontation of tyrannical and colonizing models in Herodotus' portrayal of West Greece, where 'a flight to freedom may well become an expedition of conquest or result in the oppression of others' (259).

the Zancleans' invitation and the similar betrayal that the tyrant performs here. Hippokrates cast into chains and kept in slavery the majority of the Zancleans (6.23.6), but handed over to the Samians 300 eminent citizens to be put to death. The Samians' refraining from so doing (6.23.6) seems but a meagre compensatory gesture. For over the course of the account they have colluded willingly with two tyrants in succession. They have enabled a *tyrant* to remove a *king* and enslave his people; a king, moreover, whose rule has an appearance of legitimacy both from the fact of 'the Zancleans' (apparently independently of their ruler) being those responsible for inviting the Ionians, and from the snapshot of 'people and king' acting in concord.[56] And finally they have seized for themselves the city of those whose invitation had made possible their escape from their own tyrant, enslaving most of its citizens.

Herodotus' summing-up of the tale lays bare these ironies and points to the sort of factors that overtook and relegated to the sidelines the Samians' initial noble-seeming intentions: 'Thus the Samians escaped the Medes and effortlessly acquired the extremely beautiful (*kallistēn*) city Zancle' (Σάμιοι δὲ ἀπαλλαχθέντες Μήδων ἀπονητὶ πόλιν καλλίστην Ζάγκλην περιεβεβλέατο, 6.24.2). The superlative epithet hints strongly at their ulterior motive in preferring Zancle to the merely *kalē* Aktē: thus the land-hunger motif resurfaces at the end of the story, guiding readers to consider this as an explanation for the Samians' conduct. The outcome of the story invites reassessment of the earlier statement of the Samians' motives. It arouses suspicion that their earlier displeasure at their generals' failure to support the Ionians' freedom fight at Lade, and their parallel concern to avoid slavery, may have been motivated by egotistic concerns rather than matters of principle. Their opposition was perhaps to being ruled themselves by a tyrant, rather than to tyranny per se. And yet the abruptness of the narrative shift, with the sense

[56] Skythes is described as *basileus* at 6.23.1, Hippokrates as *tyrannos* at 6.23.3. See Ferrill (1978) for the expressiveness of the *tyrannos/basileus* distinction; cf. Fisher (1992), 348 (contra Waters (1971)). Historically speaking it is unlikely that Skythes was the legitimate king of Zancle (cf. Ferrill (1978), 390): Herodotus perhaps presents him as such to underscore the ironies of the situation (including particularly the illegitimate nature of the Samians' ensuing rule). Again, the category of 'tyranny' seems to have been a slippery one from archaic times down into the fourth century, able to be applied to any ruler or regime by its discontents: Lewis (2004).

that it is partly due to pure chance—to Anaxileos making his offer—leaves open an alternative possibility, that the Samians' initial opposition to tyranny was genuine and principled, but soon extinguished by the temptations of beautiful land and additional power.

### 6.4.5  Motives of the *polis tyrannos* (5.65–78; 8.3)

The story of Samians vis-à-vis Zancleans fits into the wider pattern in the *Histories* of Greeks who set others free, only to set themselves up as tyrant. The Spartan Euryleon, for example, frees the Selinuntines from a 'monarch' only to set himself up as 'tyrant'—in a move from a neutral term to a more negative[57]—and to be assassinated (a tyrant death!). In the broader pattern of freeing others in order to become tyrant, Histiaeus 'frees' Greeks so as to become tyrant himself; Aristagoras 'frees' the Milesians (in word) because he fears for his rule and wants their willing support in his planned revolt; and Cleisthenes 'frees' the Athenian *dēmos* so as to have their support in his bid for autocratic power. The Maiandrios~Samians scenario may be interpreted as a fully fledged instance of the same pattern, though Maiandrios' original motives remain obscure, so other interpretations are possible too. In so doing, these people contravene the principles of both freedom and *to Hellēnikon*, since in the *Histories* a powerful, if frequently destablized, association is felt between these concepts (as between *to barbarikon* and tyranny[58]).

And yet one of the ironic faces of freedom, which Herodotus examines in some depth, is how it frequently appears to *entail* rule over others. It may be that a paradox is not automatically sensed, since this 'freedom to rule' was perhaps the standard ancient Greek freedom;[59]

---

[57] Ferrill (1978).

[58] Note that historically, this association probably surfaced as a consequence of the Persian Wars and not before: the King supported local governments of whatever sort, which is why he supported the sixth-century tyrants: cf. Graf (1985).

[59] Cf. e.g. Constant (1819); Larsen (1962); Austin and Vidal-Naquet (1977), 125–8. But Raaflaub (2004), esp. 118–65, 192–3, contests this notion that 'an "imperialist impulse" was firmly embedded in the Greek idea of freedom': 'On present understanding, it seems preferable to regard the deliberate and explicit linkage [in the context of Athenian empire] of freedom and rule over others…not as natural and inherent in Greek character but as the result of a specific historical constellation' (193).

and in the *Histories*, the dichotomy set forth in the final episode (9.122) is indeed between rule and being ruled. The Athenians over the course of the fifth century appear to have developed this concept that rule over others—which guarantees one's sovereignty and self-sufficiency—is a prerequisite for one's own freedom,[60] and, conversely, that freedom promotes a predisposition to rule.[61] 'Freedom to dominate' may then be regarded as being simply a stronger expression of 'freedom of self-assertion'. Indeed for the Athenians, as Jacqueline de Romilly has observed, 'the act of ruling was really considered as the perfect expression of both internal and external freedom, and, in fact, as a superior freedom.'[62] Nonetheless, both in the *Histories'* particular emphasis on 'freedom to dominate'[63]—for there *were* different possible inflections of the idea of freedom[64]—and in the implied comparison that surfaces with Persian domination, Herodotus should probably be regarded as *developing* the notion as a paradox: as heightening readers' sensitivity to it. The possibility is strengthened by Munson's argument that Herodotus 'counter(s) the contemporary tendency to view aggression as a function of defence' by presenting Scythia and Sparta as models of states that defend their own freedom while avoiding engaging in imperialism, in opposition to Athens' inability to perceive the difference between defence and aggression.[65]

The idea surfaces that these two faces of freedom, broadly representing freedom *from* (for oneself and one's wider community: defined as 'Greeks' in the case of 8.144) and freedom *to* (for oneself), may normally be felt to constitute one continuous concept, but do not do so invariably;[66] and focusing on the ramifications of their unity or separation—as through the implied comparison of Scythian

[60] See Raaflaub (2004), 181–93.

[61] See e.g. Ubsdell (1983), 135–7.

[62] De Romilly (1963), 80, with discussion there (80–2); Ubsdell (1983), 135–7 (qualifying de Romilly's observation by suggesting that this corollary was not generally held, but a specialized argument in sophistic circles).

[63] See especially Ubsdell (1983), 111–40 on the persistent connections the *Histories* makes between freedom and empire.

[64] See e.g. below, n. 68 with text (alternative possible conceptions of freedom in external relations), and ch. 6 n. 75 with text (alternative possible emphasis on the domestic benefits of freedom).

[65] Munson (2001), 212–14, quotation at 212.

[66] Compare Isaiah Berlin's (1969), 118–72 concept of negative and positive liberty, to be understood as rival, incompatible interpretations of the same political ideal.

and Spartan states with the Athenian—may generate a sense of paradox. Panhellenic rhetoric, such as the speech at 8.144, assumes that the two aspects are separable, and indeed suppresses altogether the notion of freedom *to*, unless manifestly in the context of freedom to (exercise rule) *over non-Greek outsiders*, such as Persia.[67] An important strand of Athenian propaganda emphasized the *good* Athens did her subjects in guaranteeing their internal and external freedom (offering protection from the tyranny threatened by their own oligarchs and by Persia), thus drawing attention away from her own tyrannizing.[68]

This second face of freedom ('freedom *to*') probably had sinister overtones for Herodotus' Greek readers. Thucydides concretizes the paradox,[69] but his treatment quite possibly also reflects its occasional presence even in public discussion, at least in Athenian ecclesiac contexts.[70] Herodotus engages with and develops it over the course of several anecdotes,[71] but perhaps most strikingly in Darius' assertion at the end of the Constitutional Debate:

From where did we get freedom and who gave it to us? Did it come from the *dēmos* or from an oligarchy or from a monarchy? I therefore hold the opinion that since it was a single individual who freed us (ἡμέας ἐλευθερωθέντας διὰ ἕνα ἄνδρα), it is that form of rule that we should maintain (3.82.5).[72]

---

[67] e.g. in Aristagoras' speeches at Sparta (5.49) and Athens (5.97).

[68] Raaflaub (2004), 173–7. Cf., more generally, freedom envisaged as enabling a city *to protect others* (especially suppliants): e.g. in Euripides *Heracleidae* (e.g. 197–8), and probably in the background of the Athenians' speech at *Histories* 9.27.

[69] See below, n. 78.

[70] Raaflaub (1979), (2003): the idea of '*polis tyrannos*' was a pervasive political concept at Athens, familiar also (cf. Raaflaub (1987), 224–5) in the wider Greek world; contrast Tuplin (1985), arguing for its relative rarity in fifth-century Athenian political discourse. This is too large an issue to pursue here.

[71] e.g. 5.109 (the account of the Cyprian tyrants' desire for freedom from Persia, in interaction with 4.137, recounting the Ionian tyrants' different stance); 3.65 (Cambyses' deathbed speech re. Cyrus); 9.122 (Cyrus presenting the Persians with the alternatives of ruling or being ruled).

[72] Cf. 1.210.2: Hystaspes' observation that Darius is the one ὃς ἀντὶ μὲν δούλων ἐποίησ[ε] ἐλευθέρους Πέρσας εἶναι, ἀντὶ δὲ ἄρχεσθαι ὑπ' ἄλλων ἄρχειν ἁπάντων ('who made the Persians free men instead of slaves, and rulers of all instead of being ruled by others').

Thus Darius refers to Cyrus' granting the Persians freedom *from* Median rule and *to* rule in their place (cf. 1.126); and soon after the conclusion of the speech comes the authorial observation that from that moment, Otanes' household alone in Persia remained free (μούνη ἐλευθέρη ... Περσέων, 3.83.3) rather than enslaved to the King. These different sorts of freedom, internal and external, are therefore envisaged as *able* to be divorced from one another (a circumstance that finds acknowledgment even in Darius' semi-public rhetoric), though the main point remains that they are not *naturally* so divorced.

In the digression prompted by Aristagoras' arrival at Athens (5.55), Herodotus recounts how Athens was freed from tyranny (concluding 'thus, then, the Athenians were freed from their tyrants', 5.65.5) and then turns to relate

all the things worthy of description that the Athenians, once they had been freed (ἐλευθερωθέντες), did or suffered before Ionia revolted from Darius and Aristagoras the Milesian arrived at Athens and asked for their assistance (5.65.5).

He begins, 'Athens, which even previously had been great/powerful (καὶ πρὶν μεγάλαι), once freed from her tyrants became greater still (ἀπαλλαχθεῖσαι τυράννων ἐγένοντο μέζονες)' (5.66.1). Athens' freedom from tyranny enabled her, in particular, to punish and enslave her neighbouring Boeotians and Chalcidians for aiding Cleomenes in his attack (5.77). This first narrative of Athenian military success under democracy is centred upon (and provides the *aition* for) the powerful and ironic visual spectacle of the fetters still in Herodotus' time hanging on the walls—now charred by the *Medes* (a parallel external aggressor?)—on the Athenian Acropolis. For the Athenians had defeated first the Boeotians, killing many and taking seven hundred prisoner (5.77.2), and next, on the following day, the Chalcidians, taking further prisoners to be kept under guard and in chains along with the Boeotians, and leaving behind on their land four thousand Athenian *klērouchous* (5.77.2): an action that doubtless recalled, for Herodotus' contemporary readers, the widely used—and resented— policy of the Periclean democracy.[73] In conclusion Herodotus cites the

[73] This mention in Herodotus is the earliest record of the establishment of a cleruchy: Graham (1964), 168–9; if unhistorical (cf. French (1972), 22), the terminology was perhaps chosen for its particular expressiveness.

inscription on the bronze chariot, made from a tenth part of the ransom the Athenians had demanded for the release of their prisoners, which presses once again the theme of bondage: 'the Children of Athens quenched their *hybris* in gloomy iron bonds', etc. (5.77.4).

It is at this very moment that Herodotus pauses for one of his most famous reflections on Athenian democracy:

Ἀθηναῖοι μέν νυν ηὔξηντο δηλοῖ δὲ οὐ κατ' ἓν μοῦνον ἀλλὰ πανταχῇ ἡ ἰσηγορίη ὡς ἐστὶ χρῆμα σπουδαῖον, εἰ καὶ Ἀθηναῖοι τυραννευόμενοι μὲν οὐδαμῶν τῶν σφέας περιοικεόντων ἦσαν τὰ πολέμια ἀμείνους, ἀπαλλαχθέντες δὲ τυράννων μακρῷ πρῶτοι ἐγένοντο. δηλοῖ ὦν ταῦτα ὅτι κατεχόμενοι μὲν ἐθελοκάκεον ὡς δεσπότῃ ἐργαζόμενοι, ἐλευθερωθέντων δὲ αὐτὸς ἕκαστος ἑωυτῷ προεθυμέετο κατεργάζεσθαι (5.78).

Athens, then, grew in power. And it is clear not from one thing alone but in every way that *isēgoriē* (equal freedom of speech) is an excellent thing (*chrēma spoudaion*), since the Athenians while under tyranny were no better at war than any of their neighbours, but once they had been freed from their tyrants, they became *prōtoi* (the best/first) by far. This, then, is clear, that while oppressed they fought like cowards on the grounds of working for a master, whereas once they were freed, each individual was eager to achieve for himself.

This authorial evaluation of the benefits of *isēgoriē* (along with freedom from tyranny) in exclusively military terms—as being a *chrēma spoudaion*, that is, since it bestows military supremacy[74]— fits the immediate context, and is appropriate to Herodotus' wider project as regards the Athenian military capability that will be essential in the imminent Persian conflict. It is nonetheless striking, and double-edged. We find here no praise of the internal benefits of *isēgoriē* to match Demaratus' praise of Spartan freedom under the law, besides the concluding note (αὐτὸς ἕκαστος..., 'each individual...')—and that presents democracy in terms of individuals working (egoistically) for themselves, rather than in terms, for instance, of the *dēmos*' collaborating for the good of the whole. Nor do we find an emphasis on 'the many', like Otanes' in the Constitution Debate.[75]

---

[74] See Munson (2001), 206–11 (observing that Herodotus' Athenian glosses—unlike the narrator's generalizations elsewhere—employ not ethical standards but 'the vocabulary of strategy and the useful': 208). Cf. the similar emphasis in the Hippocratic *Airs, Waters, Places* 16.

[75] e.g. **πλῆθος** δὲ ἄρχον...; βουλεύματα δὲ πάντα **ἐς τὸ κοινὸν** ἀναφέρει; **ἐν γὰρ τῷ πολλῷ** ἔνι τὰ πάντα (3.80.6). Cf. Thucydides' Pericles' emphasis on the *whole* com-

More than that, this intimate correlation between freedom from tyranny and military endeavour, with ἀπαλλαχθέντες δὲ τυράννων μακρῷ πρῶτοι ἐγένοντο ('freed from their tyrants, they became the best/first by far') encapsulating the juxtaposition found in the narrative, leaves the impression of a causal link: it calls attention to the fact that the type of freedom possessed by the Athenians is an active 'freedom *to*' (exert power over, even enslave, her neighbours[76]) rather than simply 'freedom *from*' (being ruled by others).[77] That reality was of particular poignancy for Herodotus' contemporary readers, and developed into a powerful irony by Thucydides.[78] In the rhetoric with which Miltiades appeals to Kallimachos, providing him with reasons for Athens to fight the Persians at Marathon, we find the same combination: 'if you support my opinion, your country will be free and your city the first in Greece' (ἔστι τοι πατρίς τε ἐλευθέρη καὶ πόλις πρώτη τῶν ἐν τῇ Ἑλλάδι, 6.109.6; cf. 'they became the first by far (μακρῷ πρῶτοι)', above): Athens should be moved by the prospect of securing her freedom, *but also* of becoming dominant over other cities.[79] Athens' aspiration to be *first* city of Greece has particular point in the wake of Herodotus' presentation of Sparta in

munity flourishing: 2.65.3. Ubsdell (1983), 182–98 and Romm (1998), 185–6 likewise underscore Herodotus' pragmatic rather than idealizing characterization of Athenian democracy.

[76] *Spoudaion* is generally used, in the *Histories*, of practical matters, and tends to invite an indirect object, e.g. suggesting an idea of excellence *in* or *at*; cf. 2.86.2 and 2.86.3 (embalming); 4.23.4 (the quality of the Scythians' pasture).

[77] Berlin (1969) distinguishes between these two concepts of freedom 'from' and 'to'; cf. n. 66 above.

[78] Cf. esp. Diodotus' formulation: *poleis* are tempted to run risks περὶ τῶν μεγίστων..., ἐλευθερίας ἢ ἄλλων ἀρχῆς ('when the greatest things are at stake: their own freedom, or rule over others'), Thuc. 3.45.6. Idea of *polis tyrannos*: Pericles at 2.65.2; Cleon at 3.37.2 (Athens *as* a tyranny). Van der Veen (1996), 90–110 discusses Herodotus' treatment of the negative consequences of Athenian freedom.

[79] Bornitz (1968), 93 first highlighted the striking aspect of this. As Ubsdell (1983), 33 observes, 'The promise of becoming the 'first city in Greece' is only comprehensible as a promise about power'. Cf. the alternatives in similar vein (submission to others v. being *first*: πρώτη τῶν Ἑλληνίδων πολίων) that appear earlier in the speech: 6.109.3. Stadter includes this example among others where Herodotus 'couples the courage to resist with the ambition to rule' (2006), 248, in a discussion illuminating more generally how Herodotus 'tinges with irony' (cf. 249) the relation between Athenian freedom and imperialism (247–50) (and also other instances of Greek conduct: 250–3).

that role up to this moment, with Athens playing second fiddle:[80] readers have seen in other contexts, for example that of Spartan kingly rivalry, how intolerable such a situation may be. Consequently, while from the Athenians' perspective *spoudaion* (at 5.78) bears the sense of 'good' often favoured by modern translations[81] (and it doubtless *did* seem a good thing *for Athens*), the narrative is at the same time open to the interpretation of others—especially, perhaps, her future subjects—for whom the sense must come closer to 'weighty', or 'of concern'.[82]

Thus we find the irony that being free(d) does not necessarily motivate one to help others reach the same condition, but rather the reverse: indeed, Aristagoras approached Athens, freed from her tyrants, αὕτη γὰρ ἡ πόλις τῶν λοιπέων **ἐδυνάστευε μέγιστον** ('since this city **was the most powerful** of the others' (i.e. aside from Sparta), 5.97.1).[83] This carries the implication that *this* is the sort of freedom that the Athenians have fought for; that, in their view, has been (and, under their fifth-century democracy, is[84]) *worth* fighting for. Here as elsewhere we are

---

[80] e.g. Croesus, told by Delphi to 'make the Greek his friend', sidesteps Athens (weak under tyranny) for Sparta; Aristagoras approaches Sparta first. This polarity is anachronistic (French (1972), esp. 19–20; Gray (1997); Fowler (2003), etc.), reflective rather of late fifth-century power politics, but consequently all the more expressive for Herodotus' contemporary audience.

[81] e.g. compare Godley: 'a good thing'; Nenci 'un bene prezioso'; de Sélincourt/Marincola: 'how noble a thing'; Legrand 'l'excellence'; Waterfield frames it in terms of 'the advantages', thus avoiding such ethical overtones.

[82] i.e. closer, perhaps, to the sense of τὰ σπουδαιέστερα τῶν πρηγμάτων in the first book as 'the most important/gravest of concerns', which Candaules confides to Gyges, 1.8.1, and the Persians deliberate over drunk then sober, 1.133.3; cf. Ubsdell (1983), 183–4. Aristotle plays on the two senses II.1. ('*worth serious attention, weighty*') and II.2. ('*good of its kind, excellent*') at *NE* 1176$^b$25 and 1177$^a$3: LSJ s.v. σπουδαῖος; tragedy is properly concerned with action that is *spoudaios* especially, perhaps, in the second sense, e.g. at *Poetics* 1449$^b$24.

[83] ἐδυνάστευε is a word with particularly undemocratic overtones! Cf. Thucydides' Thebans' definition of δυναστεία ὀλίγων ἀνδρῶν ('a *dynasteia* of few men') as being ἐγγυτάτω δὲ τυράννου ('most akin to tyranny', 3.62.3); Munson (2001), 53. It is therefore especially ironic that Aristagoras (if this may be read as his implied view) should see Athens' position relative to other Greek states in such terms; and even more so if it is not his own view, but the one he thinks will be best received at Athens. Cf. Nenci ad loc.: Athens is here hegemon rather than protector.

[84] Might the anachronistic note at 6.109.2 that the polemarch was selected by lot (τῷ κυάμῳ), cf. How/Wells ad loc., be intended to point the reader again (as in Otanes' references to offices selected πάλῳ, 'by lot', and *archē* as ὑπεύθυνος, 'accountable', 3.80.6) to reflect specifically on the later Athenian democracy?

left with the impression that the prospect of gaining freedom for oneself, or bestowing it on others, is not of itself powerful enough a motive to cause a state to run the attendant risks. That in turn will help us understand the attitude of those Greek states who will seem prepared to tolerate Xerxes' rule rather than oppose him; it will challenge—or at least mitigate—the harder-core authorial perspective of, for example, 8.73.3: Herodotus' observation that of the seven nations that inhabit the Peloponnese, 'the rest of the cities, apart from those I have mentioned, adopted a position of neutrality (ἐκ τοῦ μέσου κατέατο); but if I may be permitted to speak freely, by remaining neutral they in fact medized (ἐκ τοῦ μέσου κατήμενοι ἐμήδιζον)'. There are hints elsewhere in the *Histories*, too, that, although the Athenians did indeed, in Herodotus' view, prove 'saviours of Greece' (σωτῆρας . . . τῆς Ἑλλάδος, 7.139.5) in their opposition to Xerxes at Salamis, and the outcome was their freeing Greece, they were not motivated exclusively by aspirations as selfless[85] as they claim at 8.144.

We might turn, for example, to the expressive analepsis regarding Athens' motives in earlier giving over the *hēgemoniē* (chief command) to Sparta, which Herodotus sets forth after explaining why the Spartan Eurybiades had chief command of the fleet at Artemisium ('the allies said that if the Spartan did not lead they would not follow Athenian leadership, but would instead dissolve the projected campaign', 8.2.2). 'For right from the start', Herodotus observes,

ἐγένετο . . . λόγος . . . ὡς τὸ ναυτικὸν Ἀθηναίοισι χρεὸν εἴη ἐπιτρέπειν. ἀντιβάντων δὲ τῶν συμμάχων εἶκον οἱ Ἀθηναῖοι, μέγα πεποιημένοι περιεῖναι τὴν Ἑλλάδα καὶ γνόντες, εἰ στασιάσουσι περὶ τῆς ἡγεμονίης, ὡς ἀπολέεται ἡ Ἑλλάς, ὀρθὰ νοεῦντες· στάσις γὰρ ἔμφυλος πολέμου ὁμοφρονέοντος τοσούτῳ κάκιόν ἐστι ὅσῳ πόλεμος εἰρήνης. ἐπιστάμενοι ὦν αὐτὸ τοῦτο οὐκ ἀντέτεινον ἀλλ' εἶκον, μέχρι ὅσου κάρτα ἐδέοντο αὐτῶν, ὡς διέδεξαν (8.3.1–2).

There had been talk to the effect that the command of the fleet should be entrusted to the Athenians. But when the allies resisted, the Athenians yielded, deeming it of great importance that Greece should survive, and knowing that if they disputed the leadership, Greece would perish. And they judged correctly: for civil strife is worse than united war to the same degree as war is worse than peace. Knowing this, then, the Athenians did not object but yielded, but only yielded for as long as they had great need of them, as they later showed.

---

[85] See below, ch. 7 n. 50 with text.

At this point, Athens' motives in yielding leadership appear altruistic: she relinquished her power for the sake of Greece's survival; and the correctness of her reasoning in so doing (and also, in consequence, the virtue of the action) gains authorial sanction ('they judged correctly: for civil strife...'). Thus the natural understanding of the penultimate subordinate clause is 'for as long as the allies had great need of the Athenians'.

But a rather different reality is next exposed, as Herodotus continues:

ὡς γὰρ διωσάμενοι τὸν Πέρσην περὶ τῆς ἐκείνου ἤδη τὸν ἀγῶνα ἐποιεῦντο, πρόφασιν τὴν Παυσανίεω ὕβριν προϊσχόμενοι ἀπείλοντο τὴν ἡγεμονίην τοὺς Λακεδαιμονίους. ἀλλὰ ταῦτα μὲν ὕστερον ἐγένετο (8.3.2).

For once they had repelled the Persian and were no longer fighting for their territory but for his, they deprived the Lacedaemonians of the leadership, using Pausanias' *hybris* as a *prophasis* (pretext). But all this happened later.

The perspective offered on Athens' motives thus shifts swiftly from ideal, with the emphasis on her noble relinquishment of power, to selfish. She comes to appear to have desired *hēgemoniē* all along, and to have been eager to seize it the moment she ceased to be dependent on the other Greek states—for this postscript favours an alternative reading of μέχρι ὅσου κάρτα ἐδέοντο αὐτῶν, with *Athens* as its subject ('for as long as the Athenians had great need of the allies')—and had to hand an adequate pretext.[86] Herodotus thus exploits the ambivalence of his chosen wording;[87] the effect is disconcerting, and so all the more powerful.[88] The final phrase invites reflection upon what happened later (ὕστερον), later even than this, with the Delian League transforming into an Athenian *archē*.[89] And yet a disquieting note

[86] Cf. How/Wells ad loc. Asheri on 8.3.9 observes: 'Anche altrove Erodoto presenta il motivo del patriottismo disinteressato ateniese come un elemento di propaganda (VIII 144; IX 7)' ('Elsewhere, too, Herodotus presents the motive of unselfish Athenian patriotism as an element of propaganda'), *contra* Pohlenz (1937), 150.

[87] Cf. Munson (2001), 216; *pace* arguments for one exclusive reading, with 'Athenians' as subject, e.g. Stein and Asheri ad loc., or 'allies' as subject, e.g. Immerwahr (1966), 220–2 with n. 87; Harrison (2002), 575: thus in my view Herodotus does *not* 'accept...at face value' the Athenians' report of their 'noble suppression of their desire for a share in the command', ibid., but rather puts it to subversive use.

[88] A comparison might be made with Michelini (1987) on Euripides' technique.

[89] Foreshadowing of Athens' future empire-building may be felt also in Miltiades' vision of Athens as *first* of Greek cities (above, n. 79 with text) and in Themistocles' threats to Adeimantos that no Greek *polis* could repel an attack by the Athenians (8.61.2).

had in fact been sounded earlier with the mention of the allies' negative attitude towards Athens (8.2.2), which was left strangely unexplained, but turns out to have paved the way for the shift of perspective that follows.

Again, to turn to the broader sweep, we have seen that Athens was not unduly concerned to be rid of her tyrants; gained *isēgoriē* through the contrivances of an aristocrat with tyrannical associations; was prepared then as later to use her newfound military might to enslave others; and proved victor at Marathon and later saviour of Greece not on the whole through democratic processes but through the workings of ambitious individuals like Miltiades and Themistocles—individuals functioning to a large extent in a self-seeking, autocratic way. Indeed, the particular brand of Athenian egoism they display seems to be *promoted* by *isēgoriē*: for, as Herodotus framed it, 'once they had been freed, each individual was eager to achieve for himself (αὐτὸς ἕκαστος ἑωυτῷ προεθυμέετο κατεργάζεσθαι)' (5.78).[90] And again, the Athenian *dēmos* proved easier to deceive than a single person, apparently (as suggested above, 165) because it was more easily carried away by Aristagoras' evocations of the profit to be had. It comes to seem that the kind of 'desire for freedom' that has the power to be a spur to action may be specifically the freedom *to* act in one's own interests, and including—most prized of all—the exercise of rule over others. Nor is Sparta wholly innocent in this regard, though that is manifested more in relation to her individuals: the narrative hints that she was implicated, for example, in Cleomenes' bid to install tyranny at Athens, and 'the Spartans' did very nearly reinstall Hippias.[91] The question of Sparta's commitment to Greek freedom continues to come under fire (especially in her delay before Plataea), though that will be a matter more of her failing to defend it than of seeking to tyrannize others. Might we suspect that the absence of the promise of rule *for herself*— being constrained as she is by her subject population of helots—is what promotes her notorious apathy?

---

[90] Cf. the Hippocratic *Airs, Waters, Places* 23 (as noted by Stein ad loc.): ὅσοι δὲ αὐτόνομοι . . . προθυμεῦνται ἑκόντες καὶ ἐς τὸ δεινὸν ἔρχονται. τὰ γὰρ ἀριστεῖα τῆς νίκης αὐτοὶ φέρονται ('People who are independent are eager and willing to go even into danger, for they themselves take the prize of victory').

[91] Cf. also Eurykleon and Pausanias.

Thus the Athenians and Samians are not alone. Rather, the *Histories* sets forth an idea of human nature[92] that recalls Otanes' formulation, as something that inexorably leads individuals and communities to desire to possess *more*. Moreover, as we have seen in several instances, the question of whether motives are principled or pragmatic is not after all wholly clear-cut, even if that appears prima facie to be implied by Herodotus' method of ascribing *alternative* motives. It is more often a matter of progression in response to changing circumstances. An initial genuine appreciation of freedom, for example, may become perverted by the prospect of money or power; and the acquisition of either of those may in turn distort the original attitude all the more, since, as Otanes put it (3.80.3), even the best of men is soon corrupted by power and possessions. Thus we are dealing with what appears to be a *dynamic* rather than a *static* concept of motivation. Herodotus' model is flexible, allowing for change over time: what is at stake seems more complicated than simply a stable rift between surface and underlying reality. Perhaps Plutarch did not recognize this, and thus assimilated what he saw to the Tacitean innuendo with which he was familiar.[93] Once again, it comes frequently to seem a matter of *complex* psychology: of *combinations* of motives, which may indeed at times seem incongruous. Herodotus' presentation of these different possibilities, in the case of an individual, will be explored further below, in the context of his depiction of Themistocles' motives (ch. 9). In the next chapter, however, we continue our focus on group motives, exploring how Herodotus, through his suggestive portrayal of the motives and fears of the Greek states, brings out the extraordinary character of the Athenians' decision not to medize.

---

[92] *Pace* Reinhold (1985), 22. In this respect Herodotus is far closer to Thucydides than is usually admitted: see Raaflaub (2002), illuminating for example the *Histories'* 'trenchant general characterization of imperialism as a political phenomenon. It is nourished by *pleonexia*, an insatiable desire for more' (176); Lateiner (1989), 210: 'Herodotus invented political history as the modern world knows it'; and esp. Ubsdell (1983).

[93] I thank John Marincola for suggesting to me the potential usefulness to my interpretation of this distinction between 'dynamic' and 'static' concepts of motivation, and also for the idea of Plutarch's misunderstanding and assimilation to Tacitean innuendo.

# 7

## To medize or not to medize ...: compulsion and negative motives (Books VII–IX)

Readers are likely to feel sceptical (as the last chapter has indicated) about swallowing wholesale the Athenians' story at 8.144 of exclusively pure and noble motives, suspecting it represents a partly rhetorical move—and perhaps all the more so when they are next confronted with the quite different rhetorical stance of the Athenian address to the Spartans at 9.11. And yet in various ways Herodotus' narrative invites readers at the same time to appreciate what is more important, pushing this to the forefront of their minds: the fact that the Athenians did ultimately stand their ground for the sake of Greece (and themselves), *refusing*—unlike most other Greek states—to cave in to the various considerations that might well have precluded them from taking positive action, even enticed (or compelled) them actively to medize. Led by the unifying figure of their *stratēgos* Themistocles, they defied the ever-threatened 'scattering each to one's own *polis*' to instead prove true saviours *of Greece*. They sustained that resistance in holding together the Greek effort even as their city faced a second torching at Mardonios' hands. The *outcome* of the Greco-Persian Wars—thanks to the Athenians' 'holding firm' (καταμείναντες, 7.139.6)—was indeed in the interests of Greek freedom and unity. Even the volte-face in the Athenians' rhetoric at 9.11 may be explicable in context (as we shall see), and is in any case overshadowed by, in one direction, the contrast between the Athenians' profession (at least) of commitment to laudable ideals and Sparta's blatant disregard of such in the immediate aftermath; and, in another, by the (relatively) satisfactory final result (action on Sparta's part—if grossly belated).

This chapter considers how Herodotus' depiction of a range of Greek responses to the Persian threat draws attention to certain aspects of the Athenians' decision.

The earlier Ionian Revolt narrative powerfully influences readers' responses when they come to assessing the behaviour and motives of the various Greek states, including Athens, in responding to Xerxes' westwards advance. Readers are attuned to the same patterns when they resurface, and they expect similar combinations of motives. And indeed a similar picture emerges, of Greek states anything but united in democracy, and of the real and continual risk that states and individuals will put personal gain ahead of all other considerations. The backdrop of the Ionian revolt and related narratives thus leaves readers with the distinct impression that (when it comes to the later defence) it is *not at all surprising* that several Greek states choose to side with Persia, but rather entirely to be expected. For, as we have seen, it is a rare moment in that narrative when people *are* moved to action by ideals, and even then (as in the case of the Athenians' choice to fight at Marathon) those ideals are rarely distinctly separable from considerations of personal *kerdos*. What comes to seem particularly remarkable against this background is that at 7.145 several Greek states—spearheaded by Athens—*do* manage to band together against the Persian threat, dissolving their local wars and sending spies to persuade the rest of Greece to help; and that they do so on the grounds that it poses a threat *to all Greeks alike* (ὡς δεινῶν ἐπιόντων ὁμοίως πᾶσι Ἕλλησι, 7.145.2).

But also, in a different direction, the opportunity for virtual *opsis* furnished by Herodotus' text has familiarized readers with the negative considerations and motivations that might preclude states from taking action against the Great King, encouraging readerly understanding and even empathy towards their predicament. The account of the fate of Miletus in particular has helped readers to appreciate the levels of fear and apprehension that such an event inspires, as it did even a good year (possibly several) later, in the audience of Athenians watching Phrynichos' play (6.21).[1] The consequent attraction of risk-averse policies is obvious and understandable—as is the perception on the

---

[1] Rosenbloom (1993), 172 dates Phrynichos' production to 493/492–491/490, i.e., one to four years after the capture of Miletus in 494 BC.

part of some states that for survival's sake they have no choice *but* to adopt them. Readers will feel this all the more in the coming narrative as they hear recounted, for example, the terrible fate of the Phocians (8.32–3). Again, the downbeat feel of the Ionian Revolt narrative has implied more generally that a movement even in the name of freedom may not—in the light of a negative outcome, and one involving such destruction—be held to have been worthwhile.

Over the course of the initial stages of the narrative of Xerxes' invasion this second, negative aspect gains emphasis. The opposition frequently apparent in Herodotus' presentation of motives over the course of the Greek narratives of the fifth and sixth books—of ideal motives set against more pragmatic—comes gradually to be eclipsed by the different opposition of *motives* versus *necessity*. The idea that necessity (and equally, *perceptions* of necessity) circumscribes people's freedom of choice in their actions has throughout been implicit in the background,[2] but from this moment it seems to be lent increasing emphasis. Connected with this is the way in which the Xerxes' invasion narrative bears a sense of inevitability less evident in the Ionian sequence of events (which, I have suggested, had more the feel of having been *chosen*[3]).

## 7.1 NECESSITY? (7.60 ff.)

Xerxes' numbering of his army at Doriskos, after crossing over the Hellespont and into Thrace, gives Herodotus occasion to describe the contingents of the invading force. He notes the dramatic figure[4]

---

[2] e.g. in the story of Athenians under Peisistratid rule (chronologically displaced to a more expressive location within the Ionian Revolt narrative): present realities diminish the possibility of a meaningful choice of freedom over tyranny (cf. §5.4 above).

[3] Above, ch. 6 n. 47 with text.

[4] Surely to be explained in terms of ancient authors' common preference in using numbers not literally but for impressionistic effect true to contemporary perception; cf. Barron (1988), 594 n. 6: 'Hdt.'s high figures in VIII.113.2–3, 126.1 and IX.32.2 are for the present writer rhetorical, not mathematical.' (But note Rubincam's 'quantification' (2003) of Fehling (1989), 216–39, showing that 'not only is Herodotus' preference for 'typical' numbers lower than that of all but one of the poetic works [selected for the study]; it is also lower than Xenophon's and equal to that of Thucydides!' (462).) See Konstan (1987) on Herodotus' portrayal of the Persian taste for quantification.

reached by Xerxes' method—'the number of the whole land army was found to be 1,700,000' (7.60.1)—and then, taking over from Xerxes, himself recounts in detail the many and varied nations serving in his army and fleet (7.61–95). The effect produced by the account of the advance westwards of Persian conquest (of Egypt, Lydia, etc.) which structured the narrative of the earlier books—the sense of its all-consuming and overpowering nature—is here mirrored and amplified, with the presentation of so many and varied nations now at Persia's beck and call. (The effect will be repeated at 7.184–6, with Herodotus' recalculation of Xerxes' numbers before Artemisium and Thermopylae.) Most expressively, these nations now include the newly conquered Carians (7.93) and Ionian Greeks (7.94). In the narrative of Xerxes' march westwards from here, a motif that gains ground is that of the King as locus of necessity. Thus Herodotus opens this stretch of narrative: 'Xerxes marched from Doriskos to Greece, **compelling** all in his path to join his expedition (τοὺς δὲ αἰεὶ γινομένους ἐμποδὼν συστρατεύεσθαι **ἠνάγκαζε**)' (7.108.1); and he recapitulates for emphasis:

For as I earlier related, **the whole country** as far as Thessaly had been enslaved and was a tribute-paying subject of the King (ἐδεδούλωτο . . . ἡ μέχρι Θεσσαλίης πᾶσα καὶ ἦν ὑπὸ βασιλέα δασμοφόρος), through the conquests of Megabyzus and afterwards Mardonios (7.108.1).

Xerxes' advance is thus represented as compelling all in its wake into a state of subjection, with only an occasional exception to prove the rule: such as the Satrai alone of all the Thracians, whose geography and exceptionally warlike nature afford them protection (7.111.1). The Thessalians, conversely, are constrained by their geography—for they inhabit 'a land easy to take and quickly conquerable' (7.130.2)— as Xerxes' subversive investigation (confirmed by Herodotean observation, 7.129) goes to show. Xerxes' engineering project in Pieria renders similarly constrained the Perrhaiboi: 'A third of the men were cutting through the Macedonian mountains, in order that the whole army could pass by this route to the Perrhaiboi' (7.131). The immensity of Persian numbers is emphasized by the recurrent motif of rivers drunk dry,[5] and by the description of the extraordinary

---

[5] e.g. 7.109, 110.

preparations and expenditure that burden the Greek cities entertaining the King (7.118–19). Herodotus records Megakreon's apt later saying, that the people of Abdera should thank the gods that Xerxes dines just once a day: if he ate breakfast too, they would have had to flee before his advance, 'or remain and be consumed/perish (ἐκτριβῆναι) most miserably of all men' (7.120.2). All communities are encompassed, whether on land or sea.[6] *Anankē* and *piez-* vocabulary persists.[7] No longer does it seem a question of cities *choosing* to act as they so desire; to a greater extent their action is circumscribed by the necessity represented by Xerxes' purposeful advance. The idea is lent further emphasis by the notion that the Persian king is himself compelled by Persian tradition to extend his dominions.

Consequently, the authorial comment at 7.132, on the occasion of the return to Xerxes of the heralds charged with demanding the Greeks' submission (some returning empty-handed, others not, 7.131), comes as a surprise to readers. For after first listing those states who paid the tribute—'the Thessalians, Dolopians, Enienians, Perrhaiboi, Locrians, Magnesians, Malians, and Phthotian Achaeans, as well as the Thebans and the rest of the Boeotians except for the Thespians and the Plataeans' (7.132.1)—Herodotus observes:

---

[6] Cf. Herodotus' all-encompassing *men-de* phrasing as regards the Thracians in this instance: τούτων οἱ μὲν παρὰ θάλασσαν κατοικημένοι ἐν τῇσι νηυσὶ εἵποντο· οἱ δὲ αὐτῶν τὴν μεσόγαιαν οἰκέοντες ... πλὴν Σατρέων οἱ ἄλλοι πάντες πεζῇ ἀναγκαζόμενοι εἵποντο ('of these [Thracian tribes], those living on the coast followed in their ships; those dwelling inland ... all—with the exception of the Satrai—upon being compelled, followed on land', 7.110). The Scythians earlier depicted the Persians advancing against them in similar fashion: '[the Persian] subjugates all those in his path (τοὺς αἰεὶ ἐμποδὼν γινομένους ἡμεροῦται πάντας)' (4.118.5).

[7] Demaratus picks up on the idea of *anankē* in the dialogue with Xerxes after the counting of the troops at Doriskos: εἰ δὲ ἀναγκαίη εἴη ἢ μέγας τις ὁ ἐποτρύνων ἀγών, μαχοίμην ἄν ... ('if necessity were at hand or some great *agōn* (contest/aim) urging me on, I would fight ...', 7.104.3). His posture of anxious deference furthers the notion of the Persian king as locus of *anankē*: σὺ δὲ ἐπεὶ ἠνάγκασας λέγειν τῶν λόγων τοὺς ἀληθεστάτους ... ('since you compel me to speak the truest of words ...', 7.104.1), νῦν δὲ ἀναγκασθεὶς ἔλεξα. γένοιτο μέντοι κατὰ νόον τοι, βασιλεῦ ('now, then, since I was compelled, I spoke. But may it turn out as you wish, O King', 7.104.5). Cf. 7.136.1: Xerxes' guards threaten the Spartan ambassadors with *anankē* on the King's behalf. At 8.140 Alexander presents Mardonios as likewise in the grip of the necessity represented by the King (so as to make the speech ring truer to Greek ears?). But the most poignant evocation of the King as locus of necessity is 9.16, where a notable Persian weeps and informs Thersandros that many Persians follow the King aware of the fate in store but ἀναγκαίῃ ἐνδεδεμένοι ('bound in necessity', 9.16.5). πιέζ-: e.g. 7.121.1.

ἐπὶ τούτοισι οἱ Ἕλληνες ἔταμον ὅρκιον οἱ τῷ βαρβάρῳ πόλεμον ἀειράμενοι· τὸ
δὲ ὅρκιον ὧδε εἶχε, ὅσοι τῷ Πέρσῃ ἔδοσαν σφέας αὐτοὺς Ἕλληνες ἐόντες, **μὴ
ἀναγκασθέντες**, καταστάντων σφι εὖ τῶν πρηγμάτων, τούτους δεκατεῦσαι τῷ
ἐν Δελφοῖσι θεῷ. τὸ μὲν δὴ ὅρκιον ὧδε εἶχε τοῖσι Ἕλλησι (7.132.2).

Against these the Greeks who were going to war with the barbarian swore an
oath. The oath was to this effect: that once [the Greeks'] affairs were well
established [i.e. in the event of victory] they would dedicate to the god in
Delphi a tenth part of the possessions of all those [states] that had surrendered to the Persian, **unless they had been compelled.** Such were the terms
of the oath sworn by the Greeks.

The long list of communities against whom other Greeks make this
oath, qualified only by the potential exception expressed in μὴ
ἀναγκασθέντες ('unless they had been compelled'), sits oddly on the
heels of a narrative that has sketched a picture of compulsion acting
upon *everyone* in Xerxes' path (in particular upon two of the peoples
listed, Thessalians and Perrhaiboi, but readers might imagine similar
circumstances constraining other states too). Does this assumption
of general culpability represent the perspective of those Greeks who
have not yet surrendered, predominantly those further away and so
less weighed down by necessity, rather than Herodotus' own?—for
the prior narrative invites readers to dispute its justice. Or is the
participle to be felt more strongly, a sign to readers that this question—of the compulsion or otherwise of states—is a crucial one, to
be borne in mind over the course of the narrative that follows,
mitigating their potentially too harsh judgements?

Similarly surprising and discordant elements appear in the sketch
(after the digression explaining why Xerxes had not sent ambassadors
to either Athens or Sparta) of the mindset of the Greeks of each camp
vis-à-vis Xerxes' aggressive intentions towards all of Greece (7.138.1).
The Greeks, Herodotus observes, 'did not regard the situation in the
same way' (οὐκ ἐν ὁμοίῳ πάντες ἐποιεῦντο). Those, on the one hand
(οἱ μὲν), who had surrendered to Xerxes, 'were confident that they
would suffer no harm at the hands of the Persians'; whereas those (οἱ
δὲ) who had not surrendered

ἐν δείματι μεγάλῳ κατέστασαν, ἅτε οὔτε νεῶν ἐουσέων ἐν τῇ Ἑλλάδι ἀριθμὸν
ἀξιομάχων δέκεσθαι τὸν ἐπιόντα, οὔτε βουλομένων τῶν πολλῶν ἀντάπτεσθαι
τοῦ πολέμου, μηδιζόντων δὲ προθύμως (7.138.2).

were in a state of great fear, inasmuch as (ἄτε) there were not in Greece ships in a number sufficient for opposing the invader in battle, nor did the majority want to grapple with the war, but rather *mēdizontōn . . . prothumōs* (they were eagerly medizing/beginning to medize).

Is *mēdizontōn . . . prothumōs* to be understood as implying genuine desire—'eagerly collaborating with the Persians'[8]—or just as 'making haste to side with the Persians',[9] whether or not they would have wanted to?

'*Eagerly* medizing', understanding genuine desire, seems the more natural interpretation in this context of the final participial clause, i.e., after '*not wanting* to grapple with . . .' (unless that could itself imply no more than 'not willing . . .': because of practical realities rather than a real desire). But if read in those terms, as implying genuine desire, it seems an unwarranted gloss in the light both of the earlier narrative, and of the first explanation given for these Greeks' fear: for the disheartening impression of there not being sufficient ships for opposing the invader is wholly understandable (as the numbering narrative made clear). Readers might well sense that they are here entering into the *minds* of those Greeks gripped by fear who have not yet surrendered: that this perception of *willing* and *eager* medizing is the reading of a frightened—paranoid—psychology. For again, further incongruity is felt in the shift from the practical fear concerning ships, to the fear that those *at present still in the subset of those fearing and not having surrendered* should be unwilling to fight and actually keen to medize.[10] The effect may then be to remind readers of the extent to which a state of heightened anxiety may colour people's perceptions, prompting unmerited assumptions; that Herodotus' subsequent account, too, based as it is on the accounts of emotionally implicated informants, will risk such distortion.

But the alternative, less emotionally charged reading of πρoθύμως remains possible. After all, *prothumōs* in the case of the Thessalians'

---

[8] In Waterfield's translation.

[9] In Godley's translation.

[10] ἄτε appears to shift in meaning over the course of the two explanations, from implying the authorial validation we usually expect, to representing the equivalent of ὡς (that is, in a drift from certain to more questionable). ἄτε in the *Histories* can indeed have both these senses, as at 1.123: 'given that' the roads were guarded (Harpagos makes use of the ploy with the hare); and he then gives a man nets 'as if he were' going on a hunt (when in fact he is presently serving as Harpagos' messenger).

final medizing (7.174) does not suggest that it was clearly 'desired'.[11] The narrative might be taken to suggest that these Greeks are 'hurry-ing to medize' only after becoming convinced that the cause is lost, with nothing being implied as to their personal desires or motives. And a further possibility again seems to be latent between those two poles. In here being on the verge of 'eagerly medizing', the Greeks could be understood as being in the process of gradually changing their attitude in line with their perception of present realities, of the weight of necessity: a phenomenon Herodotus will explore in the coming narrative. To thus embrace actively the course of action one feels *compelled* towards seems to be a particularly human coping mechanism, and it is one dealt with, for example, by Aeschylus.[12] Notable, as Gillis observes, are the factors *not* here mentioned as causes of medism, i.e., '[b]ribery and money . . . [;] genuinely pro-Persian feelings; or desire for political stability and freedom from internecine warfare':[13] all focus is on the desire for safety. In any case, the ambivalence of Herodotus' expression draws readers' attention towards the very sorts of questions concerning motives that are to be central to the coming account. It provides an appropriate introduc-tion too to Herodotus' proleptic assessment (and the tone in which it is cast) in the following chapter (7.139) of the Athenians' key role, evident in hindsight, in the Greeks' ultimate victory.

## 7.2 NEGATIVE MOTIVES (7.145–74)

Returning to the trunk narrative at 7.145 (after the digression on the lead-up to the war in the Athenian camp: the oracles given to the Athenians, Themistocles' interpretation, etc.), Herodotus recounts how those Greeks 'with the better purpose for Hellas (περὶ τὴν Ἑλλάδα τὰ ἀμείνω φρονεόντων)' assembled and resolved to send spies to Xerxes in Sardis and messengers to Argos, Gelon in Sicily, Corcyra, and Crete to seek military support—

[11] Cf. below, §7.2.4.

[12] We may understand in these terms Aeschylus' portrayal of Agamemnon's dilemma and of Eteocles' sudden turn to desiring to fight with his brother in the *Septem.* See e.g. Gill (1990), 22–7.

[13] Gillis (1979), 60–1.

φρονήσαντες εἴ κως ἕν τε γένοιτο τὸ Ἑλληνικὸν καὶ εἰ συγκύψαντες τὠυτὸ
πρήσσοιεν πάντες, ὡς δεινῶν ἐπιόντων ὁμοίως πᾶσι Ἕλλησι (7.145.2).

taking thought whether somehow *to Hellēnikon* ('the Greek cause') might
become one, with everyone putting their heads together [/acting in concert]
towards achieving the same goal, on the grounds that the approaching
danger threatened all Greeks alike.

Herodotus' detailed coverage of these respective approaches, despite
their eventual failure, functions as an important exposition of negative motives: of the sorts of factors that readers might well expect to
deter communities from taking action; that is, to *motivate* them *not*
to take action. As well as guiding readers' expectations in assessing
the motives of both camps in the later account, it serves particularly
to indicate that a decision *not* to medize is what was exceptional.

## 7.2.1 Argives

The account of the Argives' response to the Greeks' approach presses
again the theme of close-to-home hatreds (*echthrai*) that circum-
scribe a state's freedom of action. Herodotus first recounts the
Argives' version. Learning in advance that the Greeks would be
petitioning their aid against Persia, they had (they say) sent messengers to Delphi, to ask what best to do in light of their recent defeat:
'for recently six thousand of them had been killed by the Lacedaemonians and Cleomenes son of Anaxandrides—and it was because of
this loss in fact that they had consulted the oracle' (7.148.2). Readers
are likely to recall the incident they are referring to, for it is a
memorable one: the Argives' defeat at Hespeia (Sepeia) near Tiryns
at the hands of the Spartans and Cleomenes, which Herodotus
narrated in detail at 6.75.3–78, was the prologue to Cleomenes'
sacrilegious murder of the Argives who had taken refuge in the
temple of Argos following their defeat. The Argives claim (as Herodotus twice reports, for it provides the *raison d'être* for such a
comprehensive account: 6.75.3, 84.1) that this act of impiety explains
the grisly form of Cleomenes' suicide. The narrative, and the Delphic
oracle received by Cleomenes, revolved specifically around the dual
significance of 'Argos' (Ἄργος πόλις: the *polis* Argos/Ἄργου ἱρόν: the
temple of Argos)—a further aide-mémoire of the account when

Herodotus comes to dealing again with (the *polis*) Argos here. As the Delphic oracle had earlier correctly predicted their defeat by guile at Cleomenes' hands, so here we might expect the Argives to take seriously her warning against involvement in the Greek resistance to Persia. Furthermore, in responding to their embassy in this instance Delphi addressed Argos as 'hated by your neighbours' (ἐχθρὲ περικτιόνεσσι, 7.148.3)—tapping into a theme whose seriousness readers can by now well appreciate.

And yet, the Argives continue, despite their fear of the oracle (7.149.1; *phobos*—fear—was a leitmotiv of the earlier account too (cf. 6.77.1, 3), and, as it turned out, with good reason) they remained committed to supporting the Greek cause, on two conditions only. They demanded first a share of the leadership, evidently (and as Plutarch states explicitly, 863b) so as not to serve under Spartan command: a stance that the former disaster at Spartan hands makes understandable.[14] Secondly, they demanded a thirty-year truce with Sparta, in order to give their current generation time to grow into men, as they explain; for 'in the absence of a truce … —if another disaster, in addition to the former evil, should befall them in relation to the Persian—they feared that for the future they should be subject to the Lacedaemonians' (μὴ δὲ σπονδέων ἐουσέων … , ἢν ἄρα σφέας καταλάβῃ πρὸς τῷ γεγονότι κακῷ ἄλλο πταῖσμα πρὸς τὸν Πέρσην, μὴ τὸ λοιπὸν ἔωσι Λακεδαιμονίων ὑπήκοοι, 7.149.1). The earlier narrative lends support to that consideration, too, for in the wake of the Sepeia disaster,

Argos was so bereaved of men (ἀνδρῶν ἐχηρώθη οὕτω) that their slaves took control of all affairs, ruling and administering, until the children of those who died had grown into adults (6.83.1).

In that instance it did indeed take a generation's time for the status quo to be restored. The Argives' fear for the future also seems natural in light of past events.

The earlier narrative thus implies that the two conditions are reasonable. The subsequent account strengthens that impression, since in the case of the Cretans' response to the Greek plea (soon to be narrated, at 7.169–71), Delphi's reminder of the Greeks' failure

---

[14]  Cf. Dewald *Comm.* ad loc.

to help avenge Minos' death though they had later helped avenge Menelaus, and that Crete had been rendered desolate after each incident, immediately extinguishes the possibility of their assisting: 'by reminding them of these things the Pythia restrained them, **although they wanted to help** the Greeks' (ἡ μὲν δὴ Πυθίη ὑπομνήσασα ταῦτα ἔσχε **βουλομένους τιμωρέειν** τοῖσι ῞Ελλησι, 7.171.2). This statement is made straightforwardly, without the inclusion of rival versions: we are given no reason not to accept that the Cretans really were βουλομένους τιμωρέειν. The comparison indicates the Argives' considerable commitment in even thinking of disregarding Delphi's advice, particularly in that the oracle spelt out clearly the potential dangerous ramifications—including the Argives' very fear of becoming emptied of men.[15]

The Spartan envoys replied (the Argives report) that they would bring before their assembly the matter of a truce, but that in no way could one of the Spartan kings be deprived of command. Thus

οἱ Ἀργεῖοί φασι οὐκ ἀνασχέσθαι τῶν Σπαρτιητέων τὴν πλεονεξίην, ἀλλ' ἑλέσθαι μᾶλλον ὑπὸ τῶν βαρβάρων ἄρχεσθαι ἤ τι ὑπεῖξαι Λακεδαιμονίοισι (7.149.3).

The Argives say that they would not endure the Spartans' *pleonexiē* ('selfishness/greediness'), but chose rather to be ruled by the Persians than to yield in any way to the Spartans.

This response is understandable: the narrative has underlined the fact of Spartan obduracy. Readers have seen how deadly neighbourly quarrels (and this one in particular) may be, and comprehend the legacy of resentment that results. The preference for being under the control of a distant power rather than an immediate one is familiar.[16]

According to the second version of the Argives' motives in failing to respond positively to the Greek request for aid (the *logos* 'told throughout Greece', 7.150.1), the Persians had made an earlier appeal that the Argives remain neutral on grounds of common kinship, hand in hand with the alluring promise of good future treatment at

---

[15] Cf. 7.171.1: τὴν Κρήτην ἐρημωθεῖσαν... ('Crete having been emptied/depopulated'); 7.171.2: τὸ δεύτερον ἐρημωθείσης Κρήτης... ('with Crete having been emptied for a second time...').

[16] Additionally, Persian government made little practical difference; one could not *feel* it so much: Hornblower (1983), 18.

the King's hands should he be victorious: 'I will esteem no one more highly than you' (7.150.2). Thinking much of this, the Argives made their request for a share of the leadership 'knowing that the Spartans would not grant it', so as to have an excuse to remain neutral (ἵνα ἐπὶ προφάσιος ἡσυχίην ἄγωσι, 7.150.3). On this interpretation the Argives' behaviour was far more conniving and rational (might we suspect in this a Spartan perspective? Is Herodotus focalizing the narrative through a Spartan gaze at this point?[17]). Content, so far from valuing notions of *Greek* unity, to be persuaded by arguments revolving around unity with the *barbarian*, they are motivated by the prospect of personal gain. No mention here of the pressures arising from their past defeat. And yet the confirmation of this version offered by 'certain Greeks' (τινὲς Ἑλλήνων), which Herodotus next relates, limits the possibility of censure by suggesting that if the Argives did have such a relationship with the King, others too, including the Athenians, have been similarly guilty since then. For Herodotus' audience doubtless paused at the expressively enigmatic ἑτέρου πρήγματος εἵνεκα ('for reason of other business', 7.151) in explanation of the presence in Susa in the middle of the fifth century of Kallias' Athenian delegation.

That meeting of Athenians and Argives at Susa, with its implications of a similarly compromised attitude on the part of the Athenians, in negotiating with the Persians, provides an appropriate introduction to the anecdote Herodotus next tells, of people bringing in their faults to swap, only to realize that they are preferable to others' and to take them away again. It culminates with the statement that 'thus the conduct of the Argives is not so very much more shameful than that of the others'[18] (οὕτω [δὴ] οὐδ' Ἀργείοισι αἴσχιστα πεποίηται, 7.152.3). It is a general point; but might it draw some to reflect back upon the Athenians, later in time even than the Kallias incident to which Herodotus has just referred, to

---

[17] Plutarch quotes this version without making reference, as Herodotus does, to the layer of the informants—which is crucial. Ch. 8 will consider further the presence of such implicit focalization in the *Histories*. Recent studies have explored focalization in various prose works, including Winkler (1985) on the ancient novel; Davidson (1991) on Polybius; Connor (1985); Hornblower (1994a); Gribble (1998), 58–61; Rood (1998); Dewald (1999); Morrison (2006) on Thucydides; and Dewald (1999) on Herodotus.

[18] Trans. Macan, adapted.

their 'more shameful' enslavement—though a democracy—of *Greeks*? Indeed Simon Ubsdell goes so far as to suggest that the comparison may be quite specifically with Athens rather than with other medizing states. He observes:

The traditional view of this Athenian embassy is that it represents some stage of the negotiations for the Peace of Callias, and this remains the most appealing interpretation. In that case the heteron prēgma is calculatedly reticent: Herodotus trusts his readers to spot the allusion. However, the implied significance of the embassy is the same whatever its precise business. It must be taken as an indication of how in the period after the Persian Wars Athens came less and less to see the necessity for hostility towards Persia, and even in some way or another came to terms with the Great King in order to leave her hand free for aggression against other Greeks.... While the Argives may indeed have medized out of self-interest, at least they are not guilty of the Athenians' later hypocrisy in accepting peace terms with Persia in the interests of aggression against those they had earlier called their allies.[19]

Thus—whether or not we accept such a specific referent—at the moment when the likelihood of readers reaching a severe verdict against the Argives is at its height Herodotus plants this reminder that all are human, with flaws, and any judgement must bear in mind the broader context of what others have done. The moral, as Macan (on 7.152.5) put it, 'applied pretty well all round at the time it was drawn. There was hardly a Greek state which had not compromised itself at one time or another, with Persia; they were all more or less tarred with the same brush.'

The third and final version Herodotus tells (which is framed as the least believable[20])—of the Argives actually *inviting* Xerxes into Greece, 'after the conflict with the Lacedaemonians had gone badly for them, desiring any situation over their present distress (πᾶν δὴ βουλόμενοι σφίσι εἶναι πρὸ τῆς παρεούσης λύπης)' (7.152.3)—of course in one sense presents the Argives as most culpable. And yet,

[19] Ubsdell (1983), 248–9, 251–2. For the authenticity of the Peace of Kallias, see e.g. Lewis (1992), 121–7.

[20] It is prepared for by Herodotus' statement that he is obliged to *legein ta legomena* ('say what is said') but not believe it, and by the particle ἄρα ('implying surprise'; Powell s.v. ἄρα II.2, 'introducing the improbable'; Macan on 7.152.12; cf. Denniston (1954) s.v. ἄρα III. (2), which 'conveys either, at the most, actual scepticism, or, at the least, the disclaiming of responsibility for the accuracy of the statement', 38).

significantly, what this version displays above all is the extent of the Argives' present *despair*: the note it sounds is one of pathos. The Argives' motives are here confined to the (negative) desire to avert their present circumstances. Coming to this version with the Argives' self-portrayal (as reasonable people driven to desperate lengths by Spartan intransigence) still fresh in their minds, readers may well sense that it feeds directly back into, and confirms, an important aspect of the Argives' own account, in its evocation of the extent of their desperation. Together, the first and third versions, in their interaction with the earlier narrative of Argive destruction at Spartan hands, depict the crippling pressures that may render a state more wary of a neighbour's proven and potentially imminent hostility than of a distant foreign threat. This emphasis diminishes the power even of the ever possible comparison with Athens' eventual sacrifice of her land for the greater good of all—for Athens had a ready neighbouring *refuge* in Salamis (not to mention a power base in *ships*). Moreover Athens' conflict with Aegina, by now resolved from hostility to peaceful competition,[21] was less potentially devastating than that of Argos with Sparta, which Delphi paints as still threatening.

This poignant sketch of the depths of anxiety that arise from neighbourly hatreds implies that it is not simply a question of communities *choosing* to (de-/)prioritize these as motivational forces: it is more—or at least, on the basis of past history, comes so to *seem*—a matter of survival. And when bare survival seems to be on the line, there can be no possibility of real choice, as the Gyges story in Herodotus' first book vividly depicted. In the case of Gyges, as of the Argives, Herodotus' delving into his psychology (at 1.11.2–4), revealing the despair in which he is driven to make his choice, invites readerly empathy that discourages quickly moralizing judgements.[22] Thus when Plutarch condemns the treacherous nature of Herodotus' account (863d), explaining the Argives' conduct as simply διὰ τὴν ἡγεμονίαν ('on account of the command', 863e), he overlooks the way

---

[21] Immerwahr (1966), 228 n. 110 with text discusses Herodotus' presentation of this change.

[22] Nor is there a real choice for Adrastos at 1.41–2: he is unwilling but obliged by Croesus to agree to accompany his son on the fateful hunt. Later, aware of Adrastos' remorse, Croesus demonstrates the sort of empathetic response Herodotus' text elicits from its readers, in pitying and forgiving him (1.45).

in which the narrative opens readers' eyes to a more profound (and pardonable, or at least understandable) explanation. Leadership, in Herodotus' understanding, was an issue, but a secondary one. It was not a question of the Argives desiring power per se—a typically human motive in the *Histories* (along with desire for material goods, etc.), and one that they should, in Plutarch's view, have put aside for Greece's sake (863e–f). Rather, according to Herodotus' account, the Argives' behaviour was influenced by deeper questions surrounding their relationship over time with Sparta, and their consequent fears. They were motivated not by a positive desire for command, but by the (negative) concern not to fall prey once again to this long-time enemy. Rather than being aimed, as Plutarch thought, at piquing readers' criticism (using underhand methods 'to strengthen his attacks and deepen suspicions', 863e), the effect of Herodotus' presentation is the opposite: to guide readers to *understand*.[23]

## 7.2.2 Gelon

The alternative possibilities of motives versus necessity are staged most explicitly in Herodotus' account of the Greeks' approach to the Greek tyrant Gelon and his failure to join their cause. Herodotus first records in some detail, by means of the direct speeches given by each side, the negotiations that occurred between the Greek envoys and Gelon: the tyrant's responses serve to dramatize his motives in choosing not to aid the Greeks. In responding to the Spartan address Gelon observes the Greeks' hypocrisy in calling on his aid now, when they failed to lend him aid on several earlier occasions, particularly against the equivalent barbarian army represented by the Carthaginians. But though slighted (ἀτιμίης δὲ πρὸς ὑμέων κυρήσας), he refuses to follow their example, and instead pledges significant military aid—on the one condition that he be 'general and leader of the Greeks against the barbarian' (7.158.5). In the face of the hostility of the Spartan response, however, and having duly noted the civility of his own conduct in comparison with theirs and the reasonableness

---

[23] Indeed, Legrand (1932), 31 found 'indulgence [qui] a de quoi étonner' in Herodotus' presentation of the Argives' attitude in remaining neutral.

of his desire for command (7.160), Gelon *does* suggest a compromise (ἡμεῖς τι ὑπείξομεν..., 'we will yield...'): he would be willing to command just one wing, land or sea as the Spartans choose. The Athenians, this time, refuse to waive their claim to the sea; unlike Gelon, as his wording, recalling ὑπείξομεν above, emphasizes (ἐπεὶ τοίνυν **οὐδὲν ὑπιέντες** ἔχειν τὸ πᾶν ἐθέλετε, 'since, then, **in no way yielding** you desire to have it all,' 7.162.1), they refuse to compromise. Thus Gelon bids the Greeks depart. Herodotus depicts him torn between concern for the Greeks, on the one hand, and the requirements of his pride, on the other, with the second factor ultimately weighing more heavily and moving him to take the subsequent action he does:

Γέλων δὲ πρὸς ταῦτα **δείσας μὲν** περὶ τοῖσι Ἕλλησι μὴ οὐ δύνωνται τὸν βάρβαρον ὑπερβαλέσθαι, **δεινὸν δὲ καὶ οὐκ ἀνασχετὸν ποιησάμενος** ἐλθὼν ἐς Πελοπόννησον ἄρχεσθαι ὑπὸ Λακεδαιμονίων, ἐὼν Σικελίης τύραννος, ταύτην μὲν τὴν ὁδὸν ἠμέλησε, ὁ δὲ ἄλλης εἴχετο (7.163.1).

Gelon, as regards this situation, **was fearful** for the Greeks in case they should not be able to defeat the barbarian, **but he deemed it terrible and intolerable** that he should go to the Peloponnese and *archesthai* (be ruled/commanded) by the Lacedaemonians, even though he was tyrant of Sicily. So he disregarded this path and followed the other.

Thus he considers that the honour due to him as tyrant of Sicily (ἐὼν Σικελίης τύραννος) would be compromised if he should relinquish the command to others. He instead sends Kadmos to Delphi with money to be given to the King along with earth and water should he win, but to be returned to Gelon in the case of a Greek victory.

Next, however, Herodotus recounts the story told by inhabitants of Sicily,

ὡς ὅμως καὶ μέλλων ἄρχεσθαι ὑπὸ Λακεδαιμονίων ὁ Γέλων ἐβοήθησε ἂν τοῖσι Ἕλλησι, εἰ μὴ... Τήριλλος ὁ Κρινίππου, τύραννος ἐὼν Ἱμέρης, ἐπῆγε ὑπ' αὐτὸν τὸν χρόνον τοῦτον κτλ (7.165).

that even though he was to be commanded by the Lacedaemonians, Gelon would have helped the Greeks, if... Terillos son of Krinippos, tyrant of Himera, had not brought against him at the same time...

The extremely extended tail to this sentence, offering explanation and details of the 300,000 troops brought by the expelled Terillos and led

by Hamilcar son of the Carthaginian king, gives the feel of weighty
reason indeed for Gelon's inaction vis-à-vis the Greek cause. And thus
(οὕτω δὴ), as regards his motives in sending the money, οὐκ οἷόν τε
γενόμενον βοηθέειν τὸν Γέλωνα τοῖσι Ἕλλησι ἀποπέμπειν ἐς Δελφοὺς
τὰ χρήματα ('**since he was not able to help** the Greeks, Gelon sent the
money to Dephi', 7.165). According to this version Gelon was thus
*compelled* to act as he did, prevented from offering aid since he was
already militarily stretched to the hilt by the Carthaginian attack,
although otherwise he would have helped the Greeks despite the
matter of the command. And indeed the postscript to this version
relates that Gelon's victory over Hamilcar—a worthy adversary, having
been made king κατ᾽ ἀνδραγαθίην ('on account of his bravery',
7.166)—occurred on the very same day as did the Greeks' victory
over the Persians at Salamis. The further *logos* told by the Carthaginians themselves—'making use of a plausible account' (οἰκότι
χρεωμένων, 7.167.1)—concerning the circumstances of Hamilcar's
death in that battle lends confirmation to the Sicilians' story. So too
does what is apparently Herodotus' own authorial record (derived
from personal *opsis*?) of the sacrifices offered to Hamilcar and monuments set up in his honour (7.167). The presentation of Gelon thus
shifts over the course of Herodotus' account from that of one who
chooses not to fight out of understandable if, in context, frivolous
irritation at serving under others' authority and positive desire for the
leadership himself, to one whose motives are more noble but irrelevant
in the face of necessity, for he is tied up with fighting the barbarian in
his own corner of the Greek world.[24]

And yet the first version, in being reported in Gelon's own direct
speech without the qualification of a source reference (and so leaving
the impression of authorial omniscience), retains a persuasive quality, even once the detailed psychological picture it paints has in part
been challenged by the second account. Gelon's responses remain
vivid in readers' minds. Again, the pride on display on all sides
strengthens the possibility of its presence in Gelon's case: for his
intransigence in the first version is matched by that of the Spartans
and Athenians, who refuse to compromise even after he has. In a bid

---

[24] Differently, Munson (2006), 263–5 (Herodotus undermines the claimed parallelism between Gelon's victory over the Carthaginians and that of the Greeks over the
Persians at Salamis).

to reconcile the two versions, readers might well be drawn to engage in further conjecture as to Gelon's psychology, to puzzle over the question of why he spoke as he did. Might it be that—conscious of his powerlessness at this point in time—rather than explaining the situation frankly Gelon demanded the leadership *in order* not to be given it, so as to retain his dignity by avoiding admitting inability to lend aid? The narrative again invites reflection upon the possibility that people may adapt their motives (or rather, perhaps, the motives they allege) in line with present unavoidable circumstances. The fact that such a man as *Gelon* should be impotent in the face of circumstance suggests that others will be far more so. For on the occasion of Gelon's first mention Herodotus observed that 'Gelon's power (*τὰ . . . Γέλωνος πρήγματα*) was said to be great (*μεγάλα*), greater (*μέζω*) by far than that of any other Greek state' (7.145.2); he subsequently offered a digression documenting Gelon's rise to greatness, rounded off ('by such means Gelon had become a great tyrant (*τύραννος . . . μέγας*)', 7.156.3) directly before the tale (*τότε δ' . . .*) of the Greek envoys' arrival; and the first version of those negotiations further built up an impression in readers' minds of the man's immense power and magnificence.[25]

### 7.2.3 Corcyreans

As for the Corcyreans' reaction to the Greeks' arrival and request, Herodotus first reports their immediate and enthusiastic response, which has a feeling of genuineness particularly in that they address frankly their own interests:

*οἱ δὲ παραυτίκα μὲν ὑπίσχοντο πέμψειν τε καὶ ἀμυνέειν, φράζοντες ὡς οὔ σφι περιοπτέη ἐστὶ ἡ Ἑλλὰς ἀπολλυμένη· ἢν γὰρ σφαλῇ, σφεῖς γε οὐδὲν ἄλλο ἢ δουλεύσουσι τῇ πρώτῃ τῶν ἡμερέων· ἀλλὰ τιμωρητέον εἴη ἐς τὸ δυνατώτατον* (7.168.1).

[25] e.g., 7.157.2 (the Spartan envoy speaking): *σὺ δὲ δυνάμιός . . . ἥκεις μεγάλης καὶ μοῖρά τοι τῆς Ἑλλάδος οὐκ ἐλαχίστη μέτα ἄρχοντί γε Σικελίης . . .* ('you have come to great power, and in ruling Sicily you possess a large part of Greece'), 7.162 (Gelon's comparison of Hellas deprived of an alliance with him to a year without spring—which seems to anticipate the loss of life that will thereby occur).

They immediately promised to send [troops] and to help, saying that they must not allow Greece to perish: for if she were defeated, there would be nothing else for them than to be enslaved on the following day; so they had to give as much assistance as they possibly could.

Herodotus next dismisses this, however, as being merely a specious show to be contrasted with their attitude in truth. For 'their reply thus had a specious attractiveness (ὑπεκρίναντο μὲν οὕτω εὐπρόσωπα); but when it was necessary to give help, they had other thoughts in mind (ἐπεὶ δὲ ἔδει βοηθέειν, ἄλλα νοέοντες)': they sailed out in sixty ships only to anchor off the Peloponnese and wait and see how the war would turn out, 'having no hope (ἀελπτέοντες μὲν) that the Greeks would prevail, but thinking (δοκέοντες δὲ) that the Persian would win a great victory and rule over the whole of Greece' (7.168.2). This they did on purpose (ἐπίτηδες), so as to have a plea up their sleeve for the Persians (the historian includes in direct speech their hypothetical response!); but they were ready with a different excuse for the Greeks about their failure to take part in the battle.

And yet the portrayal of the Corcyreans' psychology, particularly the evocation of their shifting emotions, points towards a rather different interpretation of their frame of mind and motives. Readers have witnessed their initial optimism that could imagine at least the possibility of Greek victory, subsequently give way to hopeless despair (cf. ἀελπτέοντες, above)—which matches well the fear displayed by everyone else too, even Gelon. From a psychological point of view, reality might be felt to strike home with ἐπεὶ δὲ ἔδει βοηθέειν (7.168.2, above): when their concrete assistance was required and they bore in mind the potential ramifications of giving it, the Corcyreans changed their tune, 'thinking other things'. Thus at this point despair took hold, preventing them from seeing through their initial (genuine) intentions. The imagined response they held in readiness for the Persians allows a further depiction of the Corcyreans' *hopes and expectations*, this time in the opposite direction (τοιαῦτα λέγοντες ἤλπιζον κτλ, 'saying such things **they hoped**...', 7.168.3): and *this* hope, Herodotus' comment—τά περ ἂν καὶ ἐγένετο, ὡς ἐμοὶ δοκέει ('which very thing would have happened, it seems to me')—seems to imply, was more practical and realizable than their unfounded optimism of earlier. Indeed, few others in this stretch of the *Histories*

appear to believe, as the Corcyreans seemed to at 7.168.1 (οὔ σφι
περιοπτέη ἐστὶ ἡ Ἑλλὰς ἀπολλυμένη..., 'they must not allow Greece
to perish...'), that their contribution could really make a difference
in enabling Greek victory. The emotional tenor of the portrait thus
challenges the authorial depiction of the Corcyreans' altogether
rational advance preparation of alternative *skēpseis* (pretexts/ex-
cuses), worked out in detail, to be used in either scenario (of Persian
or Greek victory).[26]

Two rival interpretations are therefore possible here, each of them
invited by the text. Either the Corcyreans' initial response was, as the
authorial comment suggests, entirely specious, representing an attractive assertion that the Greeks wanted to hear, but not one that the
Corcyreans really intended to carry through. The outcome in that
case was a calculated move driven all along by active motives. Alternatively, the Corcyreans' initial response was genuine and spontaneous, but modified in light of the reality of the circumstances—an
interpretation that the text's wider patterns of motivation might be
felt to support. That is, the authorial gloss is a potential and possible
interpretation of the Corcyreans' delay, and one that no doubt
was held by many Greeks in retrospect: the postscript articulates
this general Greek criticism (αἰτιωμένων...τῶν Ἑλλήνων ὅτι οὐκ
ἐβοήθεον..., 'when the Greeks accused them of not giving help...'),
to which the Corcyreans plead in their defence that they failed to
arrive in time at Salamis οὐδεμιῇ κακότητι ('through no cowardice'),
etc. (7.168.4); but the text intimates that it is not the only possible
interpretation. Readers are thus invited to understand the Corcyreans' predicament, rather than simply sharing in making accusations.
The same tension was even more evident in Herodotus' depiction of
the Argives—for while articulating trenchantly the criticisms made,
he also pressed the need for understanding by means of the anecdote
about people bringing their *oikēia kaka* ('private troubles') into the
open to swap but carrying them home again (7.152). Yes, his narrative implies, people have faults; but then so does everyone, and they
may deserve understanding, particularly if they have felt *driven* to
a particular course of action.

[26] Macan on 7.168.23 remarks upon the oddity of the Corcyreans' seeming to have
come up with their excuse for the Greeks before needing to use it.

## 7.2.4 Thessalians

Herodotus' presentation of a radical change in the Thessalians' stance vis-à-vis Xerxes, from their initial enthusiasm for the Greek cause to their eventual active medizing (even to the point of guiding Xerxes on his route: 8.33), suggests again the way in which necessity circumscribes action, and may even bring about a concomitant change in attitude and motives. At first the Thessalians seem more committed to the Greek cause than even the Corcyreans had been, in actively approaching the Greeks with their offer to lend support the moment they hear of Xerxes' intentions (ἐπείτε ... ἐπύθοντο τάχιστα μέλλοντα διαβαίνειν τὸν Πέρσην ἐς τὴν Εὐρώπην, πέμπουσι..., 7.172.1), rather than waiting to be approached like the others surveyed thus far.[27] Their location early on in Xerxes' path lends urgency. We already saw them in the grip of geographical necessity (above, 206), where Xerxes' mistaken assumption that the easily conquerable nature of their land explains their ready surrender (7.130.2) underlined their steadfastness in holding out at all. In fact it was only the Thessalians' Aleuadai rulers who had surrendered early in the piece and sent messengers inviting Xerxes to invade Greece (7.6.2): Xerxes wrongly assumed that they spoke for their whole nation (7.130.3). The Thessalian people, by contrast, had decided on their policy not 'long before' (πρὸ πολλοῦ [χρόνου], 7.130.2), as Xerxes thinks, but only recently. Now emphasized is the fact that they are in the grip of the necessity imposed by their rulers: 'the Thessalians at first medized **under compulsion** (ὑπὸ ἀναγκαίης), as their acts showed (ὡς διέδεξαν), for they were not pleased with what the Aleuadai were contriving' (7.172.1).

Herodotus reports in direct speech the Thessalians' frank exposition of the reality of the situation, their balanced phraseology underscoring the reciprocal action they expect from the Greeks in return. The pass of Olympus must be guarded, 'in order that **Thessaly and all of Greece** (Θεσσαλίη τε καὶ ἡ σύμπασα Ἑλλὰς) be sheltered

[27] Macan ad loc. notes the strangeness of the initiative coming from the Thessalians themselves, and their coming to the *already formed* Greek confederacy at the Isthmus. The Thessalians' approach must have occurred well after the Greeks' approach to the others, but Herodotus' inclusion of it at this point of the narrative allows a juxtaposition that underlines their particular zeal.

from the war' (7.172.2); they are willing to help guard it, provided the Greeks on their part send a large force (ἡμεῖς μέν νυν ἕτοιμοί εἰμεν συμφυλάσσειν, πέμπειν δὲ χρὴ καὶ ὑμέας ... ); but if not, they warn,

Be assured that we will make terms with the Persian. For it is not right that just because we lie in such an exposed place, in the first line compared with the rest of Greece, we alone should perish for your sake. And you will not be able to compel us if we do not wish to help: **for no force of compulsion is stronger than powerlessness** (οὐδαμὰ γὰρ ἀδυνασίης ἀνάγκη κρέσσων ἔφυ). We will try on our own to contrive some way of being saved (7.172.2–3).

The motif of *sheltering from war* in the oracle to the Argives as here in the Thessalians' words to the Greeks represents neutrality and even medizing as a *defensive* stance, not one taken in the hope of positive gain. In response to this appeal the Greeks resolve to defend the pass of Olympus, but do so only for a few days before abandoning the position—allegedly in the belief that Alexander had their interests at heart in advising as he did, but in truth, in Herodotus' view, motivated by fear:

It seems to me that fear was what persuaded them (δοκέειν δέ μοι, ἀρρωδίη ἦν τὸ πεῖθον), once they discovered that there was also another pass into Thermopylae by inland Macedonia, through the territory of the Perrhaiboi via the *polis* Gonnos—by which very route Xerxes' army did indeed invade (τῇ περ δὴ καὶ ἐσέβαλε ἡ στρατιὴ ἡ Ξέρξεω) (7.173.4).

Only when the Greeks fail to do as much do the Thessalians follow this course. The fact that fear, borne of the vulnerable geography of the place, should so motivate the combined Greek army to retreat underscores again the helplessness of the Thessalians' predicament. And it is a well-founded fear, as Herodotus' additional note—'by which very route...'—makes clear. The reference to the Perrhaiboi recalls Xerxes' engineering work of earlier (7.131). All this makes it all the more understandable that the Thessalians should shrink from opposing him alone. And indeed, as Herodotus concludes,

Θεσσαλοὶ δὲ ἐρημωθέντες συμμάχων οὕτω δὴ ἐμήδισαν προθύμως οὐδ' ἔτι ἐνδοιαστῶς, ὥστε ἐν τοῖσι πρήγμασι ἐφαίνοντο βασιλέι ἄνδρες ἐόντες χρησιμώτατοι (7.174).

The Thessalians, having been deserted by their allies, medized so eagerly, and no longer equivocally, that (ὥστε) they proved to be most useful men to the King in the war.

By 8.33 the Thessalians will be seen actually *guiding* Xerxes' army, and in high favour with him.

Macan's observation (ad loc.) that Herodotus with this ὥστε (with indicative) 'gives not the intentional but the actual result' is important, alighting as it does upon an area of potential ambiguity that revolves around an issue of key significance in the account of the Thessalians' motives in taking the action they do. The sentence mirrors the broader picture: for the final result (their προθύμως, 'eagerly', medizing) was by no means part of the Thessalians' initial intentions.[28] Might this circumstance explain their strangely and otherwise inexplicably *angered* response later on (at 8.31) to the Phocians' description of them as traitors of Greece (when that is patently what they have become)? Do they imagine *themselves* as the ones betrayed, forced into their predicament by the Greeks' failure to encompass them within the defence? And so again in this account Herodotus' text invites reflection upon the negative motives at play and the force of necessity, and specifically upon the way in which in the face of necessity people may adapt not only their course of action but their frame of mind, moulding their desires and motives in keeping with realities.

## 7.2.5 Thebans

The Thebans are not approached by the Greeks in the preliminaries, but do represent a further—and the final—case study of the Greek states' motives in responding as they do to Xerxes' advance and the imminent war, this time a powerful counter-example. For while Herodotus shows understanding of the other Greeks' predicament, 'To the Thebans'—as Plutarch complains—'he does not give the same understanding, though they lay under the same compulsion (τῆς αὐτῆς ἀνάγκης οὐ δίδωσι τὴν αὐτὴν συγγνώμην)' (864e). Herodotus' sketch of their motives and conduct at Thermopylae—having the four hundred stay behind with Leonidas as hostages, 'unwillingly and reluctant'

---

[28] See above, 209–10 for μηδιζόντων ... προθύμως at 7.138.2.

(ἀέκοντες ... καὶ οὐ βουλόμενοι, 7.222)—does seem a notable example of his 'choosing the worst explanation' (cf. *Malice* 855e–856a, and above, 13). His portrayal of these Thebans as *hostages* is bizarre (cf. 865a–e), rejecting what seems the more logical conclusion, favoured by modern commentators, that *this* subset of Thebans may have been genuinely loyal to the Greek cause.[29]

According to Herodotus' account, the Thebans are at first constrained by necessity to fight against the King (τέως μὲν μετὰ τῶν Ἑλλήνων ἐόντες ἐμάχοντο ὑπ' ἀναγκαίης ἐχόμενοι..., 7.233.1), but once they see that the Persians have gained the upper hand, separating out from the Greeks

χεῖράς τε προέτεινον καὶ ἤισαν ἆσσον τῶν βαρβάρων, λέγοντες τὸν ἀληθέστατον τῶν λόγων, ὡς [καὶ] μηδίζουσι καὶ γῆν τε καὶ ὕδωρ ἐν πρώτοισι ἔδοσαν βασιλέϊ, ὑπὸ δὲ ἀναγκαίης ἐχόμενοι ἐς Θερμοπύλας ἀπικοίατο καὶ ἀναίτιοι εἶεν τοῦ τρώματος τοῦ γεγονότος βασιλέϊ, ὥστε[30] ταῦτα λέγοντες περιεγένοντο· εἶχον γὰρ καὶ Θεσσαλοὺς τούτων τῶν λόγων μάρτυρας (7.233).

they stretched out their hands and approached the Persians, saying the truest of words: that they were on the Persian side and had been among the first to give the King earth and water, and that under compulsion they had come to Thermopylae, and they were guiltless of the disaster that had befallen the King. The result was that by saying these things they survived; for the Thessalians were there as witnesses of what they said.

Even if the choice to survive (ὥστε ... περιεγένοντο) is familiar, Herodotus' statement is barbed (cf. 'saying the truest of words') and condemnatory. And such conduct, moreover, in the *Thermopylae* narrative of all places—where the selfless sacrifice of other Greeks supplies a most potent foil. Thus the rhetoric of blame is not deflected in this instance; and Herodotus' presentation of the Thebans subsequently could hardly be more damning either.[31]

And yet the *Histories'* wider patterns of explanation equip readers to reach some comprehension of the Thebans' conduct: for the Theban theme, with its reminders of the legendary hostility of the brothers

---

[29] Bowen on 865a suggests that the 400 'may have been Greek loyalists; they may have been sent as Polycrates sent his Samian enemies to Cambyses'.

[30] Here following Rosén, Stein, Legrand; Hude: [ὥστε].

[31] Throughout book nine, as Flower/Marincola on 9.2.1 observe (with references to the relevant passages), they are portrayed as 'active and eager medisers'; cf. Immerwahr (1966), 227 n. 109 with text; Stadter (2006), 250–1.

Polyneices and Eteocles (and more generally of the antagonism between Argos and Thebes), has served as a paradigm for implacable
intra-Greek hostilities.³² It might recall the 'cause of Theban medism
(her hostility to Athens)'³³ set out back at 6.108, where Herodotus
recounted the origins of Athens' protection of Plataea against Thebes,
noting that Sparta promoted the relationship *specifically* so as to
embroil Athens in conflict with the Boeotians (6.108.3).³⁴ More generally it gestures towards the depths of hatred—otherwise perhaps
unfathomable—that might provoke such appalling behaviour. Elsewhere, too, in the *Histories*, we find models of how explanation on the
mythic level may take over where human explanations (in terms of
motivation and so forth) fail or prove somehow inadequate.³⁵ Thus
Herodotus does not *condone* the Thebans' actions, but to this extent he
allows readers to *comprehend* them.

## 7.3 ATHENIANS (7.139; 8.140–4)

Herodotus' shifting presentation of motives over the course of these
accounts—most markedly in the case of Gelon—exposes the degree to
which actions and decisions may be circumscribed by the absence of
sufficient freedom of will, but also may change in response to inescapable circumstances. Where circumstances leave little room for being
motivated by grand, abstract ideals, the baseline may shift: what
matters most is what one nonetheless manages to *do*. This stretch of
narrative, documenting the failure of various states to champion the
Greek cause in the face of Xerxes' advance, conditions readers' responses to the Athenians' decision, at this stage and subsequently, *not*
to medize, and to what prima facie appears their strangely altered

³² e.g. mapped on to the Cleomenes ~ Demaratus hostility: see above, ch. 6 n. 28
with text.
³³ Immerwahr (1966), 227 n. 109.
³⁴ Cf. above, 134.
³⁵ Cf. e.g. Herodotus' explanation of Mardonios' impulse (δεινὸς ... ἵμερος, 9.3) to
sack Athens a second time: twinned with *agnōmosunē* ('obstinacy')—a non-specific
explanation—Herodotus adds a second strand of motivation (Mardonios' desire to
relay the news back to Persia by means of fire signals placed on successive islands),
which through its mythic resonances, Promethean and Oresteian, opens up far wider
strands of explanation (suggestive e.g. of divine forces and cosmic inevitability).

attitude in the lead-up to Plataea. It comes to seem that it may not so much be motives that are positive (in both senses) that play a decisive role in shaping history, as negative ones: notions of freedom and unity may pervade the rhetoric, as they do especially in the Ionian Revolt narrative, but they have little motivational power if an individual or state is (or allows itself to be) constrained by other factors from choosing a particular course of action. Thus of key importance—and as 7.139 makes especially clear—is the fact that the Athenians *refused* to be motivated either by fear of the approaching danger, or by the 'frightening oracles' emanating from Delphi (given extensive narrative coverage), to abandon Greece or to side with Xerxes:

εἰ Ἀθηναῖοι **καταρρωδήσαντες** τὸν ἐπιόντα κίνδυνον ἐξέλιπον τὴν σφετέρην, ἢ καὶ μὴ ἐκλιπόντες ἀλλὰ μείναντες ἔδοσαν σφέας αὐτοὺς Ξέρξῃ.... **οὐδέ** σφεας **χρηστήρια φοβερὰ** ἐλθόντα ἐκ Δελφῶν **καὶ ἐς δεῖμα βαλόντα** ἔπεισε ἐκλιπεῖν τὴν Ἑλλάδα, ἀλλὰ καταμείναντες ἀνέσχοντο τὸν ἐπιόντα ἐπὶ τὴν χώρην δέξασθαι (7.139.2, 6).

If **through fear of the approaching danger** the Athenians had abandoned their country, or even if they had not abandoned it but remained and surrendered to Xerxes.... **But not even the frightening oracles** coming from Delphi **threw them into fear** and persuaded them to abandon Greece. They stood firm and found the courage to withstand the invader of their country.

Had the Athenians given in, Herodotus conjectures, the allies would have become subject to necessity, and so betrayed the Spartans 'not willingly but under compulsion' (οὐκ ἑκόντων ἀλλ᾽ ὑπ᾽ ἀναγκαίης, 7.139.3), as eventually the Spartans too would have been. These would either have fought nobly to the death or else, upon witnessing the rest of Greece medizing, have themselves made terms with Xerxes. The Athenians instead chose that Hellas be free (ἑλόμενοι... τὴν Ἑλλάδα περιεῖναι ἐλευθέρην, 7.139.5).

The outcome of the Greeks' approaches to Gelon and the various *poleis*, as well as the build-up to that narrative presenting Xerxes as locus of *anankē*, allows readers more fully to understand why the Spartans at 8.141 'were extremely afraid that the Athenians might make terms with the Persians' (κάρτα... ἔδεισαν μὴ ὁμολογήσωσι τῷ Πέρσῃ Ἀθηναῖοι),[36] and so immediately upon hearing of Alexander's

---

[36] Even on its own, as Barron (1988), 595 observes, 'It [Alexander's offer] was tempting: anyone could see that. More particularly, the Spartans could see.'

approach to the Athenians for that purpose (ἐς ὁμολογίην, 8.141.1) resolved to send envoys to be present at the proceedings. The prior narrative, with its staging of powerful negative motives, thus show-cases the *persuasiveness* of Alexander's speech to the Athenians at 8.140. And in relaying Mardonios' words Alexander explicitly guides his internal audience, but also readers, to think back upon that previous stretch of history (and of the *Histories*): εἴδετε μὲν γὰρ τῆς Ξέρξεω στρατηλασίης τὸ πλῆθος καὶ τὰ ἔργα, **πυνθάνεσθε** δὲ καὶ τὴν νῦν παρ' ἐμοὶ ἐοῦσαν δύναμιν ('for **you have seen** the size of Xerxes' army and what it has achieved, and **you learn** also of the forces that are now with me', 8.140a.3). It is now Mardonios who is represented as being in the grip of the necessity embodied by the King ('this is Xerxes' order, and I am compelled (ἀναγκαίως ἔχει μοι) to obey it', 8.140a.2).

Alexander casts his speech in the form of a direct report of Mardonios' words, which in turn relay (again in direct speech) Xerxes' message and offer. This Alexander urges the Athenians to accept, adding reasons for their so doing and stressing his own commitment to their cause. His presentation of the three layers of argument and advice (Xerxes', Mardonios', and his own) is effective, as well as suggesting a non-Greek pyramid of communication.[37] The speech promises (in the event of Athenian collaboration) land, autonomy, and the rebuilding of Athens' destroyed temples; it raises the spectre of the situation that will otherwise ensue; it warns of the groundless nature of any hope of overpowering the King; and emphasizes that at this time the Athenians may make peace honourably (κάλλιστα). Similar, but less comprehensive, arguments have moved others to medize or remain neutral. The offer is also plausible: readers are familiar with the Persian practice of treating well those they respect for their bravery and martial prowess,[38] and Xerxes'

[37] Cf. Pelling (2006c), 112–13.

[38] Cf. the Aeginetan marine Pytheas, saved by the Persians and honoured for his valour in fighting them aboard ship (7.181), and the later possibility (9.18) that Mardonios is testing whether the Phocians 'have any share in valour' (τι ἀλκῆς μετέχουσι). Leonidas represents a dramatic exception, but that is where Herodotus enunciates the principle (Xerxes must have been incensed against Leonidas more than against any other man, or he would not have treated his corpse as he did, 'since of all the peoples known to me the Persians are the most accustomed to honour men who are brave in war', 7.238.2), and it is all the more memorable for it.

thought processes in making it have anyhow been precisely sketched (8.136.2). Again, the Persians have proved willing to forgive the past wrongs committed against them.[39] And Greeks in the *Histories do* regularly accept such invitations from foreigners. In the most conspicuous parallel, Sparta, approached as Athens is here thanks to her martial pre-eminence among Greek states, accepted Croesus' invitation, and in part because she was flattered by the offer[40]—which is just the strategy of persuasion Alexander tries to use on the Athenians. The Lydian king, like Xerxes here, made his offer after receiving oracular advice to that effect (1.69), and framed it in terms of establishing *philia* (friendship) and *summachia* (alliance) 'without treachery and deceit' (the usual formula for international treaties[41])—much as Mardonios in Alexander's speech refers to *homaichmia* (military alliance) 'without treachery and deceit' (8.140α.4).

Thus narrative and historical patterns converge to indicate that the likeliest outcome, and the easiest option, was for the Athenians to accept Xerxes' offer. It is therefore *amazing*—surely a major Herodotean *thōma*—when they are *not* persuaded, but instead berate the Spartans for their human but inappropriate anxiety, and deliver the impassioned speech of 8.144. And although that speech makes claims of wholly ideal motives on the Athenians' part that upon reflection do invite an ironic perspective, the real emphasis at this point is not so much upon the particular composition of the Athenians' motives, as upon the surprising fact of their having chosen to defend Greece at all. Those other strands and potential interpretations—those we traced in our Ionian Revolt discussion (ch. 6) that invite readers' reflection on Athens' subsequent history, casting an ironic light—are indeed present, but by this point they have paled into relative insignificance. The effect seems much like that of Herodotus' presentation of the early Athenians' motives vis-à-vis the Pelasgians.[42] And the speech cannot be understood

---

[39] Themistocles, for example, committed a great wrong against the King but then went over to his side: Herodotus' readers quite possibly knew the story of how the King excused his κακὰ . . . πλεῖστα ('many bad deeds') of the past (Thuc. 1.137.4–138.1).

[40] 1.70.1: 'since preferring them over the rest of the Greeks (ἐκ πάντων σφέας προκρίνας Ἑλλήνων) Croesus chose them as friends'.

[41] Asheri on 8.140.22; cf. also 9.7α.1.

[42] Above, §5.3.

as being *merely* rhetorical: the narrative that follows, recounting Lykides' fate, portrays in the Athenians' conduct the same powerful emotion as felt in the speech.[43] For when Mardonios, after capturing Athens, reiterates the offer, expecting that the Athenians (now at Salamis) will change their mind (9.4.2), they demonstrate en masse their severe displeasure with a *bouleutēs* who so much as raises the possibility of accepting it. Athenian men ('not only members of the Council but also those outside, when they heard about it') stone to death Lykides; Athenian women do likewise to his wife and children (9.5).[44]

## 7.4 THE SPARTAN RESPONSE (9.6–11)

Herodotus does, however, emphasize the public and performative aspect of the Athenians' speech at 8.144, which is directed as much at the Spartans as at Alexander. The Athenians have contrived that the Spartans be present to hear their response, as Herodotus first describes, and then makes even more explicit: 'they did this on purpose (ἐπίτηδες), then, to display (ἐνδεικνύμενοι) their *gnōmē* (frame of mind, intentions) to the Lacedaemonians' (8.141.1). This conscious rhetorical aspect makes it all the more remarkable that the Athenians should have so misjudged what would be the Spartan response.

For the Athenians concluded their speech by thanking the Spartans for their generous offer to support their households, but expressing their determination to endure as best they can themselves rather than become burdensome to Sparta. Their sole plea was for urgent Spartan action:

Now then, as this is the situation, you must send out an army as quickly as possible (στρατιὴν ὡς τάχιστα ἐκπέμπετε). For as we judge, it won't be long before the Persian comes and invades our country: for he will do so as soon as he learns from our message that we will do nothing of what he has requested of us. So, before he appears in Attica, it is time for us [/'you': see n. 45] to send

---

[43] Cf. e.g. Harrison (2002), 566.

[44] In similar fashion Herodotus has Athenians generally as being responsible for the later appeals to Sparta, rather than named individuals as in Plutarch, *Aristeides* 10.2; cf. Dewald *Comm.* on 9.9–11.

an army in advance to Boeotia (πρὶν ὦν παρεῖναι ἐκεῖνον ἐς τὴν Ἀττικήν, ἡμέας⁴⁵ καιρός ἐστι προβοηθῆσαι ἐς τὴν Βοιωτίην) (8.144.4–5).

Mardonios is then shown acting in immediate fulfilment of these expectations, setting out from Thessaly and leading his army 'in haste (σπουδῇ) against Athens' (9.1). Three short chapters document his journey to Athens and its capture, the diminished narrative space heightening the sense of his speed. Readers have meanwhile been looking for imminent Spartan involvement, and at 9.6—in a stretch of narrative focalized by the Athenians who have moved to Salamis, after the failure of Spartan aid has enabled Mardonios to capture Athens a second time—they are told of the same expectation, now frustrated, on the Athenians' part. Released from their former anxiety by the Athenians' assurances, and with their confidence increasing in proportion to the rise of the Isthmus wall (in the—mistaken⁴⁶—belief it will preserve Sparta in the case of Persian attack even if Athens does medize), the Spartans have begun their excessive delay. This contrasts conspicuously with Mardonios' activity, and also with the speed at which they earlier sent messengers to Athens (κατὰ τάχος, 8.141.2). Their conduct has indeed turned wholly self-regarding, tinged with a measure of hypocritical justification that claims a religious imperative.⁴⁷

Herodotus' reflection (9.8) upon the reason for this change in the Spartans' attitude suggests that it cannot have been shared commit-

---

⁴⁵ Rosén, Stein, Asheri; Hude, Legrand: ὑμέας. Asheri ad loc. defends the transmitted ἡμέας on the grounds that the invitation to the Spartans has already been expressed in para. 4, so that ὑμέας would be superfluous. ἡμέας would also stress the fact that Athens is doing her part in shouldering the burden, in tune with the way she emphasizes her determination to support herself, and also (cf. Pelling (2006c, 120 n. 38) in assisting the wider cause of the rest of Greece. Either way, in any case, the barb points in Sparta's direction.

⁴⁶ Cf. 7.139; 9.9.

⁴⁷ As Herodotus observes at 9.7.1: 'for the Lacedaimonians were on holiday throughout this time, celebrating the Hyakinthia, and they deemed nothing more important than to provide for the god. Moreover the wall they were building at the Isthmus had reached the stage of having its parapets added'. Cf. Thucydides' Spartans, who, according to the Athenians in the Melian dialogue, 'consider what pleases them "virtuous", and what is expedient "just"' (τὰ μὲν ἡδέα καλὰ νομίζουσι, τὰ δὲ ξυμφέροντα δίκαια, 5.105.4). Readers might recall how Sparta was late for Marathon while waiting for the full moon on religious grounds (6.106), and restricted by the Karneia before Thermopylae (7.206).

ment to high-minded ideals that motivated the Spartans' initial concern 'lest the Athenians medize' (μὴ μηδίσαι Ἀθηναίους, 9.8.2; cf. 8.141.1). Their earlier profession of sympathy for the Athenians' plight (8.142.3) and promise to extend help as long as the war should last (8.144.4), and also their appeal to the Athenians' sense of *dikē* (justice), *kosmos* (propriety), and *eleutheriē* (freedom) (8.142.2–3), now appear distinctly disingenuous. Equally, their appeal to the Athenians' knowledge of foreigners' disrespect for faith or truth (8.142.5) has come to seem ironic.[48]

A gulf thus yawns between the intended outcome of the Athenian strategy at 8.144—surely to spur on Spartans (and Greeks more generally?) to fight for the Greek cause by means of this inspirational oratory, perhaps to counter the perception of imminent failure which has influenced so many Greek states to lose hope and medize? (After all, the Spartans, for their part, expect that references to similar ideals may help persuade the Athenians.) To uphold, even promote, an idea of Greek identity that deserves commitment? Even, more practically, and in keeping with what we have sensed elsewhere, to present to the Spartans the public face they could give to similar conduct on their own part?—and its actual failure. The juxtaposition of lofty ideals in the mouths of the Athenians with the cynical, self-serving nature of the Spartan response could hardly be more striking. And the Athenians' response at 8.144 *was* (consciously) altruistic: it had been made clear that they would themselves be well served by taking up Xerxes' offer, guaranteeing as it did to safeguard even their freedom (8.140a.4[49])—as they reiterate in their later speeches that again urge Spartan action.[50]

---

[48] Or rather, even more so than it already did: cf. Macan ad loc., observing how Herodotus' 'whole work belies it [the Spartans' statement], and in particular his account of Persian παιδεία, 1.136'. It was perhaps so as more effectively to tap into the resonances of the Greek/Persian opposition that Herodotus there had the Spartans speak of *barbaroi* and not *xeinoi* (which is how Spartans did historically refer to foreigners), rather than (as Asheri on 8.142.4–5 suggests) mistakenly.

[49] Although the mention of *eleutheriē* occurs in Mardonios' layer of the speech, whereas Xerxes himself spoke of the less comprehensive right of *autonomia* (8.140a.2; see Asheri on 8.140.8 for the significant difference between these terms), I suggest that Alexander contrives that Mardonios' wording eclipse Xerxes', so as to leave the stronger notion of freedom in his listeners' minds.

[50] e.g. 9.7a.2: they behave as they do 'knowing that it would be more profitable (κερδαλεώτερόν) to make terms with the Persians rather than fighting them', explicitly rejecting the *kerdaleos* ('more profitable') course of action.

Indeed the only aspect of their speech that referred exclusively to their own concerns, rather than to those of Greeks generally, was the matter of 'the statues and temples of the gods, burned and demolished'—which Xerxes had offered to rebuild (8.140α.2). Such statues and temples are anyhow (they implied at 8.144) a wider Greek concern.

## 7.5 VOLTE-FACE? (9.11)

A further surprise is in store for readers, however, when Athens, for her part, next changes her tune and appears to buy into pragmatism akin to the Spartans':

Ὑμεῖς μέν, ὦ Λακεδαιμόνιοι, αὐτοῦ τῇδε μένοντες Ὑακίνθιά τε ἄγετε καὶ παίζετε, καταπροδόντες τοὺς συμμάχους· Ἀθηναῖοι δὲ ὡς ἀδικεόμενοι ὑπὸ ὑμέων χήτεΐ τε συμμάχων καταλύσονται τῷ Πέρσῃ οὕτως ὅκως ἂν δύνωνται. καταλυσάμενοι δέ, δῆλα γὰρ ὅτι σύμμαχοι βασιλέος γινόμεθα, συστρατευσόμεθα ἐπὶ τὴν ἂν ἐκεῖνοι ἐξηγέωνται. ὑμεῖς δὲ τὸ ἐνθεῦτεν μαθήσεσθε ὁκοῖον ἄν τι ὑμῖν ἐξ αὐτοῦ ἐκβαίνῃ (9.11.1–2).

You, Lacedaemonians, remain here celebrating the Hyakinthia and making merry, betraying your allies. But for reason of being wronged by you and for lack of military support, the Athenians will make terms with the Persian as far as they are able to. And having made terms, clearly we will become allies of the King, and we will join his forces in attacking any country they lead us against. You will learn thereafter what the consequences of that will be for you.

In the contrast between the sentiments voiced by the Athenians at 8.144 and their stoning of Lycides, and their subsequent volte-face here when Sparta fails to respond, Macan found such contradiction that he was drawn to surmise independent traditions arising from Herodotus' patching together of two different sources.[51] And yet the change in the messengers' strategy is not entirely out of the blue, and is explicable in terms of patterns now familiar. Either Herodotus is tracing the Athenians' gradual and ever more explicit articulation of the necessity that

---

[51] Macan ad loc. Masaracchia on 9.11.8 finds the Athenians' language 'sorprendente' following the stoning of Lycides, but suggests that the whole episode in fact presents disconcerting aspects. Van der Veen (1996), 105 n. 266 observes that scholars have largely neglected '[t]he importance of 9.11 as the complement of Athens' democratic pretensions.'

presses them; or alternatively (or additionally?), he is documenting their use of a sophisticated rhetorical ploy—one that is likely to be all the more convincing with the Spartans in that it appeals to a historical pattern they too, like Herodotus' readers, may be expected to be familiar with. As early as 9.6 the messengers' remit included reminding the Spartans of 'everything (ὅσα) the Persian promised to give them for changing sides', and warning that 'if they refused to help the Athenians, the Athenians too would find their own way of avoiding danger' (εἰ μὴ ἀμυνεῦσι Ἀθηναίοισι, ὡς καὶ αὐτοί τινα ἀλεωρὴν εὑρήσονται).[52] At 9.7α they sketched out the reality of their situation and observed that despite its being advantageous to themselves to do so, 'we will not *willingly* make terms' (οὐ μὲν οὐδὲ ὁμολογήσομεν ἑκόντες εἶναι)—but the condition becomes expressive and mildly threatening in light of the earlier narrative of Greek states who have indeed made terms unwillingly.[53] Thus the Athenian envoys conjure up the spectre of what readers, and doubtless the Ephors, know to have happened in the case of other Greeks (particularly the Thessalians), for whom there seemed no option but to make terms with Persia after Greek aid failed to eventuate. Over the course of this stretch of narrative, then, we may be witnessing either the Athenians' gradual realization that there is likely to be no option but to cave in to Mardonios, rather as we have witnessed on the part of other Greeks; or—more likely—the Athenians' (or their messengers') attempts to give Sparta that impression: for a *further* pattern readers are familiar with is the Athenians' taste for rhetorical ploys.

Indeed, the speech at 9.11 may well be understood in terms of a strategy of persuasion.[54] Readers are familiar with the way people in the *Histories* (not to mention real life) tailor their rhetoric to suit the requirements of a situation and particularly the need to persuade, independently of their real beliefs and motives. They have witnessed the staged quality of the earlier speech; and the preceding narrative has

[52] As Flower/Marincola ad loc. observe, the future most vivid condition 'has been retained in indirect discourse to make the gravity of the Athenians' threat as immediate as possible.'

[53] The same emphasis on the compulsion acting upon them is felt in their final speech, with the reference to the Athenians making peace οὕτως ὅκως ἂν δύνωνται ('as best they can'), 9.11.1.

[54] Cf. Pelling (2006c), 113–14; *pace* e.g. van der Veen (1996), 105 n. 266; Stadter (2006), 249.

left the impression that *any* means of continuing one's resistance is to be embraced. Thus this may be *necessary* rhetoric (to be made all the more acceptable by the outcome of Sparta actually helping). It will be nothing less than Chileus' threatening reminder (9.9) of what is in Sparta's immediate interests that eventually proves effective in motivating her to take action.[55] In fact, the Athenian messengers' speech, in chiming with Chileus' appeal, might in retrospect be suspected to have contributed to Sparta's persuasion. Perhaps nothing else could by this point have been expected to work. Sparta's personal interests, whether to do with piety or security, were known to be powerful factors in motivating or circumscribing her actions.[56] The alternative counter-factuals Herodotus envisaged at 7.139—with Sparta either nobly perishing, or herself following others' example in making terms with Xerxes—served as a reminder that she is as liable as anyone else to human weakness, and not necessarily the fighting-to-the-death paragon witnessed at Thermopylae and imagined by the rosy-spectacled Demaratus. Her choice to survive ignobly rather than perish righteously would have matched that of Gyges, the Kimmerian people, the Thessalians,[57] and many others.

Again, the strategy at 9.11 may be the messengers' rather than the Athenians' (whose opposition to the notion of medizing has been vividly and recently evoked in the tale of Lykides): readers might recall a notorious previous occasion on which Athenian messengers acted independently, offering Darius tokens of subjection[58] and thereby provoking the Athenians' anger upon their return home (5.73). The messengers' persistent reference in the speech of 9.11 to 'the Athenians', using the third person plural, invites the possibility of their having a separate identity and motives from those of the Athenians they represent. (Their earlier speech at 9.7, by contrast, was reported directly, cast—after the brief opening note establishing their identity as messengers: Ἔπεμψαν ἡμέας Ἀθηναῖοι λέγοντες ..., 'the Athenians sent us to say ...'—in the first person throughout: 'We

[55] Thus the irony in the Athenians' change of tack (frequently noticed, e.g. by Harrison (2002), 566) dissolves in context.

[56] Cf. n. 47 above, for religious grounds. Concern with the helots frequently limited her involvement in international affairs.

[57] See above, §5.1.3 (Gyges and the Kimmerian people); §7.2.4 (Thessalians).

[58] A hugely significant gesture that from the Persian perspective, Kuhrt (1988) suggests, could on its own justify the attack on the rebel subject-city Athens.

Athenians . . .'.) The messengers' growing levels of frustration over the Ephors' ten-day delay in responding (9.8.1) can well be imagined, even before Herodotus specifies that they 'were intending to depart, each man to his own city' (ἐν νόῳ . . . ἔχοντες ἀπαλλάσσεσθαι καὶ αὐτοὶ ἐπὶ τὴν ἑωυτοῦ ἕκαστος, 9.11.1). Possibly more notable than their eventual threats to medize is the extent of resistance they have demonstrated first.

Equally, on the Athenians' part, what the narrative suggests may be most remarkable is the fact that these threats do not eventuate: that the Athenians *do* ultimately resist—even if narrowly, and with their frame of mind and motives remaining largely inscrutable—the very scenario played out earlier by the Thessalians (cf. above, §7.2.4). The textual reverberations between the two narratives are powerful. The Athenians' threat to make terms with Xerxes, following the Spartans' delay in coming to help, recalls closely the Thessalians'. The Athenians, like the Thessalians, present themselves as gripped by necessity in doing what they can to survive, expressing their refusal, just as the Thessalians did, simply to perish on their own. As Thessaly was excluded from the area Greece plans to fight to defend, so the Athenians (whether at Athens or Salamis) will be wholly abandoned if the Spartans choose to fight further south at the Isthmus. The Thessalians were initially eager to help out the Greek cause, and only later changed their stance; much as the Athenians initially expressed strong commitment, only now to threaten the reverse.[59] The comparison suggests how easily the Athenians might have followed the Thessalians' example. It is remarkable that they resist making terms, and at the expense of saving their city—which Mardonios delays torching in the expectation that they will (9.13.1).

The failure of Thessaly and other communities underscores the fact that the Athenians (consciously) *chose* that Greece should survive and preserve her freedom: ἑλόμενοι δὲ τὴν Ἑλλάδα περιεῖναι ἐλευθέρην (7.139.5). This important instance—'the greatest free act of the *Histories*'[60]—challenges the emphasis Thomas Harrison would lay upon the 'striking fact that very few [actions in the *Histories*] are

---

[59] 7.172 ∼ 9.11 in other ways too, e.g. 'they will find safety however they can'.
[60] Immerwahr (1954), 37; cf. e.g. Huber (1965*a*), 84–6; Solmsen (1982), 106; Lateiner (1989), 201.

clearly motivated or *willed*; very few are the result of deliberate, autonomous human decision'.[61] The significance in this case arises directly from the fact that the action was not 'robotic'[62] but chosen.

Even if readers are drawn, in the light of its aftermath, to reflect upon the degree to which the Athenians' speech at 8.144 may have been as rhetorical as that of 9.11—upon whether it may have been even more geared at persuasion than they earlier supposed, and so even less revelatory of the Athenians' real motives—any scrutiny of those motives soon gives way to appreciation of what was actually accomplished. The fact that here yet again 'Greek division and defeat were averted by a whisker'[63] makes the story all the more of a *thōma*, and the more worthy of being recorded in the *Histories*. The wider effect of Herodotus' presentation of the Athenians' opposition to Xerxes, so far from downplaying Athenian achievement or that of the Greek allies generally, as Plutarch thought, assuming *kakoētheia* on Herodotus' part, is rather the reverse.

Again, Herodotus' depiction of various Greek *poleis*' failure to join the resistance to Persia is by and large marked—in tension with some of his explicit and more judgemental authorial statements (e.g. 8.73.3, quoted at 199 above)—by an endeavour to help his readers understand,[64] rather than by the incitement of blame. While the ascription of (positive/conscious) *motives* to individuals and groups is widespread in the *Histories* (even while a parallel divine strand of causation is frequently present), leaving the impression that humans have the potential to exercise a substantial degree of self-determination, Herodotus' work is also sensitive to peoples' occasional power-lessness: to times when they are not empowered to make real choices, to frame and act upon their own motives. There is always a line to be drawn, however, and the historian must exercise his personal judgement in determining where to draw it. The Thebans' appalling behaviour, for example, evidently struck Herodotus as beyond the pale of the excusable. His account of it represents a conspicuous exception to his more usual practice of deflecting blame.

---

[61] Harrison (2003), 144 (his italics).
[62] Cf. Harrison's description of 'the majority of actions' in the *Histories* (2003), 144–5, 160.
[63] Harrison (2002), 571; cf. Flower/Marincola on 9.1–3.
[64] Thus the broader narrative invites the qualification of e.g. Bauslaugh (1991), 22.

As well as inviting readers to understand such pressures, Herodotus' narrative suggests how very different people's motivation may appear when viewed from different perspectives. The anecdote of people bringing in their own troubles (*oikēia kaka*) to exchange with their neighbours, but ultimately—after inspecting other people's *kaka*—preferring to return home with their own still in hand rather than making an exchange (7.152), vividly encapsulates this reality of differing perspectives.[65] We have noted instances where Herodotus appears to be focalizing the narrative through the gaze of a specific group,[66] and raised the possibility that readers are alerted by narrative clues to the subjective character of the interpretation. The next chapter will have occasion to explore more fully this phenomenon of 'implicit embedded' or 'deviant' focalization[67] in the context of Herodotus' presentation of Xerxes' motives. The question of authorial (and audience) sympathy in relation to any particular instance remains at issue, for, as Fowler observes,

At any point we can choose to see deviant focalisation: but we can also identify with that suppressed view, or choose to make the narrator the focaliser. . . . [T]here is always a push to unite focaliser and narrator. *It is obviously impossible to distinguish between the narrator representing a character's point of view and sympathising with it.*[68]

---

[65] Compare also its mirror image at 3.38.1–2: if one were to order all mankind to choose the best custom in the world, each group would choose its own.

[66] Above, 208, 209, and ch. 7 n. 17 with text.

[67] The former term is de Jong's (cf. ch. 2 n. 21 above—but see Rood (1998), 295 on why the concept of 'embedded focalization' is problematic), the latter Fowler's (1990), who prefers 'deviant' to describe such 'instances where in normal language we should expect focaliser and narrator to coincide but they do not' (42); '[b]ecause [such implicit focalization] is *not* explicitly signalled, whether we choose to suppose its presence in a particular instance will be a matter of interpretative choice' (44, italics in original). Dewald (1999) argues that the *Histories'* initial narratives prepare readers to 'encounter a number of different, more or less tacitly embedded, focalizations' over the course of their sequential reading (233).

[68] Fowler (1990), 58, my italics. Cf. e.g. Scodel (2002*a*), 144 on *Iliad* 24.24–30: 'we cannot completely separate the narrator from the judgements embedded in such focalizations. In choosing to give the characters' point of view through his own voice, he inevitably gives it some legitimacy'.

# 8

## Xerxes: motivation and explanation (Books VII–IX)

A study of Herodotus' presentation of Xerxes illuminates some of the ways in which motives ascribed to actors in the *Histories* interact, often to a specific powerful effect, with wider patterns of explanation. One important function is to aid the text's latent structures to surface from time to time. Herodotus' conjectures of alternative possible motives, for example, to take the most striking instance, at times appear to encapsulate in more vivid form the rival explanatory paradigms the text offers for Xerxes' behaviour. Thus they sharpen readers' awareness and active evaluation of those paradigms. Indeed, I shall argue that these statements of double unresolved motives mirror the broadly bipartite character of the *Histories'* underlying explanations regarding Xerxes. In other cases, the explanatory paradigms are themselves effective enough in guiding readers to reflect upon questions of motivation, and so they replace specific ascriptions of motives.

We have observed how Herodotus' text tends to favour structural/ explanatory schemata characterized by polarity,[1] in part no doubt because of the particular heuristic value of these. Hartog has formulated the 'rule of the excluded middle': the way in which Herodotus inverts the Persian 'Other' versus Greek opposition, for example, when he comes to deal with Amazons, enables readers to grasp the nature of the Amazons' even more extreme otherness.[2] These polarities are not stable (and this is an aspect Hartog's study played

---

[1] Above, ch. 5 n. 3.
[2] Hartog (1988).

down[3]); they are there to be undermined or qualified; but they nonetheless add intelligibility by offering readers a structure to work from and think with.[4] The discrepancies that emerge between general schema and particular instances[5] draw readers to question the extent to which the polarized schema is accurate, and to modify their conclusions accordingly. Alternatively, a single individual or situation may at times be the focus of polarized, or at least contrasted, frameworks of explanation. In this case readers are drawn into beginning a process of weighing up the alternatives. The question in their minds becomes 'which of the two' explanatory paradigms is the more convincing or useful to think with, as we shall see in the case of Xerxes. As with statements of double unresolved motives, such paring down of options to 'either-or' possibilities seems part of a strategy intended not only to simplify and thus add intelligibility, but also to engage readers all the more actively in the process of evaluation.

The attributions of motives in the Xerxes' narrative (particularly again the attributions of alternative possible motives) may alert readers also to the contrasting *perspectives*—Greek and Persian—that underlie the wider explanations. In this respect their function parallels that of Herodotus' double source citations, which likewise keep readers attuned to the way in which informants' perspectives influence the stories they tell. The motive statements do so more subtly, in a fashion better suited, perhaps, to the extensive narrative

---

[3] See Dewald's review (1990), esp. 220–1; cf. Pelling (1997); Munson (2001), e.g. 74–9, 91–133, remarking that structuralist schemes are inadequate for describing Herodotean ethnographies 'because Herodotus both is subject to cultural ways of thinking and rebels against them, is both a lover of symmetry...and contemptuous of it' (78–9).

[4] Cf. Pelling's remarks: 'Fifth-century Greeks liked binary polarities, that is clear; but they also knew that a polarity does not need to be absolute to be useful—indeed, can be *more* heuristically valuable if boundaries blur and if there are marginal cases which invite further investigation...'; a binary scheme 'is a way of exploring, not a mental straightjacket' (2000), 208.

[5] Dewald (2003), 26 finds one such discrepancy in the *Histories*' portrayal of despotism: 'The tension or inherent contradiction between the overarching structure of the ongoing narrative and the idiosyncratic autonomy of the individual *logoi* qua *logoi* both reproduces and reflects upon the tension between despotism as an organizing theme in the *Histories* and the individual portraits of highly autonomous Greek tyrants within the narrative'.

sequence. Readers frequently are tempted to assume that the contrasting suggestions of motivation do derive literally from different
sources.[6] Such ascriptions of motives thus raise readers' awareness
of the *nature* of the decision they take in prioritizing one sort of
explanation over another: for example, in prioritizing a reading that
seems Greek in flavour over one that appears distinctly Persian
(a possibility considered further below).

## 8.1 THE DECISION TO INVADE (7.3–19)

Herodotus dramatizes in striking fashion the drawn-out process by
which Xerxes comes to invade Greece. It sets the scene for the wider
Xerxes *logos* through the portrayal of a cautious and reflective, as well
as self-determining, ruler. Rather than automatically taking over his
father's campaigns, and despite the narrative pattern of everything
pressing towards Greece, Xerxes takes pause for thought, effecting a
conscious redirection in policy as regards that distant goal (7.5).[7]
Most striking is the extent to which—though beset on all sides—he
*resists* persuasion on this front.[8]

Most notably, Mardonios' strategy of argumentation—twinning
his τιμωρὸς λόγος ('vengeance argument', for invading Greece and
taking revenge on Athens for reasons of justice and defence) with a
tempting evocation of Europe's excellence and the flattering suggestion that it is worthy of Xerxes alone—has already been seen to be
effective: Aristagoras used similar rhetorical ploys in very nearly
persuading Cleomenes to an invasion of Asia (5.49). Xerxes is *not*

---

[6] This may at times be the case; in the absence of corroborating external material it
is very difficult to know. But in any case, in ascribing *motives* Herodotus was largely
working with conjectures, and these are not so dependent on sources.

[7] Cf. Immerwahr (1954): Xerxes' unwillingness to fight the Greeks 'is clearly the
negation of the whole course of Asiatic history up to this point' (30); 'One feels the
force of this unexpected attitude if one thinks back to the very beginning of Asiatic
rule where conquest is motivated almost entirely by this desire "to go always
forward"' (31).

[8] *Pace* e.g. Masaracchia (1977), xix (Xerxes is *not* '*facile* a soggiacere alle pressione
esterne' ('*quick* to succumb to external pressures'), my italics).

persuaded, however, as Herodotus adds and goes on to describe at some length (7.6.1–5), until other factors too have accumulated.

The way these link into the *Histories*' wider patterns strengthens the impression that his persuasion is inevitable. Familiar, for instance, is the way Persian kings and governors accept invitations to conquest, even from those who lack authority.[9] In this case, the Aleuadai are kings (βασιλέες), and their invitation is particularly fervent (πᾶσαν προθυμίην παρεχόμενοι, 7.6.2). A single Greek's argument has twice proved effective in persuading Darius on the two occasions that are most present to readers' minds at this point[10] (Democedes' argument on the lips of Atossa: she spoke as she did ἐκ διδαχῆς, 'from instruction' (3.134.4); and then Demaratus' on Xerxes', 7.3). The influence of this far more persistent Greek effort, one making selective use of oracles, seems even less easy to resist.

### 8.1.1 Xerxes' council

Eventually persuaded (7.7.1), Xerxes frames the case for invasion before a select group of advisers, whom he has gathered together 'in order that he might learn their opinions and himself declare before all **what he desired** (αὐτὸς ἐν πᾶσι εἴπῃ τὰ θέλει)' (7.8.1). This last expression evokes the tyrant's tendency, so well documented in the *Histories*, to foist his personal desires on others … but with it is juxtaposed the beginning of Xerxes' address, in which the king lays striking emphasis on his respect for *nomos* and plays down the relevance of his personal views (7.8α.1). Xerxes emerges not as a victim of personal lusts, but as a figure whose decisions are influenced above all by his understanding of the past. This derives both from his elders (τῶν πρεσβυτέρων) and from his own interpretation of history: he situates himself in relation to the wider category of Persian kings, as the latest in line, and as influenced primarily by his perception of the Persian *nomos* of expansion and its corroboration

[9] e.g. Aryandes' acceptance of Pheretime's invitation into Cyrene (4.167); Darius', of Syloson's invitation into Samos (3.140.5–141), etc. (cf. above, ch. 4 n. 94 with text).
[10] i.e. in the wake of 7.2–3, with its sketch of the brothers' *stasis* and Atossa's power.

in history. He is determined not to fall short of his predecessors in this respect.[11]

Xerxes points his internal audience towards evidence for the importance of this *nomos* in the peoples added to the empire in the reigns of his predecessors—evidence Herodotus' readers are equally equipped to bring to bear, since it was mapped out in the early books of the *Histories*.[12] Even as they sense the limited and rather misguided nature of an interpretation that chooses these men's careers to prove the wisdom of active conquest (for their respective attempts were by no means wholly successful), the carefully reasoned character of Xerxes' stance—which is even based on Herodotean-style enquiry[13]— is conspicuous. This contemplative aspect finds further reflection in his φροντίζ- vocabulary and the carefully reasoned progression of his thought.[14] If his fatalistic mention of the gods (with θεός τε οὕτω ἄγει, 'the god thus drives (us)', 7.8α.1) might strike some readers as ominous,[15] it also reveals his concern for divine opinion; and the more positive note on which the sentence concludes points to the complementary role of the human sphere. The gods' will is

---

[11] Fisher (1992), 370, 373 likewise lays emphasis on the pressure of tradition upon the Herodotean Xerxes (rather than focusing, as do most accounts, upon Xerxes' individual psyche); cf. Saïd (1981); Sancisi-Weerdenburg (2002) (and see n. 134 below). Fisher's argument and mine run in parallel in several respects.

[12] Cf. de Jong (2001), 106.

[13] e.g., ὡς γὰρ ἐγὼ πυνθάνομαι . . . ('for as I learn from inquiry . . .', 7.8α.1), ἐφρόντιζον ὅκως . . . , φροντίζων δὲ εὑρίσκω . . . ('I deliberated how . . . , and through deliberation I discovered . . .', 7.8α.2). Xerxes' ἐπισταμένοισι εὖ οὐκ ἄν τις λέγοι . . . ('one need not recount to those who already know . . .', 7.8α.1) parallels 3.103 (an almost matching phrase used by Herodotus speaking in his own person), van Ophuijsen/Stork ad loc.; διό occurs only once elsewhere in the *Histories*, 'very near by in H.' own narrative preceding the present speech, at the beginning of 6.4', van Ophuijsen/Stork on 7.8α.1.

[14] e.g., διό . . . ἵνα τὸ νοέω πρήσσειν ὑπερθέωμαι ὑμῖν ('on which account . . . in order that I may communicate to you what I intend', 7.8α.2); the echo of 7.8α.1 (ἐπείτε παρελάβομεν τὴν ἡγεμονίην τήνδε, 'ever since we inherited this empire') in 7.8α.2 (ἐπείτε παρέλαβον τὸν θρόνον τοῦτον, 'ever since I inherited this kingship'), which 'calls attention to the successive stages in the narrative', van Ophuijsen/Stork on 7.8α.2; 'thinking this, I did this . . .' (cf. n. above)—in contrast to the Aeschylean Xerxes' 'not understanding (οὐ ξυνεὶς) the guile of the Greek man, nor the jealousy of the gods' (*Persai* 361; cf. 373: 'he did not comprehend (οὐ . . . ἠπίστατο) what the gods had in store').

[15] Cf., noting Sophoclean parallels; Stein, How/Wells, and van Ophuijsen/Stork ad loc.; de Jong (2001), 107.

inescapable, but humans may still do well for themselves by cooperating.[16] The 'god ~ us' balance perhaps parallels the Greek proverbial wisdom on the alignment of divine causation with human uttered by Themistocles at 8.60γ.[17]

Xerxes notes his personal efforts to match past standards, before turning to focus upon matters relevant to all Persians in the present and future. Borrowing Mardonios' technique of matching idealism with concrete material benefit, he sandwiches the temptation of Greece's 'fertile land' (χώρη παμφορωτέρη) between the more abstract and idealized goals of achieving κῦδος (glory) for Persians and effecting τιμωρίη (vengeance) and τίσις (retribution, 7.8α.2). Opening the next stage of his address afresh (reiterating his reason for convening the council), he announces his intention to bridge the Hellespont and lead an army against Greece, 'so that I may exact vengeance on the Athenians for all they have done to the Persians and my father' (ἵνα Ἀθηναίους τιμωρήσωμαι ὅσα δὴ πεποιήκασι Πέρσας τε καὶ πατέρα τὸν ἐμόν, 7.8β.1).

At this point the emotional texture of the speech begins to change. The note of 'vengeance and retribution' (τιμωρίην τε καὶ τίσιν) leads naturally into the amplification of the theme of revenge that begins here, which again naturally becomes coupled with a reference to Darius. This thought of Darius pushes Xerxes on to a higher plane of emotionalism, which spills over into resentment at the fact that his father's desire for revenge was curtailed:

ὡρᾶτε μέν νυν καὶ Δαρεῖον ἰθύοντα στρατεύεσθαι ἐπὶ τοὺς ἄνδρας τούτους. ἀλλ᾽ ὁ μὲν τετελεύτηκε καὶ οὐκ ἐξεγένετό οἱ τιμωρήσασθαι· ἐγὼ δὲ ὑπέρ τε ἐκείνου καὶ τῶν ἄλλων Περσέων οὐ πρότερον παύσομαι πρὶν ἢ ἕλω τε καὶ πυρώσω τὰς Ἀθήνας, οἵ γε ἐμὲ καὶ πατέρα τὸν ἐμὸν ὑπῆρξαν ἄδικα ποιεῦντες ... (7.8β.2).

You have seen that Darius strove to campaign against these men: but he died before he managed to punish them. I, on his behalf and on behalf of the rest of

---

[16] Van Ophuijsen/Stork 7.8α.1 (observing that this is the general idea of the passage).

[17] οἰκότα μέν νυν βουλευομένοισι ἀνθρώποισι ὡς τὸ ἐπίπαν ἐθέλει γίνεσθαι· μὴ δὲ οἰκότα βουλευομένοισι οὐκ ἐθέλει οὐδὲ ὁ θεὸς προσχωρέειν πρὸς τὰς ἀνθρωπηίας γνώμας ('for humans who make reasonable plans, these generally turn out; but in the case of those whose plans are unreasonable, nor is the god likely to support their human designs'). Cf. Themistocles' description of the gods acting in support of human efforts (8.109.3).

the Persians, will not rest until I have captured Athens and burned it. For the Athenians were the initiators of unjust deeds against my father and me...

Readers' engagement in the progressive transformation of Xerxes' mood—played out in real time through direct speech—allows them to witness an understandable progression, with the King being carried away by emotion and no longer governed by the reasoned approach of earlier.[18] Alternatively (or additionally), they may find an explanation for the changing texture in the increasing levels of rhetoric Xerxes deems necessary to impress and inspire his listeners. Rulers in the *Histories* commonly *are* sensitive to the impression they make upon their audience[19], and Xerxes (as depicted in the subsequent account,[20] but also as felt in the rhetorical flourish of this speech) is no exception.

An index of the intensity of Xerxes' (show of) feeling is how he now represents Athens' burning of Sardis as a wrong against himself personally. His brief résumé of history that follows, which again engages readers in drawing comparisons with Herodotus' earlier account,[21] lacks the reasoned tone of the earlier instance. He is clearly inaccurate in referring to Aristagoras' *accompanying* the Athenian expedition to Sardis (7.8β.3), when readers know he remained in Miletus (5.99.2): Xerxes' heated mood (or desire for dramatic effect) leads him to embellish his account.[22] With ἐνέπρησαν τά τε ἄλσεα καὶ τὰ ἱρά ('they burned the groves and the temples') he employs 'the false rhetoric of war, diagnosed by [Herodotus] in 5.102.1.'[23] The attendant ἀγαθά ('good things') he speaks of are no longer simply

---

[18] Solmsen (1982), 84 likewise finds transformation here in Xerxes' state of mind, from rational to (and here we differ) megalomaniacal.

[19] e.g. Amasis, using the example of footbath turned statue to gain the Egyptians' respect (2.172); Cyrus, pleased with Croesus' advice on how to prevent his soldiers from excessive looting without inducing their hatred (1.89–90).

[20] As I shall suggest below, esp. at §8.2.

[21] Note especially Xerxes' inclusive [τὰ] ἐπίστασθέ κου πάντες ('which all of you doubtless know', 7.8β.3).

[22] Van Ophuijsen/Stork ad loc. suggest that though not literally true, the statement 'may perhaps be allowed as an effective representation of [Aristagoras'] moral leadership'. Similarly Xerxes' reference to the Greeks' burning of the groves, which did not appear in Herodotus' account (5.101), is probably a detail he invents to strengthen his case against the Greeks: de Jong (2001), 105.

[23] Van Ophuijsen/Stork ad loc.

fertile lands (cf. 7.8α.2) but rather the prospect of the Persian empire's expansion to the bounds of heaven: γῆν τὴν Περσίδα ἀποδέξομεν τῷ Διὸς αἰθέρι ὁμουρέουσαν (7.8γ.1). In view of the contrast with the first half of his speech and the psychologically credible depiction of his increasing levels of emotion, Xerxes' exaggerated expression here invites explanation at least as much in terms of his upset state or of his conscious rhetoric, as in terms of his hubristic disposition.[24] Artabanos' interpretation—for in hindsight he describes Xerxes' proposal as 'increasing *hybris*' (7.16α.2)—presents just one possibility.[25] In this state of heightened emotion Xerxes does appear more tyrant-like in observing that all, guilty and innocent alike (οἵ τε ἡμῖν αἴτιοι . . . οἵ τε ἀναίτιοι—unless, that is, we are to understand 'those answerable to us and those who are not'[26]), will be enslaved,[27] and in closing his address by speaking of how the Persians will best *please* him (τάδε ποιέοντες χαρίζοισθε . . . , 7.8δ.1).

After Mardonios' speech, reiterating several of Xerxes' sentiments and exploiting his emotional mood, has stirred the King still further, it is with the same degree of passion now turned to anger (θυμωθείς, 7.11.1) that he responds to Artabanos. A possible explanation again resides in his emotional state: we might contrast his relaxed attitude later to Demaratus' advice (7.105), so unlike Croesus' fractious response to Solon (1.33). Xerxes now goes so far as to claim that military action against Greece is necessary for defensive purposes (7.11.2–3), thus appropriating and magnifying Mardonios' earlier

[24] Though again, it might be felt that only a hubristic disposition would allow one to become so upset; cf. Cambyses' excesses of anger. See e.g. Cairns (1996), 13 for Xerxes as here demonstrating a hubristic disposition.

[25] Moreover, we should not exaggerate the force of Artabanos' expression: Herodotus' formulation here (with αὐξανούσης, 'going to increase', and καταπανούσης, 'going to abate'), van Ophuijsen/Stork ad loc. suggest, does *not* necessarily emphasize the presence of *hybris* before or while the opposed *gnōmai* were brought forward; it would tend to 'generalise the tenor of the words spoken . . . rather than just their actual effect on Xerxes' mind'. Below the possibility is raised that Artabanos' perspective may be qualified in being exclusively *Greek*. At this point his speech does seem distinctly Solonian; see n. 83 below.

[26] Cf. van Ophuijsen/Stork on 7.8γ.3, who observe that in contexts such as this one 'questions of liability, responsibility, let alone guilt are not crucial to the use of either αἴτιος or αἰτίη. In our passage too Xerxes merely means by οἱ ἡμῖν αἴτιοι men to whom an injury to him may be traced.'

[27] Cf. Croesus at 1.26.

supplementary rationale for the campaign (7.5.2). As support for his reasoning he offers a flawed argument from history (εἰ χρὴ σταθμώσασθαι τοῖσι ὑπαργμένοισι ἐξ ἐκείνων..., 'if we may judge from the actions they initiated...', 7.11.2), for there is little warrant for conjecturing as he does from the Athenians' part in the Ionian revolt—even if Aristagoras' overblown rhetoric (5.49) could conjure up the spectre of Greek conquest in Asia. ὑπαργμένοισι, 'initiated' (7.11.2; cf. ὑπῆρξαν ἄδικα ποιεῦντες, 'they began doing unjust deeds', 7.8β.2), recalls Herodotus' commentary on the Athenians' sending of the ships to help the Ionians (the ἀρχὴ κακῶν, 'beginning of wrongs', 5.97.3), but also harks back to the focus in the *Histories*' introductory chapters on identifying those responsible for beginning each new stage of conflict.[28] Xerxes' view of the situation seems a strange perversion of the Persians' in the proem. They accuse the Greeks of having escalated the conflict and have come to regard Greeks and Persians as cut off from one another (κεχωρίσθαι, 1.4.4), with the development of such ἔχθρη ('hatred', 1.5.1) rendering inevitable further conflict (i.e. the Persian Wars); whereas Xerxes now presents the situation as entailing all-out *conquest* either way, and expresses the fatalistic notion that it is impossible for either side to turn back (7.11.3). Nonetheless even at this point (at 7.11) his generalizations

match those of Artabanos, and they are not crass. Great empires are indeed threatened if they allow the small to defy them, and great kings may be under internal threats if they fail to live up to the expectations generated by a nation's past.[29]

The rhetorical force of the speech combined with the familiar pattern in the *Histories* of kings who pursue plans of conquest in the face of warnings underscores the irrevocable nature of Xerxes' decision. Wholly unexpectedly, however—his youthful temper cooled (cf. 7.13.2: ἡ νεότης ἐπέζεσε)—Xerxes resolves to heed Artabanos' advice and once more to resist the idea of a Greek campaign (7.12.1). Asking the Persians' forgiveness for his quick-changing deliberations (ὅτι ἀγχίστροφα βουλεύομαι, 7.13.2), he explains his earlier reaction in

[28] e.g. Greeks as responsible for escalating the quarrel in early days; Croesus as the first individual Herodotus can identify as responsible for the more recent conflict.
[29] Pelling (2006c), 109; cf. Saïd's (1981) emphasis on the political (as well as historical) necessity that weighs upon Xerxes.

terms of his youth and his frustration at the constant presence of others trying to influence him (7.13.2; a view which Artabanos soon corroborates: σὲ... ἀνθρώπων κακῶν ὁμιλίαι σφάλλουσι, 'the company of bad men leads you astray', 7.16α.1). This changed stance, rather than suggesting a weak personality or the arbitrary vacillation of a tyrant,[30] is comprehensible in the terms of his explanation. Indeed, it demonstrates Xerxes' ability to reflect and seize control of his anger, and modesty sufficient to admit a change of mind and follow another's advice.[31] In this he resembles Croesus, who likewise proved receptive to advice in the earlier stages of his career.

## 8.1.2 Xerxes' dream

The campaign does ultimately occur, as readers know it will, but not as a result of this individual king's wilful or hubristic decision. Rather, an apparition (ὄψις) in the form of a tall and handsome man visits Xerxes (according to the Persian account, 7.12.1) in the night following the council meeting, urging him not to abandon the expedition against Greece. This dream is insistent—appearing twice to Xerxes, and then again to Artabanos—and also violent in its threats, and it clearly implies that the gods are driving Xerxes. In finally accepting its divine origin, and thus the necessity of yielding to its command, Xerxes is again following Artabanos' advice. Thus to the notion that the campaign may in part be necessitated by Persian tradition—by the *nomos* of expansion (cf. 3.134)—is added the impression of its being divinely preordained: τὸ χρεὸν γενέσθαι ('what must be'), the vision says, must not be turned aside.[32] This supernatural element

[30] Cf. 'the most erratic (ἀναρμοστότατον) of all men' of the constitution debate (3.80.5), and Plato's tyrannical man torn apart by contradictory desires, *Republic* 577–8. Nor is 'la facilità con cui mutano i suoi orientamenti sulla spedizione' ('the ease with which his attitude to the campaign changes') to be likened to the ease with which he later turns from desiring Masistes' wife to her daughter (Masaracchia (1977), xix)—which is an entirely different situation.

[31] Cf. above, ch. 5 n. 12 (the Herodotean *topos* that counselling oneself/being advised by others are equivalent).

[32] Fornara (1990) documents the pattern in the *Histories* of dreams that portend what must inevitably occur, which trains readers to expect the same in Xerxes' case. The dream's explicit message 'was the necessity for Xerxes to submit to the will of fate, whatever his own inclinations' (165 n. 20); cf. Shapiro (1994), 253–4; Mikalson

diverts responsibility for the expedition from Xerxes himself, again indicating that it is not simply the outcome of his personal whim.[33] It also highlights his piety. We see his concern to determine whether or not the vision is divine (even if his 'testing' the deity might not seem pious to a Greek reader[34]); and ultimately he acts in accordance with the advice of Artabanos, who, concluding that Greek ruin was god-sent (θεήλατος), instructs: 'Tell the Persians about the visions sent from the god..., and make sure—since the god commands it—that you do everything you must' (σὺ δὲ σήμηνον μὲν Πέρσῃσι τὰ ἐκ τοῦ θεοῦ πεμπόμενα..., ποίεε δὲ οὕτως ὅκως τοῦ θεοῦ παραδιδόντος τῶν σῶν ἐνδεήσει μηδέν, 7.18.3). Readers cannot fail to appreciate the irony that Artabanos—the very man who has warned Xerxes about the negative effect of others' influence—should be responsible for a blatant over-reading of the phantom's words, in assuming (as is clearly *not* the case) that along with urging the invasion it foretells unequivocally the destruction of Greece.[35] The structures of Persian autocracy restrict open discussion—it is *only* Artabanos in this case who dares to offer advice, and he has consistently missed the mark in this respect[36]—and so inhibit the likelihood of receiving a balanced array of views; but Xerxes does in the end prove receptive to what advice *is* available. His growing awareness of its often warped and useless character will help explain his later move away from accepting advice.

(2003), 42. The extent of Xerxes' earlier resistance to the notion of a Greek campaign would seem to work against the possibility of reading the dream as simply confirming Xerxes' own will (cf. e.g. Huber (1965a), 142–52, 163). Solmsen (1982), 88 n. 34 counters Reinhardt's notion (1940), 172 that the dream is 'Xerxes' eigener Schicksalsdämon' ('Xerxes' own demon/*daimon* of fate'), and underlines Xerxes' efforts to resist the *daimon* (92). Differently Flower (2006), 278, suggesting it might represent divine communication *as well as* Xerxes' subconscious anxiety about losing the nobles' support if he should discontinue the campaign.

[33]  Cf. e.g. Immerwahr (1954), 33; Gärtner (1983); Giglioni (2002).

[34]  We might relate this point to the possibility (considered further below) of there being a Greek ~ Persian texture to the Xerxes narrative. Christ (1994) finds no condemnation in Herodotus' presentation of trials involving the divine, either in Xerxes' test here (the divinity is angry *before* the experiment is conducted: 197) or in Croesus' of the oracles. Lieshout (1970), 243 doubts that Xerxes can here be felt to be demonstrating 'the typically barbarian πεῖρα-attitude', since he calls up the dream a second time not out of scepticism but belief.

[35]  See e.g. Saïd (1981), 23–4; Evans (1991), 15, 28; Christ (1994), 195.

[36]  Cf. Pelling (1991).

We may pause for a moment at this point to consider an alternative potential reading. Scholars have long noted the presence of Greek and Persian elements in the narrative of Xerxes' decision to invade, finding their origins in the different stories and traditions with which Herodotus worked. Friedrich Solmsen (1982) has delineated the 'thoroughly Hellenic version' (90) of the council scene from the ensuing Persian (though Hellenized[37]) story of the devilish *devas* placing pressure upon Xerxes (89–91). Herodotus himself cites Persian informants for the story of this night-time vision (7.12.1). The possibility of an alternative reading arises, a possibility that may gain plausibility over the course of the argument pursued below: that readers are *alerted* to this move from Greek to Persian; that the 'Oriental motifs' of the dream sequence[38] are meant to be recognized as distinctly Persian. In that case, the potential *hybris* explanation arising from the council scene might be regarded as (and so limited to) a specifically *Greek* interpretation, the dream explanation, with Xerxes compelled by a Persian *daimon* to yield to the *nomos* of Persian expansionism,[39] as a specifically *Persian* one. (This may be, but is not necessarily, a *source* issue, reflecting the traditions of particular informants: it may be that Herodotus himself, in his selection and presentation of the material, is responsible for the Persian flavour.) I will argue below (§8.5.2) for the possibility of such sequential presentation in the case of Herodotus' account of the Hellespont crossing.

Thus the introductory chapters hint that this portrayal of the king may differ from those that were (surely) already familiar, of received accounts and popular imagination.[40] Xerxes seems a thinking ruler,

[37] Solmsen (1982), 90, 91 n. 44. Immerwahr (1954), 34 emphasizes the presence in the account of the dream of Greek aspects alongside Persian; cf. Huber (1965*a*), 144–5. The dream seems quite different, however, from the deceiving dream of *Iliad* 2.66: cf. Immerwahr (1954), 34–5.

[38] e.g. in the clothes exchange, the putting-on of the king's robe, the threatened punishment: see Reinhardt (1940), 171; Solmsen (1982), 89–90; further more speculative possibilities in Klees (1965), 56–8.

[39] See n. 32 above. Note Evans' (1961) interpretation of the dream as the voice of Persian *nomoi*.

[40] Herodotus' stress on the institution of Persian monarchy, and presentation of Xerxes as a reflective ruler who, at least in the initial stages of his career, resists being overwhelmed by personal emotions, contrasts with the depiction of Xerxes in the *Persai*, for example, as impulsive and youthful, unthinking (note Aeschylus' emphasis on Xerxes' lack of comprehension regarding Salamis, Herodotus' rather on the

whose actions are not to be explained as arising straightforwardly from youthful recklessness or barbarian royal *hybris*, but rather in terms of more complex motives. The immediately preceding narrative had, however, underscored the fact that he is located within a ready-made institution with its own powerful traditions: structures that restrict the individual ruler's self-determination. The account of the process by which Darius came to choose between Xerxes and Artobazanes in appointing his successor depicted a range of institutional pressures that bear down upon the Persian king, including the obligation to act in accordance with Persian custom (κατὰ τὸν Περσέων νόμον, 7.2.1), the fact that Greeks who see fit to offer advice are present at court (7.3), and the influence of family relations—most sensationally Atossa (7.3). Again, readers may recall Otanes' formulation about the corrosive effect upon the individual of absolute rule (3.80), which has been exemplified to some extent by Cambyses.[41] Readers are familiar with the historical datum of Xerxes' campaign. The question that is likely to present itself at the story's outset is therefore *to what extent* Herodotus' Xerxes will resist falling prey in either quarter (to the pressure of institutional structures or to the fact of autocracy); and what will be the *character* of the explanations that motivate the campaign that takes place.

The account of the decision to invade may be expected to influence readers' responses to the key motivational junctures in the subsequent narrative. It underlines the need to examine carefully the king's motives, rather than assuming he is driven simply by *hybris* or by tyrannical irrationality or impulsiveness.[42] Herodotus later models this approach when, in conjecturing about Xerxes' motives in ordering Leonidas' decapitation, he takes Persian custom as his point of reference, working on the assumption that there will be a reasonable explanation for any transgression on Xerxes' part:

cleverness of Themistocles' ruse), and hubristic. See further Saïd (1981). The possibility of an equivalent contrast with the Aeschylean portrait even as regards Xerxes' later action of bridging the Hellespont is raised below, n. 127 with text.

[41]  See n. 90 below.

[42]  Cf. Fisher (1992), who finds 'complex characterisation' (373). Xerxes is *not* (yet) 'the typical tyrant', his behaviour *not* 'throughout motivated by passion rather than by reason', as Immerwahr (1966), 177 holds.

δῆλά μοι πολλοῖσι μὲν καὶ ἄλλοισι τεκμηρίοισι, ἐν δὲ καὶ τῷδε οὐκ ἥκιστα
γέγονε, ὅτι βασιλεὺς Ξέρξης πάντων δὴ μάλιστα ἀνδρῶν ἐθυμώθη ζῶντι
Λεωνίδῃ· οὐ γὰρ ἄν κοτε ἐς τὸν νεκρὸν ταῦτα παρενόμησε, ἐπεὶ τιμᾶν
μάλιστα νομίζουσι τῶν ἐγὼ οἶδα ἀνθρώπων Πέρσαι ἄνδρας ἀγαθοὺς τὰ
πολέμια (7.238.2).

It is clear to me by many other proofs (*tekmērioisi*), including particularly
the following, that King Xerxes hated Leonidas, while he lived, most of all
men. For otherwise he would never have contravened custom (*parenomēse*)
in treating his corpse in this way, since of all the peoples known to me the
Persians are the most accustomed (*nomizousi*) to honour men who are brave
in war.

Thus Xerxes' behaviour is *not* to be understood simply in terms of a
tyrant's arbitrary violence, but rather in terms of wider Persian
custom—which in this case could be overridden only by a powerful
opposing factor, and very possibly a legitimate one: Herodotus leaves
readers to conjecture the source of Xerxes' anger. Striking here is how
Herodotus brings together contemporary language of proof (cf.
πολλοῖσι . . . καὶ ἄλλοισι **τεκμηρίοισι**) and knowledge of the importance of *nomoi*, customs (cf. παρενόμησε, νομίζουσι), signalling that
he is trying to make sense of this apparently barbaric act.[43] The
framework of explanation that did in large part serve for Cambyses[44]
is evidently inadequate: Herodotus could write Cambyses off as mad,
whereas he endeavours to understand Xerxes.

The account of the process by which Xerxes came to invade Greece
is a decision writ large. It supplies material that aids readers in filling
in a richer background of explanation when they come to interpreting the more bare-bones (and at times, I shall suggest, deliberately
contentious) motive statements further on in the narrative, by at-
tuning them to the sorts of factors likely to be involved. Even though
several of these do not ultimately prove operative in precipitating
Xerxes' decision to invade Greece (for the dream figure is in the end
its catalyst), the fact that they have been set before readers' minds
renders them readily available as explanations.

---

[43] Thomas (2000), 194 (comparing the parallel proof from custom Herodotus
offers at 3.38 in explanation of Cambyses' barbaric behaviour—which in that case
proves the king mad).

[44] But see ch. 4 for qualifications to this generalization.

## 8.2 THE ATHOS CANAL (7.22–5)

The keynote of the *Histories'* account of the initial stages of Xerxes' campaign is its intricate preparation. In this respect a stark contrast is felt with the abortive Ethiopian campaign Cambyses led from Egypt,[45] which Herodotus' opening reference (7.20.1) brings to mind. Herodotus sketches in outline the various contributions that were made by the many peoples involved in the campaign (ships, infantry, cavalry, food, etc., 7.21), before exemplifying Xerxes' extent of preparedness in his detailed account of the Athos arrangements (7.22–4). Only at the very end of the account, which has indicated to readers several possible explanations for Xerxes' ordering that the canal be dug, does Herodotus offer his personal opinion on the king's reason for doing so:

ὡς μὲν ἐμὲ συμβαλλόμενον εὑρίσκειν, μεγαλοφροσύνης εἴνεκεν αὐτὸ Ξέρξης ὀρύσσειν ἐκέλευε, ἐθέλων τε δύναμιν ἀποδείκνυσθαι καὶ μνημόσυνα λιπέσθαι· παρεὸν γὰρ μηδένα πόνον λαβόντας τὸν ἰσθμὸν τὰς νέας διειρύσαι, ὀρύσσειν ἐκέλευε διώρυχα τῇ θαλάσσῃ εὖρος ὡς δύο τριήρεας πλέειν ὁμοῦ ἐλαστρεομένας (7.24).

As I suppose and conclude [/find through conjecture], Xerxes ordered that the canal be dug out of *megalophrosunē* (literally, 'greatness of mind') because he wanted to display his power and to leave a memorial. For although he could have avoided all that work and had his ships dragged across the isthmus, he instead ordered that a canal be dug to the sea, wide enough for two triremes to be rowed abreast along it.

A discrepancy might be felt to emerge here between readers' constructions of Xerxes' motives and the apparently reductionist logic of the historian, since several strands in the Athos narrative have suggested alternative explanations for his behaviour than *megalophrosunē* in the sense implied by the authorial comment that follows, if it is interpreted—as it generally is—as spotlighting the superfluity and needlessness of the action. In English it is usually translated

[45] Herodotus observed that Cambyses embarked on this campaign 'without having ordered any preparation of supplies (οὔτε παρασκευὴν σίτου οὐδεμίαν παραγγείλας), nor considered that he was about to march to the far ends of the earth' (3.25.1).

'pride', or more colourfully, 'a sense of grandiosity and arrogance'.[46] However, we may have cause to wonder whether *megalophrosunē* here must inevitably be wholly negative, as such translations assume—particularly in light of the way in which the strands of the Athos narrative interact with previous perspectives (themselves feeding into wider explanatory paradigms) on Xerxes. After all, the similar quality of *megalopsychia* ('greatness of *psyche*, soul') could be extremely positive for Aristotle: *megalopsychia*, that 'crowning ornament of virtues' (κόσμος τις...τῶν ἀρετῶν, *Nichomachean Ethics* 1124ᵃ1), displayed by the man who claims much and deserves much, especially of honour: who makes *appropriately* big claims in this regard (cf. 1123ᵇ21).[47]

To begin with, Xerxes up to this point has not seemed a man driven by the sort of inordinate self-esteem or arrogance felt in this sense of the English word 'pride'. On several occasions he has defied readerly expectations of tyrant behaviour (in the Cambyses mould). He has been portrayed as deferring to the opinions of others, even excessively, and as apologetic and deferential in addressing the council after a contrary view provoked his anger (7.13; and at 7.105, as noted above, he will be remarkably easy-going in his response to Demaratus' conflicting view). Indeed as a rule he has seemed a man not at all motivated by the kind of *megalophrosunē* ('natural arrogance' in Maidment's translation[48]) that the prosecutor of Antiphon's third tetralogy thinks contributes to inciting the young to indulge their *thumos* in anger (ἐπαίρει τῷ θυμῷ χαρίζεσθαι, 3.3.2); Xerxes and Artabanos were rather ἐπαρθέντες τῇ ὄψι ('incited by the dream', 7.18.4): by an external factor quite different from pride.

---

[46] 'Pride': e.g., Godley, Powell, Legrand ('orgueil'); cf. LSJ: 'pride, arrogance'; Waterfield: 'a sense of grandiosity and arrogance'. Macan (on 7.21.1) paraphrases: 'Hdt. moralizes upon the aim and object of the Canal. It was to serve (according to him) merely as an exhibition of power and as a memorial; otherwise, he thinks, the Persian fleet might have been dragged across the isthmos. His reasoning is not very profound'. Solmsen (1982), 93 n. 50, on the other hand, suggests that Herodotus views the canal 'primarily as an admirably planned engineering feat', but finds *hybris* implied in his conjecture that *megalophrosunē* inspired it.

[47] Indeed, Aristotle's description of the *megalopsychos* ('great-souled') man (*Eth. Nic.* 1123ᵃ34–1125ᵃ35) invites comparison with the Herodotean Xerxes in several respects.

[48] LSJ translate 'pride' (of family).

Rather than being one to act on personal whims, motivated by the sort of desire for gratuitous ostentation that Herodotus has been felt to lay at his charge here, Xerxes is a man influenced above all, as we have seen, by his perception of history and the obligations it entails, and by his impression of divine will.

Herodotus' introduction of the Athos project—'in the first place, since the first expedition had met with disaster while sailing around Athos, he conducted advance preparations in regard to Athos for about three years' (καὶ τοῦτο μέν, ὡς προσπταισάντων τῶν πρώτων περιπλεόντων περὶ τὸν Ἄθων, προετοιμάζετο ἐκ τριῶν ἐτέων κου μάλιστα ἐς τὸν Ἄθων, 7.22.1)—has again left readers with a clear sense that Xerxes' motives in building the canal included a desire to learn from the past: he perhaps acted as he did to avoid the risk of a shipwreck like that which disabled Darius' fleet (even if Herodotus later mentions the further option of using the slipway, 7.24). A parallel concern not to replay Cambyses' mistakes is also promin- ent during this stretch of narrative. The emphasis on food, resources, etc.,[49] suggests a contrast with the grim circumstances that precipi- tated the cannibalism to which Cambyses' troops resorted (3.25). With the mention of an *agorē* and *prētērion* (business centre and market place, 7.23.4) a comparison is invited rather with Darius the *kapēlos* ('shop keeper', 3.89.3), noted for his efficiency and organiza- tion. The sensible and careful character of Xerxes' measures con- tinues to be indicated beyond the bounds of the Athos narrative, where Herodotus depicts him taking great care with the storing of provisions, 'in order that neither the army nor the yoke animals should suffer from hunger' (7.25.1, again in distinct contrast to the Cambyses situation, where 'once the food was gone, they used up the yoke animals too by eating them', 3.25.4), and inquiring closely (ἀναπυθόμενος: in Herodotean manner) into the most appropriate places for this. All this preparation goes to show that the invasion is by no means an *impulsive* act—as Cambyses' generally were.

Xerxes' activity at Athos, in combination with the motivation ascribed to him, suggests his awareness not only of the past but also of the future: his impulse 'to leave behind memorials' (μνημόσυνα λιπέσθαι) matches Nitokris', for example (1.184–7),

---

[49] e.g. at 7.23.4: great quantities of flour (σῖτος ... πολλὸς ... ἀληλεσμένος) imported from Asia.

and possibly even that of Herodotus himself.[50] The way the account focuses in detail on the canal's construction underlines its status as *ergon*: rather than serving simply to expose the fact of Xerxes' slave labour, Herodotus' description of the process indicates the size and magnificence of the resulting work. The similar canal begun by Psammetichos' son Nekos (2.158), and finished by *Darius*— described as being exactly like Xerxes' in breadth[51] and so perhaps inviting comparison[52]—attracts no negative authorial comment (even though 120,000 Egyptians perished over the course of its construction, 2.158.5), but instead seems to have been included in the *Histories* because it is worthy of note. Great *erga* may indeed be of tremendous interest in themselves: Herodotus cited the 'three greatest works achieved by any Greeks' at Samos as his *reason* for 'dwelling at length' upon Samian affairs (3.60.1)! Xerxes' *ergon* receives the highest commendation, too, in having the historian dwell upon it, with the implication that he counts it among the *erga megala te kai thōmasta* ('great and wondrous deeds/works') he refers to in his preface.[53] Thus Xerxes joins the ranks of those 'Greeks and non-Greeks' at 1.1 who 'display' (cf. ἀποδεχθέντα) such *erga* in parallel to the historian's own 'display' (ἀπόδεξις) of his researches.

This notion of display may prompt reflection upon a connected, but more practical factor:[54] Xerxes may be understood to 'display'

[50] Might we sense, in the resolve 'to leave a memorial', an implicit awareness of one's own mortality? (i.e. of the fact that otherwise one runs the risk of being forgotten for good?) That, too, would work against an interpretation of Xerxes' variety of 'thinking big' in terms of his hubristically regarding himself as more than human (thus complementing the rival 'Persian' strand I argue for below).

[51] εὖρος ... ὥστε τριήρεας δύο πλέειν ὁμοῦ ἐλαστρευμένας ('wide enough for two triremes to be rowed abreast'), 2.158.1; cf. εὖρος ὡς δύο τριήρεας πλέειν ὁμοῦ ἐλαστρεομένας, 7.24 (above, 254).

[52] Note Stein's suggestion (on 7.24.2) that 'Xerxes mochte seinem Vater, der den Nilkanal zum roten Meere ... ausführte ..., auch in diesem Stücke nicht nachstehen wollen' ('Xerxes did not want to be inferior in this respect, either, to his father, who constructed the Nile canal to the Red Sea').

[53] Compare the recent emphasis (in opposition to the prevailing view) on Herodotus' *pleasure* in such works of wonder of Romm (2006), e.g. 189: 'Such grand-scale reshapings of the earth's topography elicit wonder and amazement, not disapproval, from Herodotus'; Scullion (2006), e.g. 193: 'The rivers crossed and diverted, canals [including Athos: cf. his 205 n. 7], and tunnel in the *Histories* are not problematised on religious grounds and are sometimes lovingly described.'

[54] See n. 56 below.

this great *ergon* not simply with future generations in mind (which now include Herodotus' readers), but also for the benefit of his own more immediate audience. The awareness of Persian history that informs Xerxes' behaviour gives readers the key to finding an explanation for his building the canal also in the requirement that a Persian king φαίνεσθαί τι ἀποδεικνύμενον, 'be seen achieving some great (enterprise or *ergon*)', as Atossa advised Darius: νῦν γὰρ ἄν τι καὶ ἀποδέξαιο ἔργον ... ('Now is the time for you to achieve some enterprise...', 3.134.3). Xerxes formulated the principle into a *nomos* of activity and expansionism (7.8α.1–2), and came to regard his very identity as Persian king as bound up with engagement in the offensive against Athens (for otherwise, he asserted at 7.11.2, 'may I not be the son of Darius, son of Hystaspes, son of Arsames, son of Ariaramnes...').[55] From this perspective his motivation in building the canal could indeed be a matter of his desiring δύναμιν ἀποδείκνυσθαι, 'to display his power', in accordance with the authorial conjecture (7.24). However, in thus consisting of an obligation arising from Persian royal tradition (and one with a supplementary practical purpose, as we shall see), the Athos project would deserve explanation in terms other than those implied by the translation of *megalophrosunē* as simple 'pride'.[56]

For on this reading, the fact of *display*, of the ostentatious superfluity of the project—with a canal built rather than a slipway, and one in which *two* boats can fit breadthwise—would be *essential* rather than unnecessary: that is the significant point,[57] and Herodotus' conjecture draws readers to consider it. What might prima facie seem merely a moralizing comment[58] is thus put to different and constructive effect;

[55] See Immerwahr (1960), 261–90 for the flexibility of '*ergon*' in Herodotus (referring to deeds, monuments, etc.). Interestingly Herodotus postpones until here this list of Persian kings, rather than including it in his account of Darius: it is most relevant at this point, and also serves to suggest all the more effectively that Xerxes more than Darius is influenced by Persian tradition.

[56] We might note that the Egyptian *kings* of book two displayed the same twin aims as Xerxes, of leaving memorials and displaying their power, and that in their case it was usually represented as traditional rather than egotistical, as well as having an additional practical purpose.

[57] Note the importance of display in historical actuality to the Achaemenid kings: e.g. their concern to make a show of their resources, with banquets, for instance, that included contributions from all corners of the empire. The Behistun relief depicts the arrival of a great variety of nationalities of tribute bearers.

[58] Cf. Macan ad loc. (quoted above, n. 46).

readers' understanding of μεγαλοφροσύνης εἴνεκεν moves closer to the notion 'out of a sense of *appropriate* greatness/bigness'. It seems akin to the quality as understood by Socrates in Plato's *Symposium* (194b1: ἀνδρείαν καὶ μεγαλοφροσύνην, 'manliness and *megalophrosunē*', in (ironic) application to Agathon), shown by an actor as he stands confidently on the stage, unintimidated even by a large audience; indeed, about to make a *display* to his audience, in this case: ἐπιδείξεσθαι ... λόγους ('to display words/compositions'). It represents a variety of 'confidence' that goes hand in hand with *andreia*—with manifest manliness. It renders a person impressive to those watching.

Atossa's reasoning, after all, was twofold: by achieving a great enterprise the King would prove to his subjects he is a real man (ἵνα σφέων Πέρσαι ἐπιστέωνται ἄνδρα εἶναι τὸν προεστεῶτα), while they, in being worn out by war, would have no leisure to conspire against him (3.134.2). Herodotus' account makes clear that the work involved in building this canal is keeping Phoenicians, previously revolted Egyptians, and others, well occupied. At the same time the mighty *ergon* being produced is sure to be found impressive by Xerxes' wider audience of Greeks ... and may also be understood as *intended* to have that effect.[59] Xerxes will again prove sensitive to the existence of this wider audience when he puts a stop to the execution of Greek spies to instead have them shown 'the whole of his infantry and cavalry' and allowed to return to Greece (7.146). That will seem a strange and paradoxical gesture until Herodotus has Xerxes explain his motivation:

ὡς εἰ μὲν ἀπώλοντο οἱ κατάσκοποι, οὔτ' ἂν τὰ ἑωυτοῦ πρήγματα προεπύθοντο οἱ Ἕλληνες ἐόντα λόγου μέζω, οὔτ' ἄν τι τοὺς πολεμίους μέγα ἐσίναντο ἄνδρας τρεῖς ἀπολέσαντες· νοστησάντων δὲ τούτων ἐς τὴν Ἑλλάδα δοκέειν ἔφη ἀκούσαντας τοὺς Ἕλληνας τὰ ἑωυτοῦ πρήγματα πρὸ τοῦ στόλου τοῦ γινομένου παραδώσειν σφέας τὴν ἰδίην ἐλευθερίην, καὶ οὕτως οὐδὲ δεήσειν ἐπ' αὐτοὺς στρατηλατέοντας πρήγματα ἔχειν (7.147.1).

[Xerxes explained] that if the spies were killed, the Greeks would not learn in advance of the extraordinary size of his forces, nor would the Persians have done great harm to their enemies in killing three men. But if the spies returned to Greece, he said, he thought that upon hearing about his vast power the Greeks would surrender their peculiar freedom before the expedition

---

[59] i.e. rather than representing simply 'an act of pride to seek fame from posterity', Immerwahr (1954), 23, the Athos canal was a bid to engender present-day awe.

occurred. Thus the Persians would not need to trouble themselves with conducting a campaign.

The wisdom and foresight Xerxes here demonstrates (along with his misreading of the Greeks) is underscored by the manner in which the anecdote moves Herodotus to recount a further *gnōmē* of his: the time when he allowed corn ships to continue on their voyage for Greece, on the grounds that they would eventually supply his own expedition (7.147; the comparison with Croesus' advice to Cyrus that his soldiers were sacking what was now his own city (1.88) is conspicuous). Xerxes' trivializing of the Greeks' attachment to their 'peculiar freedom' suggests that he has not taken fully to heart Demaratus' view on the subject (7.104)—and yet perhaps justifiably, since Greeks do indeed change sides, many of them! Indeed the keynote of Herodotus' account is the success *against all odds* of the Greeks, thanks largely to Athens and Sparta, and even hingeing in part on individuals like Themistocles.

Xerxes' understanding of the deterrent capacity of a force of great size derives from his sensitivity to the power of perceptions,[60] and seems just as valid as the counterview voiced by Artabanos: that such a force strains resources (7.49).[61] The *Histories* earlier showed, for example, how the Samians deserted the Ionian alliance because of its disordered appearance in combination with the seeming impossibility of opposing Darius.[62] No consideration of the morally preferable option, or of abstract notions like freedom, entered into the equation; they were simply relieved at the prospect of preserving temples and homes (6.13.2).

Xerxes' interest in targeted display may thus be construed as aimed at avoiding the need to campaign at all—which is in keeping with his

[60] Xerxes' own penchant for observation (cf. Konstan (1987)) perhaps goes hand in hand with his sensitivity to perceptions generally—and especially *others'* perceptions of *him*.

[61] Rightly or wrongly Artabanos appears to withdraw his further concern, that it might also cause offence to the gods: for by the time the campaign begins, it has come to seem divinely willed to Artabanos as well as to Xerxes, cf. §8.1.2 above.

[62] ὁρῶντες ἅμα μὲν ἐοῦσαν ἀταξίην πολλὴν ἐκ τῶν Ἰώνων . . ., ἅμα δὲ κατεφαίνετό σφι εἶναι ἀδύνατα τὰ βασιλέος πρήγματα ὑπερβαλέσθαι, εὖ γε ἐπιστάμενοι ὡς εἰ καὶ τὸ παρεὸν ναυτικὸν ὑπερβαλοίατο [τὸν Δαρεῖον], ἄλλο σφι παρέσται πενταπλήσιον ('at seeing the extreme lack of discipline on the Ionian side . . ., and also because the King's forces seemed to them impossible to defeat, and they were convinced that even if they defeated Darius' present fleet another five times as large would appear', 6.13.1).

generally defensive attitude.[63] He consistently expects the Greek opposition to dissolve before him—soon after Athos, upon entering Sardis (at 7.32), and right down to Artemisium, for example, when he and his generals, at seeing the Greeks bearing down upon them with so few ships and convinced that they must have gone mad, they too launched their ships, 'expecting easily to capture them—an expectation that was entirely reasonable (ἐλπίσαντές σφεας εὐπετέως αἱρήσειν, οἰκότα κάρτα ἐλπίσαντες) . . .' (8.10.1):[64] and to a good extent it does. The Athos project thus showcases the power and bottomless resources of the King, declaring to all the magnitude of the planned expedition . . . in accordance with Persian tradition, and in the hope that no war should ultimately need to be fought. This practical dimension, and also the sense that Xerxes is not wholly free-willed in acting as he does (but responding to the constraints of tradition) works against an interpretation in terms of *hybris*.[65] This perspective will feed also into the later account of the Hellespont crossing—a connection made more explicit by Herodotus' note that the same men were responsible for bridging another river: the Strymon. It also contributes a wider explanation for the large size of the campaign generally, proposing a principle of largeness as cautionary and in accordance with Persian *nomos*, rather than as hubristic.

And yet through the Athos narrative—even prior to the authorial attribution of motivation—a rival perspective (though a less dominant one) has kept the alternative *hybris* explanation simmering in readers' minds. The passing note that the men worked under the whip (7.22.1) hinted at tyrannical coercion; and the subsequent observation of the several towns on the peninsula 'which the Persian now desired to turn into island instead of mainland towns' (τὰς τότε

[63] e.g., his care in avoiding another shipwreck, and his earlier reluctance to embark upon the Greek campaign.

[64] The Persians' view is matched by the Ionians', who 'were certain that not one [of the Greeks] would return home, so weak did the forces of the Greeks appear to them to be (οὕτω ἀσθενέα σφι ἐφαίνετο εἶναι τὰ τῶν Ἑλλήνων πρήγματα)' (8.10.2).

[65] MacDowell (1976) emphasizes the unnecessary/gratuitous nature of acts arising from *hybris* (as understood especially by Athenians—but his discussion embraces Herodotus as a non-Athenian known at Athens: 14–15), observing that '[t]he results [of *hybris*] are actions which *are, at the best, useless*, and in most cases definitely wrong' (21, my italics), and that it is by definition *voluntary*: 'Hybris means doing what one feels like doing, free from constraint, whether by other people or by oneself' (ibid.).

ὁ Πέρσης νησιώτιδας ἀντὶ ἠπειρωτίδων ὅρμητο ποιέειν, 7.22.3) fed
into the *Histories*' broader pattern of tyrants whose excesses include
not only the transgression of natural boundaries (rivers, deserts, etc.)
but even the overturning of nature itself (turning land into sea, and
vice versa).[66] The opposition of islanders and mainlanders is significant and evocative; and the theme of islanders and advice has
emerged in an earlier story.[67] This explanatory paradigm compre-
hends Xerxes' behaviour in rather different terms from the perspective we pursued above, as fitting into a wider pattern of hubristic
imperialism. Herodotus' phrasing leaves ambiguous whether the
king desired to transform mainlanders into islanders, or whether
that would simply be the outcome of his vigorous action—in
which case he demonstrates the equally tyrant-like trait of heedlessness, of failure 'to take account'.[68]

But at the same time the narrative hints that this is a specifically
*Greek* perspective: the changed identification of subject from 'Xerxes'
to 'the Persian' (ὁ Πέρσης) signals the presence of a different focalizer
whose perspective is an outsider's.[69] And the narrator continues with
the note that it was near the Greek *polis* Sane (Σάνη πόλις Ἑλλάς, as
Herodotus has just specified) that the foreigners (οἱ βάρβαροι) made
the dividing line. Macan (on 7.24.1) suggests that Herodotus and his
sources 'made too much of the Canal as a wonder-work', when it was
really 'a simple piece of engineering': 'The Greeks who controlled but
small supplies of labour viewed such works with exaggerated astonishment, and saw a hint of impiety (ὕβρις) in them'. But Herodotus
presents this as an overtly Greek point of view (perhaps paving the
way for one interpretation of his authorial conjecture of *megalophrosunē* in a similar vein), which alerts readers to its subjective nature,
reducing its authority. Equally, the Persian character of the alternative perspective is implied in the way it is rooted in a Persian
conception of *nomos*, as has been set forth in the *Histories*.

---

[66] See Immerwahr (1966), 84, 95 (on the 'river motif'); Lateiner (1989), 127–35
('"Limit", "Transgression", and Related Metaphors').

[67] Bias'/Pittakos' advice (1.27). Tyrants do not usually heed such advice.

[68] Cf. Cambyses' perseverance with the march into Ethiopia, οὐδένα λόγον
ποιεύμενος ('taking no account', 3.25.5).

[69] See de Jong (1993) for Homeric examples of such 'periphrastic denomination',
which can reflect the focalization of characters.

Readers are thus confronted with a doubleness of possible interpretations of Xerxes' motives in building the canal. The Greek perspective (following in the style of Artabanos' initial anxieties about the expedition generally) reads the action as excessive, motivated by the individual tyrant's predictable tendency to *hybris*; the rival (Persian) perspective views it as being explicable for practical reasons and justifiable in terms of Persian *nomoi*.[70] Grandiosity, in the latter case, is a traditional *attribute* of the Persian king required of him in his public role, his action one driven by tradition, with little space for the individual's self-determination. Thus, 'thinking big' in this instance *can* be construed as *hybris*,[71] but need not *invariably* be. To Greeks, Xerxes may seem 'to lay claim to a greater share of honour than a mortal should possess' (cf. Cairns (1996), 19 on the *hybris* entailed by Agamemnon's action in the carpet scene of the *Agamemnon*),[72] but the (implied) Persian view regards his action as being in keeping with the grandeur expected of the Persian King. Again (to turn from Cairns' 'dispositional' definition of *hybris* to Fisher's more 'behavioural' definition, emphasizing *hybris* as *dishonouring others*), the focus of Herodotus' account of Xerxes' conduct at Athos may be felt to be as much its effect upon Xerxes' wider audience, as its dishonouring of those involved in the canal's construction. In any case, if Xerxes' actions seem to some to display *hybris*, they do not do so straightforwardly, for it is that of the Persian imperial system,[73] and is envisaged as *nomos*.

The final authorial conjecture at 7.24 is unsettling more than confirming. Its postponement has allowed readers an opportunity to weigh up the options for themselves. They have been primed not simply to agree with it, but to consider that it too—at least if taken in a categorically negative sense—may be a subjective (Greek, and

[70] Compare the parallel tension Romm (2006) proposes on the part of Herodotus himself: 'Competing in Herodotus' mind with a sense of the inviolability of nature . . . is an esteem for human technological progress, especially when it achieves monumental changes in the landscape or in the quality of human life' (189); e.g. esp. as regards Xerxes' bridging of the Hellespont, a tragic model is present alongside a 'more progressive or *sophiē*-reverencing impulse' (190).

[71] Cairns (1996); cf. Dickie (1984), esp. 101–9.

[72] See n. 50 above for how Xerxes' desire 'to leave a memorial' might work against such a reading.

[73] Cf. Wood (1972), 163; Fisher (1992), 379.

individual) perspective. By focusing the earlier implied Greek viewpoint, the conjecture perhaps enables readers more easily to notice its
inadequacy. This contrast between Persian and Greek points of
view[74] emerges more explicitly as the account progresses, as we
shall see.

But again, readers might well be drawn to question whether
μεγαλοφροσύνης εἵνεκεν ('because of *megalophrosunē*') is really to
be understood in such a categorically negative way. Herodotus
seems deliberately to exploit the ambivalence of the expression. Its
later recurrence (and it is of Xerxes alone that the word is used in the
*Histories*)—this time in a positive sense, in explaining Xerxes' conduct in what seems an entirely different context—encourages readers
to review their understanding of the earlier instance, and by comparing the two situations to draw out possible overlap between the
two usages. For in Herodotus' analepsis back to the time when
Spartan heralds visited the King to offer their lives in atonement
for the Spartans' killing of Darius' heralds,

Ξέρξης ὑπὸ μεγαλοφροσύνης (usually translated 'magnanimously')[75] οὐκ ἔφη
ὅμοιος ἔσεσθαι Λακεδαιμονίοισι· κείνους μὲν γὰρ συγχέαι τὰ πάντων
ἀνθρώπων νόμιμα ἀποκτείναντας κήρυκας, αὐτὸς δὲ τὰ ἐκείνοισι ἐπιπλήσσει
ταῦτα οὐ ποιήσειν, οὐδὲ ἀνταποκτείνας ἐκείνους ἀπολύσειν Λακεδαιμονίους
τῆς αἰτίης (7.136.2).

[74] Van der Veen (1996) exposes the phenomenon in the *Histories* of something
being two opposite things *at once*, depending on one's perspective: Democedes at
3.137, for example, is seen to be 'both a runaway slave and a worthy citizen, according
to one's perspective' (113–14, quote at 114). Van der Veen usually frames his
discussion of perspective in terms of change over time (in accordance with Solon's
principle 'look to the end'), as in his epilogue, where he turns to consider perspective;
but Herodotus' practice of suggesting *simultaneously* differing perspectives, as here,
seems to me equally worthy of emphasis.
[75] e.g. Waterfield, Godley ('of his magnanimity'), Powell s.v. μεγαλοφροσύνη;
Mikalson (2003), 51 ('with magnanimity'); similarly de Sélincourt/Marincola
('with truly noble generosity'), Legrand 'avec grandeur d'âme'. But Immerwahr
(1966), 177 n. 86 thinks that 'comparison with 7.24.1 (where the word clearly
means "pride") shows that here also Xerxes is boasting and wants to show himself
superior to the Spartans'. In bringing out the notion of display this bears some
similarity to my preferred reading (below). The two instances of *megalophrosunē*
together, along with Artabanos' formulation at 7.10ε, suggest to van Ophuijsen/Stork
on 7.10ε that 'the word itself has not…acquired an unfavourable connotation' (see
further their discussion).

Xerxes out of *megalophrosunē* ('magnanimously'[76]) said that he would not be like the Lacedaemonians. For whereas they confounded the customs (*nomima*) of all men in executing heralds, he himself would not do that which he rebuked in them, nor would he free the Lacedaemonians from their guilt by killing [the heralds] in return.

Thus he releases the heralds rather than killing them. The literal sense of 'thinking big' opens up an area of possible common ground, since the two motives that follow suggest that this is not a matter of simple magnanimity—that is, of Xerxes acting out of pure generosity and moral superiority in sparing the heralds' lives—since he wants to do so flamboyantly, to be *seen* doing so in the eyes of the world (as his generalizing statement about human *nomos* suggests). It is not simply superior moral standards (cf. his first alleged motive) that account for his behaviour, but also (cf. the second) his ulterior objective of not letting the Spartans off the moral hook.

This aspect encourages further reflection upon the notion of display and the part it plays within the institution of Persian kingship. One possible reading of Xerxes here, as at Athos, is of a man focused on making the right impression, on (to use contemporary idiom) 'winning hearts and minds': minds through his display of a rationally insurmountable force as at Athos, hearts through the show of noble stature that proclaims his worthiness to rule. (Immerwahr's translation of *megalophrosunē*—which he views as Xerxes' 'outstanding characteristic'—as 'pride in his magnificence'[77] approaches mine, but perhaps overemphasizes the personal rather than the Persian-monarchical aspect of the word in this context.) It is this perspective that again prevails when, after the account of Xerxes' armament and extras (7.184–7), Herodotus observes: 'among all these thousands upon thousands of men, on account of his beauty and stature (κάλλεός τε εἵνεκα καὶ μεγάθεος) there was not one more worthy than Xerxes himself to hold this power (οὐδεὶς αὐτῶν ἀξιονικότερος ἦν αὐτοῦ Ξέρξεω ἔχειν τοῦτο τὸ κράτος)' (7.187.2). The king will again prove sensitive to this aspect of imperialism in his skilful use of the rhetoric of common mythic ancestry to give the Argives an acceptable motive for joining his cause (7.150).

[76] See previous note.   [77] Immerwahr (1966), 177.

## 8.3 XERXES AND ARTABANOS (7.43–52)

The opposition of Persian and Greek perspectives that emerged from
the Athos narrative crystallizes further over the course of the dialogue
between Xerxes and Artabanos at Abydos, overlooking the Hellespont. The immediately preceding account of Xerxes' act at the
Scamander river—his ascent to Priam's citadel and sacrifice there
to Athene of Ilium (7.43)—set him in the line of that king, Persians
in the line of Trojans, and in the reference to Athene pointed up a
connection between Trojans and Athenians. This Trojan background
opened readers' minds to Homer's vision of Trojans and Greeks as
equivalent to one another in virtue and humanity, setting the stage
for a conflict of equals.[78] And indeed, there is a measure both of
wisdom and of shortsightedness on both sides of the ensuing dialogue[79] (7.46–52) in which Artabanos warns of 'the worst enemies of
all' to the King's cause (land and sea) and Xerxes counters with the
advantages of decisive action that is backed up by thorough preparation. Each speaker harks back to the model of an earlier figure of
wisdom of the *Histories*: Artabanos' view is couched in overtly
Solonian style, Xerxes' in the style of his father Darius, who appeared
as a figure of wisdom at 3.38 (with his experiment proving that
*nomos* is king) and in judging Sandokes at 7.194. If Xerxes' initial
contrasting reactions as he gazes upon the scores of men below
('Xerxes counted himself happy (ἑωυτὸν ἐμακάρισε), but after this
he wept', 7.45) might for a moment invite a reading in terms of
unstable personality, his explanation soon displays instead a quite
profound insight: 'As I reflected on the brevity of all human life, it
made me feel compassion...' (7.46.2).[80] His self-*makarismos*
('counting himself happy'), unsettling to Greek sensibilities,[81] perhaps

[78] Flower/Marincola 15–16 offer a more general comparison of Herodotus' Persians with Trojans.
[79] Cf. e.g. Macan on 7.46.1; Solmsen (1982), 96–7. Contra e.g. Immerwahr (1954),
32 (who sees reason pitted against emotion in the figures of Artabanos and Xerxes
respectively). See particularly Pelling (1991), esp. 135 ff., observing the difference
between this and the usual Herodotean wise-adviser scene.
[80] Even as he accepts the more pessimistic (and more Solonian) perspective with
which Artabanos trumps this, his affirmation of the need for optimism is reasonable.
[81] Cf. Strepsiades' self-*makarismos* at Aristophanes, *Clouds* 1206.

strengthens again the impression that his perspective is distinctly Persian. Artabanos, by contrast, is of Herodotus' Persians 'most thoroughly and consistently Greek', and supplies 'a running Greek commentary on Xerxes' major decisions about the Persian Wars', as Mikalson observes.[82] His perspective in this instance, too, remains pervasively Solonian[83] right down to the final note of caution on which he ends, when he recalls an old saying: 'the end is not always clear at the beginning' (τὸ μὴ ἅμα ἀρχῇ πᾶν τέλος καταφαίνεσθαι, 7.51.3).

The responses of Xerxes—who in sightseeing at the Hellespont follows Darius' example at the Bosphoros (4.85–8)—recall those of Darius to Otanes in the lead-up to the conspiracy of the seven. Darius there urged the principle of securing *to kerdos* (profit) through action rather than delaying with speeches or deliberation; here Xerxes, while displaying moderation in accepting the reasonableness of Artabanos' desire for caution (7.50.1), counters similarly:

ἀτὰρ μήτε πάντα φοβέο μήτε πᾶν ὁμοίως ἐπιλέγεο. εἰ γὰρ δὴ βούλοιο ἐπὶ τῷ αἰεὶ ἐπεσφερομένῳ πρήγματι τὸ πᾶν ὁμοίως ἐπιλέγεσθαι, ποιήσειας ἂν οὐδαμὰ οὐδέν. . . . τοῖσι τοίνυν βουλομένοισι ποιέειν ὡς τὸ ἐπίπαν φιλέει γίνεσθαι τὰ κέρδεα, τοῖσι δὲ ἐπιλεγομένοισί τε πάντα καὶ ὀκνέουσι οὐ μάλα ἐθέλει (7.50.1–2).

Don't fear everything or give equal attention to all alike. For if you were to think equally over everything that ever occurred, you would never do anything. . . . Profitable results (*ta kerdea*) usually occur for those, then, who are willing to act; whereas for those who weigh up everything and hesitate, such results are not at all likely to happen.

He notes that this view finds corroboration in the past history of the Persian kings; and readers are well primed to recall Darius' success in adopting this approach in the coup. As far as foreign affairs are concerned, Darius' model is less salutary,[84] but Xerxes points to

[82] Mikalson (2003), 160–1.
[83] e.g. in his speaking of human *eudaimonia*, αἱ συμφοραὶ προσπίπτουσαι ('disasters that befall'), αἱ νοῦσοι συνταράσσουσαι ('illnesses that harrass'), ὁ θεὸς φθονερός ('the jealous god') (7.46.3–4), etc. See e.g. Stein ad loc.; How/Wells ad loc.; Harrison (2000), 48–51 for the Solonian echoes of Artabanos both here and in his earlier advice to Xerxes at 7.10δ.1–ζ; Mikalson (2003), 39, 160 for additional Greek poetic parallels.
[84] Cyrus' is far more so. Atossa and others in her wake reasonably look back upon him as a great early imperialist, for as well as reclaiming rule from the Medes, he secured fame and further territories for the Persians—even if he ended badly at Tomyris' hands.

elements that differentiate his own campaign against Greece from his father's Scythian (and Cambyses' Egyptian) expedition.[85] Xerxes' pilgrimage to Troy has illustrated again his sensitivity to the past, and it is this that shapes his responses to Artabanos: in following in the footsteps of his predecessors he may expect to win success (7.50.4). It is in responding to Artabanos' secondary area of anxiety (the Ionians' involvement) that Xerxes' view appears less tenable: for as How and Wells (on 7.52.1) observe, the Ionian tyrants' fidelity at 4.137 'was founded on self interest . . . , and was but a poor proof of the loyalty of their people when opposed to brother Hellenes'. Thus having appropriated Darius' theory of self-interest (*kerdos*), Xerxes seems to fail to give it the consistent application it deserves. And yet he does have hostages as a supplementary, more practical guarantee of the Ionians' good faith (7.52.2); and history will in the end prove him largely correct.[86]

So, Xerxes' arguments display once again the 'Persian' philosophy of ceaseless activity and endeavours—and of emulating one's forefathers (ἡμεῖς . . . ὁμοιεύμενοι ἐκείνοισι, 7.50.4) in this respect—in contrast to Artabanos' 'Greek' philosophy of caution and moderation. (Of course this polarity is not stable: significantly the Athenians' adoption of the more active ethos, led by Themistocles, is what will precipitate Greek success.[87]) The 'Persian' perspective regards the campaign as the inevitable outcome of a pattern of history, and as likely to meet with success in consequence of its full preparation in various practical ways.[88] The 'Greek' perspective, on the other hand,

---

[85] e.g., 7.50.4: τοῦτο μὲν γὰρ αὐτοὶ πολλὴν φορβὴν φερόμενοι πορευόμεθα, τοῦτο δέ, τῶν ἄν κου ἐπιβέωμεν γῆν καὶ ἔθνος, τούτων τὸν σῖτον ἕξομεν· ἐπ' ἀροτῆρας δὲ καὶ οὐ νομάδας στρατευόμεθα ἄνδρας ('We are taking a good quantity of provisions with us on the march, and moreover we'll get food from the inhabitants of whatever land and community we reach. The men we are campaigning against are farmers, not nomads').

[86] For the most part the Ionians fail to desert to the Greeks, apart from at Mycale. Themistocles' plan does not appear to have worked. See Pelling (1991), 136.

[87] Thucydides will develop this polarity in characterizing Athenians in opposition to Spartans.

[88] I am not convinced by Harrison's view that 'the thoroughness of Xerxes' preparations, . . . lavishly described, is a signal that the campaign is bound to end in failure: as Artabanus recognizes, their numbers will work against them' (2000), 61: this preparation can equally be viewed as distinguishing Xerxes' campaign from Cambyses' unprepared (and unsuccessful) prequel; the size of the expedition does indeed play some role in demoralizing the Greeks; and Artabanos' view is only one of those available.

views it with an attitude resembling Solon's towards Croesus' belief in the enduring nature of his own prosperity: as exhibiting an unfounded degree of confidence that perhaps even verges on *hybris*. The subsequent account will demonstrate the *near* truth of Xerxes' opinion on the human level (for many Greeks *are* cowed into submission, and the army copes with food supply problems on the way to Greece), but the truth of Artabanos' opinion on the *divine* level[89]—in the one area, that is, about which Xerxes was resigned to the impossibility for men to have knowledge: 'How can one that is only human know with certainty? (εἰδέναι δὲ ἄνθρωπον ἐόντα κῶς χρὴ τὸ βέβαιον;)—I think it's impossible' (7.50.2), though his frequent sacrifices suggest he does his best.

## 8.4 THE PYTHIOS EPISODE (7.27–9, 38–40)

On the heels of the Athos narrative comes the account of Xerxes' encounter with Pythios. Here we may observe with particular clarity Herodotus' practice of setting forth rival templates, in this case (irrational, hybristic) 'tyrant' ∼ (rational, pious) 'king' (mapping broadly on to the Cambyses ∼ Darius models of motivation/behaviour).[90] The possibility again arises that these alternatives may imply contrasting perspectives (e.g. Persian ∼ Greek), and again these perspectives might—but do not necessarily[91]—reflect different traditions. 7.27–9 relate Pythios' generosity in entertaining Xerxes and his army, and Xerxes' pleasure at this and generosity in return. 7.38–40

[89] Cf. Sancisi-Weerdenburg (2002): 'Herodotus' description of the event [i.e., Xerxes' weeping at Abydos] and the subsequent conversation with his uncle Artabanus signals less the hybristic monarch than a man who is prepared to take reasonable risks and follow in the footsteps of his predecessors on the Persian throne (7.8). Fate… meanwhile has decided that things will happen differently from what could be foreseen' (587); Pelling (1991), 138: the 'cosmic register… turns out to be the vital one'.

[90] For Herodotus' use of such 'templates' see esp. Dewald (2003). As Dewald (2003), 34 remarks, Cambyses 'most completely fulfills all the items in Otanes' picture of the despotic template' (cf. 43: only Cambyses 'acts as the Compleat Tyrant, according to the model of the Constitutional Debate'). See e.g. Heni (1977), 129–32 for Cambyses' developing 'tyrant' aspects.

[91] Cf. remarks above, n. 6 with text; cf. 251 above. See Masson (1950) on the probable Near Eastern background of the episode of Pythios.

recount the grim postscript: frightened by the eclipse and encouraged by Xerxes' gifts, Pythios secures the promise of a favour before requesting his eldest son's leave of absence from the war (7.38). Angered, Xerxes has the son sliced in two and each half set on either side of the road out of Sardis for his army to march through.

From one angle, the Sardis setting of this stretch of the *Histories* recalls the earlier arrival there of Solon and his advice to Croesus—which hints from the very beginning of the episode that Pythios' excessive prosperity, like Croesus', may not endure. The impending loss specific to Pythios is in keeping with the pervasive theme in the *Histories* thus far of the *apaidia* (childlessness) that accompanies material prosperity.[92] Indeed his introduction—'Pythios the Lydian, son of Atys' (7.27.1)—brings to the fore this network of associations, for Atys is the name of the son of Croesus whom Adrastos accidentally killed (1.43). The immediately preceding mention of Apollo (7.26.3) might draw attention to the Pythian aspect to his name. The talk of numbers recalls both the quantity of Croesus' riches, and, more specifically, Solon's tour de force of arithmetic in proving the disaster-prone nature of men (1.32). This perspective rather equates Pythios with the earlier Lydian king, implying that the reversal of his fortune may be inevitable. Thus it sets forth (as did the dream sequence in Susa) the notion of Xerxes as an agent of some greater force, not to be held personally responsible.

On the other hand, the stark juxtaposition of the opposed episodes surrounding Xerxes and Pythios seems to many commentators expressive of Xerxes' unstable, tyrannical character[93]—and in broad outline that, too, is certainly an available perspective. The stories that intervene between the two parts of the Pythios narrative pave the way for such an interpretation by showcasing the extreme character of the king's reactions: his rewarding a plane tree for its beauty with adornment of gold and an Immortal to guard it (7.31) contrasts with his subsequent punishment of the Hellespont with lashings and fetters (7.35) for its

---

[92] e.g. Croesus' wealth then loss of Atys; Ameinocles' fortune after Salamis then loss of his son (7.190), etc.

[93] e.g. Dewald *Comm.* on 7.37–43 (quoted below, 275); Hohti (1976), 55 (with his n. 1): 'the extreme nature of these incidents illustrates Xerxes' capriciousness'; Solmsen (1982), 93 (observing 'the despotic volte-face in [Xerxes'] dealings with Pythius'); Ubsdell (1983), 15–16.

destruction of the bridges. Hints at Xerxes' tyrant aspect are felt also in the foregrounding of the transgression of boundaries (with, for example, the crossing of the Halys (7.26) noted just prior to the first mention of Pythios, Croesus' boundary pillar (7.30) observed just after it[94]), and in the note of the king's 'pleasure' at Pythios' words.

Xerxes' shifting responses to Pythios recall those especially of his tyrant precursor Cambyses; and beyond this general impression readers may note points of similarity in the particulars too. Xerxes' angered order (κάρτα τε ἐθυμώθη ..., 7.39.1) that the body of the son of a previously most favoured man whose words had pleased him (Ξέρξης δὲ ἡσθεὶς τοῖσι εἰρημένοισι, 7.28.3) be sliced in half (μέσον διαταμεῖν, 7.39.3), and then displayed before the father's eyes, recalls specifically Cambyses' analogous treatment of the son of his favourite Prexaspes (τὸν ἐτίμα τε μάλιστα..., 'whom he honoured most of all...', 3.34.1). There, angered (θυμωθέντα, 3.34.3, ὀργῇ, 3.35.1) at the apparent reversal of the Persians' earlier judgement and Croesus' comment which had pleased him (ἥσθη, 3.34.5) particularly, Cambyses shot the boy right in the heart (μέσης τῆς καρδίης, 3.35.2) then had him sliced open before his father's eyes. However, this basic similarity of situation lends prominence to some significant areas of *difference*. The Prexaspes anecdote served as an example of Cambyses' mad dealings with Persians generally (3.34.1, following on from examples of his acts of madness concerning his own household), whereas in Xerxes' case the preceding narrative[95] has conditioned readers to expect an explanation founded upon reason. Thus readers are encouraged to reflect carefully upon his motives at this point, and specifically upon what might differentiate this situation from its Cambyses prototype, rather than to accept the explanation of mental instability that is implied by the surface comparison. In this way, even as the 'tyrant' explanation we have outlined remains present and possible, it is challenged by an opposing strand of the narrative that invites a counter-interpretation.

The most notable divergence between the two scenarios is the fact that in the Cambyses situation the link between the Persians'

[94] Note too the details of other rivers and of roads that pervade the narrative at this point.
[95] e.g. the decision to invade and the Athos narrative, discussed above.

offending action and his own counteraction is tenuous and illogical. Indeed, the king's (inaccurate) perception that the Persians have accused him of madness motivates an action that—so far from proving them wrong, as he intends—ironically displays his insanity all the more.[96] Cambyses' accusation of lying on the Persians' part is unfounded, whereas Xerxes' similar accusation of inconsistency—of a promise not kept—is well explained and justified: for Pythios has indeed failed to live up to his promise, and to the expectations aroused by a relationship of *xeiniē* (guest-friendship). The first Pythios episode foregrounded the notion of reciprocal *xeiniē*. The two-pronged character of Pythios' initial gesture—*xeiniē* for the men and Xerxes, twinned with concrete financial aid (7.27.1)—was matched by Xerxes' recognition of Pythios as his *xeinos* (guest-friend), plus his gift of a large sum of money (7.29.1–2). Important, as Xerxes' words indicated, was not only the magnitude in financial terms of Pythios' gift, but also the generous spirit in which it appeared to have been made: Pythios had acted thus αὐτεπάγγελτος, 'of his own accord'. Xerxes' phraseology highlights the idea of reciprocity.[97] His reciprocal *gerea* ('gifts of honour, privileges') consist of both a return of material goods and the establishment of a bond of friendship. Before continuing with his journey he makes clear the mutual expectations established by this relationship, advising Pythios: 'Keep what you already possess, and make sure that you always remain such a man as this (ἐπίστασό τε εἶναι αἰεὶ τοιοῦτος): for you will never regret this kind of behaviour, either now or in the future' (7.29.3).

Pythios later fails to provide the unqualified support signalled by his initial gesture when, encouraged by Xerxes' gifts, he hopes to withdraw one of his sons from the expedition—and so neglects the wider obligation entailed by the relationship those gifts denoted. He secures Xerxes' promise of a favour (for the king 'thought that he would ask for anything rather than what he actually requested', πᾶν μᾶλλον δοκέων μιν χρηίσειν ἢ τὸ ἐδεήθη (7.38.2)—presumably taking

[96] Cf. Heni (1977), 132.
[97] e.g., σὺ δὲ καὶ ἐξείνισας μεγάλως στρατὸν τὸν ἐμὸν καὶ χρήματα μεγάλα ἐπαγγέλλεαι. σοὶ ὦν ἐγὼ ἀντὶ αὐτῶν γέρεα τοιάδε δίδωμι ... ('You have both magnificently entertained my army and offered large sums of money. To you therefore I, in return for these things, give the following gifts of honour', 7.29.1–2).

for granted that it would accord with the obligations of their mutual
*xeiniē*) before spelling out his request. Xerxes angrily observes that he
is campaigning in person, taking with him his sons, brothers, relatives and friends (φίλους), whereas Pythios—who should be doing
the same but is not—has the gall to plead for his son (φίλους reminds
us that he too should now be regarding himself as numbered among
Xerxes' friends). In voicing anxiety Pythios also overlooks the importance to the King's project of a show of total support. In branding
him a slave (ἐὼν ἐμὸς δοῦλος) Xerxes underscores the fact that
Pythios has proved himself unworthy of the former reciprocal relationship, which, moreover, was an exceptional honour: Demaratus is
the only other individual in the *Histories* who appears as Xerxes'
*xeinos*, 'guest-friend' (7.237.3). Xerxes nonetheless respects his own
side of the bargain in bearing in mind *ta xeinia* ('hospitality') of
earlier when he metes out a more lenient punishment than he
considers deserved (7.39.2). Herodotus has the king explain his
motivation, setting forth the logic behind his changing responses to
Pythios' actions:

ὅτε μέν νυν χρηστὰ ποιήσας ἕτερα τοιαῦτα ἐπηγγέλλεο, εὐεργεσίῃσι βασιλέα
οὐ καυχήσεαι ὑπερβαλέσθαι· ἐπείτε δὲ ἐς τὸ ἀναιδέστερον ἐτράπευ, τὴν μὲν
ἀξίην οὐ λάμψεαι, ἐλάσσω δὲ τῆς ἀξίης (7.39.2).

At the time when you performed good services and promised more, you will
not boast that you outdid the King in the generosity of your benefactions.
But now that you have turned to behaving shamelessly, you will get not what
you deserve, but less.

Xerxes' second response was thus not arbitrary, nor dictated by
(tyrannical) extremes of personality[98] or even by anger *tout court*,
but comes rather to appear an 'exemplary gesture' of the sort studied
by Christopher Gill: it seems an eminently appropriate response
to kill the favourite son of a *philos* in return for his violation of
the obligations of *philia*.[99] Indeed, the later 'Captain's Reward'

[98] The fact that the second response is not an entirely opposite action to the first
but rather one arising from Xerxes' same quality (his high regard for *xeiniē*), hinders
us from regarding it, as do Immerwahr (1966), 182 and others, as exemplifying his
contradictory character.
[99] Compare Gill's discussion of the rationality of Medea's murder of Jason's (and
her) children to punish him for his devaluation of their relationship; indeed, Gill
regards the 'second-order' reasoning which precipitates her 'exemplary gesture' as

story—according to which Xerxes exhibits extremes of behaviour similar to those involving Pythios (in close sequence rewarding and then punishing the captain of his ship), only this time coupled with an indisputable measure of irrationality and arbitrariness—Herodotus refuses to believe (οὐδαμῶς ἔμοιγε πιστός . . ., 8.119). For when the ship is overloaded Xerxes, according to this version, has Persians rather than slaves jump overboard; and his contradictory acts concerning the captain—'since he had saved the life of the King, Xerxes gave the captain a golden crown, but since he had caused the deaths of many Persians, he cut off his head' (8.118.4)—are not envisaged as sequential, logical responses to changing circumstances, but as being almost simultaneous, arising from conflicting and perverse urges within the King.[100] Herodotus does not, as Flory observes, object to 'the story's most unbelievable feature, the combination of award and execution. Should Herodotus not ask of what use a golden crown will be to a man with no head?'[101] But the historian is perhaps purposefully leaving unexplained this further signal of the extreme irrationality of the imagined situation, for the attentive reader to enjoy elucidating.

Darius, too, pervades the background in the Pythios affair (much as Cambyses' father Cyrus did in the Prexaspes scenario, where at issue was the question of Cambyses' standing in relation to his father). The Persians quickly identify Pythios for Xerxes as 'the man who gave your father Darius the golden plane tree and vine' (7.27.2; might filial nostalgia prompt the later plane tree affair?), and he in tallying up his fortune refers to his 'four million **Daric** staters (στατήρων Δαρεικῶν)' (7.28.2). An obvious touchstone for Xerxes'

possibly more rational than her (emotional, last-minute) urge to save them (1996), 216–26, esp. 225. Might Xerxes' whipping of the Hellespont be understood as an exemplary gesture too? He does have his men say that it is done ὅτι μιν ἠδίκησας οὐδὲν πρὸς ἐκείνου ἄδικον παθόν ('because you did him wrong/treated him unjustly although you had suffered no wrong/injustice from him', 7.35.2); and we know that Darius, for example, is very concerned with justice.

[100] Flory (1987), 58 notes that Herodotus uses this anecdote to make Xerxes' cruelty on the way to Greece (in the Pythios episode) mirror his cruelty on the way back, but overlooks the way in which this basic mirroring points up a significant difference between this account (not to be believed) and its structural counterpart. See below, n. 108 with text, for a different significance. Dewald and Kitzinger suggest a further level of truth again: Xerxes 'did indeed seat Persian grandees at the oars of the ship of state' (2006), 128 n. 7.

[101] Flory (1987), 62.

dealings with Pythios is Darius' with the Persian Oiobazos in the lead-up to the Scythian expedition. To Oiobazos' request that one of his three sons, all serving in the army, might be left behind, Darius replied that 'since he was a friend and making a moderate request (ὡς φίλῳ ἐόντι καὶ μετρίων δεομένῳ), he would leave behind all his children' (4.84.1). Oiobazos rejoiced, imagining his sons were released from service; Darius had them all put to death; and, Herodotus concluded, 'these were left behind there [in Susa]—with their throats cut' (4.84.2). Darius, like Xerxes, is motivated in exacting this harsh punishment by the flouting of a bond of friendship, as his ironic reply indicates, which suggests rather that Oiobazos' request is *not* μέτριος—moderate or tolerable—on the part of a friend. The parallel that emerges between the two episodes brings out all the more clearly this common pattern: the two are mutually illuminating, with the Xerxes episode prompting reflection back upon its Darius counterpart.

But commentators note the more gruesome nature of Xerxes' treatment of the son's body. Dewald (*Comm.* on 7.37–43) remarks:

Xerxes' treatment of Pythius here suggests a certain instability in Xerxes himself.... His act is the same as his father's in 4.84, but the coupling of it with the earlier effusive praise and grand gesture is not. Again, the army's departure through the two halves of the severed body of Pythius' son strikes an ominous note.

And yet Darius' punishment is the more severe, for he destroyed Oiobazos' line, rendering him wholly *apais* (without children), whereas Xerxes allows Pythios to remain in possession of four of his five sons. Xerxes' 'effusive praise and grand gesture' serves to amplify (in keeping with the greater length and detail of that account) the theme of his established bond of reciprocal friendship with Pythios—which was swiftly but nonetheless clearly indicated (with ὡς φίλῳ ἐόντι, 'on the grounds that he was a friend') in the Darius version. Xerxes at least sets out his justifications for the punishment before exacting it, whereas Darius left the wretched Oiobazos with the impression that his request had been successful, leaving him to work out in retrospect the significance of the King's action. It is Xerxes not Darius who emulates the latter's moderate earlier behaviour (at 7.194.2, which Herodotus seems implicitly to

approve) in weighing up the man's rights and wrongs in assessing his
due punishment, taking account of his earlier virtue (7.39).[102]

Readers *are* compelled, however, to confront the question of why it
is that Xerxes has the body exposed in the macabre way he does—
since his moderation in putting to death just one son,[103] along with
the reasoned quality of his other responses, indicate that an explanation solely in terms of tyrannical excess (as might have suited the
Cambyses situation) will be inadequate. The temptation to write it
off it as being motivated simply by a barbarous character[104] is fore-
stalled by the tale of matching Greek atrocity that Herodotus has
chosen to recount just a few chapters earlier (directly after the first
Pythios episode): Xanthippos and the Athenians' 'crucifixion [alive]'
of Artaÿctes (7.33).[105] The familiar patterns of motivation and action
regarding Xerxes might well guide readers, searching for a reasonable
explanation, to return to the notion of display. His punishment of
Pythios caused less human tragedy than did Darius' of Oiobazos, but
it nevertheless made clear to all—to the whole army—that desertion
in any form would not be tolerated.[106] Herodotus' text thus leaves
open the possibility that Xerxes' action was motivated by his sensitivity to the practical use of a display of punishment: an 'exemplary'

[102] Compare the similar trajectory of Kurke's interesting argument (1999), 81–3
that Cambyses' treatment of Sisamnes (5.25–6) may be viewed, from one of the
available perspectives, as representing a punishment more logical and in accordance
with Persian *nomos* than is Darius' of Sandokes (which is based upon financial profit).

[103] Contrast also Darius' granting Intaphrenes' wife the life of only one family
member, subsequently bolstered to two (versus Xerxes' depriving Pythios of just one life).

[104] e.g. as 'an exhibition of the unbounded cruelty and caprice of the oriental
despot, from whose rule Hellas had been saved at Salamis', Macan ad loc.

[105] Desmond (2004), 32–6 brings out the disquieting character of this episode,
with the form of the punishment perhaps being expressively reminiscent of Persian
impaling.

[106] Compare Xerxes' 'numbering of the host by the sheep-pen method' (in Hammond's expression), which might be interpreted as much in terms of the (traditional
Persian) requirement for an impressive *show* of great numbers as being, as Hammond
argues, one of Herodotus' 'indirect comments on the folly of excess in mustering over
five million men' (1988), 536. Indeed, Xerxes' decision to do so at Doriskos in
emulation of Darius (for Herodotus postpones until then (7.59.1) this information
regarding Darius' Scythian campaign) seems a gesture of continuity of tradition, of
filial imitation of his father. The Persian predilection for quantification, discussed by
Konstan (1987) in terms of its opposition to *intrinsic* virtue/*aretē*, might perhaps
equally, in some instances (and from a 'Persian' standpoint), be viewed in terms of the
Persian traditional requirement to *display* (i.e., with an external audience in mind).

gesture in a second sense.[107] The *exemplary* aspect has particular relevance on the way to Greece, while others are present to encourage and impress. Here a suggestive contrast may be felt with the 'Captain's Reward' story which, even though unbelievable, is expressive in its portrayal of Xerxes' conduct on the *return* journey as diminished into *nothing* but a 'gesture'.[108] In any case, as Fisher suggests, the Pythios episode 'should be seen as much as a comment on the system of power in the Empire and the pressures on the King to exact absolute obedience from all his "slaves", as it is a comment on Xerxes'.[109]

Thus in this instance, rather than offering an explicit statement of Xerxes' motives, Herodotus' method is to leave readers to draw inferences themselves, guided in so doing by the divergences that become apparent from previously established Persian King templates with their accompanying explanatory paradigms. These floating explanations make specific motive statements unnecessary. There is not the implication—as there might well be in a parallel situation in Thucydides[110]—that because Herodotus is unable to supply a specific motivation (or disinclined, wishing to keep before us various possibilities), therefore the behaviour is inexplicable: for Herodotus has trained his readers to accompany him in the search for explanations. While Herodotus may thus shy from offering a specific explanation, he equips his readers to consider the possibilities. And in this case the questions that suggest themselves to readers are couched in 'motive' terms, as 'either-or' alternatives: is one or other particular, reasonable motive at work, or is the king's behaviour to be explained more in terms of an irrational tyrant mentality? Broadly we may speak in terms of the 'Darius' and 'Cambyses' behavioural models (while recognizing that the *Histories* qualifies that opposition: ch. 4). Both templates are brought into play in a manner that sensitizes readers to significant aspects of Xerxes' case, through comparison as well as contrast. The Xerxes scenario maps on

---

[107] i.e. as aimed not simply at the individual who is the focus of punishment, but also at the widest possible further audience. Thomas Friedman (1990) writes interestingly on the historical importance of this in the Middle East; cf. Foucault (1977).

[108] I owe this nice point to Chris Pelling.

[109] Fisher (1992), 378–9.

[110] Cf. e.g. Rood (1998), 143: 'Thucydides' silence explains why [Paches' suicide] cannot be explained'.

to both templates in outline, but less so when readers move to considering the specifics. The Cambyses ('tyrant') template is certainly significant—in that it serves as a foil for a what is a more subtle picture in Xerxes' case: for we *are* expecting reasons, rational ones, for this King's behaviour.[111] Herodotus' narrative at times evokes the tyrant template, only to show that it is not quite so simple as that.

### 8.4.1  Epitaph on a tyrant? (9.108–13)

And yet as the *Histories* progress and some of these patterns recur, readers find Xerxes coming to fit more easily into the Cambyses-tyrant template, and are drawn to wonder whether something along the lines of the Otanes formula (3.80) may be playing itself out. The motif of the tyrant's heedlessness has perhaps already surfaced in Xerxes' failure to take account of an omen (7.57.2) or (earlier) to perceive the shortcomings of the Magi's interpretations (of the *vanishing* crown of Xerxes' third dream (7.19) and the eclipse at 7.37.2–3). More strikingly, with Xerxes' reward of the man who saves his brother Masistes' life (9.108) will be juxtaposed the beginning of the account (9.108 ff.) in which he himself precipitates Masistes' death, a tale marked by his changing lusts and disregard for familial *nomos*. Here the Pythios pattern plays itself out again in a context that underscores readers' impression of more unqualified tyrannical behaviour. The motif of the binding request recurs. But whereas Pythios was encouraged by Xerxes' pleasure in him into asking an unspecified favour to which the King initially agreed but withdrew upon learning its nature, it is Xerxes himself who, enraptured by Artaÿnte, offers to grant her whatever she wishes and is eventually obliged to grant her request.[112] Amestris in turn awaits the feast day on which the King is constrained by *nomos* to grant any favour, before requesting that he grant her Masistes' wife. Xerxes, this

---

[111] Waters' argument (1971) is useful in reminding us that tyrant patterning should not be pressed too far.

[112] Ξέρξης δὲ πᾶν μᾶλλον δοκέων μιν χρήσειν ἢ τὸ ἐδεήθη... ('Xerxes, thinking that he would ask for anything rather than what he actually requested...', 7.38.2) ∼ ὁ δὲ πᾶν μᾶλλον δοκέων κείνην αἰτήσεσθαι... ('he, thinking that she would rather ask for anything else...', 9.109.2).

time fully understanding her purpose (9.110.3), nonetheless unwill-ingly yields (9.111.1). He thus brings about the terrible mutilation (and doubtless the death[113]) of his brother's innocent wife at Ames-tris' hands. It is an even more brutal treatment, in that it is drawn out, than that suffered by Pythios' son.

The motif of the binding request expresses the increasingly de-structive effect upon Xerxes of others' influence, while the feast day *nomos* expresses that of Persian tradition—both furthering themes we have seen developing from Xerxes' first appearance, which once again sideline the role of his motives. And yet Xerxes does to some extent persist in working against the grain of these seemingly in-escapable patterns—if only in a more passive capacity, by demon-strating a degree of moderation. For instance, although in tyrant fashion he succumbs to lust for family members on whom he has no claim, first his brother's wife and then her daughter—much as Cambyses fell for two of his sisters in succession, in contravention of Persian *nomos*—Xerxes scrupulously avoids all use of force against the women:[114] 'he did not use force (οὐδὲ βίην προσέφερε), out of respect for his brother Masistes; and in fact this was precisely what was restraining the woman, too, for she knew well that she would not be subjected to violence (εὖ γὰρ ἐπίστατο βίης οὐ τευξομένη)' (9.108.1; unlike Cambyses at 3.32, or the typical tyrant of 3.80.5 who βιᾶται γυναῖκας, 'violates women'[115]). Indeed Herodotus thus im-plies that the woman's knowledge of Xerxes' principle on this score enables her, too, more easily to resist his advances: she was perhaps not so entirely innocent after all.[116]

Again, even if Xerxes' heavy sense of obligation as regards the particular feast day custom is strangely discordant with the flouting of family *philia* that his consequent action entails, he nevertheless persists in acting in accordance with *nomos*[117] (again in contrast with Otanes' notion of the tyrant, who 'disturbs a country's ancestral

[113] Flower/Marincola on 9.113.1.     [114] Cf. Sancisi-Weerdenburg (2002), 586.
[115] Cf. ch. 5 n. 90.     [116] Cf. Masaracchia on 9.108.4–5.

[117] As Sancisi-Weerdenburg (2002) observes: 'Xerxes' relations with women, as reported by Herodotus, is much more a tragic story of a king caught between duty and fate, than of the lecherous monarch modern commentators have found in the Artaynte-story. In the situation described it is not so much the seductive powers of women which place Xerxes in a difficult situation, but the obligation to adhere to his royal duty and not to go back on his promise' (586). Contra e.g. Masaracchia (1977), xix.

customs', νόμαιά τε κινέει πάτρια, 3.80.5). In this respect he follows rather in the vein of Darius, especially at 3.38, whose name has surfaced several times over the course of the account, than he does in the vein of Cambyses, who could ignore *nomoi* indiscriminately.[118] Moreover Herodotus' account brings out Xerxes' feeling for his brother and frustration at a sequence of events that seems to him to be beyond his control. Like Cambyses he—likewise succeeding an established father—is shaped by the considerable pressures of the fully fledged institution of monarchy, which determine the parameters of his actions. And yet, rather than responding in frustration by choosing to ignore the institution and its *nomoi* entirely (as Cambyses appeared to do—in letting his emotions overrule him, having his brother killed, and so on), he retains a degree of respect for both, and manages to keep his emotions more in check.

## 8.5 CONCERNS OF PIETY

### 8.5.1 Hellespont offerings (7.54–6)

In other cases, rather than guiding readers to work from general to particular (from broad templates to specific corollaries), Herodotus problematizes the question of motivation more directly through the presentation of alternative possible motives, each of which feeds back again into the wider patterns. We introduced above[119] the possibility of 'Greek' versus 'Persian' explanatory paradigms: the one helpful in understanding the near success of the expedition, the other in comprehending its ultimate failure, each implying a different understanding of Xerxes' attitude in executing it. Such awareness and promotion of an alternative, non-Greek perspective would be in keeping with Herodotus' intense curiosity in the rest of the *Histories* about different peoples' customs, regarding which

---

[118] Again, this opposition is not absolute: Darius, too, could ignore others' *nomoi* (as in the Chorasmian plain episode, 3.117), and Kurke (1999), 82–3 detects a strand of Herodotus' account of Sandokes suggesting that Darius prioritizes financial gain over traditional royal justice.

[119] 251 (council and dream sequence), 262–4 (Athos canal).

[h]e models for his listeners an attitude of charitable observation; when he does not lead them to the realization of unexpected likeness, he promotes the discovery of understandable difference and creative solutions.[120]

In this final section I aim to demonstrate that the 'Greek'/'Persian' explanatory paradigms surrounding Xerxes are mirrored in, and encapsulated by, some of the more specific double unresolved motives Herodotus attributes to the King. The specific attributions highlight the presence of those paradigms.

Soon after Artabanos' departure for Susa, in preparation for the crossing of the Hellespont, Herodotus recounts Xerxes' prayer to the sun at sunrise and libation from a golden bowl into the sea, followed by an action for which two possible motives are suggested:

ἐσέβαλε τὴν φιάλην ἐς τὸν Ἑλλήσποντον καὶ χρύσεον κρητῆρα καὶ Περσικὸν ξίφος, τὸν ἀκινάκην καλέουσι. ταῦτα οὐκ ἔχω ἀτρεκέως διακρῖναι οὔτε εἰ τῷ ἡλίῳ ἀνατιθεὶς κατῆκε ἐς τὸ πέλαγος, οὔτε εἰ μετεμέλησέ οἱ τὸν Ἑλλήσποντον μαστιγώσαντι καὶ ἀντὶ τούτων τὴν θάλασσαν ἐδωρέετο (7.54.2–3).

He threw into the Hellespont the bowl, a golden krater and a Persian sword, which they call the *akinakēs*. I cannot decide with certainty whether he was making an offering to the sun in casting these items into the sea, or whether he repented of whipping the Hellespont and so in compensation for this was giving them as gifts to the sea.

The objects represent a mixture of the familiar in Greek terms (golden bowls and kraters) and the more exotic and specifically Persian (the Persian *akinakēs*, which requires the authorial gloss).[121]

The action may be interpreted from an implicitly Persian perspective, according to which Xerxes is motivated by concerns of piety in sacrificing to the sun in accordance with Persian custom (as he has been seen doing several times previously in the *Histories*), which was after all the explicit object of his prayer. Alternatively, as seen from a more judgemental—and perhaps implicitly Greek—perspective, the action represents the King at long last repenting of his earlier hubristic stance in whipping the Hellespont. This alternative recalls the earlier anecdote of the whipping, and Xerxes' reported command for

---

[120] Munson (2001), 141.
[121] Compare the triple suggestions of motive for Cyrus' placing Croesus on the pyre (1.86.2), which similarly draw the audience across a spectrum of explanation ranging from the extremely exotic to the familiar and Greek.

his men 'to speak barbarous and reckless words' ($\lambda\acute{\epsilon}\gamma\epsilon\iota\nu$ $\beta\acute{\alpha}\rho\beta\alpha\rho\acute{\alpha}$ $\tau\epsilon$ $\kappa\alpha\grave{\iota}$ $\mathring{\alpha}\tau\acute{\alpha}\sigma\theta\alpha\lambda\alpha$, 7.35.2) at the river. The doubleness to some extent also maps on to the Darius-king versus Cambyses-tyrant paradigm. The historian's expression of inability to decide which reading of Xerxes' motives he prefers, together with its accompanying paradigm—that of pious leader or (only now) repentant tyrant (as Cambyses was eventually remorseful about murdering his brother)—becomes a model for the reader's. Or rather, it guides the reader to think carefully about the possibilities and reflect upon likely combinations, with a view to reaching a more profound understanding of Xerxes' reasons for action. Herodotus' purpose goes much further than offering two variants simply to increase readerly belief in the common core (that is, the Hellespont offerings), or to introduce a note of praise or blame.[122]

## 8.5.2  The Hellespont crossing (7.55–6)

The expansion of the narrative that the dwelling on possible alternatives produces also prolongs this significant moment heralding Xerxes' transgression of boundaries: his move over the Hellespont and into Europe. And the doubleness of perspective perhaps goes some way towards explaining the enigma of Herodotus' account of the crossing that ensues,[123] which seems more readily comprehensible if we understand it as being told twice over in different versions. Herodotus first relates what seems a discrete account (7.55) of the crossing as taking place over two days: on the first, the ten thousand Persians ($\mathring{\epsilon}\sigma\tau\epsilon\phi\alpha\nu\omega\mu\acute{\epsilon}\nu\sigma\iota$ $\pi\acute{\alpha}\nu\tau\epsilon\varsigma$, 'all wearing garlands') and the army mixed up of all the different peoples ($\acute{o}$ $\sigma\acute{\nu}\mu\mu\iota\kappa\tau\sigma\varsigma$ $\sigma\tau\rho\alpha\tau\grave{o}\varsigma$ $\pi\alpha\nu\tau\sigma\acute{\iota}\omega\nu$ $\mathring{\epsilon}\theta\nu\acute{\epsilon}\omega\nu$) cross over; on the second, the horsemen and those who carry their spears reversed; the sacred horses and sacred chariot ($\sigma\mathring{\iota}$ $\tau\epsilon$ $\mathring{\iota}\pi\pi\sigma\iota$ $\sigma\mathring{\iota}$ $\mathring{\iota}\rho\sigma\grave{\iota}$ $\kappa\alpha\grave{\iota}$ $\tau\grave{o}$ $\mathring{\alpha}\rho\mu\alpha$ $\tau\grave{o}$ $\mathring{\iota}\rho\acute{o}\nu$); Xerxes' himself, the spearmen and the

---

[122] As Flory (1987), 75 suggests.

[123] Over which many commentators have puzzled. Macan ad loc. came to the conclusion that '[t]his passage is of value as showing how little Hdt. recks of the contradictions and inconsequences in his various sources: he does not really know (or much care) whether Xerxes crossed last, or midst, or, as this passage [7.56.1] implies, among the first; nor whether the crossing took two days, or "seven days and seven nights without pause"!'

thousand cavalry; and finally the rest of the host. The account is marked by brevity and understatement, with few details or qualifiers included apart from those that underscore the piety of the expedition (the *garlanded* Persians and *sacred* chariot team). Herodotus rounds it off, in what is a characteristic closural manner of his, with an alternative possibility: 'I once heard a version in which the King crossed over last of all' (7.55.3).

However, following directly on from this seemingly finished account comes the narration of a separate, more sensational version (which does however require the assumption of one of the alternatives proposed in the preceding account: that Xerxes was *first* to cross[124]).

Ξέρξης δὲ ἐπεὶ διέβη ἐς τὴν Εὐρώπην, ἐθηεῖτο τὸν στρατὸν ὑπὸ μαστίγων διαβαίνοντα. διέβη δὲ ὁ στρατὸς αὐτοῦ ἐν ἑπτὰ ἡμέρῃσι καὶ [ἐν] ἑπτὰ εὐφρόνῃσι, ἐλινύσας οὐδένα χρόνον. ἐνθαῦτα λέγεται Ξέρξεω ἤδη διαβεβη-κότος τὸν Ἑλλήσποντον ἄνδρα εἰπεῖν Ἑλλησπόντιον· Ὦ Ζεῦ, τί δὴ ἀνδρὶ εἰδόμενος Πέρσῃ καὶ οὔνομα ἀντὶ Διὸς Ξέρξην θέμενος ἀνάστατον τὴν Ἑλλάδα θέλεις ποιῆσαι, ἄγων πάντας ἀνθρώπους; καὶ γὰρ ἄνευ τούτων ἐξῆν τοι ποιέειν ταῦτα (7.56).

When Xerxes had crossed into Europe, he viewed his army as it crossed under the whip. The army made the crossing in seven days and seven nights, never ceasing. There is a story that after Xerxes had now crossed the Hellespont, a Hellespontine local said: 'O Zeus, why, if you wish to devastate Greece, do you do so in the likeness of a Persian man, and taking the name Xerxes instead of Zeus, and leading all mankind with you? For you could achieve that goal even without these things.'

What we have here is the sketch of a far more drawn-out affair, involving tyrannical severity (e.g., ἐλινύσας οὐδένα χρόνον, 'never ceasing') including lashings, and redolent of *hybris*. For where the first account indicated pious care with the details of religious form (note that the sacred chariot remains empty), here Xerxes has himself taken on the appearance of a god disguised. All this is focalized in striking fashion through the gaze of a Greek onlooker. Thus the reader is tempted to recognize at work the same sort of alternative possibilities—and associated perspectives, Greek and Persian—as

[124] This is not unusual in Herodotus: cf. e.g. 3.44–9 (discussed above §4.2.1); 8.84–94 (the Salamis narrative, accepting the version that the Corinthians did not take part, although an alternative version is subsequently recorded: 8.94.4).

those dramatized in the preceding instance of double unresolved motives. The *Histories'* preface set the scene for this doubleness of available perspectives in its impartial object to record ἔργα μεγάλα τε καὶ θωμαστά, τὰ μὲν Ἕλλησι, τὰ δὲ βαρβάροισι ἀποδεχθέντα ('great and wondrous deeds performed by Greeks and non-Greeks').[125] Furthermore, the observation (back at 1.131) that Persians do not set up statues and temples and the like, and count as fools those who do so (τοῖσι ποιεῦσι μωρίην ἐπιφέρουσι—an explicitly Persian focalization)—because, Herodotus supposes, they do not anthropomorphize their gods as the Greeks do (οὐκ ἀνθρωποφυέας ἐνόμισαν τοὺς θεοὺς κατά περ οἱ Ἕλληνες εἶναι, 1.131.1)—would suggest to an attentive reader that this could *only* be a Greek perspective. The book one Persian ethnographic narrative constantly depicts Persian versus Greek perspectives on various subjects,[126] and thus sets the stage for recognizing similar (if less explicit) Greek-versus-Persian focalization in the later book. All this doubleness naturally feeds back into two possible ways—'Greek' and 'Persian'—of explaining the *raison d'être* as well as the outcome of the campaign.[127]

### 8.5.3  Sacrifice on the Acropolis (8.54–5)

A similar strategy appears to be at work in Herodotus' later ascriptions of alternative possible motives in explaining Xerxes' ordering a sacrifice on the acropolis of Athens. For soon after seizing control of the city, Xerxes commanded that the Athenian exiles in his train

τρόπῳ τῷ σφετέρῳ θῦσαι τὰ ἱρὰ ἀναβάντας ἐς τὴν ἀκρόπολιν, εἴτε δὴ ὦν ὄψιν τινὰ ἰδὼν ἐνυπνίου ἐντέλλετο ταῦτα, εἴτε καὶ ἐνθύμιόν οἱ ἐγένετο ἐμπρήσαντι τὸ ἱρόν (8.54).

---

[125]  Note that βάρβαρος may, as here, mean 'non-Greek', as a neutral equivalent for 'Persian'; at times, as when it appears in adjectival form accompanied by ἀτάσθαλα ('arrogant, reckless', 7.35.2, cf. 282 above), it may have had the pejorative sense closer to our 'barbarian'/(adj.) 'barbarous' (which I have been associating with the perspective of an outsider/Greek). See Powell s.v. βάρβαρος.

[126]  See esp. Munson (2001), 149–56.

[127]  Thus again, cf. n. 40 above, the (Aeschylean) explanation in terms of Xerxes' *hybris* does not have absolute authority. Cf. Scullion (2006) and Romm (2006), questioning the prevailing view that Herodotus' attitude to Xerxes' bridging the Hellespont was wholly negative and underlining points of contrast with Aeschylus' presentation.

climb the acropolis and sacrifice victims in their own manner. Perhaps he gave these orders because he had seen some vision in a dream (*enhupniou*), or perhaps his burning of the temple was weighing on his mind (*enthumion*).

The first conjectured motive reminds readers of Xerxes' earlier dream, and with it of the role played by his perception of divine will (influenced by others' interpretations) in precipitating his decision to campaign. It thus highlights the external pressures bearing down upon the King. From this perspective, his action was piously in keeping with his impression of divine will. Indeed, the way he commanded the Athenians to carry out the sacrifice 'in their own manner' has again implied a man respectful of others' *nomoi*, and specifically those concerning the gods. The earlier reference to Xerxes' sacrifice to Athene of Ilium (7.43), plus the way in which the second motive recalls the episode of Alyattes and the temple of Athene of Assesos (1.19)[128]—Athene, to the tale about whose miracle olive shoot this anecdote serves as a transitional device, as Herodotus tells us explicitly (8.55)—make this supernatural strand even more prominent. Xerxes here might approximate to the Darius of 3.38 (conducting the experiment on Indian and Greek funerary customs Herodotus uses to illustrate that *nomos* is king), rather than the mad custom-transgressing Cambyses of 3.28–9—who is tellingly juxtaposed with Darius in that part of book three.

The alternative motive focuses instead upon Xerxes' personal responsibility in determining a particular outcome (*enthumion* contrasts effectively with *enhupniou*): he has himself come to the view that the burning of the temple was impious and desires to make amends. It contrasts with the perspective voiced by Persians elsewhere, according to which this represents just and pious retribution for the Greeks' burning of Persian temples in the Ionian revolt.[129]

---

[128] Herodotus uses an almost equivalent statement of motives in Alyattes' case: following the (accidental) burning of the temple and his sickness, Alyattes sent to Delphi for advice, εἴτε δὴ συμβουλεύσαντός τευ, εἴτε καὶ αὐτῷ ἔδοξε . . . ('whether because someone advised him, or because he himself thought it a good idea...', 1.19.2).

[129] e.g. 5.105; 7.8β.3; 8.102. The suggestion made at 5.102.1 that this was merely a pretext—the Greeks' burning of Sardis with its temple of Cybebe, τὸ σκηπτόμενοι οἱ Πέρσαι ὕστερον ἀντενεπίμπρασαν τὰ ἐν Ἕλλησι ἱρά ('which the Persians later made their excuse for retaliatory burning of temples in Greece')—seems to be just one available perspective, rather than the full story.

The directly preceding account of the Persians' slaying of suppliants, plundering the temple, and burning the Acropolis (8.53), struck a strong note of impiety. This was followed by further expectation of a reversal of fortune in the mention of the messenger sent to Susa to announce Xerxes' 'present success' (τὴν παρεοῦσάν σφι εὐπρηξίην)— recalling Aeschylus' depiction of tragic reversal (Xerxes' first message in the *Persai* was soon followed by its reverse), and reminding readers familiar with the *Histories'* Solonian wisdom that such success is likely not to endure. In keeping with this sentiment the second motive statement presses again the disquieting aspect of Xerxes' action. In bringing to mind other such scenarios, including Alyattes' burning of the temple of Athene at Assesos, it hints once more at ominous consequences. Occurring at such a key moment, and in connection with one of the campaign's central justifications, it casts a shadow of impiety also over the aims and outcome of the wider expedition. Thus not only the motives, but also the grounding of those motives, is at stake.

The double unresolved motivations thus encapsulate the doubleness we have noticed throughout Herodotus' portrayal of Xerxes. Macan (on 8.54.3) notes that the alternatives εἴτε δὴ ὦν... εἴτε καί... ('perhaps..., or perhaps [his burning of the temple was] *also*...') are not mutually exclusive, although translations generally take them that way; and indeed these conjectures of motivation are compatible, even if each suggests a rather different perspective on Xerxes. Taken together, they replicate the sequence of debate plus dream of 7.8–19.[130] The notion of a mixture of human and divine motivation working in parallel is of course familiar.[131] Herodotus presents the options in such a way that readers may engage all the more with the different sorts of pressures under which humans act. Once again, it is not simply a matter of his allocating moral praise or blame: of giving us 'two reasons for sympathizing with Xerxes at the very moment when his actions are likely to have stirred the reader's antipathy'.[132] Herodotus rather guides readers intellectually to come to some understanding, opening their eyes to the way in which different perspectives may lead to different interpretations and conclusions.

---

[130] Discussed above, §8.1.
[131] See above, ch. 1 n. 18.
[132] Flory (1987), 76.

The question of greatest moment for Herodotus' Greek audience is ultimately that of why Xerxes failed in his attempt to conquer Greece. Any answer must depend in part on readers' interpretation of the role played by Xerxes: of his own motives, and of the relation of those to wider patterns of explanation, over the course of the whole story. The Xerxes that emerges from Herodotus' pages is a 'reflexive actor': his actions are shaped by the circumstances and institutions in which he is located, and yet are not entirely determined by those, since he retains the capacity to respond and adapt to them.[133] As second in line like Cambyses, he has more institutional pressures to deal with than the *novus homo* Darius; but he manages to interact with and respond to those, rather than choosing, as Cambyses did, to ignore them entirely. Possibly the personal skills inherited from Darius (the hereditary model) enabled him to do this.[134]

But our question perhaps cannot be answered definitively, since it always comes down to a matter of interpretation. Herodotus' account displays frankly the fact that history is not neutral: it is always being put to use for a purpose, always involving an implied perspective or agenda. The subjectivity of historical interpretation has emerged as a theme: readers are introduced to Xerxes', Mardonios', and Artabanos' differing interpretations of Persian military history, and encouraged to weigh those interpretations up against their own (whether derived from earlier sections of the *Histories*, or from their independent knowledge of the past).

We have seen how Herodotus' account dramatizes the fact that the past can invite contrasting interpretations: for example, how the story of Xerxes' campaign could be used to argue either that Artabanos was nearly right on the subject of caution and resources... or

[133] Herodotus' interpretation thus finds a role for both structure and personality (or agency); cf. Anthony Giddens' (1984) notion of 'structuration', which sets out a sensible middle path between a view of the individual as entirely self-determining, and that of the institution as determining the behaviour of the individual. (The term 'reflexive actor' is Giddens'.)

[134] My view of Herodotus' portrayal of Xerxes is in sympathy with that of Heleen Sancisi-Weedenburg, in her excellent article (2002) countering modern over- and mis-interpretations of aspects of Herodotus' account—from which has derived the 'almost general agreement as to history's verdict on Xerxes: a second rate personality and not really worthy of the throne of his father' (581); cf. Wiesehöfer (1996), 51–2.

that Xerxes was, in his views on the importance of bold action (for the *Histories* has shown the importance of perceptions in determining outcome). This theme alerts readers to the difficulties involved in interpreting history, and to the challenge faced by Herodotus—and subsequently by his readers—in interpreting Xerxes.

# 9

## Themistocles: constructions of
## motivation (Books VII–IX)

Interpreting the *Histories'* Greek protagonist presents similar challenges. Our final case study addresses Herodotus' presentation of
Themistocles' motives. It aims to draw together some of the strands
of earlier chapters, particularly so as to illuminate further Herodotus'
technique of presenting readers with various and shifting perspectives on questions of motivation. We also reconsider the possibility
(aired especially in chapters one and three) that Herodotus makes
use of unreliable narratorial comments.

### 9.1 THE *THŌMA* OF 8.109–10

Herodotus recounts how, in the immediate aftermath of the victory
at Salamis, the Greeks chased Xerxes' fleet as far as Andros, then—
having lost sight of it—held a council to debate their next move.
Themistocles argued first for continuing the pursuit and dismantling
the Hellespont bridges, Eurybiades for returning to Greece—with
which view the rest of the Peloponnesian *stratēgoi* all agreed. At this
point Herodotus sets down in direct discourse Themistocles' speech
dissuading the Athenians from persevering in pursuit, and then
explains his motivation:

ταῦτα ἔλεγε ἀποθήκην μέλλων ποιήσεσθαι ἐς τὸν Πέρσην, ἵνα ἢν ἄρα τί μιν
καταλαμβάνῃ πρὸς Ἀθηναίων πάθος ἔχῃ ἀποστροφήν· τά περ ὦν καὶ
ἐγένετο. Θεμιστοκλέης μὲν ταῦτα λέγων διέβαλλε, Ἀθηναῖοι δὲ ἐπείθοντο
(8.109.5–110.1).

he said this with the intention of laying up a store of favour with the King, so that if ever some calamity should befall him at the Athenians' hands, he would have a refuge. And in fact this is exactly what happened. Themistocles was deceiving (*dieballe*[1]) in speaking as he did, but the Athenians were persuaded.

Scholars tend to regard this verdict, along with much of the *Histories'* Themistocles material, as issuing from Herodotus' reliance upon hostile sources: his narrative ignores the possibility that the general

> may quite well have been honestly in favour of breaking down the bridge and stirring up revolt among the Greeks of Asia, and yet have resolved to sacrifice the project rather than make a breach in the alliance with the Peloponnesians.[2]

However, Herodotus' account over these paragraphs, when assessed in the context of the rest of the Themistocles narrative, hints that something more sophisticated is going on here than can be explained simply as the reproduction of his sources' bias. The speech shows clear marks of Herodotean fashioning: if it bears any relation to an actual speech delivered on the occasion, then that material appears to have been thoroughly reworked.

The effect of this statement of Themistocles' motivation is jarring. Plunging readers into reflection upon the general's later disgraceful career (indeed it is the only point in the *Histories* where Herodotus alludes to that explicitly), it shocks them out of their captivation with the noble rhetoric of the speech it follows. It also presents a contrast with the impression of Themistocles' character and motivation garnered from the broader movement of the narrative so far. For Themistocles, however wily and cunning a figure, has until now been characterized as a catalyst of Athenian, and Greek, unity in the face of divided opinion, and as one who uses oratorical skill to achieve that end. Is that not exactly what he is again accomplishing here?

---

[1] But see n. 44 below for alternative possible translations of *dieballe*, e.g. 'was hiding his intentions'.

[2] How/Wells ad loc.; cf. Cawkwell (1970), 42; Macan ad loc.; Stein ad loc.; contra Frost (1980), 9: the theory of Alcmaeonid influence 'attributes to Herodotus a naïveté he nowhere else reveals', Fornara (1971), 66–7.

## 9.2 THEMISTOCLES AS CONTRIVER OF UNITY
## (7.143–4; 8.4–5, 123–4)

At his first appearance in the *Histories*, Themistocles was portrayed settling the debate between the principal contrasting interpretations of the oracular 'wooden wall,' proposing a reading that 'the Athenians' found more convincing even than that of the professional seers (so when the Persians reach Athens they come across only 'some few Athenians', τινας ὀλίγους ... τῶν Ἀθηναίων, still clinging to an alternative, 8.51.2). By overriding the seers' view that the Athenians should offer no resistance and evacuate Attica (7.143), he singlehandedly ushered in the conditions necessary for Athens' subsequent championing of Greek unity in face of the foreign threat.[3] His reading diverged only moderately from that of the professionals,[4] and so was likely to inspire consensus. Next, Herodotus offered a digression back to when another of Themistocles' opinions 'was the best at an important moment' (ἐς καιρὸν ἠρίστευσε, 7.144.1):[5] his persuading the Athenians that the Laurium silver strike should go not to *private* pockets but towards building up their fleet in the *polis*' *collective* interest (to benefit the Athenians in their war with Aegina;[6] but in the end serving the cause of the united Greeks).

[3] Cf. the saviours of Greece passage (8.139).

[4] Stein on 7.143.4 emphasizes this point: in Themistocles' view, the seers were only mistaken as to the oracle's reference.

[5] Such 'mastery over the *kairos*' is a hallmark of the man of *mētis*: Detienne and Vernant (1991), 16. The quality is highlighted in Thucydides' obituary of Themistocles (Thuc. 1.138.3).

[6] Themistocles intended that the ships be used ἐς τὸν πόλεμον, τὸν πρὸς Αἰγινήτας λέγων ('for the war, mentioning the war against the Aeginetans', 7.144.1)—which leaves unclear whether he was himself looking forward to the Persian Wars: speaking to the assembly of this war (but having in mind another). Cf. Moles (2002), 45: Herodotus' subtle wording allows that possibility, 'Aegina being Themistocles' *public* argument', contra Macan ad loc.; Stein ad loc.; Cawkwell (1970), 40–1; Harrison (2003), 146. Later authors make explicit the notion that the general was thinking ahead. Many Greeks had contact with Persia, and information regarding an impending invasion certainly reached Greece well in advance (cf. 7.138), thus Herodotus' audience will not have had reason to suspect that Themistocles' premonition indicated treacherous intimacy.

Similarly during the war Themistocles has been shown to advocate decisions in the interests not merely of individual *poleis*, but of all the Greeks; or rather, to enable *polis* interests (which realistically had to be catered for) to correspond with wider Greek ones. In engineering the Greek defence at Artemisium, he reconciled the interests of the Euboeans, who wished the Greeks to remain where they were in defence of the island, with those of the rest of the Greeks: for fighting there did indeed bring success. Modern commentators, like Plutarch (867e), object to the ignoble spur to action given Themistocles for advocating what was 'both honourable and strategically right',[7] again invoking hostile (Alcmaeonid) sources. But Themistocles' reconciling those interests with his own (in gaining a large bribe, 8.4.2) may perhaps have struck Herodotus' original audience as rather enhancing his achievement.

The succinctness of the narrative at this point, in contrast with the slower descriptive texture of the foregoing lines, conveys the efficiency of the operation. The Euboeans 'persuaded Themistocles with a bribe of thirty talents, on the condition that the Greek fleet should remain there and fight in defence of Euboea. And Themistocles held the Greeks to that in the following way...' (8.4.2–5.1): no sooner said (and persuaded) than he effects what is necessary. His doling out of only part of the money to those *stratēgoi* still resisting[8]—five talents to Eurybiades ('as if giving it as his own', ὡς παρ' ἑωυτοῦ δῆθεν διδούς), two to Adeimantos—leaving them to suppose that the Athenians had sent the money for that purpose, is suave and effective, with its added benefit of improving interstate relations. The

---

[7] Cawkwell (1970), 41. As modern studies emphasize, there will have been little option but to remain at Artemisium while the defence continued at Thermopylae (cf. e.g. Asheri on 8.4.5); it may be that Themistocles used his influence with Eurybiades to clarify to him that reality.

[8] Difficulties surround any interpretation of this anecdote in historically literal terms: for one (cf. Macan ad loc.), Eurybiades must have had nine colleagues. Herodotus is apparently distorting actualities for the sake of his theme (perhaps being obliged anyhow to work from scanty information), much as Moles (1993) envisages him doing in reporting the fictitious Persian constitutional debate. In that case, '[a]bandonment of historicity is counterbalanced by other factors' since the debate 'provides an excellent focus for the exploration of several of Herodotus' major themes' (119–20). Indeed, Moles suggests, '[n]o serious ancient historian was so tied to specific factual truth that he would not sometimes help general truths along by manipulating, even inventing, "facts"' (120).

'delightful inconsequence' Macan (on 8.4.9) detects—that the Euboeans wish Eurybiades to remain 'for a short time' (χρόνον ὀλίγον, 8.4.2), but Themistocles instead has the Greeks fight three battles on three successive days—points to the way in which the bribery is outweighed in the narrative by the actual result. Might that suggest that Themistocles did not contrive that outcome simply because of the bribe, but that the Euboeans' request planted in his mind the seeds of a more dramatic plan?—or that he had had such a plan in mind all along? Herodotus highlights the Euboeans' desire that this battle take place at Artemisium (the troops should remain there at least 'until they had removed their children and households to safety', ἔστ᾿ ἂν αὐτοὶ τέκνα τε καὶ τοὺς οἰκέτας ὑπεκθέωνται, 8.4.2), as at 8.40 he will draw attention to the Athenians' interest in that battle taking place at Salamis ('in order that they should bring their children and wives to safety', ἵνα αὐτοὶ παῖδάς τε καὶ γυναῖκας ὑπεξαγάγωνται, 8.40.1). Since in the latter case we subsequently hear of solid strategic and tactical reasoning (8.60) that must have played a part in the decision of where to fight, the parallel seems to imply that the same should have been understood here.

Herodotus sums up the tidy elegance of the manoeuvre: 'The generals were won over by gifts/bribes, the Euboeans were pleased, and Themistocles himself profited (ἐκέρδηνε) by secretly taking the rest [*sc.* of the money]' (8.5.3). Thus on a personal level everyone wins, and the final outcome is united opinion on the Greek front—and only a chapter earlier (8.3) Herodotus has set forth a serious reflection on the benefits of united war (πολέμου ὁμοφρονέοντος) over civil strife. As Frost reminds us, this was the generation of Athenians that praised and spoiled the young Alcibiades. They, at least,

would have remembered Themistocles with appreciation. His ambition, his quick wits, his ability to make a little money on the side—these were all qualities they admired, and if he accomplished his goals by means that were sometimes devious, it was because the world was a hard and devious place.[9]

We might remember too that Athene, in the words of that wooden wall oracle itself (7.143), appeared 'beseeching Olympian Zeus with many words and with shrewd *mētis* (cunning)' (7.141.3). As she, the

---

[9] Frost (1980), 10; cf. Fornara (1971), 72.

daughter of Mētis, admired that quality in her protégé Odysseus,[10] so Athenians at least could be expected to admire it in their latter-day hero. Plutarch's version of the episode (*Themistocles* 7.6), in which the general passes the whole bribe on to Eurybiades (so as to make the action demonstrate 'not fraudulent deception, but prudent intervention'[11]), misses much of Herodotus' point. As for Themistocles' plain use of bribery, even the Alcmaeonids' own Pericles, as everyone knew, was not averse to such an act if it resolved efficiently the state's military problems.[12]

Later, in obliging the Greeks to fight at Salamis by means of his first message to the King (8.75), Themistocles cut short the disagreements about withdrawing and the related threat of Greek disunity: for wise advisers on both sides had forewarned of the danger of dispersal should the Greeks retreat to the Isthmus,[13] as Salamis was the last stand where a battle on behalf of all Greece might still notionally occur. The way the message, in Herodotus' version, is as much designed to outwit fellow Greeks as the Persians (though that is probably an unhistorical detail[14]) does not inevitably cast a strongly negative shadow over the admiral.[15] Again after the campaign, the majority (8.123.2) of the Greeks, despite themselves, will be united in awarding Themistocles second place in the polls of achievement. Thus paradoxically he attracts consensus in the face of the intense individualistic rivalry that compelled each man to award himself first place.

The magnitude of Themistocles' service to the Greeks in this role of unifier is lent emphasis by the persistent threat that the Greek cause could be lost through the disagreements of quarrelling groups. The Persian Wars are played out on a background of Greek disintegration: of foiled attempts by Sparta and Athens to win the support

---

[10]  *Od.* 13.287–97; cf. Fornara (1971), 72–3.

[11]  Marr (1998), 88–9.

[12]  His notorious 'necessary expenditures': Plutarch, *Pericles* 23.1–2; Aristophanes, *Clouds* 859; cf. Thuc. 2.21.1.

[13]  See n. 17 below.

[14]  Macan ad loc.

[15]  Cf. Frost (1980), 10 (in reference to Ion of Chios' story, Plut. *Cimon* 9): 'The noble Cimon's favourite memory was not of butchering Persians but of fooling fellow Greeks.'

of other states.[16] The failure of such direct appeals for unity leaves the impression that *mētis* may be indispensable in dealing with such wrangling collections of individuals and contrasting agendas. The outcome of the whole war might otherwise have followed the pattern of Thermopylae, where divided counsels—with no Themistoclean figure to contrive unity—issued in actual disintegration of the Greek force, and ultimately defeat:

ἐνθαῦτα ἐβουλεύοντο οἱ Ἕλληνες, καί σφεων ἐσχίζοντο αἱ γνῶμαι· οἱ μὲν γὰρ οὐκ ἔων τὴν τάξιν ἐκλιπεῖν, οἱ δὲ ἀντέτεινον. μετὰ δὲ τοῦτο διακριθέντες οἱ μὲν ἀπαλλάσσοντο καὶ διασκεδασθέντες κατὰ πόλις ἔκαστοι ἐτράποντο, οἱ δὲ αὐτῶν ἅμα Λεωνίδῃ μένειν αὐτοῦ παρεσκευάδατο (7.219.2).

Thereupon the Greeks held a council, and their opinions were divided: some argued for not abandoning their post, but others put the opposite case. Afterwards, once the meeting had broken up, some of the Greeks departed and scattered, each returning to his own *polis*, while others prepared to remain where they were with Leonidas.

Though disunity was not the cause of the defeat at Thermopylae, in the narrative it becomes inevitably associated with it (and the very language here, of divided counsels and scattering each to one's own *polis*, is found on the lips of wise advisers foretelling disaster for the Greeks should that occur[17]). Interpreted against this background, a most natural explanation of the Andros speech is that Themistocles had earlier set forth his genuine opinion, but now—upon realizing that he would not be able to persuade the majority (ὅτι οὐ πείσει τούς γε πολλούς, 8.109.1)—deferring democratically to that majority verdict, he puts his rhetorical skill to the end of upholding it, again valuing unity above all. And his speech persuades the Athenians: after it 'the Greeks' (οἱ Ἕλληνες) are shown once again to be acting as one (8.111.1).

Thus the perspective of plot guides readers to draw different conclusions about Themistocles' motivation than those drawn explicitly. It runs counter to the view on Herodotus' portrait of Themistocles that has long been *communis opinio* (following Stein's judgement a hundred years ago), that:

[16] See ch. 7 above. Immerwahr (1966), 225–34 discusses Herodotus' presentation of Greek divisiveness, concluding that '[t]he motif that binds the Greek accounts together is…disunity' (234); cf. Corcella (1984), 199–200. See also §6.3 above.
[17] e.g. 8.57.2 (Mnesiphilos), 8.68β.2 (Artemisia to Xerxes).

Von seinen unleugbaren Verdiensten spricht er [Herodotus] überall mit auffallender Kühle, manche verschweigt er ganz, andere erwähnt er nicht als die seinigen...,[18] und während er das momentane Eingreifen des Aristeides zu einem unbeschränkten Lobe dieses Gegners benutzt..., hat er für jenen und seine weitfassende unermüdete Tätigkeit kaum ein Wort der Anerkennung; nur in List und Verschlagenheit erkennt er ihm den Vorrang zu...[19]

For as we have seen, Herodotus does in fact make clear the magnitude of Themistocles' achievement, through both oratorical brilliance and talent in human relations, in contriving Greek unity. It is Themistocles above all who drives forward the plot at its key turning points in the stretch of narrative that leads to victory at Artemisium and then at Salamis. Moreover, the dimensions of the plot may have made a greater impression upon Herodotus' audience, who were versed in the traditions of oral narrative, than did the sort of evaluative statements with which he praises Aristeides.[20] The portrayal of his 'weitfassende unermüdete Tätigkeit' ('far-reaching, untiring activity') is perhaps an indication of merit just as powerful as any explicit evaluative comment might have been, especially in light of Herodotus' stated purpose, to preserve ἔργα μεγάλα τε καὶ θωμαστά, 'great and wondrous deeds'. Likewise, the depiction of repeated action may have exercised a more powerful effect on the historian's listening audience than any 'Wort der Anerkennung' ('word of recognition').[21] Even where causal relations are not set

[18] On this, see below, n. 39.

[19] Stein on 8.4.11 ('Everywhere Herodotus speaks with striking coolness of his undeniable merits. Some he conceals completely, others he mentions not as his..., and while he makes use of Aristeides' momentary intervention to give absolute praise of this opponent, he has for Themistocles and his far-reaching, untiring activity scarcely a word of recognition: only in cunning and slyness does he award him precedence'); cf. e.g. How/Wells on 8.4.2; Gillis (1979), 54; Masaracchia on 8.41.2–3 for the antithemistoclean reserve in book 8. But Fornara (1971), 66–73 and Blösel (2001), (2004) find a more positive dimension to Herodotus' portrait; cf. Asheri on 8.1–23.

[20] Axel Olrik, in his study of the 'Epic Laws' (characteristic elements of oral narrative) speaks of 'plot constraint on the narrative': '[a]ny ability of a character or a thing must be expressed in action; otherwise it has no importance for the narrative.... The characteristics of the narrative and its view of life lie in the plot itself' (1992), §63.

[21] Cf. Olrik's observation that '[o]ral narrative composition does not know detailed description and thus cannot use it to express the nature and meaning of the plot. What must be shown to be important is depicted through repetition': Olrik (1992), §61. Running through the Themistoclean episodes are repeated themes and

out explicitly, Herodotus at times uses his literary art to underline Themistocles' importance in driving the unfolding plot. John Moles observes this tactic in the account of Themistocles' management of the Laurium silver strike, where

[t]he interaction between Herodotus' own claim [that the ships would be used in the Persian Wars] and the narrative creates a causal chain: the Aeginetan war, the building of the navy, the Athenians' acceptance of Themistocles' interpretation of the oracle and their heroic stand, a chain whose single and brilliant artificer is Themistocles.[22]

More generally Themistocles is 'the dominant figure in [Herodotus'] account of Xerxes' War': thus we are equipped to recognize his importance.[23]

As for Themistocles' 'List und Verschlagenheit' ('cunning and slyness'), Herodotus gives no hint, as we saw above, that anything else could have worked. In dealing with men of *mētis*, like the Greeks (and especially the Athenians), greater *mētis* may be the only effective tool.[24] And *mētis* was by no means necessarily negative. As Detienne and Vernant argue, Christianizing ideals as well as the concept of Platonic truth have led to the negative associations with 'cunning intelligence' that are alien to fifth-century Greek thought. Charles Fornara has proposed that Herodotus' primary intent in his depiction of Themistocles at Andros was indeed positive, 'to show Themistocles' great capacity for the clever ruse'. In Fornara's expression, 'Themistocles did not deceive the Greeks; he fooled Xerxes'—since his false claim to have stopped the Greeks' pursuit gained him credit with the King; '[o]bviously [the Athenians] had to be dissuaded'[25]—as we suggested above. The characteristic man of *mētis* among fifth-century sophists and politicians was one who, like Themistocles, 'knew better than anyone how to adapt himself to the time, the

---

patterns of action: e.g. in the motif of the Greeks in panic contemplating flight (see Masaracchia on 8.18.5–6 for this *topos*; cf. Blösel (2001), 184; Plutarch observes it bitterly, 867e), juxtaposed with the calm brought by Themistocles, and the prominent theme of Themistocles as source of unity.

[22] Moles (2002), 45; cf. n. 6 above.
[23] Fornara (1971), 67.
[24] See Detienne and Vernant (1991), 5 on the need to master *mētis* with greater *mētis*.
[25] (1971), 71 n. 17 with text.

place and his audience and how to give the best reply in all circumstances'[26]—an expert in audience response. Indeed Herodotus surely prided himself on being just such an expert (as we suggested in chapters one and three).

## 9.3  THE SPEECH AT ANDROS: TWOFOLD PERSUASION (8.109)

A closer look at the speech with which Themistocles persuades the Athenians at this key moment after Salamis points again to his expertise in audience response and the power of his seductive rhetoric—which even as it persuades, however, must alert the audience to the danger of such persuasiveness. Of the three speeches that figure at this point of the narrative, Herodotus summarized briefly the opinion expressed by Themistocles in the first, then reported Eurybiades' response indirectly (8.108); but here his choice of the direct mode of discourse in reporting Themistocles' second speech places his extratextual audience (probably listening to the text as it is read aloud) in the same situation as the Athenian audience in the text who—angry at the Persians' escape and keen, even without the other Greeks' assistance, to chase them to the Hellespont—are listening to Themistocles. Along with the Athenian *stratēgoi* (who evidently are moved to change their mind: at 8.111 the Greeks generally—*οἱ Ἕλληνες*—have resolved not to pursue the barbarian or break the bridges), the reader too must be convinced, for not only is the speech eloquent in style and sensible in matter, but it reiterates several of the *Histories'* persistent themes.

The difference in ground covered by this speech, as compared with Eurybiades', makes manifest its two-pronged persuasiveness (to suit these two audiences). Eurybiades' manner was calm and practical, his speech focusing on the potentially devastating outcome for Greece should the Persians be forced to remain (*εἰ . . . ἀναγκασθείη ἀπολαμφθεὶς ὁ Πέρσης μένειν*, 8.108.3). Themistocles alludes initially to this line of reasoning, reproducing the platitude that beaten men,

---

[26]  Detienne and Vernant (1991), 313.

driven to necessity (ἐς ἀναγκαίην ἀπειληθέντας, 8.109.2), may well recover an earlier defeat. Thus he draws a thread of continuity between Eurybiades' line of argument and his own, rather as his interpretation of the oracle at 7.143 grew from that of the seers. But he then goes on to produce further arguments tailored to the psychology of his different audience: the angry Athenians will find greater satisfaction in his emphasis on the magnitude of the Greek achievement thus far (the fact of having repelled νέφος τοσοῦτον ἀνθρώπων, 'such a great cloud of men') and in his impassioned tirade against the Great King's *hybris*. His exhortation that for the moment (νῦν μὲν) they should order their affairs at home, and chase after the Persians the following year instead (ἅμα δὲ τῷ ἔαρι, 'with the coming of spring', 8.109.4)—a proposal of postponement not cancellation— could be expected to be mollifying.

So the speech is a model of audience response, carefully crafted to appeal to the psychological state of its in-text listeners. It is its astonishing effect upon that audience that Herodotus goes on to underline in his emphasis on the fact of their complete persuasion (Ἀθηναῖοι δὲ **ἐπείθοντο** ... πάντως ἕτοιμοι ἦσαν λέγοντι **πείθεσθαι** ... ὡς δὲ οὗτοί οἱ **ἀνεγνωσμένοι ἦσαν** ..., 8.110.1–2).[27] This foregrounding of the speaker-listener dynamic, which is sensationalized through the equation of Themistocles' persuasion with deceit (διέβαλλε),[28] invites us to assume that in writing this section Herodotus may have been especially sensitive to his own audience's response. The possibility is lent support by the way the speech seems designed to be

[27] ('The Athenians were persuaded ... they were wholly ready to be persuaded by him speaking ... when these men had been persuaded by him ...'.) Thucydides appears to note this theme and turn it around ironically, in reporting the Athenians' equally brisk persuasion on the matter of Themistocles' guilt (1.135.3). Thus he brings to the fore the Janus-faced potential of rhetoric (which even Spartans can use to good effect!), as well as implying that the Athenians are as fickle as Themistocles: both themes of Herodotus' *Histories* (cf., for the latter theme, n. 65 below).

[28] It is all the more sensational in that it brings into play the wider Herodotean associations of the *diabolē-peithō* pairing, e.g. Aristagoras' deceitful persuasion of the Athenians, dramatized with the suggestive moral that it is easier to deceive many than one (πολλοὺς ... εὐπετέστερον διαβάλλειν ἢ ἕνα, 5.97.2), which led to the sending of the ships that spelt the beginning of evils (5.97.3) for Greeks and Persians; or the way in which Histiaeus (exactly as we are told of Themistocles) μὲν δὴ λέγων ταῦτα διέβαλλε, Δαρεῖος δὲ ἐπείθετο ('in saying these things was deceiving, but Darius was persuaded', 5.107).

equally convincing for the *Histories'* contemporary readership as for the audience in the text. In Themistocles' opening statement— 'I myself have seen many instances of this, and many more times have I heard that it is so...' (Καὶ αὐτὸς ἤδη πολλοῖσι παρεγενόμην καὶ πολλῷ πλέω ἀκήκοα τοιάδε γενέσθαι..., 8.109.2)—the dual appeal to *opsis* (his personal experience) and *akoē* (hearsay)—in that order—as providing confirmatory evidence for the assertion he goes on to make, mirrors the historian's own historical method. In matter, too, readers are drawn in further by the thematic connections they detect with sentiments uttered elsewhere with authorial sanction. Themistocles' observation that the Greeks' victory was the chance discovery of a piece of good luck, and hint ('all is well **for the present** (ἐς τὸ παρεὸν)', 8.109.4) that present luck will not necessarily endure, reiterates a theme that is central throughout the *Histories*. Likewise the notion that the gods and heroes are responsible for the defeat must recall Herodotus' own narrative of the wars up to this point, which has shown specific heroes to be (thought) responsible for Greek success at various points, and underlined the important role played by the gods in human affairs.

### 9.3.1  Echoes of Xerxes' council

The extra-textual audience is struck also by the way in which this exchange echoes that between Mardonios and Artabanos at another council, the one of Persian nobles which Xerxes called together having resolved to campaign against Greece (7.8; discussed above, §8.1.1). There, as here, the issue tabled concerned the merits of aggressive action: of undertaking the invasion of Greece that Darius had set in motion. The thematic and linguistic echoes that stretch across the speeches of the two councils suggest that each is intended to shed light upon the other. In the earlier Persian council, Xerxes explained his resolution to follow up the attack on Greece, Mardonios offered a speech in support, and Artabanos one in opposition that urged caution. When the failure of the King's campaign gives rise to a similar Greek council, Herodotus could expect his audience to recall that third speech, which warned of the possibility of a defeat at sea (which readers have of course known all along will occur), and of its being followed by the destruction of the Hellespont bridges (which Themistocles' proposal at the council will imply was a real possibility[29]). Themistocles' proposal for pursuit and destruction of the bridges, though it receives brief narrative coverage, thus brings into play for the audience the wider range of supporting material that Artabanos had earlier raised. The fact too that part of Artabanos' warning presents a pre-play of history (of the victory at Salamis, in a sea battle) lends historical plausibility to the second half of the scenario: to the fear that the Greeks should pursue and break the bridges. The manner in which Themistocles' first proposition answers precisely to that fear, though it undergoes development in characteristic Themistoclean style,[30] indicates again his uncanny foresight, as well as the plausible nature of his proposal.[31]

When Themistocles next argues the opposite case, persuading the Athenians to act in accordance with Eurybiades' view, he again touches upon themes familiar from Artabanos' speech. Where the Persian had dwelt upon the notion that the gods smite down the great (trees, houses, men) and observed that a god may out of jealousy ($\phi\theta o\nu\acute{\eta}\sigma\alpha s$) contrive that a numerous army be destroyed by a lesser (7.10ε), Themistocles states that gods and heroes 'were jealous ($\grave{\epsilon}\phi\theta\acute{o}\nu\eta\sigma\alpha\nu$) that one man should rule Asia and Europe' (8.109.3). Again his brief coverage of the point gains conviction from the earlier fuller exposition. Thus both his speeches, even though they set forth opposed views, replay the wisdom of the wise adviser. Even in switching arguments as he does, Themistocles has a precedent in Artabanos' behaviour (7.18.4). The parallel between the two figures brings to the fore the possibility that Themistocles' reasons for his about-turn may have been as compelling as Artabanos' (whose supernatural warning

[29] Although perhaps it was not: see e.g. Macan and Asheri on 8.108 (*pace* Masaracchia ad loc.) on how the Greeks cannot have contemplated chasing the Persians; cf. Hdt. 8.132.3.

[30] Themistocles adds the suggestion that the Greeks should hold their course through the islands. The way in which the proposition ascribed to him seems to combine three unrelated plans (to Macan's dissatisfaction, ad loc.) can be seen in terms of the topos of Themistocles' borrowing something and extending it with his own contributions, as he does with Mnesiphilos' arguments. His transformation of givens illuminates his originality.

[31] Cf. the parallel between Themistocles' rock-engraved appeal to the Ionians (8.22) and 7.51, 'where the same point and the same moral are urged by Artabanos' (Macan on 8.22.5), which makes Themistocles' idea seem all the more intelligent.

could not be ignored): perhaps more extensive or complex than (or even different from) those which Herodotus has delineated explicitly.

Eurybiades' response to Themistocles' first speech similarly replays several of the ideas expressed at the earlier council by Xerxes and Mardonios (7.8–9). His speech arises from an analogous vision of the dynamic and expansionist character of Persia: if cut off in Greece, he argues, Xerxes and his army will avoid being inactive; and if they remain active, every city and people of Europe may join their cause, by conquest or treaty (8.108.3). The effect of this echo is somewhat qualified, because the surrounding narrative (in the Persian council scene) revealed the selfish machinations from which the Persians' arguments arose and thus diminished their conviction. Egotistical desires led Mardonios to persuade Xerxes (7.6.1), who was at the same time beset by others' self-seeking attempts, even though he had initially been unwilling to attack Greece.[32] The narrator explained that Mardonios 'thus made plausible (ἐπιλεήνας) Xerxes' opinion', and that other Persians dared not voice contradictory views (7.10.1); but their later rejoicing at the king's change of mind (7.14) emphasized those private misgivings. Again, the audience knows, or will learn from Herodotus' narrative, that the destruction of the bridges (which does indeed happen, caused by storms: 8.117.1; cf. 9.114.1) will by no means be 'the greatest of all harms' that could be done to Greece, as Eurybiades claims. Eurybiades' final argument (that it is better that a country other than one's own be at stake in a fight) has elsewhere been heard on another wise adviser's lips,[33] but the outcome in that case was disquieting. Nonetheless, the wider narrative of the *Histories* lends strong support to Eurybiades' opinion: Persia's expansionist character has been vividly portrayed, and various peoples have already been depicted joining Xerxes' cause (cf. 8.108.3, 'the whole of Europe might go over to him—city by city and people by people'). To Herodotus' audience Eurybiades' proposal that the conflict be transformed into one over the *King's* land (τὸ ἐνθεῦτεν δὲ περὶ τῆς ἐκείνου ποιέεσθαι ἤδη τὸν ἀγῶνα, 8.108.4)

---

[32] See above, ch. 8 n. 8 with text.

[33] Croesus warned Cyrus to fight on Tomyris' side of the river, not his own (1.207). The story occurs far earlier in the *Histories*, but is memorable. (The end result is Cyrus' death; but in accordance with Croesus' advice the Massagetae remain within their territory rather than attempting to conquer that of their attackers.)

may even have seemed prophetic of future *Athenian* action in Asia— which would occur in the years following 478 BC. In changing tack in his second speech, and going along with Eurybiades' argument, Themistocles may therefore be viewed as once again recognizing and putting into action what is the best advice[34] (and what will indeed turn out to be in Athens' future interests).

## 9.3.2 A twofold emotional response?

So, as we have seen, Themistocles' speech before the Athenian admirals after Salamis engages both audiences (internal and external) in intellectual appraisal. I would like to suggest further that it works to engage both groups *emotionally*, too. Readers first observe the Athenians from outside, as a group who are 'much aggrieved most of all at those who had escaped' (8.109.1)—unlike the others present at Andros or the readers themselves, who, with their extra-textual knowledge of the fact that the Persian campaign is not quite dead but will continue under Mardonios, can see the prudence of Eurybiades' view. But readers are soon drawn into and captivated by Themistocles' *logos* to the extent that they become an audience *alongside* the Athenians. In being reported in direct discourse, the general's words mirror real time as closely as possible: the vivid re-enactment breaks down the barrier between external audience and in-text characters, encouraging them to share the viewpoint of and empathize with the Athenians in the text.[35] As the heated rhetoric, all the more effective in a live performance setting, begins to work on the emotions of the external audience, it pushes them closer towards experiencing the Athenians' anger and indignation, as well as the uplifted feeling

---

[34] Cf. Marincola (2006), 20: Themistocles' genius, according to Herodotus, resides in his ability to *recognize* good advice and to put it into *action*. The implied *future* outcome, which will be favourable for Athens, works against the way the narrative shows Peloponnesian interests (in opposition to Athenian ones; and perhaps this is why Herodotus prefers the version with the Spartan Eurybiades as Themistocles' opponent, rather than Aristeides) determining the course of *present* action: it is the Peloponnesian *stratēgoi* who are said to favour Eurybiades' view. Spartan insularity and selfishness is a clear theme in Herodotus' narrative of the war, cf. §7.4 above. Themistocles' achievement in nonetheless effecting a profitable outcome for Athens thus becomes all the more apparent.

[35] Cf. Gill's (1990) 'personality viewpoint'.

(fostered by the talk of abstract morals and great achievement) that the speech seems to be aiming to replace it with. This emotional response on the part of Herodotus' external audience is buttressed by their simultaneous, cognitive appraisal, which arises from their awareness of the textual pattern underlying the threat of disunity[36] along with their fuller retrospective understanding of the situation. Both factors invite them to appreciate that the persuasion of the Athenians at this point in time is beneficial in the broader scheme.[37] At its end the speech opens out into future time, inviting listeners of both audiences to imagine it: a time when the Athenians will have rebuilt and reorganized their homes, crops, and lives, and become secure in the knowledge of having 'driven the foreigner wholly away' (παντελέως ἀπελάσας τὸν βάρβαρον, 8.109.4). The note of renewal is reiterated in the final clause: with the coming of spring they will set sail eastwards. Eurybiades used sensible argumentation to persuade the majority, but Themistocles has here tailored his speech to listeners in a different mood, and played with their emotions to an extent that the other's speech, less emotive and indirectly reported (and so not intended to affect *readers* to such a degree, anyhow), could not.

## 9.4  A MASTER OF RHETORIC? (8.58–63)

But the stirring closing vision—shared by the reader at this juncture (for the absence of authorial comment has left the words to speak for themselves)—is next shattered by the cynical suggestion that a quite different, utterly unidealized glance to the future is what has actually motivated this speech: it has been uttered 'in order that if ever any calamity should befall him at the Athenians' hands, he would have a refuge' (ἵνα ἢν ἄρα τί μιν καταλαμβάνῃ πρὸς Ἀθηναίων πάθος, ἔχῃ ἀποστροφήν, 8.109.5). At this point the reader is pulled back once again to a position of external observation: 'In speaking these things,

---

[36] See above, §9.2.

[37] Cf. Levene's (1997) distinction between the former variety of 'audience-based' emotion and the latter 'analytic' emotion. Herodotus' technique here seems illustrative of Levene's observation that '"audience-based" emotions are not only derived from, but may reinforce and underpin, the moral and historical analysis' (134).

Themistocles was deceiving, but the Athenians were persuaded' (Θεμιστοκλέης μὲν ταῦτα λέγων διέβαλλε, Ἀθηναῖοι δὲ ἐπείθοντο, 8.110.1). Thus the audience has been seduced by Peithō—drawn in along with the in-text audience—and then suddenly exposed to the fact that that has occurred. The technique is familiar in modern film, where, as here, it causes the audience to re-enact themselves the mental state of the in-text subject(s). (*A Beautiful Mind* (2001), for example, is focalized largely through the gaze of its schizophrenic subject John Nash, and so viewers are made to experience his delusions and *see* the phantoms of his imagination; and there too they are disquieted when they are made aware of the fact.) Here, readers *feel* how contemporaries were drawn in: how they themselves in that situation might also have been persuaded. The ascription of motivation prompts them (as they seek to comprehend the event by contextualizing it) to shift perspective from the close-up focus on Themistocles' words to a more distant vantage point, so as to take in the wider perspective of the sequence before Salamis—with, indeed, its pronounced theme of Themistocles' mastery of rhetoric. His chameleonic oratorical ability was particularly on show when, pleased with Mnesiphilos' advice, he set about persuading the relevant parties to reverse their decision and fight to defend Salamis, carefully tailoring each approach to circumstance and audience (as we shall see in the following section, §9.4.1). He achieved his desired result despite the fact that a formal resolution[38] had only just been passed (in favour of defence of the Isthmus), and that, barely (in the face of blind panic and the premature departure of some of the captains: 8.56). Herodotus' detailed coverage of this sequence, fallacious in historically literal terms—for some at least of the arguments put forward must have been raised in the debate that preceded the original resolution—indicated its thematic importance.

### 9.4.1 Touchstone: before Salamis (8.56–64)

Themistocles first proceeded with restraint and in keeping with convention in approaching the admiral Eurybiades. Only after explaining his purpose and receiving an invitation to enter and

---

[38] Cf. Macan and Masaracchia ad loc.

speak, 'he repeated all the arguments he had heard from Mnesiphilos (ἐκεῖνά τε πάντα τὰ ἤκουσε Μνησιφίλου), making them out to be his own' (aware that his own authority will have greater sway than an unknown's[39]), 'adding many other arguments besides (καὶ ἄλλα πολλὰ προστιθείς)' (thus framing the argument in even more convincing terms—which are left to the reader's imagination—than did Mnesiphilos), 'until he persuaded him (ἐς ὃ ἀνέγνωσε)...' (8.58.2). But next, before the council of admirals, Themistocles pre-empted the formal presentation of the matter to the council with his vehement defence of its importance (8.59), presumably aware of the men's likely resentment at this late-night reassembly.[40] Before this audience he selected different arguments:

he no longer put forward any of the arguments he had spoken earlier (ἔλεγε ἐκείνων μὲν οὐκέτι οὐδὲν τῶν πρότερον λεχθέντων).... For, in the presence of the allies, it would not have been fitting for him to make accusations (οὐκ ἔφερέ οἱ κόσμον οὐδένα κατηγορέειν) (8.60.1).

More appropriate at that point was his newly upbeat tone and emphasis on Eurybiades' potential to save Greece. He matched his assessment of the strategic viability of the respective options—which contemporary readers' extra-textual knowledge might prime them to find plausible—with an emotive reference to the saving of women and children if they choose Salamis. He underlined the advantage to everyone of this scenario: Eurybiades will find profit (χρηστὰ εὑρήσεις), and the allies

---

[39] Commentators, e.g. Plutarch (869 d–e), Stein ad loc., tend to read as disparaging Herodotus' apparent emphasis (cf. Frost (1980), 6–7) on the fact that Themistocles passes off another's advice as his own. Frost offers some apologetic: 'If he seems to detract from Themistocles' *euboulia* by saying that he was merely passing on another man's advice as his own, he no doubt believed that this was so, and had witnesses to back it up' (11). But the phenomenon is best understood in terms of Themistocles' rhetorical skill: cf. 8.80, when again he is aware of the importance of the speaker's authority, urging Aristeides to address the Greeks himself since he is more likely to be believed. Cf. Jocelyn (1967) on Ennius fr. 84.9 q.v., citing inter alia Euripides, *Hecuba* 294–5 (λόγος γὰρ ἔκ τ' ἀδοξούντων ἰὼν | κἀκ τῶν δοκούντων αὐτὸς οὐ ταὐτὸν σθένει, 'for the same argument/speech does not have equal strength coming from men without repute as from men of reputation'), 'the substance of [which] ... was a commonplace both in the fifth century and later'.

[40] Herodotus' Themistocles frequently displays sensitivity to the men's psychology when he addresses them, as when he knows just how much to reveal to them about the slaying of the Euboean flocks: ταῦτα μέν νυν ἐς τοσοῦτο παρεγύμνου ('these things to this extent he disclosed', 8.19.2). Cf. above, ch. 3 n. 30 with text.

will achieve 'that which you desire most of all' (τοῦ καὶ περιέχεσθε μάλιστα (8.60β); the plural, as Macan (ad loc.) observes, avoids accusing Eurybiades of partiality), the defence of the Peloponnese. The allies would thereby save not only Megara and Aegina but also Salamis—'in which place an oracle predicts you will overcome your enemies' (8.60γ)—and thus their action would accord with divine will. The observation recalled his own triumph on the earlier occasion (should not the listeners trust his opinion now as the Athenians did then?). His concluding *gnōmē*, that heaven is most likely to favour reasonable designs, pointed again to the concordance that both internal and external audiences have already witnessed between the plans and actions of this clever, rational man, and those of the gods (as when, in ordering the seizure of the Euboeans' flocks, Themistocles acted in accordance with an oracle once given to them but long forgotten[41]).

But at this point in the earlier sequence the Themistoclean rhetoric again changed, becoming less diplomatic and more threatening. Rebuked by Adeimantos a first time, on a procedural matter, for the moment (τότε) he had responded ἠπίως, 'gently' (8.60.1); but attacked again on the subject of his very entitlement to vote and taunted about Athens' capture, this time (τότε δή), Themistocles

responded with many insults against Adeimantos and the Corinthians (κεῖνόν τε καὶ τοὺς Κορινθίους πολλά τε καὶ κακὰ ἔλεγε), and made clear that the Athenians still had a *polis* and a country—and one greater than theirs—so long as they had 200 ships manned, since none of the Greeks could repel them should they choose to attack (8.61.2).

Although previously extremely careful not to offend the allies, this time Themistocles opted instead to underline Athens' military significance among Greek cities. *Polis* politics and rivalry were brought to the fore with the inclusion of Adeimantos' fellow Corinthians; and thus readers were reminded of the varied composition of Themistocles' audience. The high profile of this threesome (Athenians, Spartans,

---

[41] Compare how, in contriving that the battle take place at Salamis (by prompting the Persians' encirclement of the Greeks), Themistocles acts in accordance with the oracle of 8.77—which Herodotus cites immediately after reporting the ruse. Cf. 8.117: a storm destroys the bridges and prevents the retreating Persians from using it in strange concordance with Themistocles' earlier (not activated) plan. As divine involvement was surmised in the case of an earlier storm (8.13), the same may be imagined here.

and Corinthians) in the pre-Peloponnesian War politics of Herodotus' listeners must have impressed upon them with particular immediacy the challenges involved in addressing such a group. Where
Herodotus' version thus paints a multitextured audience that demands carefully tailored responses, Plutarch's—which has Eurybiades take Adeimantos' place as Themistocles' only opponent
(*Themistocles* 11)—diminishes the theme of persuasive rhetoric and
so deprives it of much of Herodotus' point.

When he turned for a final time to Eurybiades, speaking more
vehemently than before (8.62.1), Themistocles bestowed upon him
personal moral responsibility for any future defeat ('if you remain
here (Σὺ εἰ μενέεις αὐτοῦ) you are a brave man, but if not, you will
ruin Greece (ἀνατρέψεις τὴν Ἑλλάδα)', 8.62.1); threatened that the
Athenians would leave the Greeks to their fate and voyage to Siris
unless Salamis be defended; and concluded portentously (again
widening his address with the plural): 'once you (ὑμεῖς) have been
abandoned by such allies as we are, you will remember my words'
(8.62.2). Fear of that prospect is what finally persuaded Eurybiades to
change his mind. Thus the many different rhetorical stances tried out
do in the end achieve their purpose. The two parts of Themistocles'
address have together been judged by modern commentators to have
been given such beautiful structure and narrative weight that they
must articulate Herodotus' personal interpretation of events,[42] but
they are more naturally viewed as showcasing Themistocles' rhetoric.[43] When the time comes to address all the Greek fighters before
the battle of Salamis, the admiral again displayed his skill at choosing
the right speech for the occasion, excelling all others with the patriotic harangue which Herodotus summarizes (8.83).

[42]  Cf. Masaracchia on 8.60.6: '[i] discorsi hanno uno spazio e un peso eccezionali
negli ultimi tre libri delle *Storie*. Attraverso di essi, Erodoto avanza la sua personale
interpretazione degli eventi narrati e delle decisioni che li provocarono, costruisce
grandiosi quadri di carattere.' ('The speeches have an exceptional space and weight in
the final three books of the *Histories*. By their means Herodotus advances his personal
interpretation of the events narrated and the decisions that provoked them, and
constructs grand character portraits'.)

[43]  Also showcased, over the course of the sequence, is the travesty of *logos* that
Themistocles' changing rhetorical stances promote, cf. Pelling (1997) and (2006c),
112—for Themistocles does not speak his mind. We consider further this subversive
flipside of his rhetorical skill below, §9.6.

### 9.4.2 After Salamis: rhetoric at Andros (8.109)

And Themistocles seems to be doing the same again in the speech at Andros, which—though imagined as delivered spontaneously—displays the oratorical flourish of a set piece. We may note, for example, how the initial notion of the enemy's potential to *recover* or stand up from their earlier defeat finds subtle reflection in the *an(a)* alliteration—ἄνδρας ἐς ἀναγκαίην ἀπειληθέντας νενικημένους ἀναμάχεσθαί τε καὶ ἀναλαμβάνειν τὴν προτέρην κακότητα ('beaten men, driven to necessity, **renew** the fight and **make amends for** their earlier cowardice', 8.109.2)—which leads into further repetition (εὕρημα ... εὑρήκαμεν) underlining the notion of the victory as merely a chance result. But such demonstration of the power of *logos*—not merely to persuade an audience to change their intellectual stance, but even to transform their mood—leaves the audience well aware that the rhetorical skills that have achieved this are also those of Herodotus himself. Does this consciousness about the power and persuasive, even deceptive, potential of *logos* undermine in some sense, or leave open to doubt, the authorial verdict at 8.110.1 (that 'Themistocles was deceiving' in the speech in which he dissuaded the Athenians from pursuing Xerxes)? Or does it at least invite readers to approach it with scepticism? Might it signal to the reader that the authorial voice, too, may be capable of misleading representations?

   Indeed, even at this point a simple reading remains elusive, for the ascription of motivation draws readers simultaneously in two different directions: not only to reassess their previous impressions of the speech, but also to critique the ascription, despite its apparent authorial validation. For the observation that in being so persuaded the Athenians were being deceived is somewhat undercut by the explanation then given for that reaction:

ἐπειδὴ γὰρ καὶ πρότερον δεδογμένος εἶναι σοφὸς ἐφάνη ἐὼν ἀληθέως σοφός τε καὶ εὔβουλος, πάντως ἕτοιμοι ἦσαν λέγοντι πείθεσθαι (8.110.1)

since even previously Themistocles had been thought to be wise (*sophos*), and now he showed himself to be truly wise (*sophos*) and well counselled (*euboulos*), they were wholly ready to be persuaded by whatever he said

—an explanation that harmonizes so well with the narrative so far as to leave the impression that not only was the Athenians' being persuaded understandable, but that they were quite *right* so to have been (since their leader was yet again advocating the wisest action). That is, διέβαλλε ('he was deceiving') is perhaps misleading, or at least demands reconsideration.[44] Peisistratus' 'deception' of the Athenians (1.59.5), as suggested above (158), might be similarly construed. Here as there, we should perhaps lay emphasis on the notion of the Athenians' *allowing* themselves to be persuaded.[45]

## 9.5 THE DEMOCRATIC TEXTURE

Moreover, another perspective emerges with Herodotus' detail that the Athenian audience appreciated Themistocles' *euboulia* ('good counsel', 8.110.1). This suggests that the fact of his expressing a changed view, usually regarded by modern scholars as a sign of double-dealing, may be no clear condemnation, since the capacity to accept others' advice is a hallmark of Herodotean wise men. Furthermore the Athenians' reasoning in these lines links the two virtues: the man has proved himself σοφός τε καὶ εὔβουλος ('wise and well counselled').[46] Artabanos, in the very stretch of narrative in which he delivers the speech that Themistocles' echoes, made the same equation: 'I judge it equivalent to have good ideas oneself or to be willing to be persuaded by someone else who has good advice (φρονέειν τε εὖ καὶ τῷ λέγοντι χρηστὰ ἐθέλειν πείθεσθαι)' (7.16α). The importance of *euboulia* to the discourse of democracy (in which leaders must accept the people's view, the people, experts' advice) has been illuminated through the contrast with Xerxes' behaviour in his parallel councils of war—for the Great King has been

---

[44]  e.g. in view of the emphasized Spartan-Athenian contrast (which is mapped on to their respective leaders: Eurybiades as cautious Spartan, Themistocles as bold and adaptable Athenian), is Themistocles only 'deceiving' the Athenians in that he elects to go along with the Spartan strategic vision? Or, as Blösel (2004), 263 suggests, should we translate διαβάλλειν here as 'seine Absichten verschleiern' ('hiding his intentions') (since Themistocles is saying what is best for the Athenians, though not revealing his extra vested interest)? Cf. already Fornara (1971), 71 n. 17: 'His deception of the Athenians was his concealment from them of his further intentions'.

[45]  A possibility captured by the translations of 8.110.1 of Asheri ('gli Ateniesi si lasciarono persuadere') and Legrand ('les Athéniens se laissèrent persuader').

[46]  See above, ch. 5 n. 12.

seen to accept no opinion that does not mirror that which he already holds.[47] Mnesiphilos earlier claimed that if his advice not be followed, Greece would perish ἀβουλίῃσι, 'through *aboulie* (want of counsel)' (8.57.2): just as Themistocles saw the wisdom of that advice and so changed his view (having that evening been among 'those left behind' who resolved to fight in defence of the Isthmus,[48] 8.56), so here in this council after Salamis he is perhaps genuinely persuaded by Eurybiades' argument. The way in which Themistocles takes something from Eurybiades' argument but adds much more of his own besides recalls his earlier use of Mnesiphilos', repeating much but ἄλλα πολλὰ προστιθείς ('adding many other arguments besides', 8.58.2). On this reading, in each instance it is upon realizing the wisdom of the alternative plan that the general does what he can to make it succeed. Thus Herodotus uses the Athenians' perspective to suggest to his readers a comparison with the earlier episode, and thus to point them towards drawing out a meaning quite different from that which the authorial voice lays out explicitly.

But if readers interpret Themistocles as remaining privately convinced that pursuit is in the Greeks' best interest (and Artemisia's advice to Xerxes at 8.68 will echo Mnesiphilos': that leader will appreciate the queen's suggestion, but not follow it, and his army will suffer the consequences), the narrative works in other ways to suggest that his second speech is not the result of deception. When the Greeks reached Andros (having initially decided on pursuit: ἐδόκεε ἐπιδιώκειν—persuaded in that by Themistocles, we are left to wonder?),

ἐβουλεύοντο. Θεμιστοκλέης μέν νυν γνώμην ἀπεδείκνυτο.... Εὐρυβιάδης δὲ τὴν ἐναντίην ταύτῃ γνώμην ἐτίθετο.... ὡς δὲ ἔμαθε ὅτι οὐ πείσει τούς γε πολλοὺς ... μεταβαλὼν πρὸς τοὺς Ἀθηναίους ... ἔλεγέ σφι τάδε (8.108.1–109.1).

they held a council. Themistocles declared his opinion.... Eurybiades gave an opinion opposite to this.... When Themistocles realized that he would not (be able to) persuade the majority, he changed tack and addressed the Athenians as follows: ...

---

[47] At least in the later stages of his career; the 'decision to invade' sequence presents a different picture (cf. above, §8.1).
[48] Contra Macan on 8.57.1, who assumes that 'if any such meeting had been held, if any such decision arrived at, Themistokles had been there and against the making of it'.

312    *Themistocles: constructions of motivation*

Thus the two speeches are framed in a context of sophistic—or even specifically *democratic*—processes (for Themistocles is Athens' quintessential representative, and post-Persian Wars, democratic Athens begins to surface at this point of the narrative as a potent absent presence—as we shall see further below). A council was called, two speakers argued opposing positions, the majority view was ascertained (perhaps through a vote), and the decision was binding on all. The implication is that Themistocles may genuinely have held the position for which he initially argued, but was obliged in democratic spirit to support wholeheartedly the majority resolution.[49]

The emphasis on sophistic/democratic process may suggest to readers that Themistocles' expression of an alternative *gnōmē* (opinion) should also be viewed positively: that in an isegoric (or specifically democratic) system it is desirable for a variety of options to be available (though an adversarial system tends to limit these to two), so that an informed decision may be made. That reading is brought to the fore by the contrast the narrative builds up between the texture of the discourse of Greek *isēgoriē* (equal freedom of speech) and that of the discourse of Persian autocracy. Herodotus' general method of setting readers in the role of judge between alternative accounts, each of which (even the less plausible) is shown to be worthy of telling through its being recorded, must render his audience acutely conscious of this sort of process. The lively discourse on the Greek side— the constant calling of councils, wordy jousting, divided opinions, possibility for even a private individual like Μνησίφιλος ἀνὴρ Ἀθηναῖος ('Mnesiphilos, an Athenian man': an 'everyman', given no patronymic—or even the 'Stellvertreter aller Athener'[50]) to have his opinion brought before the generals for debate,[51] and so on—presents

[49] Cf. Blösel (2004), 260. Eurybiades as admiral will in fact have made the actual decision (cf. Macan on 8.109.2; Hdt. 8.64): Herodotus perhaps sought to emphasize the isegoric nature of the Greek council in contrast to the Persian.

[50] Blösel (2004), 361 ('representative of all Athenians').

[51] By contrast, Mnesiphilos' counterpart on the Persian side, the Athenian exile Dikaios, would be executed if his views were reported to the King: 8.65.5. The conspicuous exception to the general rule of willingness, on the Greek side, to bring questions before the assembly for debate is the execution of Lykides (and his family) for suggesting that the King's offer be brought before the people (9.5): but this is recounted as a unique instance; it represents an opinion that if followed would deprive the very institution of its power; and it accords with the Athenian legal charge of *graphē paranomōn*.

a stark contrast with the stifled state of *logos* at the Persian court. The descriptions of the parallel councils of war invite comparison (as suggested above, §9.3.1): the vigorous debates of the Greeks, in which individuals may break into others' speeches or fail to follow the usual programme (as Themistocles jumps in at 8.59), and which are followed by a vote, are a foil to the Persian model.[52]

For the King, before Salamis, communicates to his councillors indirectly, through Mardonios, from on high. His councillors are themselves hierarchically arranged in accordance with their standing with him. Far from making a genuine request for advice, Xerxes is 'trying' his men (ἀποπειρώμενος, 8.67.2—using the same sort of sinister behaviour that the Lydian despot knew Gyges expected of him, 1.9.1). He has already made a decision on the issue before calling the council.[53] The term *anakrisis* (8.69.1) chosen to describe Artemisia's response, a word used of the examination of parties concerned in a legal suit, underlines the necessarily defensive quality of her reply.[54] The advisers speak only that which they believe the king wants to hear, as we see by their surprise at Artemisia's unusually candid (even if deferential and flattering) words. And their concern is well founded. Artabanos earlier got off lightly thanks only to a tie of kinship with the king (7.10), despite having introduced his opinion with an apologetic and defensive insistence on the desirability of opposed views being expressed (7.10α); and that was before Xerxes had become fully immersed in the ways of Persian monarchy, and had no doubt grown to appreciate the frequently warped nature of the advice that is on offer.[55] And finally the king proclaims his decision. The nature of the situation is illuminated by the ironic syntactical movement at 8.69.2 from a democratic-seeming outcome, to the king's real motivation. Though greatly pleased with Artemisia's words,[56] Xerxes bids that '**the majority**

[52] Cf. Pelling (2006c), 111.

[53] Cf. 7.8, with Pelling (2006c), 108–9 and below, n. 57.

[54] Such use of fifth-century Greek legal terminology might be remarked by contemporary readers, prompting further reflection on the anti-isegoric nature of Xerxes' methods.

[55] Cf. above, 249.

[56] κάρτα τε ἥσθη τῇ γνώμῃ τῇ Ἀρτεμισίης ('he was extremely pleased with Artemisia's opinion', 8.69.2), cf. Themistocles at Mnesiphilos' words (8.58.1; cf. at Aristeides', 8.80.1): the similar wording draws attention to fundamental differences

should be followed' (τοῖσι πλέοσι πείθεσθαι ... )—but this is because their advice, as readers discover only in the final clause, happens to coincide with his own premeditations.[57]

Thus the speech at Andros works in tandem with the movement of the text as a whole to undercut the authorial judgement. We find a similar strategy in the narrative of Themistocles' message to the king (8.110.2–3), which is recounted directly after the statement that the Athenians were being deceived, apparently as corroborating evidence for that. But Herodotus' contemporary readers, as easily as later historians, may have seen other possible interpretations, options left quite open and accessible by the way the speech stands alone in direct discourse, attracting no further authorial comment or explanation. Even Plutarch's opinion that the plan was a clever stratagem intended to get the king quickly out of Greece (and so deceiving *him*), one that actually worked,[58] is a possibility unspoken in the *Histories* but nevertheless implicit to the extent that readers are left free to engage with it. This is especially the case after the first Sikinnos message, which was intended to hasten the King into action, to Greek advantage. Blösel points to a suggestive parallel between how with his first message to the King, Themistocles *deceived* the King (into a precipitate attack at Salamis) by speaking the *truth* about the Peloponnesians' desire to retreat, and how at Andros he 'deceives' the Athenians in speaking the truth about what is indeed the best policy (i.e. not to destroy the bridges).[59] The parallel might be extended to the second message too, with Themistocles there once again speaking the *truth* (about what he has achieved in persuading the Athenians) in order to *deceive* the King into an even more precipitate departure from Greece.

---

between the Greek and Persian situations, even if (as Pelling (1997) well brings out) there is also travesty of *logos*—of a different sort—on the Greek side, cf. n. 43 above.

[57] With equal irony Xerxes is said to summon the Persian nobles to a council, ἵνα γνώμας τε πύθηταί σφεων καὶ αὐτὸς ἐν πᾶσι εἴπῃ τὰ θέλει ('in order to discover their opinions and himself declare publicly his desire', 7.8.1): the parallel placement of the separate subordinate clauses suggests that the others' views will have no effect upon his own.

[58] Plutarch, *Themistocles* 16.4–6; *Aristeides* 9.6–10.1.

[59] Blösel (2004), 263–4.

## 9.6 THEMISTOCLES' MOTIVATION
## AND READER RESPONSE

The effect of delaying authorial judgement until after Themistocles' address—the same technique Herodotus uses in his narration of the Alcmaeonid shield incident (discussed in chapter one[60])—is to leave readers to work out for themselves, and make their own assumptions about, the speech's *raison d'être*. Wolfgang Iser suggests that such temporary withholding of information increases the suggestive effect of details, 'stimulating a welter of possible solutions'[61] in readers' minds. Indeed, as we have seen, the preceding account has pointed readers to a variety of alternative explanations for Themistocles' motivation in delivering the speech at Andros beyond that offered by the authorial conjecture at its conclusion. Herodotus himself models this interpretative method for his readers through his frequent suggestions of possible alternative motivations for the behaviour of actors in his text.

With the additional observation that τά περ ὦν καὶ ἐγένετο ('and in fact this is exactly what happened'), Themistocles' later history is dramatically brought before readers' minds—which was hardly necessary, and so can be no simple reminder. The effect is perhaps to implant a sharper realization that those later events may have contributed to the retrospective interpretation given here of Themistocles' motives, and thus to prompt reflection upon whether that is really what was motivating him at the time, and whether other possibilities present themselves. Certainly, as we have seen, Herodotus does not simply ignore the possibility that Themistocles sacrifices his project for the sake of maintaining the alliance with the Peloponnesians: readers may find it themselves in the patterns in his text. Contemporary readers' awareness of the historical fact that under Themistocles' influence all continued after this point to turn out favourably for the Athenians for some time must also be a factor powerfully influencing their interpretation (a paradox intensified by their knowledge that Themistocles himself will be less fortunate). Thus Fornara and Frost rightly emphasize the importance of considering contemporary (440s)

---

[60] §1.4.     [61] Iser (1989), 11.

views on Themistocles, and ways in which Herodotus is working with those.⁶² More potent again is the keen awareness on the part of Herodotus' contemporary audience of *Athens'* post-Persian Wars trajectory:⁶³ her power and influence in the islands and Asian cities, amassing of tribute, and also—in striking congruence with Themistocles' ambiguous dealings via Sikinnos with the King—her use and misuse of her 'anti-Persian' stance.⁶⁴ Indeed, a conspicuous—and (as suggested further below) disquieting—parallel surfaces between Themistocles and Athens.⁶⁵ Readers' independent knowledge of events described and their aftermath—from personal experience, oral accounts, or other texts' treatment—thus provides accounts of their recent history with a further, and powerful, perspective. This meets and confronts those main perspectives of (fictional) narrative that Iser identifies (cf. §1.3 above).

If the statement of motivation is not intended to be taken at face value and swallowed whole, it nevertheless provides much food for thought. In particular, it offers a further impression of Themistocles' character (thus illuminating a different sort of historical truth), and hints at ways in which the same qualities may be ambivalent. The man's astonishing ability to conjure up on the spot a speech that argues so persuasively the opposite view from that of his first brings to mind the sophists' verbal dexterity and the flexible moral stance that might accompany it. But the same quality—that of the man of *mētis*—is what Herodotus shows has led the Greeks to victory in the Persian Wars. It was that same spontaneous adaptability that enabled the Athenians, specifically, quickly to become a seafaring people, and then (led by Themistocles) to make the most of their position in the battles at Salamis, despite smaller numbers, and even to use that to their advantage in fighting in the straits. Through the juxtaposition

---

⁶² Fornara (1971), 69–74; Frost (1980), 8; cf. Munson (1988) and (2001).

⁶³ See especially Raaflaub (1987); Stadter (1992); Moles (1996); and Blösel (2001), (2004).

⁶⁴ Rosalind Thomas alerts me to this point.

⁶⁵ Athens, like Themistocles, is shown to act out of self-interest; cf. above, esp. §6.4.5. Immerwahr (1966), 223–5, 287–8, Wood (1972), 185–6, Munson (1988), 100–2, and Asheri (2003), xix discuss Themistocles as personifying Athens and Athenian character. Ubsdell (1983), 44–5 observes how his same qualities are seen working both to good and to ill. For Blösel, (2001) and (2004), he mirrors fifth-century Athens vis-à-vis Greece in his trajectory from positive to negative.

of Themistocles' publicly expressed plans for the future (in his speech) with his alleged secret ones (in the authorial comment), Herodotus vividly sets forth the two sides of that same coin: the same capacity to look to the future might always be turned against the Athenians. The man of *mētis*—just like the city he hails from—looks to his own security first.

But *mētis* is Odyssean; it is cunning, working in opposition to brute force; in its presence 'the defeat of the weak and the frail is not a foregone conclusion':[66] so the reader is somewhat perturbed when, straight after Themistocles' speech and the decision not to pursue Xerxes, the language of *bia* (force) emerges in the narrative of the treatment of the Andrians (8.111). Themistocles, up to this point *Peithō* (Persuasion) personified, now adds *Anankaiē* (Necessity, Constraint) to the formula, threatening the Andrians with the fact that the Athenians possess 'two great gods, *Peithō* and *Anankaiē*' (8.111.2)—for, the narrator observes, Themistocles 'did not cease being greedy' (οὐ ... ἐπαύετο πλεονεκτέων, 8.112.1). Having failed to provide money, they are besieged; other islanders, made fearful, hand it over promptly. Themistocles collects all the funds, 'escaping the notice of the other commanders' (λάθρῃ τῶν ἄλλων στρατηγῶν, 8.112.3). So the wandering viewpoint has moved on: the incident causes readers to reflect again upon his earlier instances of persuasion, and whether they were in any sense sinister as well; perhaps even upon the extent to which *peithomai*, up to this point, has shaded into its sense 'to obey'. (Sophists such as Gorgias, after all, could link *Peithō* with *Bia*.[67]) But still the text hints, too, at an alternative reading: that the islanders are fearful because they have indeed medized (it is upon learning that Andros was besieged for this offence that they offer the money). Furthermore, when the narrative resumes after a digression on Persian affairs and Xerxes' return home, the earlier tale is rounded off: 'After the Greeks were unable to capture Andros, they first made their way to Karystos and devastated their land, and then returned to Salamis' (8.121.1). There is no mention of Themistocles here; he is but one of the others. Was the

---

[66] Detienne and Vernant (1991), 28.

[67] e.g. Gorgias, *Helen* 6; cf. (a generation earlier) Aeschylus, *Agamemnon* 385, where *Peithō* uses *bia*. See Goldhill (2002), 56–7; Asheri on 8.111.8–9.

earlier action really motivated by his personal *pleonexiē* (greed)? The narrative subtly calls into doubt any simplistic conclusions.

Herodotus' text contains layers of differing response-inviting structures. Readers are prompted to engage with the material and actively work to combine the different strands, with (in Iser's expression) the 'wandering viewpoint' changing as the narrative progresses and new perspectives shed light on the old. The emerging impression of Themistocles' motivation is one of complexity and studied ambivalence, which encourages readers to engage with the issues and paradoxes involved. To evaluate the representation of the man's character more generally as either wholly negative (issuing wholesale from biased sources), or as simply or straightforwardly patterned (for example, in terms of a 'bipartite division' like Blösel's, for whom Themistocles' 'egoism and his hubris after Salamis are obviously contrasted with his patriotism and uncompromising struggle for Greece up to that point'),[68] may risk overlooking the subtlety of Herodotus' treatment. The historian implies that the differing contemporary opinions of Themistocles, as well as the complex range of motivations he may well actually have had, defy simplistic interpretations. The way Herodotus, in this instance, provokes his readers to work with the evidence and to struggle with the incongruities that become apparent is a small example of what he does elsewhere, and one way the contrary 'source citations' seem intended to work. (These, if purely literary, work as a tool to engage the reader with conceptual difficulties, and if literal, with actual source difficulties.[69])

Readers of the *Histories* have recently become more alert to its narrative sophistication, an aspect of which is how it may invite readers to challenge an interpretation that prima facie seems most obvious. This growing awareness of ways in which the narrative itself points readers towards a sceptical stance vis-à-vis the oral traditions it preserves makes ever clearer the fact that Herodotus' claim to 'record whatever is said' (7.152.3) is far from being the full story.[70] Ernst Badian argues that the account of Alexander I of Macedon

---

[68] Blösel (2001), 196.

[69] Luraghi (2001), esp. 160 discusses Herodotus' source references as metaphors, not intended to be understood literally. See further above, ch. 1 n. 31 with text.

[70] See above, ch. 5 n. 9.

preserves the original sources' philhellenic apologetic, but so far from himself reproducing that rhetoric unquestioningly, Herodotus 'has used his literary art to guide the reader to what seemed to him a just verdict on Alexander's duplicity by stylistic and compositional devices.'[71] On each of the occasions in the *Histories* where Alexander appears pretending to be benefiting the Greeks, the narrative (Badian suggests) subtly indicates that he is in fact acting as a loyal subject of the King: for instance at Tempe, where the account of Alexander's disclosure to the Athenians of Mardonios' plans (9.44–5) is followed by the narrative of the Persian retreat after their defeat at Plataea—where Herodotus 'has nothing to say about Macedonia except that Artabazus passed through Macedonia by the shortest route, and . . . that he was not attacked until he got to Thrace'; thus 'Herodotus is once more leaving the reader to draw the obvious conclusion' (i.e. that Macedonia remained friendly to Persia), 'without giving positive offence to a powerful ruler.'[72] Wolfgang Blösel describes this phenomenon as 'contamination, or . . . invention directed towards criticizing the mighty',[73] and recognizes a similar technique in Herodotus' treatment of the anecdotal traditions that surrounded Themistocles. The modification and rearrangement of the anecdotes at his hands transforms their original significance as stand-alone stories, so that taken together they come to present a bipartite characterization of Themistocles:

Der jähe Umschlag des Wollens und des Handelns des Herodoteischen Themistokles—in Zeiten der Bedrohung kompromißloser Einsatz für die Sache aller Griechen, danach jedoch ungezügelte Befriedigung der Selbstsucht—, bildet das *tertium comparationis*, über das der Blick des Publikums auf das eigentliche Objekt der Kritik gelenkt werden kann: die Herrschaft der Athener im Seebund.[74]

---

[71] Badian (1994), 121.

[72] Badian (1994), 117–19 (quotation at 119).

[73] Blösel (2001), 180.

[74] Blösel (2004), 365 ('The sudden change of the intentions and the actions of the Herodotean Themistocles—at the time of the threat, uncompromising dedication to the cause of all the Greeks, afterwards however [i.e. following the council at Andros where, in Blösel's view, he so readily abandoned his initial plan of pursuing the Persians after the Salamis victory] unbridled fulfilment of self-interest—forms the basis of comparison, as a result of which the gaze of the audience can be directed to the actual object of criticism: the Athenians' rule in the Delian league').

Indeed, it was primarily in order to make that criticism that Herodotus chose to include the anecdotes.[75]

These scholars' work is extremely illuminating in the close attention it pays to detail and to the processes of Herodotus' narrative, and its recognition of the *Histories*' narrative sophistication and of the crucial role played by its contemporary audience in its interpretation. However their emphasis on Herodotus' deliberate manipulations of his sources and the narrative in order to champion a single clear message (that Alexander medized, or that Themistocles mirrored Athens in the transformation of his motives from ideal to self-serving)—on his use of *suppressio veri* to (for Badian) smooth over inconvenient truths or (for Blösel) produce a particular significant pattern[76]—seems out of keeping with the opening up and problematizing of such challenging questions that we have found to be characteristic of Herodotus' technique. We have seen that this is especially the case on occasions when attitudes and motives are at issue. In the case of Alexander's presentation, the complexities of Herodotus' account, to which Badian responds, might be viewed rather as giving readers a sense of the difficulties involved in explaining his conduct over time: in interpreting his motives generally, and specifically the extent to which he was pro-Persian or otherwise. Herodotus lays out the rather contradictory strands for his readers to reflect upon. The evidence available to him cannot have been simple and clear, for that is not the nature of collective memory and the oral traditions it transmits—which are likely to be unstable and various as well as partisan.[77] Herodotus could more easily ascertain what Alexander *did*; his motives cannot have been so

---

[75] Blösel (2001), 194. Blösel (2001), (2004) also offers detailed, highly speculative suggestions as to the content and flavour of each individual anecdote as heard by Herodotus, which he believes has been transformed. He suggests that the minimal historical worth of the sources available on Themistocles must have seemed to Herodotus to justify a wholesale reconstruction of events according to his personal judgement: cf. e.g. (2001), 194.

[76] This, in Badian's view, is 'quite typical' in the *Histories*: (1994), 126 n. 19. Blösel's Herodotus knows full well the pitfalls of patriotic Athenian oral traditions but chooses to follow them nonetheless in his account of the first half of Themistocles' career (cf. e.g. (2004), 101) for the sake of the clear-cut rise-and-fall picture that most effectively recalls contemporary Athens.

[77] See e.g. Thomas (1989) and (1993); and more generally Fentress and Wickham (1992); Schudson (1995).

evident, for example (to return to the example mentioned above) in informing the Athenians of Mardonios' plans; and they were presumably also complex. The emphasis elsewhere (5.221) on Alexander's claim of Greek identity might, for example, allow readers to envisage a measure of nostalgia playing a part in motivating his conduct in this instance (indeed one of the alternative explanations Herodotus conjectured for Demaratus' conduct in warning the Greeks in advance of Xerxes' action (7.239: *eunoia*, goodwill) could serve readers as a model for such an interpretation). Likewise Blösel's black-and-white portrayal of the Herodotean Themistocles' motives—as wholly positive before, wholly negative after the turning point represented by the Andros episode where he turns to focusing on his own interests in resolving 'to lay up a store of favour with the King' (8.109.5)—seems to iron out some of the rich complexity of Herodotus' presentation.

Again, the political implications of such use of narrative techniques to prompt the audience to draw conclusions (faced with Badian's 'subtle silences') potentially different from those laid out explicitly by the narrator have been emphasized to the neglect of the historian's wider intellectual and historiographical concerns. This seems especially so with regard to the *Histories'* coverage of more recent historical material in the narrative of the Persian Wars. What Badian responds to in Herodotus' method of characterization may be less a subtle means of expressing unsavoury views without treading too heavily on sensitive and politically still-powerful toes, than a way of engaging readers with the challenging nature of the intellectual inquiry involved in assessing the past. Blösel's assertion that Herodotus' principal concern in his account of Themistocles is with awarding praise and blame—with presenting an obvious contrast between the admiral's genuine patriotism before Salamis and his egoism and *hybris* afterwards, so as to present a criticism of contemporary Athens—sidelines the way in which his narrative works on readers on an intellectual as well as a more narrowly political level. This traditional moral focus, upon the degree to which Themistocles' portrayal is positive or otherwise, neglects the rhetorical texture of the account and the questions it raises about discourse and persuasion. The rhetorical aspect qualifies any such clear-cut judgement of Themistocles' character and motivation.

In arguing for *exclusive* readings—for keys that promise to unlock the 'true' interpretation, or Herodotus' single and central 'message'—such approaches disregard the ways in which the *Histories* promotes an approach to the past that acknowledges the difficulty, even impossibility, of alighting upon such absolute truth. Any reading of human history—which is inevitably complex, so many and varied are the factors that impinge upon its manifold series of outcomes—is necessarily subjective, depending on the interpreter's own identity and location in time. All the more so when inextricably bound up with an interpretation of the motives of such an individual as Themistocles: a particular enigma, whose famed rhetorical skill made his real intentions all the more evidently difficult to evaluate. Such an individual's motives may be profitably puzzled over and conjectured—and this process leads to deeper understanding of the period—but conclusions remain provisional and qualified. Herodotus' narrative opens up different interpretative possibilities.

# Epilogue

Herodotus has laboured under the criticism of being naïve. Our discussion, building upon and corroborating recent research, strengthens further the suspicion that the *naïveté* is rather that of his critics. His *Histories* is the work of an author acutely aware of the problems of historiography; of one possessing the extra perceptions available to the careful analyst, who is deeply mindful of the contested nature of the past, and sensitive to the opposing views it provokes.

Herodotus sought to communicate not only what happened (*ta prachthenta/ta genomena*), but also the background of thoughts and perceptions that both *shaped* those events and became critical to their fair interpretation in retrospect. People's ideas and motives are by their nature less easy to pin down than hard facts. Herodotus' narrative technique when it comes to this aspect of the historical record, inspired by that of Homer but then thoroughly developed, is sophisticated. His ascriptions of motives seem in keeping with the 'open' ending of the work as a whole. Indeed, in its subtle treatment of motivation the *Histories* invites comparison with fifth-century tragedy, which likewise is preoccupied with questions of motivation and complicates simple judgements, and whose characteristic ποικιλία (variation),[1] I would argue, elicits a similar sort of response as the *Histories*, and to similar purpose. But that is another story.

Herodotus' is a Janus-faced view, directed not only backwards in time to past events, but forward, to readers of the future. The result is that the *Histories*' meaning remains living and contested: it is never to

---

[1] Cf. Dionysius of Halicarnassus, *Letter to Gnaeus Pompeius* 11.

be set in stone, let alone to become τῷ χρόνῳ ἐξίτηλον, 'faded away in the course of time', like the monumental inscription evoked in its preface;[2] but readers may continue to uncover its further layers of significance.

[2] Cf. Moles (1999), §8.

# References

Note: texts, translations, commentaries, and lexica that are cited without date (by the name of the scholar) are to be found in the list of Abbreviations.

Abrams, M. H. (1953), *The Mirror and the Lamp: Romantic Theory and the Critical Tradition* (London, New York, and Oxford).

Andersen, Ø. (1990), 'The Making of the Past in the *Iliad*', *HSPh* 93, 25–45.

Auerbach, E. (2003), *Mimesis: The Representation of Reality in Western Literature*, tr. W. R. Trask, 50th Anniv. Edn. (Princeton; German orig. 1953).

Austin, M. M. (1990), 'Greek Tyrants and the Persians, 546–479 BC', *CQ* 40, 289–306.

——and Vidal-Naquet, P. (1977), *Economic and Social History of Ancient Greece: an Introduction*, tr. and revised by M. M. Austin (London; French orig. 1972).

Badian, E. (1994), 'Herodotus on Alexander I of Macedon: A Study in Some Subtle Silences', in Hornblower (1994*b*), 107–30.

Bakker, E. J. (2002*a*), 'The Making of History: Herodotus' *Histories Apodexis*', in Bakker, de Jong, and van Wees (2002), 3–32.

Bakker, E. J. (2002*b*), 'Khrónos, Kléos, and Ideology from Herodotus to Homer', in M. Reichel and A. Rengakos (eds.), *Epea Pteroenta: Beiträge zur Homerforschung: Festschrift für Wolfgang Kullmann zum 75. Geburtstag* (Stuttgart), 11–30.

——, Jong, I. J. F. de and Wees, H. van (2002) (eds.), *Brill's Companion to Herodotus* (Leiden, Boston, and Cologne).

Bakker, M. P. de (2007), 'Speech and Authority in Herodotus' *Histories*' (PhD diss., University of Amsterdam).

Barron, J. P. (1988), 'The Liberation of Greece', in Boardman, Hammond, Lewis, and Ostwald (1988), 592–622.

Bauslaugh, R. A. (1991), *The Concept of Neutrality in Classical Greece* (Berkeley and Oxford).

Benardete, S. (1969), *Herodotean Inquiries* (The Hague).

Berlin, I. (1969), *Four Essays on Liberty* (Oxford).

Bischoff, H. (1932), *Der Warner bei Herodot* (Leipzig).

Bloomer, W. M. (1993), 'The Superlative *Nomoi* of Herodotus' *Histories*', *ClAnt* 12, 30–50.

Blösel, W. (2001), 'The Herodotean Picture of Themistocles: A Mirror of Fifth-Century Athens', in Luraghi (2001), 179–97.

—— (2004), *Themistokles bei Herodot: Spiegel Athens im fünften Jahrhundert* (Stuttgart).

Boardman, J., Hammond, N. G. L., Lewis, D. M., and Ostwald, M. (1988) (eds.), *The Cambridge Ancient History* ², vol. 4: *Persia, Greece and the Western Mediterranean* (Cambridge).

Boedeker, D. (1987), 'The Two Faces of Demaratus', in Boedeker and Peradotto (1987), 185–201.

—— (2000), 'Herodotus's Genre(s)', in M. Depew and D. Obbink (eds.), *Matrices of Genre: Authors, Canons, and Society* (Cambridge, Mass. and London), 97–114.

—— (2001), 'Heroic Historiography: Simonides and Herodotus on Plataea', in Boedeker and Sider (2001), 120–34 (orig. *Arethusa* 29 (1996), 223–42).

—— (2002), 'Epic Heritage and Mythical Patterns in Herodotus', in Bakker, de Jong, and van Wees (2002), 97–116.

—— (2003), 'Pedestrian Fatalities: The Prosaics of Death in Herodotus', in Derow and Parker (2003), 17–36.

—— and Peradotto, J. (1987) (eds.), *Herodotus and the Invention of History* (*Arethusa* 20; Buffalo).

—— and Sider, D. (2001) (eds.), *The New Simonides: Contexts of Praise and Desire* (Oxford and New York).

Bornitz, H.-F. (1968), *Herodot-Studien. Beiträge zum Verständnis der Einheit des Geschichtswerks* (Berlin).

Braund, D. (1998), 'Herodotos on the Problematics of Reciprocity', in Gill, Postlethwaite, and Seaford (1998), 159–80.

Brock, R. (2004), 'Political Imagery in Herodotus', in Karageorghis and Taifacos (2004), 169–77.

Burkert, W. (1990), 'Herodot als Historiker fremder Religionen', in G. Nenci and O. Reverdin, *Hérodote et les peoples non grecs* (Entretiens Hardt 35; Geneva), 1–39.

Cairns, D. L. (1996), 'Hybris, Dishonour, and Thinking Big', *JHS* 116, 1–32.

Cartledge, P. (1982), 'Sparta and Samos: A Special Relationship?' *CQ* 32, 243–65.

—— and Greenwood, E. (2002), 'Herodotus as a Critic: Truth, Fiction, Polarity', in Bakker, de Jong, and van Wees (2002), 351–71.

Cawkwell, G. L. (1970), 'The Fall of Themistocles', in B. F. Harris (ed.), *Auckland Classical Essays* (Oxford), 39–58.

Chiasson, C. C. (1986), 'The Herodotean Solon', *GRBS* 27, 249–62.

Christ, M. R. (1994), 'Herodotean Kings and Historical Inquiry', *ClAnt* 13, 167–202.

—— (2006), *The Bad Citizen in Classical Athens* (Cambridge).

Cobet, J. (1971), *Herodots Exkurse and die Frage der Einheit seines Werkes* (*Historia Einzelschriften* 17; Wiesbaden).

—— (1974), review of D. Fehling, *Die Quellenangaben bei Herodot. Studien zur Erzählkunst Herodots* (Berlin, 1971), in *Gnomon* 46, 737–46.

Cohn, D. (1990), 'Signposts of Fictionality: A Narratological Perspective', *Poetics Today* 11, 775–804.

Connor, W. R. (1984), *Thucydides* (Princeton).

—— (1985), 'Narrative Discourse in Thucydides', in Jameson (1985), 1–17.

—— (1987), 'Tribes, Festivals and Processions: Civic Ceremonial and Political Manipulation in Archaic Greece', *JHS* 107, 40–50.

—— (1993), 'The *Histor* in History', in R. M. Rosen and J. S. Farrell (eds.), *Nomodeiktes: Greek Studies in Honor of Martin Ostwald* (Ann Arbor), 3–15.

Constant, B. (1819), *On the Liberty of the Ancients Compared with that of the Moderns* = B. Fontana (tr. and ed.), *Benjamin Constant, Political Writings* (Cambridge, 1988), 307–28.

Corcella, A. (1984), *Erodoto e l'analogia* (Palermo).

Danek, G. (1998), *Epos und Zitat: Studien zu den Quellen der Odyssee* (Vienna).

Darbo-Peschanski, C. (1985), 'Les *logoi* des autres dans les *Histoires* d'Hérodote', *QS* 22, 105–28.

—— (1987), *Le discours du particulier: Essai sur l'enquête Hérodotéenne* (Paris).

Davidson, J. (1991), 'The Gaze in Polybius' *Histories*', *JRS* 81, 10–24.

Davis, T. F. and Womack, K. (2002), *Formalist Criticism and Reader-Response Theory* (Basingstoke).

Dawson, D. (1996), *The Origins of Western Warfare* (Boulder).

Denniston, J. D. (1954), *The Greek Particles*[2] (Oxford).

Derow, P. and Parker, R. C. T. (2003) (eds.), *Herodotus and his World* (Oxford).

Desmond, W. (2004), 'Punishments and the Conclusion of Herodotus' *Histories*', *GRBS* 44, 19–40.

Detienne, M. and Vernant, J.-P. (1991), *Cunning Intelligence in Greek Culture and Society*, tr. J. Lloyd (Chicago; French orig. 1974).

Dewald, C. (1981), 'Women and Culture in Herodotus' *Histories*', in H. P. Foley (ed.), *Reflections of Women in Antiquity* (New York and London), 91–119.

—— (1985), 'Practical Knowledge and the Historian's Role in Herodotus and Thucydides', in Jameson (1985), 47–63.

—— (1987), 'Narrative Surface and Authorial Voice in the *Histories*', in Boedeker and Peradotto (1987), 147–70.

Dewald, C. (1990), Review of F. Hartog, *The Mirror of Herodotus* (Berkeley and London, 1988), in *CPh* 85, 217–24.

—— (1993), 'Reading the World: The Interpretation of Objects in Herodotus' *Histories*', in Rosen and Farrell (1993), 55–70.

—— (1997), 'Wanton Kings, Pickled Heroes, and Gnomic Founding Fathers: Strategies of Meaning at the End of Herodotus's *Histories*', in D. Roberts, F. Dunn, and D. P. Fowler (eds.), *Classical Closure: Reading the End in Greek and Latin Literature* (Princeton), 62–82.

—— (1998), 'Explanatory Notes' to R. Waterfield (tr.), *Herodotus: the Histories* (Oxford).

—— (1999), 'The Figured Stage: Focalizing the Initial Narratives of Herodotus and Thucydides', in T. M. Falkner, N. Felson, and D. Konstan (eds.), *Contextualizing Classics: Ideology, Performance, Dialogue* (Lanham and Oxford), 221–52.

—— (2002), ' "I didn't give my own genealogy": Herodotus and the Authorial Persona', in Bakker, de Jong, and van Wees (2002), 267–89.

—— (2003), 'Form and Content: The Question of Tyranny in Herodotus', in Morgan (2003), 25–58.

—— and Kitzinger, R. (2006), 'Herodotus, Sophocles and the woman who wanted her brother saved', in Dewald and Marincola (2006), 122–9.

—— and Marincola, J. (2006) (eds.), *The Cambridge Companion to Herodotus* (Cambridge and New York).

Dickie, M. W. (1984), '*Hēsychia* and *Hybris* in Pindar', in D. E. Gerber (ed.), *Greek Poetry and Philosophy: Studies in honour of Leonard Woodbury* (Chicago), 83–109.

Dihle, A. (1962), 'Herodot und die Sophistik', *Philologus* 106, 207–20.

Dillery, J. (1992), 'Darius and the Tomb of Nitocris (Hdt. 1.187)', *CPh* 87, 30–8.

—— (1996), 'Reconfiguring the Past: Thyrea, Thermopylae and Narrative Patterns in Herodotus', *AJPh* 117, 217–54.

Dover, K. J. (1973), *Thucydides* (Oxford).

Duff, T. (2003), *The Greek and Roman Historians* (London).

Edmunds, L. (1975), *Chance and Intelligence in Thucydides* (Cambridge, Mass.).

Erbse, H. (1991), 'Fiktion und Wahrheit im Werke Herodots', *Nachrichten der Akademie der Wissenschaften in Göttingen* 4, 131–50.

—— (1992), *Studien zum Verständnis Herodots* (Berlin and New York).

Evans, J. A. S. (1961), 'The Dream of Xerxes and the "*Nomoi*" of the Persians', *CJ* 57, 109–11.

—— (1976), 'Herodotus and the Ionian Revolt', *Historia* 25, 31–7.

—— (1991), *Herodotus, Explorer of the Past* (Princeton).

Fehling, D. (1989), *Herodotus and his 'Sources': Citation, Invention, and Narrative Art*, tr. J. G. Howie (Leeds; German orig. 1971).

Fenik, B. (1974), *Studies in the* Odyssey (Wiesbaden).

Fentress, J. and Wickham, C. (1992), *Social Memory* (Oxford).

Ferrari (1994/5), 'Heracles, Pisistratus and the Panathenaea', *Métis* 9/10, 219–26.

Ferrill, A. (1978), 'Herodotus on Tyranny', *Historia* 25, 385–98.

Fisher, N. R. E. (1992), *Hybris: a Study of the Values of Honour and Shame in Ancient Greece* (Warminster).

Flory, S. (1987), *The Archaic Smile of Herodotus* (Detroit).

Flower, M. A. (1994), *Theopompus of Chios* (New York).

—— (2006), 'Herodotus and Persia', in Dewald and Marincola (2006), 274–89.

Foley, H. P. (1982), 'The "Female Intruder" Reconsidered: Women in Aristophanes' *Lysistrata* and *Ecclesiazusae*', *CPh* 77, 1–21.

Foley, J. M. (1991), *Immanent Art: From Structure to Meaning in Traditional Oral Epic* (Bloomington).

Fornara, C. W. (1971), *Herodotus: An Interpretive Essay* (Oxford).

—— (1990), 'Human History and the Constraint of Fate in Herodotus', in J. W. Allison (ed.), *Conflict, Antithesis, and the Ancient Historian* (Columbus), 25–45.

—— and Samons, L. J. (1991), *Athens from Cleisthenes to Pericles* (Berkeley and Oxford).

Forrest, W. G. (1979), 'Motivation in Herodotus: The Case of the Ionian Revolt', *International History Review* 1, 311–22.

Forsdyke, S. (1999), 'From Aristocratic to Democratic Ideology and Back Again: The Thrasybulus Anecdote in Herodotus' *Histories* and Aristotle's *Politics*', *CPh* 94, 361–72.

—— (2001), 'Athenian Democratic Ideology and Herodotus' *Histories*', *AJPh* 122, 333–62.

—— (2002), 'Greek History, c. 525–480 BC', in Bakker, de Jong, and van Wees (2002), 521–49.

Foucault, M. (1977), *Discipline and Punish: The Birth of the Prison*, tr. A. Sheridan (London; French orig. 1975).

Fowler, D. P. (1990), 'Deviant Focalisation in Virgil's *Aeneid*', *PCPhS* 216, 42–63 (repr. in *Roman Constructions: Readings in Postmodern Latin* (Oxford, 2000), 40–63).

Fowler, R. L. (1996), 'Herodotos and his Contemporaries', *JHS* 116, 62–87.

—— (2003), 'Herodotos and Athens', in Derow and Parker (2003), 311–12.

—— (2004) (ed.), *The Cambridge Companion to Homer* (Cambridge).

—— (2006), 'Herodotus and his Prose Predecessors', in Dewald and Marincola (2006), 29–45.

Fox, M. (1993), 'History and Rhetoric in Dionysius of Halicarnassus', *JRS* 83, 31–47.

French, A. (1972), 'Topical Influences on Herodotos' Narrative', *Mnemosyne* 25, 9–27.

Friedman, T. (1990), *From Beirut to Jerusalem* (London).

Frost, F. J. (1980), *Plutarch's* Themistocles: *a Historical Commentary* (Princeton).

—— (1999), 'The "Ominous" birth of Peisistratos', in F. B. Titchener and R. F. Moorton (eds.), *The Eye Expanded: Life and the Arts in Greco-Roman Antiquity* (Berkeley), 9–18.

Gärtner, H.A. (1983), 'Les rêves de Xerxès et d'Artabane chez Hérodote', *Ktèma* 8, 11–18.

Gaskin, R. (1990), 'Do Homeric Heroes Make Real Decisions?', *CQ* 40, 1–15.

Genette, G. (1988), *Narrative Discourse Revisited*, tr. J. E. Lewin (Ithaca NY; French orig. 1983).

Gibert, J. (1995), *Change of Mind in Greek Tragedy* (Hypomnemata 108; Göttingen).

Giddens, A. (1984), *The Constitution of Society* (Cambridge).

Giglioni, G. B. (2002), *Erodoto e i sogni di Serse* (Rome).

Gildersleeve, B. L. (1899), *Pindar: The Olympian and Pythian Odes* (New York).

Gill, C. (1990), 'The Character-Personality Distinction', in C. B. R. Pelling (ed.), *Characterization and Individuality in Greek Literature* (Oxford), 1–31.

—— (1996), *Personality in Greek Epic, Tragedy, and Philosophy: The Self in Dialogue* (Oxford).

—— (1998), 'Altruism or Reciprocity in Greek Philosophy?', in Gill, Postlethwaite, and Seaford (1998), 303–28.

——, Postlethwaite, N., and Seaford, R. A. S. (1998) (eds.), *Reciprocity in Ancient Greece* (Oxford).

Gillis, D. (1979), *Collaboration with the Persians* (*Historia Einzelschriften* 34; Wiesbaden).

Gilula, D. (2003), 'Who Was Actually Buried in the First of the Three Spartan Graves (Hdt. 9.85.1)? Textual and Historical Problems', in Derow and Parker (2003), 73–87.

Giorgini, G. (1993), *La città e il tiranno: il concetto di tirannide nella Grecia del VII–IV secolo a.C.* (Milan).

Goldhill, S. (1999), 'Reading Differences: The *Odyssey* and Juxtaposition', in I. J. F. de Jong (ed.), *Homer: Critical Assessments*, vol. 4: *Homer's Art* (London and New York), 396–431 (orig. *Ramus* 17 (1988), 1–31).

—— (2002), *The Invention of Prose* (Oxford).

Gould, J. (1989), *Herodotus* (London).

—— (1991), *Give and Take in Herodotus. The Fifteenth J. L. Myres Memorial Lecture* (Oxford) (repr. in Gould (2001), 283–303).

—— (1994), 'Herodotus and Religion', in Hornblower (1994*b*), 91–106 (repr. in Gould (2001), 359–77).

—— (2001), *Myth, Ritual, Memory, and Exchange: Essays in Greek Literature and Culture* (Oxford).

Graf, D. F. (1985), 'Greek Tyrants and Achaemenid Politics', in J. W. Eadie and J. Ober (eds.), *The Craft of the Ancient Historian* (Lanham), 79–123.

Graham, A. J. (1964), *Colony and Mother City in Ancient Greece* (Manchester).

—— (1996), 'Themistocles' Speech before Salamis: The Interpretation of Herodotus 8.83.1', *CQ* 46, 321–6.

Gray, V. J. (1995), 'Herodotus and the Rhetoric of Otherness', *AJPh* 116, 185–211.

—— (1996), 'Herodotus and Images of Tyranny: The Tyrants of Corinth', *AJPh* 117, 361–89.

—— (1997), 'Reading the Rise of Pisistratus: Herodotus 1.56–68', *Histos* 1: <http://research.ncl.ac.uk/histos/Histos_BackIssues1997.html> accessed 14 September 2007.

—— (2001), 'Herodotus' Literary and Historical Method: Arion's Story (1.23–24)', *AJPh* 122, 11–28.

—— (2003), 'Herodotus in Two Minds', in J. Davidson and A. Pomeroy (eds.), *Theatres of Action: Papers for Chris Dearden* (*Prudentia* Suppl.), 43–62.

Gribble, D. (1998), 'Narrator Interventions in Thucydides', *JHS* 118, 41–67.

Griffin, J. (1980), *Homer on Life and Death* (Oxford).

Groten, F. J. (1963), 'Herodotus' Use of Variant Versions', *Phoenix* 17, 79–87.

Hammond, N. G. L. (1988), 'The Expedition of Xerxes', in Boardman, Hammond, Lewis, and Ostwald (1988), 518–90.

Harrison, T. (2000), *Divinity and History* (Oxford).

—— (2002), 'The Persian Invasions', in Bakker, de Jong, and van Wees (2002), 551–78.

—— (2003), 'The Cause of Things: Envy and the Emotions in Herodotus' *Histories*', in D. Konstan and N. K. Rutter (eds.), *Envy, Spite and Jealousy: the Rivalrous Emotions in Ancient Greece* (Edinburgh), 143–63.

Hart, J. (1982), *Herodotus and Greek History* (London).

Hartog, F. (1988), *The Mirror of Herodotus*, tr. J. Lloyd (Berkeley, Los Angeles, and London; French orig. 1980).

Häsler, B. (1978), *Plutarchi Moralia*, vol. 5 (Leipzig).

Heni, R. (1977), *Die Gespräche bei Herodot* (Heilbronn).

Herington, J. (1991), 'The poem of Herodotus', *Arion* 3, 5–16.

Hesk, J. (2000), *Deception and Democracy in Classical Athens* (Cambridge).

Hignett, C. (1963), *Xerxes' Invasion of Greece* (Oxford).

Hohti, P. (1976), *The Interrelation of Speech and Action in the* Histories *of Herodotus* (Helsinki).

Holt, P. (1998), 'Sex, Tyranny, and Hippias' Incest Dream', *GRBS* 39, 221–41.

Holub, R. (1984), *Reception Theory* (London).

Hornblower, S. (1983), 'Phthonos (envy) and the origin of the Delian League', in *The Greek World 479–323 BC* (London), 15–31.

—— (1987), *Thucydides* (London).

—— (1991), *A Commentary on Thucydides*, vol. 1 (Oxford).

—— (1994*a*), 'Narratology and Thucydides', in Hornblower (1994*b*), 131–66.

—— (1994*b*) (ed.), *Greek Historiography* (Oxford).

—— (2004), *Thucydides and Pindar: Historical Narrative and the World of Epinikian Poetry* (Oxford).

Huber, L. (1965*a*), *Religiöse und politische Beweggründe des Handelns in der Geschichtsschreibung des Herodot* (Tübingen).

—— (1965*b*), 'Herodots Homerverständnis', in H. Flashar and K. Gaiser (eds.), *Synusia. Festgabe für Wolfgang Schadewaldt* (Neske), 29–52.

Hunter, V. J. (1973), *Thucydides: The Artful Reporter* (Toronto).

—— (1982), *Past and Process in Herodotus and Thucydides* (Princeton).

Hunzinger, C. (1995), 'La notion de θῶμα chez Hérodote', *Ktèma* 20, 47–70.

Immerwahr, H. R. (1954), 'Historical Action in Herodotus', *TAPhA* 85, 16–45.

—— (1956), 'Aspects of Historical Causation in Herodotus', *TAPhA* 87, 241–80.

—— (1957), 'The Samian Stories of Herodotus', *CJ* 52, 312–22.

—— (1960), '*Ergon*: History as Monument in Herodotus and Thucydides', *AJPh* 81, 261–90.

—— (1966), *Form and Thought in Herodotus* (Cleveland).

Isager, S. (1999), 'The Pride of Halicarnassus', *ZPE* 123, 1–23.

Iser, W. (1974), *The Implied Reader: Patterns of Communication in Prose Fiction from Bunyan to Beckett* (Baltimore).

—— (1978), *The Act of Reading* (London; German orig. 1976).

—— (1989), *Prospecting: From Reader Response to Literary Anthropology* (Baltimore and London).

Jameson, M. H. (1985) (ed.), *The Greek Historians: Literature and History. Papers presented to A. E. Raubitschek* (Saratoga).

Jocelyn, H. D. (1967), *The Tragedies of Ennius: The Fragments* (Cambridge).

Jong, I. J. F. de (1987), *Narrators and Focalizers: The Presentation of the Story in the* Iliad (Amsterdam).

—— (1992), 'The Subjective Style in Odysseus' Wanderings', *CQ* 42, 1–11.

—— (1993), 'Studies in Homeric Denomination', *Mnemosyne* 46, 289–306.

—— (1994), 'Between Word and Deed: Hidden Thoughts in the Odyssey', in I. J. F. de Jong and J. P. Sullivan (eds.), *Modern Critical Theory and Classical Literature* (Leiden, New York, and Cologne), 27–50.

—— (1999), 'Aspects narratologiques des *Histoires* d'Hérodote', *Lalies* 19, 217–74.

—— (2001), 'The Anachronical Structure of Herodotus' *Histories*', in S. J. Harrison (ed.), *Texts, Ideas, and the Classics* (Oxford), 93–116.

—— (2002), 'Narrative Unity and Units', in Bakker, de Jong, and van Wees (2002), 245–66.

—— (2004), 'Herodotus', in de Jong, Nünlist, and Bowie (2004), 101–14.

——, Nünlist, R., and Bowie A. M. (2004) (eds.), *Narrators, Narratees, and Narratives in Ancient Greek Literature* vol. 1 (Leiden and Boston).

Jörgensen, O. (1904), 'Das Auftreten der Götter in den Büchern i–m der *Odyssee*', *Hermes* 39, 357–82.

Kallet, L. (2003), '*Dēmos Tyrannos*: Wealth, Power, and Economic Patronage', in Morgan (2003), 117–53.

Karageorghis, V. and Taifacos, I. (2004) (eds.), *The World of Herodotus* (Nicosia).

Katz, M. A. (1991), *Penelope's Renown: Meaning and Indeterminacy in the Odyssey* (Princeton).

Klees, H. (1965), *Die Eigenart des griechischen Glaubens an Orakel und Seher. Ein Vergleich zwischen griechischer und nichtgriechischer Mantik bei Herodot* (Stuttgart).

Konstan, D. (1987), 'Persians, Greeks and Empire', in Boedeker and Peradotto (1987), 59–73.

Kuhrt, A. (1988), 'Earth and Water', in A. Kuhrt and H. Sancisi-Weerdenburg (eds.), *Achaemenid History III: Method and Theory* (Leiden), 87–99.

Kurihara, A. (2003), 'Personal Enmity as a Motivation in Forensic Speeches', *CQ* 53, 464–77.

Kurke, L. (1999), *Coins, Bodies, Games, and Gold: The Politics of Meaning in Archaic Greece* (Princeton).

Lada, I. (1993), '"Empathetic Understanding": Emotion and Cognition in Classical Dramatic Audience-Response', *PCPhS* 39, 94–140.

—— (1996), 'Emotion and Meaning in Tragic Performance', in M. S. Silk (ed.), *Tragedy and the Tragic* (Oxford), 397–413.

Lang, M. L. (1968), 'Herodotus and the Ionian Revolt', *Historia* 17, 24–36.

—— (1984), *Herodotean Narrative and Discourse* (Cambridge, Mass. and London).

Lanza, D. (1977), *Il tiranno et il suo pubblico* (Turin).

Larsen, J. A. O. (1962), 'Freedom and its Obstacles in Ancient Greece', *CPh* 57, 230–4.

Lateiner, D. (1976), 'Tissaphernes and the Phoenician Fleet (Thucydides 8.87)', *TAPhA* 106, 267–90.

—— (1982), 'The Failure of the Ionian Revolt', *Historia* 31, 129–160.

—— (1989), *The Historical Method of Herodotus* (Toronto).

—— (2002), 'The Style of Herodotos: A Case Study (7.229)', *CW* 95, 363–71.

Lateiner, D. (2004), 'The *Iliad*: An Unpredictable Classic', in Fowler (2004), 11–30.

Lavelle, B. (1993), *The Sorrow and the Pity* (Stuttgart).

Ledbetter, G. M. (2003), *Poetics before Plato* (Princeton and Oxford).

Legrand, P. E. (1932), *Hérodote: Introduction* (Paris).

Lendon, J. E. (2000), 'Homeric Vengeance and the Outbreak of Greek Wars', in H. van Wees (ed.), *War and Violence in Ancient Greece* (London), 1–30.

Lesher, J. H. (1981), 'Perceiving and Knowing in the *Iliad* and *Odyssey*', *Phronesis* 26, 2–24.

Lesky, A. (1961), *Göttliche und menschliche Motivation im homerischen Epos* (Heidelberg).

Levene, D. S. (1997), 'Pity, Fear and the Historical Audience', in S. M. Braund and C. Gill (eds.), *The Passions in Roman Thought and Literature* (Cambridge and New York), 128–49.

Lewis, D. M. (1992), 'The Thirty Years' Peace', in D. M. Lewis, J. Boardman, J. K. Davies, and M. Ostwald (eds.), *The Cambridge Ancient History*², vol. 5: *The Fifth Century B.C.* (Cambridge), 121–46.

Lewis, S. (2004), 'Καὶ σαφῶς τύραννος ἦν: Xenophon's Account of Euphron of Sicyon', *JHS* 124, 65–74.

Libero, L. de (1996), *Die Archaische Tyrannis* (Stuttgart).

Lieshout, R. G. A. van (1970), 'A Dream on a *kairos* of History: An Analysis of Herodotus' *Hist.* VII. 12–19, 47', *Mnemosyne* 23: 225–49.

Lloyd, A. B. (1975), *Herodotus, Book II: Introduction* (*Études preliminaires aux religions orientales dans l'empire romain* 43; Leiden).

Lloyd, G. E. R. (1966), *Polarity and Analogy* (Cambridge).

Long, T. (1987), *Repetition and Variation in the Short Stories of Herodotus* (Frankfurt).

Loraux, N. (1986), *The Invention of Athens: The Funeral Oration in the Classical City*, tr. A. Sheridan (Cambridge; French orig. 1981).

Luraghi, N. (2001*a*), 'Local Knowledge in Herodotus' *Histories*', in Luraghi (2001*b*), 138–160.

—— (2001*b*) (ed.), *The Historian's Craft in the Age of Herodotus* (Oxford).

—— (2006), 'Meta-*historiē*: Method and Genre in the *Histories*', in Dewald and Marincola (2006), 76–91.

Macdowell, D. M. (1976), '*Hybris* in Athens', *G&R* 23, 14–31.

Mailloux, S. (1991), review of Iser (1989), in *Modern Philology* 89, 312–16.

Malkin, I. (2001) (ed.), *Ancient Perceptions of Greek Ethnicity* (Center for Hellenic Studies Colloquia 5; Washington).

Marincola, J. (1987), 'Herodotean Narrative and the Narrator's Presence', in Boedeker and Peradotto (1987), 121–37.

—— (1994), 'Plutarch's Refutation of Herodotus', *AncW* 25, 191–203.

—— (1996), Introduction and Notes to A. de Sélincourt (tr.), *Herodotus: The Histories* (New York and London).

—— (1997), *Authority and Tradition in Ancient Historiography* (Cambridge).

—— (2006), 'Herodotus and the Poetry of the Past', in Dewald and Marincola (2006), 13–28.

Marr, J. L. (1998), *Plutarch: Lives. Themistocles* (Warminster).

Masson, O. (1950), 'A propos d'un rituel hittite pour la lustration d'une armée. Le rite de purification par le passage entre les deux parties d'une victime', *Revue de l'histoire des religions* 137, 5–25.

Michelini, A. N. (1987), *Euripides and the Tragic Tradition* (Madison).

Mikalson, J. D. (2002), 'Religion in Herodotus', in Bakker, de Jong, and van Wees (2002), 187–98.

—— (2003), *Herodotus and Religion in the Persian Wars* (Chapel Hill and London).

Missiou, A. (1992), *The Subversive Oratory of Andokides* (Cambridge).

Mitchell, B. M. (1975), 'Herodotus and Samos', *JHS* 45, 75–91.

Moles, J. (1993), 'Truth and Untruth in Herodotus and Thucydides', in C. Gill and T. P. Wiseman (eds.), *Lies and Fiction in the Ancient World* (Austin), 88–121.

—— (1996), 'Herodotus Warns the Athenians', *Papers of the Leeds International Latin Seminar* 9, 259–84.

—— (1999), '*Anathema kai Ktema*: the Inscriptional Inheritance of Ancient Historiography', *Histos* 3: <http://research.ncl.ac.uk/histos/Histos_BackIssues1999.html> accessed 14 September 2007.

—— (2002), 'Herodotus and Athens', in Bakker, de Jong, and van Wees (2002), 33–52.

Montiglio, S. (2000),'Wandering Philosophers in Classical Greece', *JHS* 120, 86–105.

—— (2005), *Wandering in Ancient Greek Culture* (Chicago).

Morgan, K. A. (2003) (ed.), *Popular Tyranny: Sovereignty and its Discontents in Ancient Greece* (Austin).

Morrison, J. V. (1992), *Homeric Misdirection: False Predictions in the* Iliad (Ann Arbor).

—— (2006), *Reading Thucydides* (Columbus, Ohio).

Müller, D. (1981), 'Herodot—Vater des Empirismus? Mensch und Erkenntnis im Denken Herodots', in G. Kurz, D. Müller, and W. Nicolai (eds.), *Gnomosyne: Menschliches Denken und Handeln in der frühgriechischen Literatur. Festschrift für Walter Marg zum 70. Geburtstag* (Munich), 299–318.

Munson, R. V. (1988), 'Artemisia in Herodotus', *ClAnt* 7, 91–106.

—— (1991), 'The Madness of Cambyses (Herodotus 3.16–38)', *Arethusa* 24, 43–65.

Munson, R. V. (1993), 'Three Aspects of Spartan Kingship in Herodotus', in Rosen and Farrell (1993), 39–54.

—— (2001), *Telling Wonders: Ethnographic and Political Discourse in the Work of Herodotus* (Ann Arbor).

—— (2006), 'An Alternate World: Herodotus and Italy', in Dewald and Marincola (2006), 257–73.

Murray, A. T. (1995) (tr.), *Homer:* Odyssey², 2 vols., rev. by G. E. Dimock (Cambridge, Mass.).

—— (1999) (tr.), *Homer:* Iliad², 2 vols., rev. by W. F. Wyatt (Cambridge, Mass.).

Murray, O. (1988), 'The Ionian Revolt', in Boardman, Hammond, Lewis, and Ostwald (1988), 461–90.

Nagy, G. (1987), 'Herodotus the *Logios*', in Boedeker and Peradotto (1987), 175–84.

—— (1990), *Pindar's Homer: the Lyric Possession of an Epic Past* (Baltimore and London).

Naiden, F. S. (1999), 'The Prospective Imperfect in Herodotus', *HSPh* 99, 135–49.

Olrik, A. (1992), *Principles for Oral Narrative Research*, tr. K. Wolf and J. Jensen (Bloomington; German orig. 1921).

Olson, S. D. (1995), *Blood and Iron: Stories and Storytelling in Homer's* Odyssey (Leiden).

Osborne, R. (2002), 'Archaic Greek History', in Bakker, de Jong, and van Wees (2002), 497–520.

Ostwald, M. (1969), Nomos *and the Beginnings of the Athenian Democracy* (Oxford).

Payen, P. (1990), 'Discours historique et structures narratives chez Hérodote', *Annales (ESC)* 45, 527–50.

—— (1997), *Les Îles nomades: Conquérir et résister dans l'enquête d'Hérodote* (Paris).

Pearson, L. (1941), 'Credulity and Scepticism in Herodotus', *TAPhA* 72, 335–55.

—— (1947), 'Thucydides as Reporter and Critic', *TAPhA* 78, 37–60.

Pelling, C. B. R. (1991), 'Thucydides' Archidamus and Herodotus' Artabanus', in M. A. Flower and M. Toher (eds.), *Georgica: Greek Studies in Honour of George Cawkwell* (London), 120–42.

—— (1997), 'East is East and West is West—Or Are They?' *Histos* 1: <http://research.ncl.ac.uk/histos/Histos_BackIssues1997.html> accessed 14 September 2007.

—— (2000), *Literary Texts and the Greek Historian* (London).

—— (2002), 'Speech and Action: Herodotus' Debate on the Constitutions', *PCPhS* 48, 123–58.

—— (2006*a*), 'Educating Croesus: Talking and Learning in Herodotus' Lydian *Logos*', *ClAnt* 25, 141–77.

—— (2006*b*), 'Homer and Herodotus', in M. J. Clarke, B. G. F. Currie, and R. O. A. M. Lyne (eds.), *Epic Interactions: Perspectives on Homer, Virgil, and the Epic Tradition Presented to Jasper Griffin by Former Pupils* (Oxford), 75–104.

—— (2006*c*), 'Speech and Narrative', in Dewald and Marincola (2006), 103–21.

—— (unpublished paper), '*De Malignitate Plutarchi*: Plutarch, Herodotus, and the Persian War'.

Pohlenz, M. (1937), *Herodot der erste Geschichtschreiber des Abendlandes* (Leipzig).

Powell, J. E. (1937), 'Puns in Herodotus', *CR* 51, 103–5.

Raaflaub, K. A. (1979), '*Polis Tyrannos*: zur Entstehung einer politischen Metapher', in G. Bowersock, W. Burkert, and M. Putnam (eds.), *Arktouros: Hellenic Studies presented to B. M. W. Knox on the occasion of his 65th birthday* (Berlin and New York), 237–52.

—— (1984), 'Athens "Ideologie der Macht" und die Freiheit des Tyrannen', in W. Schuller (ed.), *Studien zum attischen Seebund* (Konstanz), 45–86.

—— (1987), 'Herodotus, Political Thought, and the Meaning of History', in Boedeker and Peradotto (1987), 221–48.

—— (2002), 'Philosophy, Science, Politics: Herodotus and the Intellectual Trends of his Time', in Bakker, de Jong, and van Wees (2002), 149–86.

—— (2003), 'Stick and Glue: The Function of Tyranny in Fifth-Century Athenian Democracy', in Morgan (2003), 59–93.

—— (2004), *The Discovery of Freedom in Ancient Greece*, tr. R. Franciscono (Chicago and London; German orig. 1985).

Rawlings, H. R. (1975), *A Semantic Study of Prophasis to 400 B.C.* (*Hermes Einzelschriften* 33; Wiesbaden).

Redfield, J. (1985), 'Herodotus the Tourist', *CPh* 80, 97–118.

Reinhardt, K. (1940), 'Herodots Persergeschichten', in C. Becker (ed.), *Vermächtnis der Antike: Gesammelte Essays zur Philosophie und Geschichtsschreibung* (Göttingen) (repr. in W. Marg (ed.), *Herodot: Eine Auswahl aus der Neueren Forschung* (Darmstadt, 1962), 320–69).

Reinhold, M. (1985), 'Human Nature as Cause in Ancient Historiography', in J. W. Eadie and J. Ober (eds.), *The Craft of the Ancient Historian* (Lanham, New York, and London), 21–32.

Renehan, R. (1987), 'The *Heldentod* in Homer: One Heroic Ideal', *CPh* 82, 99–116.

Richardson, S. (1990), *The Homeric Narrator* (Nashville).

Romilly, J. de (1963), *Thucydides and Athenian Imperialism*, tr. P. Thody (Oxford; French orig. 1947).

Romm, J. (1998), *Herodotus* (New Haven).

—— (2006), 'Herodotus and the Natural World', in Dewald and Marincola (2006), 178–91.

Rood, T. (1998), *Thucydides: Narrative and Explanation* (Oxford).

—— (2004), 'Thucydides', in de Jong, Nünlist, and Bowie (2004), 115–28.

—— (2006), 'Herodotus and Foreign Lands', in Dewald and Marincola (2006), 290–305.

Rosen, R. M. and Farrell, J. S. (1993) (eds.), Nomodeiktes: *Studies in Honor of Martin Ostwald* (Ann Arbor).

Rosenbloom, D. (1993), 'Shouting "Fire" in a Crowded Theatre: Phryni-chos' Capture of Miletus and the Politics of Fear in Early Attic Tragedy', *Philologus* 137, 159–96.

Rösler, W. (1991), 'Die "Selbsthistorisierung" des Autors: zur Stellung Herodots zwischen Mündlichkeit und Schriftlichkeit', *Philologus* 135, 215–20.

Rubincam, C. (2003), 'Numbers in Greek Poetry and Historiography: Quantifying Fehling', *CQ* 53, 448–63.

Russo, J. (1997), 'Prose Genres for the Performance of Traditional Wisdom in Ancient Greece: Proverb, Maxim, Apothegm', in L. Edmunds and R. W. Wallace (eds.) *Poet, Public, and Performance in Ancient Greece* (Baltimore and London), 49–64.

Rutherford, R. B. (1986), 'The Philosophy of the *Odyssey*', *JHS* 106, 145–62.

Ryberg, I. S. (1942), 'Tacitus' Art of Innuendo', *TAPhA* 73, 383–404.

Saïd, S. (1981), 'Darius et Xerxès dans les *Perses* d'Éschyle', *Ktèma* 6, 49–75.

Sancisi-Weerdenburg, H. (2002), 'The Personality of Xerxes, King of Kings', in Bakker, de Jong and van Wees (2002), 579–90 (orig. publ. in L. de Meyer and E. Haerinck (eds.), *Archaeologia Iranica et Orientalis Miscellanea in Honorem Louis Vanden Berghe* vol. 1 (Gent, 1989), 549–60).

Schadewalt, W. (1959), *Von Homers Welt und Werk* (Stuttgart).

Schneider, C. (1974), *Information und Absicht bei Thukydides* (Göttingen).

Schudson, M. (1995), 'Dynamics of Distortion in Collective Memory', in D. L. Schacter (ed.), *Memory Distortion: How Minds, Brains, and Societies Reconstruct the Past* (Cambridge, 1995), 346–64.

Scodel, R. (1999), *Credible Impossibilities: Conventions and Strategies of Verisimilitude in Homer and Greek Tragedy* (Stuttgart).

—— (2002*a*), *Listening to Homer: Tradition, Narrative, and Audience* (Ann Arbor).

—— (2002*b*), review of I. J. F. de Jong, *A Narratological Commentary on the Odyssey* (Cambridge, 2001), *BMCR* 2002.06.12.

—— (2004), 'The Story-Teller and his Audience', in Fowler (2004), 45–55.

——(2005), review of de Jong, Nünlist, and Bowie (2004), *BMCR* 2005.07.48.

Scott, L. (2005), *Historical Commentary on Herodotus Book 6* (Leiden and Boston).

Scullion, S. (2006), 'Herodotus and Greek Religion', in Dewald and Marincola (2006), 192–208.

Scully, S. (1984), 'The Language of Achilles: the ὀχθήσας Formulas', *TAPhA* 114, 11–27.

Shapiro, S. O. (1994), 'Learning through Suffering: Human Wisdom in Herodotus', *CJ* 89, 349–55.

Shrimpton, G. S. and Gillis, K. M. (1997), 'Appendix 1: Herodotus' Source Citations', in G. S. Shrimpton, *History and Memory in Ancient Greece* (Montreal and London), 229–65.

Silk, M. (2004), 'The *Odyssey* and its Explorations', in Fowler (2004), 31–44.

Sinos, R. H. (1993), 'Divine Selection: Epiphany and Politics in Archaic Greece', in C. Dougherty and L. Kurke (eds.), *Cultural Poetics in Archaic Greece: Cult, Performance, Politics* (Cambridge), 73–91.

Solmsen, F. (1982), 'Two Crucial Decisions in Herodotus', in *Kleine Schriften III* (Hildesheim, Zürich, and New York), 76–109 (orig. *MAWBL* 37 (1974), 1–33).

Solmsen, L. (1943), 'Speeches in Herodotus' Account of the Ionic Revolt', *AJPh* 64, 194–207.

——(1944), 'Speeches in Herodotus' Account of the Battle of Plataea', *CPh* 39, 241–53.

Sourvinou-Inwood, C. (2003), 'Herodotos (and others) on Pelasgians: Some Perceptions of Ethnicity', in Derow and Parker (2003), 103–44.

Stadter, P. A. (1992), 'Herodotus and the Athenian *Arche*', *ASNP* 22, 781–809.

——(2006), 'Herodotus and the Cities of Mainland Greece', in Dewald and Marincola (2006), 242–56.

Stahl, H.-P. (1975), 'Learning through Suffering? Croesus' Conversations in the History of Herodotus', *YClS* 24, 1–36.

——(2003), *Thucydides: Man's Place in History* (Swansea; German orig. 1966).

Stanford, W. B. (1968), *The Ulysses Theme: A Study in the Adaptability of a Traditional Hero*[2] (Ann Arbor).

Steiner, D. (1994), *The Tyrant's Writ* (Princeton).

Strasburger, H. (1955), 'Herodot und das perikleische Athen', *Historia* 4, 1–25.

——(1972), *Homer und die Geschichtsschreibung. Sitzungsberichte der Heidelberger Akademie der Wissenschaften. Philosophisch-historische Klasse* (Heidelberg).

Szegedy-Maszak, A. (1987), 'Narrative Voice and the Persona of the *Histor*: Response to Dewald', in Boedeker and Peradotto (1987), 171–4.

Thomas, R. (1989), *Oral Tradition and Written Record in Classical Athens* (Cambridge).

—— (1993), 'Performance and Written Publication in Herodotus and the Sophistic Generation', in W. Kullmann and J. Althoff (eds.), *Vermittlung und Tradierung von Wissen in der griechischen Kultur* (Tübingen), 225–44.

—— (2000), *Herodotus in Context* (Cambridge).

—— (2001), 'Ethnicity, Genealogy, and Hellenism in Herodotus', in I. Malkin (ed.), *Ancient Perceptions of Greek Ethnicity* (Washington), 213–33.

—— (2003), 'Prose Performance Texts: *Epideixis* and Written Publication in the Late Fifth and Early Fourth Century', in H. Yunis (ed.), *Written Texts and the Rise of Literate Culture in Ancient Greece* (Cambridge), 162–88.

—— (2004), 'Herodotus, Ionia and the Athenian Empire', in V. Karageorghis and I. Taifacos (eds.), *The World of Herodotus. Proceedings of an International Conference held at the Foundation Anastasios G. Leventis* (Nicosia), 27–42.

—— (2006), 'The Intellectual Milieu of Herodotus', in Dewald and Marincola (2006), 60–75.

Thompson, W. E. (1969), 'Individual Motivation in Thucydides', *C&M* 30, 158–74.

Tölle-Kastenbein, R. (1976), *Herodot und Samos* (Bochum).

Tozzi, P. (1978), *La rivolta ionica* (Pisa).

Tuplin, C. J. (1985), 'Imperial Tyranny: Some Reflections on a Classical Greek Political Metaphor', in P. A. Cartledge and F. D. Harvey (eds.), *Crux: Essays in Greek History presented to G. E. M. de Ste. Croix on his 75th Birthday* (London), 348–75.

Ubsdell, S. (1983), 'Herodotus on Human Nature', (diss., DPhil University of Oxford).

Veen, J. E. van der (1995), 'A Minute's Mirth . . . : Syloson and his Cloak in Herodotus', *Mnemosyne* 48, 129–45.

—— (1996), *The Significant and the Insignificant* (Amsterdam).

Veyne, P. (1987), preface to C. Darbo-Peschanski, *Le discours du particulier: Essai sur l'enquête Hérodotéenne* (Paris).

Vlastos, G. (1953), 'Isonomie', *AJPh* 74, 337–66.

Walbank, F. W. (2002), 'The Problem of Greek Nationality', in T. Harrison (ed.), *Greeks and Barbarians* (Edinburgh), 234–56 (orig. *Phoenix* 5 (1951), 41–60).

Waters, K. H. (1971), *Herodotus on Tyrants and Despots: A Study in Objectivity* (Wiesbaden).

West, M. L. (1998–2000), *Homeri Ilias*, 2 vols. (Stuttgart, Leipzig, and Munich).

West, S. R. (1991), 'Herodotus' Portrait of Hecataeus', *JHS* 111, 144–60.

Westlake, H. D. (1989), 'Personal Motives, Aims and Feelings in Thucydides', in *Studies in Thucydides and Greek History* (Bristol), 201–23.

Wheeler, S. M. (1999), *A Discourse of Wonders: Audience and Performance in Ovid's Metamorphoses* (Philadelphia).

Wiesehöfer, J. (1996), *Ancient Persia from 550 B.C. to 650 A.D.*, tr. A. Azodi (London and New York; orig. 1993).

Winkler, J. (1985), *Auctor and Actor: A Narratological Reading of Apuleius' Golden Ass* (Berkeley).

Wiseman, T. P. (1983), 'The Credibility of the Roman Annalists', *LCM* 8, 20–2.

—— (1995), *Remus* (Cambridge).

Wood, H. (1972), *The Histories of Herodotus: An Analysis of the Formal Structure* (The Hague and Paris).

Woodman, A. J. (1988), *Rhetoric in Classical Historiography: Four Studies* (London and Portland).

# General Index

Alyattes 16 n. 43, 91, 125–6, 285–6

Amasis
  and the shrine 143
  Cambyses' treatment of remains
    of 116
  ending friendship with Polykrates
    7, 87–8
  motivation for dissolution of
    friendship with Polykrates
    7, 87
  motivation for marrying a woman of
    Cyrene 126
  Phanes and 111

Amazons 240

ambiguity 11, 151 n. 84, 168, 225, 262
  expressive syntactical 168, 200,
    209–10, 262

Amestris 97 n. 49, 278–9

Ammonians, Cambyses' expedition
  against 112, 115

Amphimedon 40, 43 n. 27, 44, 52, 53

analepsis 6, 163, 199–200, 264, 291

anachronism 178–9, 195 n. 73, 198 n. 84

Anaxandros 78

Anaxileos 190, 192

Andersen, Ø. 41

Andocides 20

Andrians 143 n. 63, 317

Andros, Greek debate at 289
  democracy in 310–12
  echoing Xerxes' council 300–3
  Themistocles' speeches at 289–90,
    295, 298–304, 301, 309
    emotional response to 303–4
    engaging internal and external
      audiences 299–300, 303
    motivation for 304, 315–16 and
      ch. 9 *passim*
    rhetoric in 304–10

anger 90–1, 97 n. 49, 103, 112–15, 155,
  245–7, 271, 273

*apaidia* (childlessness), material
  prosperity and 270

Apis bull, Cambyses and 117–18

Archias 94–5

Argeia 174

Argives, medizing of 178, 211–17, 222,
  224
  Xerxes' persuasion of 265

Arion 16

Aristagoras 61, 163, 192, 199
  and Cleomenes 61, 167–70, 242
  as instigator of the Ionian
    Revolt 167–70, 183–5
  evocations of *kerdos* 165
  persuasion of Cleomenes compared to
    Mardonios' persuasion of
    Xerxes 242

Aristeides 296

Aristodemos 75, 173–4

Aristogeiton 27 n. 78, 153–4, 170–1

Aristotle 17, 198 n. 82, 255

Arkesileos 130, 166

Artabanos 249, 266–9, 300, 310, 313
  advice to Xerxes 248–9, 250
    parallel to Themistocles' Andros
      speeches 301–2
  Greek perspective of 267
  on size of the Persian army 260
  on Xerxes' proposal to invade 247

Artaphrenes 167, 170, 172–3, 183, 184

Artaxerxes 11 n. 27, 178

Artaÿnte 278

Artemisia 61–2, 311, 313

Artemisium, Greek defence at 292,
  293, 296

Artobazanes 252

ascription of motivation, *see* motives,
  ascription of

Asheri, D. 92 n. 40, 94 n. 44, 99 n. 51,
  105 n. 65

Athenians
  adaptability of 316
  and Aristagoras' speech 167
  as 'saviours of Greece' 175, 199,
    203, 237–8
  Athenian character
    as displayed in Pelasgian
      digression 143–4
    as exemplified by
      Themistocles 143, 312,
      316–17
  attitude to Peisistratid
    tyranny 148–59
  cleverness of 157
  crucifixion of Artaÿctes compared to
    Xerxes' treatment of Pythios'
    son 276
  desire to be first 143 n. 63, 197–8,
    200 n. 89
  freedom from tyranny 31, 157–9,
    195–7 and §5.4 *passim*

Fisher, N. R. E.  244 n. 11, 252 n. 42, 263, 277
Flory, S.  124, 152, 154, 156–7, 274
Flower, M. A.  14 n. 35, 226 n. 31, 235 n. 52, 250 n. 32, 266 n. 78
focalization  41, 58, 214 n. 17
  and periphrastic denomination 262 n. 69
  Greek versus Persian 284
  implicit embedded/ deviant 239 n. 67
  in Homer 41
  in proem 12 n. 31
  of Athenians at Spartan delay before Plataea 232
  of Greek states at medizing states 208–9
  of Greeks at Xerxes' building of Athos canal 261–2
  of Greek onlooker at Xerxes' crossing of Hellespont 283
  of Megacles' daughter 152
  of Spartans 214
  of Persians on anthropomorphism in religion 283–4
  *see also* perspectives; narratology
Foley, J. M.  23 n. 69
Fornara, C.W.  28 n. 81, 249 n. 32, 297, 310 n. 44, 315–6
Forrest, W. G.  165 n. 10
Forsdyke, S.  150 n. 79
Fowler, D. P.  12 n., 15 n. 40, 18 n. 50, 239
freedom
  as motivation  133, 167
    versus desire for power 178–9
    versus desire for benefits 182
  Athenians and  31, 147, 148–59, 237–8
  contesting of association with Greek identity 179, 189, 190, 192
  Demaratus' speech on Greek devotion to  161, 176
  Dionysius' speech in the name of  188
  expressed through rule over others 180, 192–3, 201
  freedom *from* versus freedom *to*  193–5, 197
  in rhetoric  147–8, 154, 167, 192, ch. 6 *passim*

Ionian communities' desire for  186, 169
  ironies in Herodotus' treatment of 89–90, 95, 162
  Otanes and  195
  Spartans and liberation rhetoric 89–90, 94–5
Frost, F. J.  293, 315–16

Gelon, medizing of  210, 217–20, 227, 228–9
Genette, G.  33 n. 97
Gill, C.  130, 273, 303 n. 35
Gillis, D.  32 n. 92, 210
Gillos  120–1
Gilula, D.  179
gods
  divine causation  7, 115, 307 n. 41
    for Xerxes' invasion 249–50, 256
    in parallel to human motivation 126
  divine motivation, in Homer 126 n. 13
  limited human knowledge of 269
  misunderstanding of mortals 46
  *see also* impiety
Goldhill, S.  40–1, 43
Gorgias  20–1, 317
Gould, J.  8 n. 20, 131 n. 33
Gray, V. J.  16, 125, 142–3
Greeks
  and *kerdos*  148
  compared to Persians  110, 112, 121
  discourse of, compared to Persian autocracy 312–3
  disintegration of  173, 294–5
  Greek ∼ Persian opposition  122 n. 3, 233 n. 48
  contested  88, 107, 110, 111–12, 121
  lack of common identity 175
  pattern of attracting Persian invader 177–8
  *see also* unity, Greek; disunity, Greek; identity, Greek
Griffin, J.  37–8
Grinnos  166
Gyges narrative  73–4, 216
  *kerdos* motivation in 131

Hamilcar  21

354 *General Index*

motives/ motivation (*cont.*)
  outcome different in character
    from 171, 190, 225
  outcome disproportionate to 86,
    87–8, 98, 100–1, 104, 108, 118
  outcome taking priority over 141,
    203
  ranking of 180
  reciprocity model 156
  shifting depictions of 43, 95–6,
    101–6, 134–6, 149, 189–92
    and ch. 7 *passim*
  *see also* alternative motives;
    multiplicity of motives;
    negative motives; idealism in
    motivation; human nature/
    character; *pleonexiē*; jealousy;
    hatred(s); anger; fear; despair;
    vengeance
multiplicity of motives
  in Herodotus versus Thucydides 85
  of Cambyses 86–7
  of Cyrus 66–7, 281 n. 121
  of Maiandrios 106
Munson, R. V. 17, 18 n. 47, 29, 31–2,
    62 n. 22, 136 n. 43, 172 n. 25,
    190 n., 193, 196 n. 74, 200 n.
    87, 219 n. 24
Murray, O. 164, 169 n. 21
Myrinaians 140

Nagy, G. 18 n. 47
narrative *passim* and
  adversarial presentation 17–20
  Homer as model for 35–6
  sophistication 30, 318–20
narrative patterns, patterning 5, 137
    n. 48, 240
  ascriptions of motives and 52, 53, 204
  dreams 249 n. 32
  in Homer 43–4, 53
  of betraying cities for personal
    gain 177
  of freedom and tyranny 192
  of Persian expansionism 11, 242–3
narratology, theory of 6
  *see also* focalization; analepsis;
    prolepsis
narrator, Herodotean

as conscientious historian 57
as distinguished from implied
  author 6, 33
compared to Homeric human
  narrators 49–51, 58
double persona of 55–9
exposing disreputable motives 58
stance of non-committal 33
unreliability 32–3, 34 n. 98, 58–9,
  80, 135
use of irony 21, 105, 151 n. 86, 159
*see also* Herodotus
narrator, Homeric 36, 37–44
compared to Herodotean
  narrator 41, 50 n. 51, 53–4
omniscience of 37–8
compared to human
  narrators 46–8
narrators, human 46–7, 49–50
Nash, John 305
Nausicaa 42 n. 22, 48
necessity (*anankē, anankaiē*)
  and changes in motives 210, 220,
    223–5
  of medizing 205–10, 228
  under which the historian
    writes 79 n. 62
  versus free will 125, 129, 228,
    132–3, 162
  versus motives 205, 207 and ch. 7
    *passim*
  Xerxes as locus of 206–7, 228, 229
negative motives 14–15, 95–6, 134,
    156, 227–8
  for Histiaeus' instigation of Ionian
    Revolt 183–4
  for medizing 204–5, 208–11
    Argives 211–17
    Corcyreans 220–2
    Gelon 217–20
    Thebans 225–7
    Thessalians 225–5
  Herodotus' favouring of 13–14,
    132–6, 162
  Plutarch on 132–3, 162
  *see also kerdos*; jealousy; fear
Nekos 257
Nikodromos 177
Nitokris 62–4, 73, 79, 129, 256–7

Solon
  Artabanos' style as Solonian 266,
    267 n. 83
  Croesus and 52, 127
  Herodotus and, parallels 55 n. 2
*sophistēs* (sophist), definitions of
    55–6
sophists
  and knowledge of the past 20
  and rhetoric 23
  meaning for Herodotus 55–6
  *mētis* and 297
  persuasion methods of 56
  Plutarch's definition of 57
  techniques used by Herodotean
    narrator 80
  *see also epidexis*; fifth-century
    context
sources of the *Histories, see* informants;
    oral tradition
source citations 18, 318
  double unresolved motives compared
    to 241–2
  scholarship on 12
Sourvinou-Inwood, C. 144 n. 64
Spartan campaign against Samos
  double motivation for 89–91
  Plutarch on 133
  role of Samian exiles 95–6
  synchronicity with Cambyses'
    Egyptian invasion 88
Spartans
  acceptance of Croesus' invitation 230
  Argives and 211
  delay of involvement at Plataea 232–3
    compared to Marathon and
      Thermopylae 232 n. 37
  dual kingship of Cleomenes and
    Demaratus 173–4
  given chief command 199
  piety versus pragmatism of
    motivation 71 n. 44,
      232 n. 47, 236
  power and land as motivation 166
  response to Athenians' speech 231–4
  selfishness of 303 n. 34
speeches, compared to Homeric
    soliloquies 36; *see also*
      rhetoric

spies
  of Cambyses in Ethiopia 112–13
  of Darius in Greece 120
  Xerxes' return of Greek 259–60
Stadter, P. A. 164, 189 n. 54, 197 n. 79
Stahl, H.-P. 82 n.
Stein, H. 69 n. 39, 70 n. 40, 257 n. 52,
    291 n. 4, 295–6
Steiner, D. 63, 102 n.
Strasburger, H. 32
Strymon river 261
'subtle silences', *see* Badian
survival motif 204–5, 216, 236,
  implied in Kimmerians' decision to
    flee 132, 145
  in Gyges narrative 74
  in Thermopylae narrative 74
Syloson 106, 120–1
  compared to Maiandrios 103
  as link between Persian and Samian
    stories 100
  return to Samos 102
  invitation of Darius 100, 178 n. 36,
    242 n. 9
Szegedy-Maszak, A. 18 n. 50

Table of the Sun 113
Tacitus, Tacitean innuendo 28 n.79, 202
Telemachus 52, 53
  and Penelope 46
  motives for visiting Pylos 45–6
Terillos 218
Thebans 68
  as reverse image of Spartans 77
    at Thermopylae 65, 70
  hostage explanation for presence at
    Thermopylae 71–2
  medizing of 76, 225–7
Themistocles 119, 289–322
  adaptability of 316
  as contriver of unity 291–8
  as driving force of plot 296
  as representative of Athens 143, 312,
    316–17
  bipartite characterization of 319,
    321
  *euboulia* (good council) and 310–11
  interpretations of bribe taken by
    292–3

# Index of Citations

*Index of Citations*

HIPPOCRATES

*Airs, Waters, Places*
23: 201 n. 90

HOMER

*Iliad*
1.33: 37 n. 6
1.65: 49
1.93–100: 49
1.94–5: 46
1.213–14: 46
2.315–16: 45 n. 35
2.325 ff.: 45 n. 35
2.325–9: 45
4.175–7: 45
6.86–95: 45
6.113–15: 45
6.335–6: 46
7.437: 146
7.449–50: 146 n. 68
7.451–3: 146
7.458–63: 147
8.97: 42
8.152–7: 43 n. 27
9.260 ff.: 45 n. 33
9.313: 45
9.352–4: 40
12 ff.: 146
12.7–8: 146
12.10–33: 147
13.85–7: 146
15.721–3: 40
19.572–87: 40
24.24–30: 239 n. 68
24.167–9: 40
24.235–40: 43

*Odyssey*
4.240–64: 40
4.269–89: 40
4.317 ff: 46
4.349: 49
4.351–585: 49
4.712–14: 46
7.263: 47
9–12: 47 n. 39, 58
9.20: 58 n. 12
9.102: 48
9.196 ff.: 39
9.229: 48

9.339: 47 n. 40
9.366–7: 39
10.34–6: 48 n. 43
10.95: 39
10.147: 48
10.415–17: 49
10.419–20: 49
10.448: 49 n. 47
11.544–5: 47
12.49: 44
12.389: 49
13.209–16: 49
13.287–97: 294 n. 10
14.389: 48 n. 41
23.97–103: 46, 53
23.160: 44
24.121–90: 52 n. 59
24.192–202: 52 n. 58

LIVY

*Ab Urbe Condita*
1.6.3–7.3: 146 n. 70
1.7.2: 146 n. 68

PINDAR
fr. 228: 135

*Pythian*
11.22–5: 137

PLATO

*Republic*
571–9: 150 n. 80
577–8: 249 n. 30

*Symposium*
194b1: 259

PLUTARCH

*Aristeides*
9.6–10.1: 314 n. 58
10.2: 231 n. 44

*Cimon*
2.4–5: 56, 56 n. 5
9: 294 n. 15

*Greek Questions*
199c–d: 146 n. 70

*How to tell a Flatterer from a Friend*
51c–d: 11 n. 26

Printed in the USA/Agawam, MA
May 17, 2012